The Birth of Nobility

The Birth of Nobility

Constructing Aristocracy in England and France 900–1300

David Crouch

Harlow, England • London • New York • Boston • San Francisco • Toronto • Sydney • Singapore • Hong Kong
Tokyo • Seoul • Taipei • New Delhi • Cape Town • Madrid • Mexico City • Amsterdam • Munich • Paris • Milan

PEARSON EDUCATION LIMITED

Edinburgh Gate
Harlow CM20 2JE
United Kingdom
Tel: +44 (0)279 623623
Fax: +44 (0)1279 431059
Website: www.pearsoned.co.uk

First edition published in Great Britain in 2005

ISBN 0 582 36981 9

British Library Cataloguing in Publication Data
A CIP catalogue record for this book can be obtained from the British Library

Library of Congress Cataloging in Publication Data
Crouch, David.
The birth of nobility : social change in England and France : 900–1300 / David Crouch.
p. cm.
Includes bibliographical references and index.
ISBN 0–582–36981–9 (pbk.)
1. Nobility–Great Britain–History–To 1500. 2. Nobility–France–History–To 1500. 3. Aristocracy (Social class)–Great Britain–History–To 1500. 4. Aristocracy (Social class)–France–History–To 1500. 5. Great Britain–Social life and customs–1066–1485. 6. France–Social life and customs–To 1328. 7. Social history–Medieval, 500–1500. I. Title.

HT653.G7C75 2005
305.5′2′0941–dc22

2004060072

10 9 8 7 6 5 4 3 2 1
09 08 07 06 05

Set by 3, in 10/13.5pt Sabon
Printed and bound in Malaysia, KHL (CTP)

The Publishers' policy is to use paper manufactured from sustainable forests.

Al mielz qe soy e poy l'ay certes ordiné;
Sachez de controvere n'ay rien ajusté.
Si jeo rien i ay mis qe seit superfluité,
Amende le donc qui siet, ou del tut seit osté.

Thomas of Kent, *The Anglo-Norman* Alexander (*Le Roman de Toute Chevalerie*) ed. B. Foster (2 vols., Anglo-Norman Text Society, xxix–xxxi, 1976–77) i, ll. 6653–56.

Contents

List of Plates

(*In central plate section*)

Acknowledgements

We are grateful to the following for permission to reproduce copyright material:

Plates 1 and 6 © Archivo Iconografico, S.A./CORBIS; Plate 2 © Historical Picture Archive/CORBIS. Photo: Philip de Bay; Plate 3 © Angelo Hornak/CORBIS; Plate 4 reproduced by permission of the British Library, London; Plate 5 courtesy of The Bridgeman Art Library; Plate 7 © Bettmann/CORBIS; Plate 8 © The British Library, Institution Reference: Shelfmark ID: Cotton MS Tiberius A.VI Folio No: 71. Image courtesy of the Heritage Image Partnership; Plate 9 Sir Frank Stenton Collection, © University of Reading; Plate 10 courtesy of Musee Conde, Chantilly, France, Lauros / Giraudon / www.bridgeman.co.uk.

In some instances we have been unable to trace the owners of copyright material, and we would appreciate any information that would enable us to do so.

Foreword

Explaining medieval aristocracy to generation after generation of undergraduates has a cumulative effect. Time and again it has sent me back to basic ideas, and, each time I repeat the exercise, I am sent back deeper and deeper into the historiographical wilderness out of which they have emerged. This book is then a travelogue in history. It is a journal of my own explorations of a vast continent of sources and the tribes and cities of debate which have arisen upon it. Medieval though the period is, it is not a small space to explore. Its horizons recede before us as yet more studies and debates are published and become annexed to it, so I have to begin by saying that this travelogue cannot illustrate more than a small part of its wonders and curiosities. But there is this to it. The history of medieval aristocracy over the centuries has by no means been written in vain. Scholars have successfully mapped the essentials of its shape and its structure and this book is an overdue essay in recognising these great pioneers and their achievements.

Any such study accumulates debts, and I must acknowledge here help and advice received at various times from Andew Ayton, Richard Abels, Martin Aurell, David Bates, Martha Carlin, Sam Clark, Peter Coss, Thomas Deswarte, Robin Fleming, Natalie Fryde, John Gillingham, Lindy Grant, Julian Haseldine, Derek Keene, Chris Lewis, Nick Marshall, Nicholas Vincent and Ann Williams. I gladly and gratefully acknowledge the very wise and pertinent advice about this book's structure and content contributed by Maurice Keen, which has much improved its tone and organisation. I must also acknowledge with great gratitude support received in research and writing from L'Institut Universitaire de France, the Centre des Études Supérieures de Civilisation Médiévale (CNRS) at the University of Poitiers, the Leverhulme Trust, and the British Academy. The collections and librarians of the University of Hull, the Institute of Historical Research of the University of London and the Brotherton Library, University of Leeds, were as always invaluable. Parts of this work featured as papers given to the Haskins society at Cornell University, and to colloquia at Poitiers in 2002 and 2004 and at Göttingen in 2003. I offer my thanks to those scholars who contributed observations and apologies for not identifying them individually here.

A final point. When I chose the title of this book for a proposal several years ago, it was well before K-F. Werner's work *Naissance de la noblesse* (1998) came to my attention. I am a great admirer of Professor Werner's comparative work, but the title of this book is not flattering it by imitation.

Scarborough
September 2004

Introduction

I have organised this book into several categories by which the subject of aristocracy has been analysed in the past: conduct, family structure, class feeling and domination. These categories have emerged almost naturally from centuries of scholarship. In one of those intimidating philosophical phrases: past work has created a clear epistemology. Within each category I have discussed what historians have said about it, and on occasion looked at sociological concepts which have become part of the historiography. I have added to this reflections on the same category drawn from the primary source material, in the manner of a dialectic between sources and historiographical assumptions.

The last chapter in the last section is different from the rest. It encapsulates a study of noble women. It is placed in Part Four because the comparatively shallow historiography of noble women has largely focussed on power and powerlessness. Nonetheless, it is a different chapter from the others. The historiography of medieval women was constructed in these latter decades when the study of history has changed radically from what it was in past generations. It is therefore a subject which has a wider bearing than perhaps its place indicates.

The book is organised as an exercise in comparative history. I have looked at two principal national historiographies on the subject, British and French. Any study of medieval aristocracy which did not feature the French contribution would be of course useless. As you will see, the customs, attitudes and structures which came to define aristocracy appeared principally in northern and central France between 900 and 1300. Pre-conquest England was by no means immune to French influence, but after 1066, English aristocratic society was self-consciously a proud northern extension of a dominant French culture. It happens that there has been a cross-fertilisation between modern French and British historiographies of the subject, although not as often as one might hope. Very often, the two traditions have diverged radically. The American historiography of medieval aristocracy is by no means inconsiderable or unimportant, but it either favours that of Britain, as in the nineteenth and early twentieth century, or that of France, as in the last half-century. It has on occasion developed arguments independent of both, and these contributions will be noted in the appropriate places, but, in general, American historiography is dealt with as extensions of the British and French and is not part of the direct comparison. German historiography is of a different order entirely, and is not dealt with here except where it has directly affected the British and French. In part this was because German schools do tend to be independent. In part also I have shied away from Germany was because space simply did not permit it – a Franco-British comparison is complex and challenging enough, God knows. But it also has to be said that Franco-German comparative history on aristocracy has already been well served by eminent scholars and fruitful studies in ways that Franco-British history simply has not been.

The apparent indifference of the one national tradition to the other is peculiar enough. There have been isolated exceptions. One of Helen Cam's earliest (and least successful) studies was a directly comparative study, *Local Government in England and Francia* (1912). Of medievalists in Britain it is those of the earlier centuries who have been active in drawing comparisons between Britain and the Continent. It is enough here to cite the names of Donald Bullough, Janet Nelson and J.M. Wallace-Hadrill against any charge of insularity in that sector. The 'insularity' is found on the other side of the Channel. But the eleventh, twelfth and thirteenth centuries are a different matter. Apart from the special case of the Norman Conquest, which has drawn serious comparative historians since the time of Augustin Thierry at the beginning of the nineteenth century, there have been very few deliberate attempts to reconcile the aristocratic histories of 'the Continent' and 'Outre-manche'. In recent years, only Richard Kaeuper, *War, Justice and Public Order: England and France in the later Middle Ages* (1988) and Samuel Clark's *State and Status: the Rise of the State and Aristocratic Power in Western Europe* (1995) have made frontal assaults on the subject, each from different perspectives. The reasons why this has been so will be explained in the proper place. But it will be maintained here that noble society in England and France (outside Occitania) was in fact very similar, and each national aristocracy was closely comparable with the other. Indeed, it is clear that there was as much or as little difference between the aristocratic aspirations of England and the Ile-de-France as there was between those of the Ile-de-France and Poitou in the high middle ages.

A final introductory point is about the words 'nobility' and 'aristocracy'. They are different things. The difference is a finicky business, but it is important. The late Tim Reuter summed it up neatly. A nobility is a dominant group whose status is legally defined, while an aristocracy is the same group defined sociologically. So a nobility is a socially privileged group, whose privilege set it apart from others and was evident to contemporaries. An aristocracy, on the other hand, was a dominant group in society which drew its importance from its economic and social weight. As a group it is usually wider than the nobility in any generation, and its nature is more often evident to historians than to contemporaries.[1] This book is about the stratification of aristocracies and how social dominance became self-conscious hierarchical social class. So it is about how aristocracy became structured into nobility.

By this definition, the end of the process this book deals with came in France in the reign of King Philip IV (1285–1314). It is easy to demonstrate this because the French government of the time devised a procedure for 'ennobling' commoners, and thus endowing them with the privileges of nobility, even if they did not possess the accepted qualifications of lineage and noble connections (or 'parage'). A century before, this had been possible simply by knighting a man, as the writer Andrew the Chaplain said early in the 1180s. But by the mid-thirteenth century it was necessary first to be noble before a man could be knighted, so the rules had changed. In the first year of his reign, Philip IV of France began issuing a series of letters patent of ennoblement, apparently with the intention of raising money through the fees paid for them (his father had issued the earliest-known in 1270). Some of the newly formalised privileges that went with noble status in France were already ancient by the 1280s and had long belonged to knights (notably freedom from paying tolls while travelling), but some were new. These included the privilege of wearing high status clothing, as defined by emerging sumptuary legislation, and exemption from the heavy taxation on knights' fees held by non-nobles.[2]

In England, the situation of the noble and the appearance of a nobility is less easy to define. No medieval English king ever issued letters of ennoblement, so by a strict definition it might be said that England never had a nobility; the English just muddled along with their vague and unarticulated idea of aristocracy. In England it can seem that the only workable definition of a medieval nobleman remained a man who dressed and acted like a nobleman and was not laughed at.[3] But there have been suggestions that

[1] T. Reuter, 'The Medieval Nobility in Twentieth-Century Historiography' in, *Companion to Historiography*, ed. M. Bentley (London, 1997), 178–80.

[2] M. Aurell, *La noblesse en Occident, v^e^–xve siècle* (Paris, 1996), 95–7.

[3] D. Crouch, *The Image of Aristocracy in Britain, 1000–1300* (London, 1992), 2–3.

this is not the whole story. A definition of nobility as residing in the privileged court aristocracy in England, is a workable, if highly exclusive, one. K.B. McFarlane, in the 1953 Ford Lectures, suggested as much when he defined the privileged nobility in late medieval England as those men summoned by name to Great Councils and parliaments.[4] Indeed we find a consciousness amongst the higher English baronage as early as the mid-thirteenth century that it formed a social group of 'peers' set apart from the rest of society.[5] Such a minimalist approach does not comprehend the several thousands of late-medieval Englishmen who acted and lived in a noble style. However, the search to find an alternative and more exclusive definition has found no simple answers, just a series of criteria relating to birth, knighthood and noble service. The most productive and suggestive work in defining English nobility has only recently appeared. This is Peter Coss's cogent argument that in England the display of a heraldic device (and its eventual award by letters patent) was a workable way of defining who was or was not noble, and which groups within society could be considered to be part of the nobility.[6] Accepting this, we can describe both English and French societies around 1300 as having reached a self-consciousness that there was a nobility at the head of each. The business of this book is to work out how it got there.

4 K.B. McFarlane, *The Nobility of Later Medieval England* (Oxford, 1973), 142–5.

5 Ibid., 104–5.

6 P.R. Coss, 'Knighthood, Heraldry and Social Exclusion in Edwardian England' in, *Heraldry, Pageantry and Social Display in Medieval England*, ed. M. Keen and P.R. Coss (Woodbridge, 2002), 39–68, esp. 67–8.

PART ONE

NOBLE CONDUCT

CHAPTER 1

Reconstructing Chivalry

There was once a thing called chivalry. Unlike 'feudalism', for instance, it is not an invention of scholars; men once knew it, felt it, explained it to each other and practised it, after their fashion. When they did so, and what it was that they practised, are proper questions for historians. And the historical debate on chivalry is an ancient one. It could be said that it stretches back to the time of chivalry itself, for, as an ideal, it was a long time dying. Many Elizabethan gentlemen and Caroline courtiers wanted to be considered chivalric in their conduct and aspirations. Because it is an idea with this sort of continuity behind it, the debate on chivalry is a curious one. It became historically 'scientific' in Voltaire's France, at a time when reason alone was thought pure, and noble conduct and hypocrisy were regarded as one and the same thing. In the 1730s and 1740s antiquarian scholars began to investigate chivalry as a cultural phenomenon which was thought at the time to be dead and gone. But these first autopsies on a past system of values were made difficult by the refusal of the corpse to lie down. In England and France alike, other eighteenth-century people developed a curious nostalgia for the pastoral and heroic, especially what was heroic in the medieval past. Its simple and manly ideals were admired in days which people regarded as effete and corrupt. In England, the conscious concept of the 'gentleman' complicated things further, for the eighteenth- and nineteenth-century 'gentleman' regarded himself as the living lineal representative of the Plantagenet knight and the Stuart cavalier.

The result of this was that many early writers on medieval chivalry cannot be entirely trusted as historians. They sometimes have a polemical purpose which colours their prose. In this chapter, I have broadly divided the study of chivalry into two periods. The first, which lasted into the twentieth century, was a time of didactic writing on the subject. Even the most rigorous of early writers, such as Charles Mills, might have a teaching purpose in mind as they wrote. For Mills, it was to demonstrate that the Regency gentleman was the ethical heir of a great moral estate, and to provide an inventory of its treasures. The extreme examples are those of the ultramontane Catholic writers Kenelm Henry Digby and Léon Gautier. For them chivalry was a means to transform their corrupt and secular worlds. Gautier constructed his massive analysis of medieval chivalry on purpose to expose the moral bankruptcy of the secular Third Republic, and to provide the ammunition for a moral revolution in France.

The age of polemical and didactic writing on chivalry ended, as much else, with the Great War. Chivalry lost ground as a living concept and polemicists went elsewhere in search of ideas to reform society. It was only after this that sober academic historians gingerly approached the corpse. The great medievalists of the nineteenth century had ignored chivalry as being a light subject, tainted by amateurs and romantics. It took several decades for the subject to attract serious historians, and it is no exaggeration to say that the academic study of chivalry did not really come alive as a debate until the 1980s. Historiographers will hardly be surprised that – just as the debate began – the idea of chivalry itself began to undergo deconstruction. What was the basic impulse that created noble conduct? 'Chivalry' was certainly a self-conscious medieval concept, but not until the first quarter of the thirteenth century.

What was noble about conduct before then? A sub-group of historians have now set up the secularised concept of 'courtliness' or 'cortoisie' as a more accurate tool to analyse distinctive noble conduct. It seems entirely appropriate that the study of chivalry might well fall beneath the swords of its critics, in the moment when it has triumphantly raised its bright banner above the ivory towers of Academe.

Preaching Chivalry

Nineteenth-century English gentlemen were quite conscious of how savage were their Anglo-Saxon ancestors. They had an explanation for how that savagery had been tamed so as to produce their urbane world: it had been by the discipline of feudalism and the inspiration of its good angel, chivalry. The idea of chivalry as a code of conduct to be admired or ridiculed was already deeply embedded in English literary culture by the nineteenth century. The tendency to admire or to ridicule chivalry was there as early as the seventeenth century, depending on whether you took Sir Philip Sidney or Cervantes's Don Quixote de la Mancha (first published in English in 1620) as your hero. The eighteenth century, in its patrician and Augustan way, was inclined to admire it, rather than ridicule it.

The founding father of reasoned eighteenth-century views on chivalric culture was Jean-Baptiste de la Curne de Sainte-Palaye (1697–1781), whose studies first appeared in print in the 1740s, and whose great work, *Mémoires sur l'ancienne chevalerie* was published in 1759–60.[1] Sainte-Palaye was by no means the first serious writer on chivalry, but he stands at the head of the lineage of analytical historians who looked at it as a historical phenomenon to be explained.[2] He drew on later medieval sources (particularly his beloved Froissart) to offer his readers an interpretation of chivalry as a pageant of heraldry, jousting and deeds of heroism; following a generic knight from childhood to the grave. Sainte-Palaye was not all that concerned to give the origins of chivalry a full historical treatment, although he had a vague belief that it came from the Teutonic forests of the days of Tacitus and eventually fell into ultimate decadence. But he did regard chivalry as having 'laws' and as being a self-conscious code. His book is at the root of all subsequent French and English scholarship on the subject, and is one reason why much of it is so very florid.

As it rose, the great literary wave of romanticism carried the idea of chivalry foaming on its crest, and picked it up very early. Many take the *Letters on Chivalry and Romance* (1762) of the literary critic, Bishop Richard Hurd (1720–1808), as the romantic movement's first conscious stirrings, and a mild sort of nostalgia for 'the Gothic chivalry' was a notable theme in the earliest of Hurd's twelve letters, although it was Spenser ('the great master of Chivalry himself') and Elizabethan court culture that he truly admired. Hurd's views were formed under French influence: he had read Montesquieu who convinced him that eleventh-century 'feudal government' was warlike and unstable, and so Hurd deduced that chivalry arose out of the courts of feudal princes who were

1 First published as, *Mémoires sur l'ancienne chevalerie* (2 vols, Paris, 1759–60), and in English as *Memoirs of Ancient Chivalry*, trans. Susanna Dobson (London, 1784). Sainte-Palaye was familiar to English readers as the first modern editor of Froissart, from whose chronicles he drew much of the material for his book on chivalry. He first presented his ideas in memoirs published in the *Histoire de l'Académie des Inscriptions et Belles-lettres* in 1743 and 1746, for the background, see V.M. Hamm, 'A Seventeenth-Century French Source for Hurd's *Letters on Chivalry and Romance*', *Publications of the Modern Language Association*, lii (1937), 820–8.

2 Sainte-Palaye was preceded by at least two French antiquarian writers keen to locate and publish chivalric texts: François Menestrier, *De la chevalerie ancienne et moderne* (Paris, 1683), whom Hurd had read, and P. Honoré de Sainte-Marie, *Dissertations historiques et critiques sur la chevalerie* (Paris, 1738).

imposing order on their world. He had gratefully read Sainte-Palaye, so he believed that chivalry was an improving moral code and that knights were brought up in it from their childhood. It was the nostalgia of Bishop Hurd that was behind Edmund Burke's declaration that the 'age of chivalry was dead' in 1791 when he condemned the revolutionaries' treatment of Marie Antoinette; but poets and playwrights of the 1790s were also obsessed with the morality and language of the lost 'days' or 'age' of chivalry. By the time that Walter Scott rode the wave with the publication of *Ivanhoe* (1819), 'chivalry' had long been historicised; that is, it was understood to be a social movement with origins and a historical line of development.

It was in 1825, partly in response to Scott's loose way with evidence, that the young lawyer Charles Mills (1788–1826) offered a first historical account in English of how 'feudalism' and its guardian angel, 'chivalry', had taken the ancestors of the gentlemen of his day out of the 'rudeness and gloom' of the Teutonic forests, in his bestseller, *The History of Chivalry*, published just before his premature death.[3] Mills charmed his public (and indeed Sir Walter Scott himself) by making a direct – and not entirely inaccurate – connection between the chivalry of the age of Froissart and Caxton and the living civilized virtues of the Georgian gentleman (who read Froissart in Sainte-Palaye's edition). Mills drew a line to connect Sir John Chandos with Mr Darcy and Mr Knightley. He was not particularly original in his thinking. He had – and acknowledged – predecessors, notably Sainte-Palaye. But he was not entirely happy with Sainte-Palaye's work. He was irritated by the Frenchman's failure to tell the full story and his airy belief that knighthood 'had been the ornament merely of his own country' (he was by no means the last English-speaking historian to feel that particular cause of irritation with the French).

A new impulse behind Mills's work was his concern to draw a historian's distinction between the 'chivalric character' of the middle ages and the literary extravagance that informed most people's understanding of it. A thick and increasingly turgid stream of pseudo-medieval verse and fiction had been clogging English minds since the publication of the ancient ballads collected by Bishop Thomas Percy (1729–1811) and Thomas Warton the younger (1728–90). Where Charles Mills did a great service to medieval studies was in setting up a clear historical model of the development of chivalry in English. He declared that chivalry was a social, not a military phenomenon, and he tried to identify its key features: gen-

[3] C. Mills, *The History of Chivalry or Knighthood and its Times* (London, 1825), 3–5, 13–17.

erosity, fidelity, liberality and indeed courtesy. His influence had a long-term impact.[4] When the English historian J.E.A. Jolliffe wrote about his understanding of what defined a twelfth-century feudal baron in *Angevin Kingship* (1955), he consciously echoed Sainte-Palaye and Mills in seeing the baron as a relic of the Teutonic forest, still possessed by a generic Northern *saevitas*, or savagery, at odds with the emerging concept of the monarchical state. For Jolliffe, like Mills, the twelfth century was 'a raw, ingenuous age, as yet imperfectly Christian and political'. Jolliffe's book was reissued in 1963 and still features on university reading lists (including my own).[5]

Studying chivalry with historical detachment was not always enough for some people. Many writers contemporary with Mills were all too keen to take chivalry as a moral and religious programme to counter the social problems of their own age. From the 1760s till the 1940s there were writers who believed that chivalry had a lot to teach their own day, whether it was in civic virtue, private manners, attitudes to the female sex or religion. Sir Walter Scott and Mills were historians in their approach, and although they both admired the ideal of chivalry from a distance they thought its relics had been long transformed into the modern gentleman. But others, like the romantic baronet, Sir Kenelm Henry Digby (1800–1880), in his influential and inspirational work, *The Broad Stone of Honour* (1822) made chivalry the basis of a passionate and unsubtle critique of their own England of Utilitarianism, satanic mills and the Reform Act. Digby's reception into the Catholic church in 1825 led to his book's reissue in an even more rarified and spiritualised form. This idealism reached perhaps its greatest absurdity when the concept of chivalry was absorbed into the romanticised, conservative politics of Disraeli's Young England movement.[6] The tendency by authors to preach chivalry at their

[4] Another contribution that Mills made to the study of medieval chivalry was his conscious method. He quoted Scott with approval: 'We have no hesitation in quoting the romances of chivalry as good evidence of the laws and customs of knighthood. The authors, like the artists of the period, invented nothing, but, copying the manners of the age in which they lived, transferred them without doubt or scruple to the period and personages of whom they treated.' *History of Chivalry*, 5.

[5] J.E.A. Jolliffe, *Angevin Kingship* (2nd edn., London 1963), 169.

[6] The effloresence of early nineteenth-century romantic chivalry in Britain is best observed through M. Girouard, *The Return to Camelot: Chivalry and the English Gentleman* (New Haven, 1981), esp. ch. 5, but see also the bibliographical essay in, F.J.C. Hearnshaw, 'Chivalry: its Place in History', in, *Chivalry: A Series of Studies to Illustrate its Historical Significance and Civilizing Influence*, ed. E. Prestage (London, 1928), 29–33.

own age lasted well into the twentieth century, and inspired and confused several generations of British youth. But the sublimity of Digby and his like had another impact. It made chivalry a subject beneath, or above, the consideration of the sober empiricism of the history school at Oxford in the 1860s and 1870s. History dons tended to ignore chivalry as being a subject for the lightweight and romantic student of the middle ages. The romanticism which infected the idea of chivalry quarantined it academically till as late as the inter-war years. There long remained a belief that the selflessness of chivalry should still be held up for admiration, and might be experienced on the playing fields of the greater English public schools or in the ranks of the Boy Scouts, in the air with Bigglesworth of the Royal Flying Corps and the Red Baron, or in the mythical Scotland of John Buchan.

The climax of chivalric rhetoric within the historical profession came at the end of the nineteenth century in France with the work of the right-wing Catholic archivist and historian, Léon Gautier (1832–97). In one sense, Gautier's *La Chevalerie* (1884) is simply a more focussed and extensive essay on the lines of Sainte-Palaye, whom he quotes extensively and whose basic structure he borrowed for his own work. It is the richness of its trawl of the literary and historical sources that makes Gautier's work still so valuable, as well as its focus on the formative years of the eleventh and twelfth centuries (he rarely trespassed beyond 1223 and the death of Philip Augustus). Despite his trenchant francocentric approach, his basic evolutionary outlook and his reconstruction of chivalry was little different to that of Mills, who had defined chivalry's full appearance as the point when knighthood took the Church under its protection. Gautier said much the same, if in a more ultramontane way: knighthood emerged from the Teutonic forests and was tutored into civilisation and chivalry by the Catholic Church, of which Gautier was such a partisan.

The principal difference between the reactionary Gautier and (say) his contemporary, the reactionary English historian Edward Augustus Freeman, was the extent to which Gautier was prepared to enthuse about Christian chivalry as a living social force. He seems not to have known anything of Kenelm Henry Digby: if he did, he ignored his fellow enthusiast as a trespasser in what was a French field. However, Gautier preached much the same social sermon on his chivalric gospel: both men saw their own time as a corrupt and effete one, and the revival of a religious and idealistic chivalry was the cure for its ills. Readers know where they are with Gautier from the start. The title page of his massive quarto work is adorned with an armed knight with downcast eyes holding a scroll bearing the word 'Credo'. He dedicated his book to the memory of Cervantes – of all people. Digby naturally despised Cervantes, but Gautier found a way to recruit him to the cause of chivalry. It is to Cervantes the veteran of Lepanto, the latter-day crusader, that he dedicates his book, not Cervantes the creator of Don Quixote 'who delivered the fatal blow to chivalry'.

It was his disgust with the bourgeois secularism and political selfishness of the Third Republic that powered Gautier's hypnotic rhetoric. He was a simple reactionary in the age of General Boulanger. He bristled at the thought that the intellectual élite of his nation, led by influential thinkers like Frédéric Le Play, was fixated on the modern example of the United States as a solution for French social and political problems. He wanted Frenchmen to look rather to their own ancient glories: the crusades, the vernacular epics of Charlemagne and the field of Bouvines. His book is illustrated in the manner of a plush picture Bible, and it is the serpent of secularity and modernity that the celestial proto-chevalier, St Michael, is slaying on the illustrated end-piece to his book. One of his final exhortations was that 'a nation which has fallen in love with its own comfort is a nation lost'.[7]

It is very easy to mock Gautier's ultramontane earnestness but to do that is to miss the major historical point of his work. True, he went far beyond the evidence in sacramentalising chivalric practices. He made the ceremony of dubbing a form of ordination into a collegiate knighthood. He was at his most apparently bizarre when he came out of his study like Moses in a frock coat to offer his own reconstructed 'ten commandments' for the chivalrous knight. But it is in fact at this point that Gautier needs to be taken most seriously. He was a fine literary scholar – more accomplished than many who have followed him – and his decalogue of chivalry was not entirely a figment of an obsessed mind. Although he was offering a non-existent medieval code of ten chivalric commandments to instruct the youth of the Third Republic in national pride and public virtue, he had a literary basis for it: a passage in the mid-thirteenth-century romance *Gaydon* listing the qualities that noble knights should *not* possess.[8] If theologians can argue the nature of God from what he is not, then Gautier could certainly argue a code of chivalry from what was not thought chivalrous at the time. The idea has been explored here too in suggesting the

[7] Gautier, *La chevalerie*, p.782: 'Une nation que aime avant tout le confort est une nation perdue'.

[8] Ibid., 31–34, 88. Sainte-Palaye too tried to define laws of chivalry, but he based it on the twenty-six articles of the oath taken by knights of the Order of the Holy Spirit founded by King Henry III of France (1574–89), *Memoirs of Ancient Chivalry*, 74.

existence of an archetypical 'anti-preudomme' (see pp.46–52). There is an eccentric greatness in Gautier's work which cannot be denied, and it has a significance as an historiographical turning-point in both England and France. His work was the last outpost of over a century of scholarship on chivalry, using still the methods and ideas developed in the eighteenth century. His *Chevalerie* was indeed very like a fortress built on the edge of a principality; the marchlands beyond it, into which historians of chivalry now ventured, were to be more debatable and uncertain places.[9]

Chivalry in Retreat, 1884–1984

The twentieth century rapidly turned away from chivalry as a phenomenon of relevance to its own time, which is perhaps a comment on the twentieth century itself. But the debate on medieval chivalry continued at a subdued and academic level: subdued because, in England at least, historians were not supposed to find it a concept sufficiently weighty for serious study. A curious feature of the century after Gautier is that, despite holding diverse views on the subject, historians seemed often to assume that they were all talking about the same thing when they talked of chivalry, even when they were not. This is very much the symptom of intellectual fragmentation and the absence of true debate. There were some general beliefs inherited from earlier writers. For most of the century it was still generally agreed that the chivalrous knight emerged into view out of the dark and violent times of the European Dark Ages under the tutelage of the Church. Chivalry was accepted to have been a consciously-taught code of virtues (Mills gave five, Gautier eight) instilled in a violent social group by a teaching Church, which took over the rite of passage of the fully-instructed squire into knighthood. But then the international consensus fragmented. The English empirical tradition tended to play down the influence of chivalry as no more than a hypocritical veneer concealing the brutal and unscrupulous nature of the medieval aristocracy.[10]

[9] For a brief critique of Gautier see, J.D. Adams, 'Modern Views of Medieval Chivalry, 1884–1984', in, *The Study of Chivalry: Resources and Approaches* (Kalamazoo MI, 1988), 46–9.

[10] Twentieth-century English writers were still capable of producing Pre-Raphaelite works on chivalry that dwelt on its romance and pageantry, notably that of the Scottish herald A.R. Hope Moncrieff, *Romance and Legend of Chivalry* (London, 1913); reasonable and sceptical English academic writers were still seduced into tracing its story down to the idealised conduct taught in the greater public schools, see Girouard, *Return to Camelot*, ch. 15; Hearnshaw, 'Chivalry: its Place in History', 21–2.

This dismissive view was also to be found beyond England. *The Waning of the Middle Ages* (1924), the great work on later medieval society by the Dutch historian, Johan Huizinga (1872–1945), had a very jaundiced view of chivalry. The hollowness of chivalry is a major theme of his book. He believed that chivalry was the only world view late medieval historians had. So when they launched into their chronicles, chivalric principles were their shallow substitute for the vast economic and social forces twentieth-century historians acknowledged as the moving forces in their history. Chivalry was 'the best they had in the way of general political ideas'. Naturally the professions of chivalry in their work fail to correspond with the butchery and treachery which they describe in their pragmatic political world. So to that extent chivalry was hypocrisy. Huizinga was not by any means a cynical historian. Echoing the polemical writers on chivalry of his own day, he was willing to recognise a genuine ideal of noble, masculine self-denial in chivalry. He paid a sort of homage to it (although he believed that it invariably became 'hideously corrupted'). Influenced by the philosopher William James and his famous work, *The Varieties of Religious Experience* (1904), Huizinga historicised chivalry as another example of an impulse towards idealised male behaviour found in ancient and eastern cultures.[11] But, these qualifications aside, Huizinga's critical and detached views still reinforced the trend in English professional historiography to devalue the study of chivalry. It concentrated instead on the practicalities of knighthood and its 'feudal' mechanics.

Twentieth-century French historians, even Marc Bloch, remained more caught up in the power of the concept of chivalry, perhaps in part because of the dying embers of the fervour of Gautier's rhetoric, perhaps also because early French literature largely consists of scores of chivalric epics and romances. This does account for the broad range and output of French literature on knightly life, even if it tended to be less focussed than in contemporary English studies. By the time of the Second World War, French and some French-influenced Anglophone scholarship was reaching common ground. The American historian, Sidney Painter, led the way. He was both amused and inspired by Gautier when he wrote his colourful and influential essay *French Chivalry* (1940). Painter had no conscious political agenda, and was certainly not hyper-religious in his treatment of the subject, but he saw more than hypocrisy in chivalry. His broader and more academic approach is evident in his formulation of new distinctions

[11] J. Huizinga, The *Waning of the Middle Ages*, trans. F. Hopman (repr. Harmondsworth, 1990), chs. 4–5.

between 'the courtly ideal', 'feudal chivalry' (that is, military and sporting) and 'religious chivalry' (that is, moral and introspective). It was a way of avoiding Gautier's glaring failure to reconcile all his medieval sources into the one universal model of Christian chivalry he was seeking. As far as Painter was concerned, Gautier only wrote about 'religious chivalry'.[12] Painter's distinctions were and remain useful, especially as the tendency at the end of the twentieth century has been to look to 'courtliness' as the proper word for the medieval aristocratic social code, not 'chivalry'. It was Painter who first broached in any conscious way the subject of courtliness as a major component of chivalry.

Marc Bloch gave *chevalerie* its own treatment in the exploration of what he called the 'second feudal age' in his *La Société Féodale* (1940–44). To him, as to English historians, the Church had been the agency which transformed the early medieval warrior into the twelfth-century knight and redefined it as an 'order'. He was willing to use Gautier's image of a 'new decalogue' to describe a self-conscious code of chivalry. But, like Painter, he made distinctions to improve on Gautier. In Bloch's case he made something of the change he saw in the contemporary literature. From the writings of Chrétien de Troyes he deduced that there was an age of secular courtly chivalry in late twelfth-century France. From the ethical and devotional writings of the likes of Raoul de Houdenc and Philip de Novara, he deduced that chivalry became spiritualised in the thirteenth century, that is, it provided material for theological reflection on lay life. He called this second stage 'prudhommie'.[13] Bloch and Painter between them set the tone for most of the subsequent Anglo-French coverage of chivalry. Indeed, a new entente was formulated quite early on in the work of Bloch's former senior colleague at Strasbourg, the literary historian Gustave Cohen (1879–1958): in 1949 he offered a synthesis between Bloch's views and those Painter had published. Cohen honoured Sainte-Palaye as the pioneer of chivalric studies but predictably passed over Gautier and his ten commandments of chivalry: Gautier's great work was a place 'from which you could draw a little, but ignore much': a comment in which we can sense the revulsion from Vichy and its Catholic chauvinism of a French Jew who had been a wartime refugee in Canada and the United States.[14]

[12] See comments in S. Painter, *French Chivalry* (repr. Ithaca NY, 1967), 168. Gautier, for instance, could not come to terms with what young twelfth-century ladies are said by the romances to have got up to: he was too shocked by the subject seriously to consider the erotic side of courtly romance.

[13] M. Bloch, *Feudal Society*, trans. L.A. Manyon (2nd edn, London, 1962) ii, 316–19.

[14] G. Cohen, *Histoire de la chevalerie en France au moyen âge* (Paris, 1949), esp. p. 7 on Gautier's work, 'où il y a un peu à puiser, mais beaucoup à laisser'.

For all his huge output on noble society, Georges Duby (1919–96), the most twentieth-century of medieval historians, had a limited and somewhat traditional outlook on chivalry when he engaged with the concept at all, which he did surprisingly infrequently. Perhaps he assumed that chivalry was subsumed into the over-arching *mentalité* of the age, which was his principal area of investigation. Nonetheless, he did have a particular outlook on chivalric conduct. In his 1976 preface to an edition of the *Roman de la Rose*, he linked it, like Bloch, with the growth of formal conduct in feudal courts in the twelfth century. But for Duby it was all one with the transforming effect of feudalism on society. Chivalry was a projection into social conduct of the growing wealth and possibilities of an aristocracy in the process of transformation, as it found ways of distinguishing itself from the poorer and lower orders which had become subjected to it. Chivalry drew its instructors from amongst the clergy educated in Ovid, Statius and Lucian, and by 1220 aristocratic society and its clergy had created a sophisticated and literary secular elite.[15] In his much-admired 1978 study *Les trois ordres* (*The Three Orders*) Duby's chapter on *chevalerie* has a lot to say about the ceremony of knighting and the 'order' of knighthood, but simply repeats what he had already said about courtly culture (*la culture courtoise*). It is not until his 1984 analysis of the ethics of the profession (*la morale de son ordre*) of William Marshal, 'the best knight in all the world', that Duby offers something explicit and less general on chivalry. Here he categorised knightly behaviour under several headings. It says how little the subject had moved in France that his breakdown of chivalry was not far distant from that of Gautier: the Marshal, he says, showed liberality, courtesy, honour, valour and loyalty.[16]

Duby did not therefore offer anything very new in defining chivalry's qualities. What he did do was to offer a new chronology for the transforming effect it exerted on the military aristocracy, and a new reason for regarding it as a secular phenomenon. Gautier had believed that knights were a pre-existing élite who became noble and pristine Christian chevaliers at the beginning of the twelfth century. Nobility simply became chivalric. Bloch agreed with this. The qualification for him was that the nobility which became chivalric in the early twelfth century was an upstart and violent one. Duby's treatment of knighthood was more sophisticated.

[15] G. Duby, 'Le Roman de la Rose', repr. in, *Mâle moyen âge: de l'amour et autres essais* (Paris, 1990), 83–117.

[16] G. Duby, *Les trois ordres ou l'imaginaire de féodalisme* (Paris, 1978), pt. 5, ch. 2; idem, *Guillaume le Maréchal ou le meilleur chevalier du monde* (Paris, 1984) ch. 4.

He separated the idea of nobility from knightliness. Knights in the twelfth century aspired to be noble, but they were subservient courtiers excluded by their betters. For him the nobility and knighthood did not come together in France till the beginning of the thirteenth century (a chronology which is still generally accepted). Nobility became chivalric for Duby when the ceremony of *adoubement* became the admission into a noble order. Then all three concepts: chivalry, knighthood and nobility fused into a new social class.

Duby also offered a new model for the secular culture which lay behind chivalry. He saw youth as a factor. In a short and brilliant essay, he demonstrated that there was a secular, heedless and playboy style of life which arose out of the young and rootless members of the warrior caste, and which kings and princes were happy to adopt and patronise in their courts.[17] This was what he meant by *la culture courtoise*. Lords and their men shared a common outlook: they were all horseback warriors. In a few generations this common outlook fused the behaviour of knights and their lords so that in the end there was nothing to tell them apart. All that was lacking to this theory was the empirical work to justify it. Duby's pupil, Jean Flori, offered in the 1970s and 1980s numerous studies to support the Duby chronology. The summation of them was offered in his *Essor de la Chevalerie* (The Rise of Knighthood) published in 1986.

Flori makes up for the previously limited French academic treatment of chivalry, and presents a uniquely detailed and integrated scheme as to how Anglo-French society in the twelfth century gave rise to a number of attempts to define a knightly ethic. A key part of his early work rests on the meaning of the word *chevalerie*, how by the year 1200 it was beginning to mean more than horsemanship and deeds-at arms, and had the additional meaning of a social and moral behaviour appropriate to noble knights.[18] The word was extended to describe the behaviour of all nobles.

[17] G. Duby, 'Au xiie siècle: les 'jeunes' dans la société aristocratique dans la France du nord-ouest', *Annales. Economie, société civilisation*, 5 (1964), 835–64, translated as, 'Youth in aristocratic society: northwestern France in the twelfth century', in, *The Chivalrous Society*, trans. C. Postan (London, 1977), 112–22.

[18] A view first formulated in, 'La notion de chevalerie dans les chansons de geste de xiie siècle: étude historique de vocabulaire', *Le Moyen Âge*, 81 (1975), 211–44, 407–44. G.S. Burgess, The Term "Chevalerie" in Twelfth-century French', in, *Medieval Codicology, Iconography, Literature, and Translation: Studies for Keith Val Sinclair*, ed. P.R. Monks and D.D.R. Owen (Leiden, 1994), 343–58, points to the relative rarity of the term in twelfth-century texts, and the lack of any firm instance of the ideological use of the word by 1180, other than the employment of the term 'order' by Stephen de Fougères to describe it.

Flori's treatment of chivalry is subtle and nuanced, but still admirably clear. For him, as for Duby, knighthood and nobility were originally separate concepts which had fused at the end of the twelfth century. The period from 1100 to 1200 saw the status and conduct of knights modified by a variety of agencies, notably the needs of the Church to make the protectors of Christendom socially acceptable despite their violence. Knighthood rose socially, and chivalry was the hot air in its balloon. The rise involved a complete ethical makeover for knights, which was taught and preached by a variety of twelfth-century clerical luminaries of whom the key figures were perhaps Bernard of Clairvaux and John of Salisbury. Threatened, particularly in the Plantagenet realms, by a rising merchant class and the professional mercenary, the knights assisted this process of adaptation from within their social group. They staked a claim to legitimate use of violence and juridical primacy over competing social groups. The literature which knights sponsored depicted ideal worlds where social order was (not surprisingly) dependent on their swords, and where kings and princes competed for their services.[19]

Such for Flori was the origins of chivalry, or as he terms it, *l'idéologie chevaleresque*. It was born out of the struggle for social hegemony in a vaguely Weberian world of competing classes and social ideologies. It should be noted that it has thus taken well over a century-and-a-half for social evolutionism to be deployed to analyse the phenomenon of chivalry. Ironically, if Gautier had analysed chivalry in a wholly descriptive eighteenth-century way, Flori analysed it in a way that was the cutting-edge social thought of the late nineteenth-century. It seems entirely appropriate that writing on chivalry has always lagged well behind the mainstream in historiography. Flori's prolific subsequent work has maintained this view, grafting on to it ideas about technological change in military life which made the knight more important on the battlefield.[20]

Coincidentally, exactly a century after Gautier's great work, a further landmark work on chivalry was published. This was Maurice Keen's *Chivalry* (1984). Keen's book took the same wide canvas as Sainte-Palaye, and surveyed the entire period when chivalry was a developing and developed social code. Unlike Sainte-Palaye, and indeed any other scholar of chivalry in three centuries, Keen provides a thorough synthesis between

[19] J. Flori, *L'Essor de la Chevalerie, xie-xiie siècles* (Geneva, 1986).

[20] Later recensions of his theories can be found in, *La Chevalerie en France au Moyen Âge* (Paris, 1995); *La Chevalerie* (Paris, 1998); *Richard Coeur de Lion: Le roi-chevalier* (Paris, 1999).

literary and historical sources for the extensive period he surveys, and not just in England and France, but in all the early western nations. The book remains a unique and perhaps unrepeatable exercise in the analysis of a major cultural and social theme in the medieval and early modern period. Keen and Flori share a methodology, which is surprising in view of the national traditions in which they wrote. In Keen's case his work method is predictable. He employs the patient empirical methods which originated in the Oxford school founded by William Stubbs. It was this same British school which marginalised the study of chivalry in the 1860s and 1870s. At that time, chivalry was seen as a medieval fantasy world at odds with the hard realities of the medieval society which could be reconstructed from legal and historical records. Chivalry was then also too popularised and confused with modern ideologies to be a respectable arena for a late nineteenth-century British scholar. By the 1980s, the slow percolation of French ideas and methods had changed the emphasis of British historical writing from institutions to mentalities, so chivalry was a subject ripe for reconsideration in Britain. Flori's adoption of the same nominalist and evidential method is more surprising, in view of the Annalist domination of French historiography and the Duby school's adherence to it, but it is evident that Flori had read English work where such methods are taken as the norm; he also acknowledged a debt to the methodology of François-Louis Ganshof. The pragmatic nature of Ganshof's writings on knighthood and feudalism always made him the Francophone historical scholar of choice in post-war England. The same may account for Flori's growing popularity in current Anglophone scholarship.

Maurice Keen's analysis of chivalry is one of the finest applications of British humanistic scholarship to a cultural theme. It provides a line of development of a chivalric code from its origins to its mutation into something new in the early modern period: Keen avoids eighteenth-century rhetoric about the 'decay' or 'decline' of chivalry, rhetoric drawn ultimately from Cervantes. Keen presents a narrative of chivalry fashioned out of two centuries of international scholarship, as well as a wide and critical knowledge of the historical and literary sources superior to anything ever previously deployed in the field. This is his principal achievement, and its significance should not be underestimated. Otherwise Keen's *Chivalry* is a summation of current scholarship; it redirects but does not overturn it. Like Painter he sees both secular and spiritual strands in the weave of chivalry, the difference from Painter being that he has taken Duby's ideas about the youth of the eleventh and twelfth centuries and found there the source of the courtly culture that dominated the late twelfth century. To him, like Duby and Flori, it is the secular strand that it is the thickest in the fabric of chivalry; something christianised rather than Christ-inspired. Indeed, he goes further than Flori, and denies the Church had any plan to sacramentalise and control the ceremony of *adoubement*, it merely offered some ideological scaffolding for a secular ideal. In this way Keen asserts and summarises what is the major difference between nineteenth- and twentieth-century views on chivalry. The nineteenth century saw chivalry as a device of the Church to tame the feudal warrior. The twentieth century increasingly saw chivalry as a code of conduct which arose within the warrior caste, and which absorbed a few ethical norms from the Church's teaching on what was godly authority and what was tyranny.[21]

As with Gautier in 1884, so with Keen in 1984. His book too stands like a border post looking out on an uncertain country. The reason in this case is that subsequent writers have not been entirely happy that what we call 'chivalry' is the right word for noble conduct. Keen and Flori are together responsible for this, although neither writer doubted that chivalry existed and noble conduct could be comprehended by the word. Keen is responsible because he brought to the fore the secular side of chivalry, and so opened new avenues of investigating noble conduct. Flori is responsible because he made the troubling observation that the word 'chevalerie' was not applied to noble conduct until the end of the twelfth century. Flori opens up the question as to what was noble conduct before chivalry became the word for it.

Towards Secularism : The Kingdom of Courtliness

Some clues to the lie of the new land may already exist. Keen, as I have said, helped trigger a major redirection in the study of chivalry in the 1980s. At issue was the old question of chivalry's part in the civilising process; a question first raised explicitly in the 1820s. A sociologist provided the bomb with a long time-fuse which has eventually exploded and diverted historical debate. It was Max Weber (1864–1920) who in his posthumously-published work *Wirtschaft und Gesellschaft* (1922) articulated an idea which led ultimately to a suggested medieval social transformation in terms of conduct. For him, 'feudal' society took the charismatic warrior lordship of primitive medieval societies and tamed it, making it 'routine' or 'workaday' (the process of *Veralltaglichung*).[22]

[21] See useful observations in J.D. Adams, 'Modern Views of Medieval Chivalry', 68–70.

[22] M. Weber, *The Theory of Social and Economic Organization*, trans. A.M. Henderson and T. Parsons (New York, 1947), 329–35.

German historians took the lead in articulating this idea of taming and social routinization and applying it to the middle ages. So Otto Hintze in 1929 took the already ancient observation that feudalism tamed warrior society, but gave it a finer edge by saying that feudalism therefore prepared the way for the evolution of the Weberian disciplined, bureaucratic state.[23]

For our purposes, what the German scholar Norbert Elias (1897–1990) did in 1939 with Weber's insight was more relevant to the social history of France and England. For Elias, the appearance of the feudal princely court compelled those attracted to it to modify their unconstrained, autonomous and violent impulses and accept artificial and non-violent norms of conduct. Elias had adopted Weber's idea that the origins of the state lay in the establishment by princes of a monopoly on physical coercion; so for Elias the prince's court was the germ from which the state grew. In this way, according to Elias, courtly chivalry civilised society.[24] It should be noted that deep beneath Weber and Elias's work is a Marxian assumption that the mainsprings of the process were secular and socio-economic. To examine chivalry and medieval culture in their way was to come down from the rarified spires of religious ideology and pass into the counting-house of secularism.

When Sidney Painter produced his Anglo-French synthesis on chivalric society in 1940 he showed no awareness of this materialist and Weberian angle. He did, however, work on a parallel line. Painter made the social observation that the knight was a step forward in the domestication of masculine ethics, which he defined in a nineteenth-century way as the evolution of the modern gentleman from the hero of Germanic legend.[25] In this Painter was following at a distance the ideas of medieval social and cul-

[23] O. Hintze, 'Wesen und Verbreitung des Feudalismus', *Sitzungsberichte der Preussischen Akademie der Wissenschaften, phil-hist. Klasse*, 20 (Berlin, 1929), 321–30, translated as, 'The Nature of Feudalism', in, *Lordship and Community in Medieval Europe: Selected Readings*, ed. F.L. Cheyette (New York, 1975), 22–31.

[24] N. Elias, *Über den Prozess der Zivilisation* (2 vols, Basel, 1939), published in English as *The Civilizing Process*, trans. E. Jephcott (Oxford, 1994), see esp. pt.3: 'Feudalization and State Formation'. Similar and unrelated observations about the influence of the court on warrior behaviour were being made centuries before Elias, as for instance in Richard Hurd's third letter on chivalry: 'For the castles of the barons were ... the courts of these little sovereigns, as well as their fortresses; and the resort of their vassals thither, in honour of their chiefs, and for their own proper security, would make that civility and politeness, which is seen in courts and insensibly prevails there, a predominant part in the character of these assemblies', *Letters on Chivalry and Romance* (London, 1762), 15–16.

[25] S. Painter, *French Chivalry: Chivalric Ideas and Practices in Mediaeval France* (Baltimore, 1940), 28–9.

tural transformation of his own master, Charles Homer Haskins, which are set out in his *Twelfth-Century Renaissance* (1927). Haskins, like Weber, had simply absorbed by intellectual osmosis the old idea, as old as Sainte-Palaye and Boulainvilliers (and qualified by Montesquieu) that early medieval society was violent and unrestrained, and that feudal chivalry made it less so. Haskins found the engine for change in the twelfth-century French rediscovery of the study of the models of behaviour offered by classical literature, a theme which would eventually resurface in later work. Painter, for his part, explored a different possible mechanism for the growth of civilised behaviour. He proposed the idea that it was the courtly romances of the later twelfth century which achieved it by producing a new variant of chivalry, one in which aristocrats were obliged to honour women, and interact socially with them to the benefit of their prowess. In this way social behaviour was softened and disciplined, although, as far as Painter was concerned, violence continued because men tried to impress women by fighting hard to show themselves at an advantage. Still, the new courtly knight of the twelfth century would have proved himself as of some use outside the battlefield: if he could learn to please women by fair words, he could learn to please princes too; this for Painter was 'courtly chivalry'.[26]

The idea that the princely court was the school of restrained conduct was therefore reached independently by several minds in the first half of the twentieth century, but it took a while for it to be articulated in relation to the middle ages. The social consequences of the need for subordinates to please princes had of course been treated at length by Elias the year before Painter published *French Chivalry*. But Elias's work did not gain much currency in the English-speaking world before the 1970s. It was not until the 1980s – that key decade in the historiography of chivalry – that a writer reinterpreted medieval aristocratic behaviour in the light of what Elias had to say about the power of the court to modify the innate violence of warrior leaders. The scholar in question was the American scholar of medieval German culture, Stephen Jaeger, who published his influential work, *The Origins of Courtliness* in 1985, the year between Keen and Flori's landmark books. Jaeger's thesis was extensively argued, but still essentially a simple one. The ultimate engine of social change was not the rediscovery of classical learning by the early twelfth-century French scholastics (as Haskins proposed); nor was it the influence of the late twelfth-century courtly romance (as Painter proposed); nor was it the

[26] Ibid., 148.

convergence of knighthood with ecclesiastical ideals around 1200 (as Duby and Flori proposed). To Jaeger it all happened much earlier. It happened in late-tenth-century Ottonian Germany, when imperial clergy devised from classical models a new social code to appeal to the emperor and his chancellor, and so gain the glittering prizes of the imperial court. From tenth-century Germany, this artificial secular model of courtly behaviour filtered into southern and then northern France, being taught to the knights of France and England by the clergy of the late twelfth and thirteenth century.

Jaeger leaves only a little space for 'religious chivalry' in his model, although he acknowledges it had some influence. His book does not engage directly with Keen, which is perhaps not surprising in view of the date of publication. But his failure to engage with Flori's ecclesiastical model of knightly transformation and his failure to note the significance of Duby's secular model of courtly youth does tend to devalue his own theories.[27] Nonetheless, Jaeger proposed several new and exciting ideas, and his book has attracted much attention. The first radical departure is Jaeger's willingness to project back civilised behaviour to courts as early as the beginning of the tenth century, at least for clerics. Previous scholarship, as far back as the Enlightenment, had tended to look to the twelfth century for evidence of culture and civilisation at court. This was the consequence of the francocentric and literary nature of chivalric scholarship from Sainte-Palaye onwards (although it might be noted that Montesquieu, although vague about chronology, seems to suggest that the Church and Monarchy were trying to counteract feudal indiscipline as early as the ninth century). Jaeger also offered the idea of self-conscious courtliness (*curialitas*) as a package of ideas in which the ambitious layman could seek instruction from the secular clergy who promoted it. Thirdly, he leaves us in no doubt that he sees medieval chivalry as 'a neo-classical institution', a statement which is at odds with most of the past three centuries of historiography (with the exception of Haskins). Jaeger's willingness to assert something so radical seems largely due to a lack of much engagement with

[27] See his prefatory notes in, C.S. Jaeger, *The Origins of Courtliness: Civilizing Trends and the Formation of Courtly Ideals, 939–1210* (Philadelphia, 1985), p. xii. The subsequent study by Aldo Scaglione, *Knights at Court: Courtliness, Chivalry and Courtesy from Ottonian Germany to the Italian Renaissance* (Berkeley CA, 1991), chs. 2–3, takes a similar line, although he is a little more interested in previous debate on chivalry (at least he mentions Duby, Flori and Keen) and fits the Jaeger thesis within a bigger, non-Germanic frame (see criticisms in ibid., 62–3) but he insensibly reinvents Painter's threefold compartmentalisation of chivalry.

non-German literature – either modern or medieval – at the time he wrote in the early 1980s, although that should not stand against his propositions, which he has not modified since.

Jaeger's work is directed at a wider field than just chivalry, although he clearly considers his work a contribution towards its study. His *Origins of Courtliness* is focussed rather on clerical culture, as is most of his subsequent work. So he believes that clerical thinking and teaching influenced lay behaviour, but as he does not particularly concentrate on chivalry, he does not test this assumption by exploring what pre-existing aristocratic culture might have been. He is not interested either in whether clergy themselves might have been profoundly influenced in their turn by the secular conduct of the households in which they grew up. But his great and abiding achievement is to offer a compelling and very accessible study of 'courtliness': behaviour appropriate for a medieval court. The systematic analysis of the components of a self-conscious courtliness is now a developing concern for students of chivalry.

Courtliness for Jaeger arose out of a clerical culture which had colonised the courts of princes. The late twentieth century has seen other views emerge, opposed to those of Jaeger. A principal one is the view that courtliness was a secular movement which rose out of knightly culture itself. Maurice Keen's work does itself lead in that direction, but subsequent work in English has gone much further. Richard Kaeuper, like Jaeger, begins with Norbert Elias's 'civilising process', although he is unimpressed by Elias's limited acquaintance with medieval sources and studies. Kaeuper's principal aim is to assess the degree to which concepts of honour and stubborn personal autonomy pushed medieval aristocrats towards violence. In that sense he is putting the emphasis back on the innate violence of the medieval aristocracy, and saying that the court's influence in taming it was limited. Kaeuper's treatment of chivalry places it in opposition to the ideologies of Church and State: to him it was an aggressive and secular ideology. In his work, religious ideals were an external (and sometimes resented) influence on knightly conduct. Anticlericalism was a natural response in knights to their own alienation from the rival clerical sphere of life. He does not believe (from the evidence of romance literature) that there was spiritual depth in knightly Christianity. Antagonism, anticlericalism and opposition to kings defined chivalry: which is why so many writers were determined to reform it from the eleventh century to the late middle ages. Chivalry, for Kaeuper, was not a force for mannered restraint in a military aristocracy.[28]

[28] R.W. Kaeuper, *Chivalry and Violence in Medieval Europe* (Oxford, 1999).

There is much in common between Kaeuper and Jaeger at one level. Both see knights as detached from clerical culture. They believe that, to the clerks, knights were a dangerous social force to be contained. Jaeger was more willing to think that the clerks had the upper hand in the struggle. At best for them both, knightly allegiance to Christianity was distant and conventional. And here is the major change in historiography on the threshold of the twenty-first century, a willingness to look elsewhere than Christian teaching to explain the ethos of chivalry. Another group of writings from the 1990s reinforces the impression that, since Maurice Keen's *Chivalry*, secularity has become the lens through which medieval chivalry is to be viewed. The works of the British historians, John Gillingham and Matthew Strickland, are more limited in ambition than those of Kaeuper and Jaeger, but they do share a common secularity, drawn ultimately from Keen himself. Their concept of chivalry is as a self-generated, internal aristocratic code which applied only to kings and nobles: 'chivalry', says Gillingham, 'was essentially an aristocratic business'. For Gillingham, constrained social behaviour begins to become apparent amongst the mid-eleventh-century Norman aristocracy and was imported into England by the Conqueror. The contrast of French aristocratic behaviour with the continuing iron-age morality of the indigenous English and Welsh social élites is very instructive. There had been a social change in eleventh-century Normandy (and by implication, in France too) which had failed to happen in Britain. What was the nature of that change? It was nothing to do with religion, it was all to do with the multiplication of socio-economic assets, such as towns and castles, which could be exchanged for the sparing of their lord's life and limbs.[29]

Gillingham's is a pragmatic and non-ideological chivalry; he marginalises the religious and epistemological concerns of earlier generations of writers in favour of a concentration on secular questions, such as pinpointing the time when warfare became less barbarous. He is apt to cite

[29] J. Gillingham, '1066 and the Introduction of Chivalry into England', in, *Law and Government in Medieval England and Normandy: Essays in Honour of James Holt*, ed. G. Garnett and J.G. Hudson (Cambridge, 1994), 31–55, quote from p. 51. Gillingham had already broached the instructive contrast between fringe Celtic cultures and the Francocentric ones in, 'Conquering the Barbarians: War and Chivalry in Twelfth-century Britain', *Haskins Society Journal*, 4 (1992), 67–84. Gillingham made a case for pre-Conquest English thegns embracing some of Jaeger's courtly virtues, although they did not have the forbearance of the contemporary French knightly ethic of mercy, see J. Gillingham, 'Thegns and Knights in Eleventh-Century', *Transactions of the Royal Historical Society*, 6th ser., 5 (1995), 147–51.

what he calls a 'code of honour' amongst warriors, for which he sometimes uses Painter's word, 'courtesy' and sometimes the concept of 'chivalry'. He has explored some aspects of what that sort of chivalry was, and quite how old it was, in a valuable analysis of Geoffrey Gaimar's *Estoire des Engleis* (*c.*1139). He found there the same sorts of values and noble behaviour as Jaeger found in his analysis of late twelfth-century courtly literature: liberality, witty good humour and restraint. Gillingham concludes that Gaimar was writing to defend the reputation of William Rufus, seeing him as a pattern chivalric king to set against his brooding, ruthless father, the Conqueror.[30] The secular, military view of chivalry is equally evident in the more extensive work of Matthew Strickland, notably in his *War and Chivalry* (1996). Strickland's chivalry is as much a warrior ethic as is Gillingham's; chivalrous qualities are for him an idealization of what makes a warrior admirable, or indeed serviceable: honour, loyalty, courage and generosity. Within this context Strickland is uncomfortable with Christianity as a central factor in the formulation of medieval warrior ethics – although indeed thirteenth-century writers believed otherwise (see below, p. 82). He points out (in unconscious echo of Kenelm Henry Digby) that, in their day, pagan Viking, and Christian Anglo-Saxons and Franks all seemed to belong in the same warrior world, whereas Christian Celtic warriors showed less restraint in battle than contemporary Anglo-Norman knights.[31] For both Gillingham and Strickland, chivalry is restraint of violence amongst fellow warriors. Naturally, therefore, both would reject the chronology of Jaeger, and neither then needs to engage with other aspects of the 'code'.

The declining emphasis that scholars are inclined to place on Christian ideals as an influence on chivalry is one defining feature of twentieth-century historiography. Another – which has ultimately perhaps a lot to do with Gautier – is the readiness to concentrate on the period 1050 to 1220 as the period which is of key importance in the development of a conscious chivalric code. This is certainly true of French historiography, although perhaps less so of Anglophone scholars, especially since the work of Maurice Keen and his admirers. A third, and perhaps long-lasting factor is the tendency to hive off the discussion of noble behaviour into a separate

30 J. Gillingham, 'Kingship, Chivalry and Love. Political and Cultural Values in the Earliest History written in French: Geoffrey Gaimar's *Estoire des Engleis*', in, *Anglo-Norman Political Culture and the Twelfth-Century Renaissance*, ed. C.W. Hollister (Woodbridge, 1997), 33–58. For more on this see below, p. 37ff.

31 *War and Chivalry : the Conduct and Perception of War in England and Normandy, 1066–1217* (Cambridge, 1996), esp. 19–30.

category of 'courtliness' or 'courtesy', and in the case of certain British scholars, to distinguish those concepts from the ethics of the warrior-knight. It was for them career strategy and warrior freemasonry. Time will perhaps tell if this secular impulse is no more than historians doing what they are so good at doing: being creatures of their own times, in this case 'post-Christian' times.

It is only right then the last word on all this should belong to an eleventh-century warrior: that remarkable eleventh-century count, Fulk le Réchin of Anjou. Count Fulk was a literate, well-read and reflective man; he wrote his own autobiography. In the 1080s he himself wrote a letter to the dean of St-Laud of Angers from his siege camp around Château-du-Loir, which he had just taken by storm. Jesus Christ, he wrote, had just given him the palm of victory. He had led his army against the castle on a Friday, and he had observed that it had fallen at the very hour Christ had died on the cross on another Friday. He seems to have put down the rapid fall of the fortress to the fact that its crossbowmen had been provided with leaves from a bible to make flights for their bolts, given them by the treasurer of Le Mans, who was sheltering there. Fulk had personally arrested the cringing treasurer as the castle fell, and taken from him the collection of relics he and his chaplains were trying to take out of the castle. He broke the locks and pulled out the various bones within, including the jaw of St Julian of Le Mans, which he handled reverently and kissed. He was shocked when his own jaw promptly and painfully dislocated. His men, he said, quailed at this and suggested he hand the dangerous relics back. He refused and vowed instead that he would keep them with honour in his own church. At this, Christ had taken all the pain quite away, although his jaw remained out of place. So he sent the relics to the church of St-Laud, for the Friday on which Château-du-Loir fell was his feast day.[32] The post-Enlightenment mind will find Count Fulk's to be superstititious and credulous. But we should reflect more on the way that this eleventh-century warrior rationalised events against a spiritual and not a pragmatic frame, and that he did so without any evident hypocrisy. As the castle fell, he was observing the hours of the passion. It was the canon treasurer of the cathedral of Le Mans who was pragmatic and irreligious, not him. To understand medieval warriors, we have to bear in mind that they included men like Count Fulk, meaning that there were knights who were wide open to moral and religious, as well as pragmatic arguments.

[32] *Cartulaire du chapitre de Saint-Laud d'Angers*, ed. A. Planchenault (Angers, 1903), 97–8.

CHAPTER 2

From *Preudommie* to *Chevalerie*

The abiding question about chivalry, as we have seen, is the question of its origins. Right at the beginning of the debate, Sainte-Palaye assumed that there was always the potential for noble behaviour to be found amongst free warriors, even in the ancient Teutonic war bands. For him, the rough warrior virtues were there before they were refined and moulded by Christian teaching. Early medieval writers had in fact preceded Sainte-Palaye in this belief. The elegiast of Jumièges who in 942 lamented the death of William Longsword, count of Rouen, reflected that the count was born outside France to a pagan father, but that he became the model of a virtuous Christian prince. It followed that the potential nobility of William Longsword was there, even before he was a Christian. His baptism opened up his moral horizons. The fact that medieval writers believed in the existence of noble pagans and noble Saracens meant that for some of them the potential for noble conduct was universal. But equally, Sainte-Palaye believed that it was the Church which took the rough warrior in hand and slowly educated him in new and higher ideals. Some voices in the present debate on courtliness would not echo this belief, as we have seen. Whether the influence was fear of the disfavour of the prince, the freemasonry of a warrior elite, or emulation of the humanistic ideals of the Ancient world, some writers on courtliness would look elsewhere than the Church for the origins of chivalry.

In this chapter I will focus closely on early noble conduct. We are now obliged to do so. As we have seen, Jean Flori set off a historiographical mine by proving that the word 'chivalry' itself is not as old as the concept of an aristocratic conduct that it labels. The question as to what exactly came before it follows on naturally from Flori's insight. We have to wonder if there was anything 'chivalric' before 'chivalry' became chivalrous around 1200. Flori says that there was. Before 1200 there was a pattern of conduct which was chivalry's prehistory, and he looked to find out what it was in the body of ethics preached at the princes of the eleventh century. Can we go further? Was there before 1200 a more focussed ideal of noble conduct than the concept of a 'chivalric prehistory' admits? This chapter will argue that there was. There is a character in the sources whom the historians of chivalry have so far overlooked (with one distinguished exception). As early as 1100, there was an ideal type of mature, discreet and wise conduct, and it was to be found in the conduct of the proverbial *preudomme*. The *preudomme* summed up in himself all the best expectations which society laid on its leaders and protectors. This is why he features so strongly in the proverb collections of the twelfth and thirteenth century. That a *preudomme* did this or did that was the way that proper conduct was taught to the young, and all the young aspired to be recognised in time as a *preudomme*.

The *preudomme* appeared fully formed in the emerging vernacular sources at the end of the eleventh century. He was in existence as the model of noble conduct a century before the knight was admitted to be noble simply because he was a knight. The *preudomme* remained an important measure of lay conduct through the twelfth and into the fourteenth century: he was known to St Louis and to Geoffrey de Charny. But by the time of Charny the *preudomme*'s essential qualities were also those expected of the *preu chevalier*, and so in due course the older ideal faded away. In modern French, a *prud'homme* is now little more than a legal term for a responsible adult male. However before the *preudomme* faded away, he had achieved much. It was on the foundation of what the *preudomme* did that much of the later code of chivalry was erected in the thirteenth century.

Noble Conduct before Chivalry: The *Preudomme*

We are not of course all that well-off for sources which describe the proper conduct of the eleventh-century lay person. The starting point for such a study has to be the epic *Song of Roland*, which arose out of eleventh-century lay culture and was committed to parchment around 1100, perhaps in England. An important point that can be quickly established is that the *Song* has an ideal of an aristocrat expressed as the *prozdom* or *preudomme*. The word pervades the *Song* and – it might be said – also pervades the literary sources of the next two centuries, and although this has been noticed, it has not been much commented on; when it has, it has been dismissed as too broad a designation to count as a social category. Marc Bloch, however, long ago made the link between the *preudomme* and *cortoisie*. He believed that a *preudomme* was a synonym for the courtly man, and this opinion has long asked for closer scrutiny.[1]

The *prozdom* was a man who was, of course, *proz* or *preuz*. The word is a compound of three French words 'preuz' 'de' and 'homme'. The nearest English equivalent would be the old Hollywood Irish description for a likely fellow, 'a broth of a boy'. A *preudomme* was a '*preuz* of a man'. Well into the thirteenth century it was a popular word, with its root meaning still commonly understood. Later writers played with the meaning. They would talk amiably of a '*preuz* of a woman' or '*preuz* of a squire'.[2] Knowing that there was this current label does not get us very far in assessing aristocratic conduct, for *preuz* is as difficult a term to define as 'noble'. 'Valiant', 'useful', 'worthy' and 'notable' are suggested by various translators; the likeliest root of the word is the Latin *probus* (upstanding, honest) and philologists reject the attractive suggested alternative, *prudens* (instructed, discreet, judicious).[3] In the *Song*, men are called *prozdom* when they assist their lords with good counsel (ll. 26, 604) and when they strike manfully against their enemies (ll. 1288, 1557). In one case *proz* (sound) counsel is opposed to *fols* (reckless) counsel (ll. 1193, 1209) and elsewhere it qualifies names and deeds which confer prestige (ll.

[1] M. Bloch, *Feudal Society,* trans. L.A. Manyon (2 vols., London, 1962) ii, 305–6. Some of the following material was explored by me in, D. Crouch, 'Loyalty, Career and Self-Justification at the Plantagenet Court: the Thought World of William Marshal and his Colleagues' in, *Culture Politique des Plantagenet (1154–1224)*, ed. M. Aurell (Poitiers, 2003), 229–40.

[2] The Burgundian author of the *Prose Lancelot* talked occasionally of 'preudebacheler', 'preudechevalier' and even 'preudeserjanz', as well as 'preudeshomes', although the last term is by far the more common in the work. In the last quarter of the twelfth century Chrétien de Troyes (in *Le Chevalier au Lion (Yvain)*, ed. M. Roques (Classiques français du moyen âge, 1982) l. 786 'de prode fame et de prodome') and the author of the *Song of Aspremont* noted also a category of 'prodefeme'; good wives who are wise and undaunted in council. Another definition of a 'prodefeme' according to a late twelfth-century proverb was that they refrained from calling their maidservants whores when they were annoyed.

[3] See in this regard the views of Andrew the Chaplain, that a man who had 'probitas' above that of others had a claim to be considered truly noble, even if his birth was undistinguished, *On Love*, ed. and trans. P.G. Walsh (London, 1982), 76–8.

221, 597).[4] The composite *prozdom* of the late eleventh century was therefore a man of mature sense and wisdom, an experienced and effective soldier, and a valued supporter of his prince. To be called a *prozdom* was to receive the respect and deference of your fellows at court and on the field of battle.

In the *Song*, one of the most obviously *proz* of men is Count Oliver, *li proz e li gentilz*, the companion of Roland. He has the courage and skill in arms to command respect in a military aristocracy, but also he is *sages* (a man of wisdom and good counsel), more so than his friend, Roland. Oliver reveals the qualities of the complete *prozdom*. He knows the hearts of men; he knows that Roland's aggression and misjudgement make him a danger to himself. Oliver is restrained in language, sound in judgement and objective in any situation. When the French see the Saracen army at Roncesvalles, it is Oliver who makes an accurate assessment of the enemy strength and deduces the chain of betrayal that has brought them there: he has *mesure*. It is Oliver who pragmatically advises Roland to summon assistance, and is of course ignored. As the *Song* says, Roland is *proz* but Oliver is *sages*.[5] A thorough *prozdom* had to be both these things, and the irony at the heart of the *Song* is that command is entrusted to a man who is *proz* but also *pesmes* (ill-judging) and who leads his men to a brave and holy, but unnecessary death. The *Song* seems undecided in the end as to whether Roland is the more admirable for his undaunted courage or Oliver for his sound judgement, but it is certainly aware of the tragedy that may follow when the true *prozdom* is ignored. Indeed, before he dies, Oliver has the chance (ll. 1723–26) to rebuke a repentant Roland for his rashness (*legerie*) and to praise moderate judgement (*mesure*) over recklessness

[4] The argument of G.J. Brault, '*Sapientia* dans la Chanson de Roland', *French Forum*, 1 (1976), 111, goes too far in attempting to make *proz* and *sages* synonymous, even on the evidence of the *Song*.

[5] For the dramatic significance of the opposed pair of heroes, J. Subrenat, 'e Oliver est proz', in, *Études de philologie romane et d'histoire littéraire offertes à Jules Hovrent*, ed. J-M. d'Heur and N. Cherubini (Liège, 1980), 461–7, which judges Oliver to be the author's real hero '. . . lui seul dans la *Chanson de Roland* est entouré d'une telle tendresse' (p.466). Interestingly, as far as medieval perceptions of Oliver are concerned, in the Tournament of Antichrist (*c.*1230) Roland's name was incised with Gawain's on the front of the helmet of Courtoisie, *Li Torneiemenz Antecrit*, ed. G. Wimmer and trans. S. Orgeur (2nd edn., Paris, 1995), ll. 1840–1. Fierce temper and passion were certainly forgiveable in a *preudomme*; see the opinion of the wise senator in, Philip de Remy, *La Manekine*, ed. H. Suchier (Société des anciens textes français, 1884), ll. 6033–4, that 'anger and distress are things that happen in good measure to many *preudome*'.

(*estultie*). To that extent, the *Song* is an anthem in praise of the complete *prozdom*.[6]

The *preudomme* can be said on this evidence to have been an 'ideal type' (to borrow a concept of Max Weber). It was already recognisable to lay people in the year 1100, and must certainly have been known in the preceding century too. Like any ideal type, the *preudomme* had a fitful relationship with reality; few men fitted all the requirements to be considered one. But it provided a model of conduct, something to aim at in the competition for status in medieval male society and something to use to criticise the behaviour of others. To paraphrase Walter of Arras: you know one when you've met one (see below n.10). Walter tells us something about the way the ideal of the *preudomme* was defined and taught in his society. Walter's work preserves scores of contemporary proverbs, most with a moral and social point. In a society which had low levels of lay literacy, it was by proverbs that norms and expectations were taught to the young. From late-twelfth-century proverbs we learn that behaviour in power was the true test of the *preudomme*; that you must trust a *preudomme*'s advice and follow his example; that his reputation is proof against detractors, and that the road to earning the status of a *preudomme* is a hard one. The point of all these is that there was a status that men could aim for, and which offered a socially healthy ambition to fulfil. It depended on the recognition of their peers, and behind this were expectations of conduct which fed the recognition.[7]

The *preudomme* was a consistent and persistent ideal of aristocratic virtue throughout the twelfth century: he was the practised soldier and

[6] For the contrast, E. Steidl, '*Meilz valt mesure*: Oliver, the Norman Chroniclers and the Model Commander', *Romance Philology*, 45 (1991/2) 251–68. J.H.M. McCash, '*Scientia* and *Sapientia* in the Chanson de Roland', *Medievalia et Humanistica*, new series, 11 (1982), 131–47, finds in the *Song* an exploration of Augustinian ideas about worldly wisdom as opposed to divine inspiration, and sees Roland as the exponent of the latter, and Oliver the former. She sees Roland as the true hero as being led to holy martyrdom by his actions. The point is certainly arguable, but only if the *Song* arose out of a clerical mentality; a lay and military mind would have looked at Roland's actions differently, and indeed the *Song* disapproves his military decisions in no uncertain terms, note Oliver's rebuke: 'Your prowess will destroy us all, Roland!' (l. 1731).

[7] For the proverbs concerned: *Proverbes français antérieurs au xve siècle*, ed. J. Morawski (Classiques français du moyen âge, 47, 1925), nos. 47,414, 505, 546, 1610, 1725, 1817. For their appearance and reflection in late twelfth-century literature, and their didactic function: E. Schulze-Busacker, *Proverbes et expressions proverbiales dans la littérature narrative du moyen âge français: recueil et analyse* (Paris, 1985), 45, 155, 178, 198, 205, 229, 268, 278.

man of affairs. Writers between 1100 and 1260 offer numerous incidental observations to support that belief. In the late 1130s the description was by no means confined to laypeople. For Geoffrey Gaimar, St. Aidan of Lindisfarne 'was a bishop *pruz* and valiant', while St. Wilfrid was a *prohom* because of his integrity and courage. In that same decade the anonymous author of the epic, the *Couronnement de Louis*, decided that God 'who rules and reconciles us all' was also a *prodom*. (It was not the Victorian period which decided God was a gentleman; medieval people even gave him a coat of arms.) But for the most part being *pruz* was a lay characteristic. King William Rufus of England in his wealth and stately grandeur was to Geoffrey Gaimar both *prodome* and *curteis*. The qualities the early-twelfth-century *prodom* needed were those which made a man 'chivalrous' a century later. When, in the *Couronnement de Louis*, the great hero, William of Orange, rode out to confront the Saracens attacking Rome, all marvelled at '*la bel chevalier, et pro et sage, corteis et enseignié*' (that handsome knight, valiant and wise, courtly and skilled).[8] The next generation had much the same ideal. According to Bishop Stephen de Fougères of Rennes in the mid 1170s, the *prodome* was the best of the inhabitants of the royal court, the sort that sordid flatterers and backbiters tried to overthrow. King and bishop alike must be *prodom* in their dignity, integrity and concept of public duty.[9] Walter of Arras, Bishop Stephen's contemporary in the Capetian realm, also believed that the *preudomme* was the pinnacle of virtue in public affairs: 'No-one knows what a man is worth until he has been elevated among others. When he has gone as high as he can, that is the point that he shows whether he is a *preudom*'.[10] Chrétien de Troyes made the socially telling point that a man could not be a *preudomme* who did not show largesse, which tells us that above-average wealth was regarded by some as a qualification for the description.[11]

[8] Geoffrey Gaimar, *L'Estoire des Engleis*, ed. A. Bell (Anglo-Norman Text Society, 1960), ll. 1316–17, 1617–19; *Le Couronnement de Louis*, ed. E. Langlois (Classiques français du moyen âge, 22, 1984), ll. 36, 608–9. The use of *preudom* to describe a holy man persisted: it is applied to the charismatic hermit who became King Arthur's confessor and spiritual adviser, *Lancelot do Lac*, E. Kennedy (2 vols, Oxford, 1980) i, 285.

[9] *Le Livre de Manières*, ed. R.A. Lodge (Geneva, 1979), cc, 21, 42, 86.

[10] *Eracle*, ed. G. Raynaud de Lage (Classiques français du moyen âge, 1976) ll. 1999–2002: 'Nus ne set home que il valt ançois qu'il soit montés en halt; quant il est montés dusqu'en som, lors primers pert s'il est preudom'.

[11] *Cligés*, ed. A. Micha (Classiques français du moyen âge, 1957), ll. 188–213.

Preudomme remained the defining French vernacular word for a virtuous and worthy aristocrat for centuries after the *Song of Roland*, and, as we have seen, writers began consciously to number and define the qualities the word evoked. By 1200 the urge to define ideal noble conduct was becoming increasingly powerful, as the boundaries of social groups were beginning to coalesce in people's minds. Conduct was one way to establish who was or was not noble. Strangely, it seems to have been contact with noble warriors who were not Christian which helped in part to solidify in medieval minds the qualities of a noble man. It was as if knowing that there were admirable emirs forced Christian noblemen to think what it was that they admired in each other, and how they defined virtue. So around 1190 the crusading writer of the *Song of Aspremont* described the noble Saracen knight Gorhan:

It is no wonder that he was a proud man, for he was wealthy and the possessor of great honors. He was pros, *tough and a very skilled horseman* (cevalerous). *He could play a good game of chess or backgammon. He was knowledgable about hawks, falcons and their use in the fens. No huntsman knew more than he did about woodcraft. In deciding court cases he was wise and insightful. To the proud he was indomitable and remorseless, but he behaved with humility and consideration to lesser folk. He was not greedy for possessions and was generous to important and humble people alike. In body he was well-proportioned and an object of admiration.'*[12]

A similar, but even better, example comes around 1220, when a writer in north-eastern France wrote a tract which has much to say about the *preudomme*, a work he called – significantly – the *Ordene de Chevalerie*. The example concerns another well-known admirable Saracen, in this case Saladin.

The *Ordene* depicts 'King' Saladin as being curious about Christian knighthood, and determined to take tuition from one of his prisoners, Hugh de Tabarie, prince of Galilee, a historical figure. The *Ordene* begins in terms familiar from the *Song*. Hugh teaches that the *preudomme* is wise (*sages*) and not indiscreet (*fols*). Although the tract then goes on to relate the *preudomme* to the precepts of biblical Wisdom literature – indicating that the author is working in the twelfth-century Latin clerical tradition of moralising on knighthood – the author nonetheless does have a secular

12 *La Chanson d'Aspremont*, ed. L. Brandin (2 vols, Classiques français du moyen âge, 1923–4) i, ll. 2212–23.

ideal before him. Hugh had outstanding qualities: he was full of bravery (*hardement*) and knightliness (*chevalerie*) and was a proper man to instruct others in the qualities of a knight. Hugh illustrates that he is a *preudomme* by the fearless frankness and assurance of his behaviour to Saladin; but, like Oliver, he is also prudent, and sensitive as to how far he can go in defying the king. He does not persist in his refusal to teach the 'pagan' king about Christian knighthood, and does not defy him when the king refuses to allow him to ransom other crusaders, because he could tell that Saladin was getting angry. The *preudomme* Hugh is assuredly a courtier and courtly man and, as the author says, King Saladin 'honoured him much because he found him to be a *preudomme*, and caused much honour to be done to him'.[13] If we wish to find a catalogue of what it was that Saladin recognised in Hugh, it is to be found in the contemporary moral lecture that the young Lancelot repeated for the Lady of the Lake on the 'merits, virtues and qualities' of a *preudome*: they included courtesy, wisdom, distinguished bearing (*debonaireté*), loyalty, valour, generosity and bravery – 'none can be reckoned a *preudome* who has them not in his heart'.[14]

But the *Ordene* is an essay on inauguration into the social degree of *chevaler*, not of *preudomme*. The *preudomme* is related in it to the *chevaler*, as the best sort of knight, but since no one could be admitted into an order of *preudomme*, then it was pretty much useless as a marker for admission into a noble social group. Also, as we have seen, a *preudomme* might as easily be a noble and pious clerk as a noble and wise layman. With the appearance and dissemination of the *Ordene*, the days of the *preudomme* as avatar of noble conduct began to be numbered. Most subsequent treatises on self-conscious noble conduct were written as essays on *chevalerie*, and it was *chevalerie* that ultimately gave its name to codified noble conduct. However, it would still be many decades before the ideal of the *preudomme* lost its force. The Hennuyer poet, Baldwin de Condé, could still write a poem in praise of the *preudomme* in the mid-thirteenth century. Baldwin's *preudomme* was a man who kept his promises and who gave generously; he had no fear or envy of others; he sought to do good whenever he could; he hated wickedness and loved justice; he would do no wrong so as to get on in the world, and he was courtly (*cortois*). Above all,

[13] *The Anonymous* Ordene de Chevalerie, ed. and trans. K. Busby (Utrecht Publications in General and Comparative Literature, 17, Amsterdam, 1983), 105–19, quotation from ll. 485–7.

[14] *Lancelot do Lac*, i, 141–2.

the *preudomme* loved prudent conduct (*mesure*) – 'the proper compass of life' – and respected sense (*raison*). Such a man would gain salvation after death, he said, and since Baldwin addressed his meditations to 'lords and ladies', it is clear enough that his *preudomme* was meant to be a lay ideal, not a clerical one.[15]

The *preudomme* was certainly an ideal of noble manhood which still very much concerned the court of Louis IX of France (1226–1270). When the poet Rutebeuf lamented the death of Count Eudes of Nevers in 1266, he lamented the death of a knight who was *preudome et sage*.[16] Count Eudes was the king's cousin, and their children had married. Louis IX himself gave much thought to what qualities a *preudomme* possessed, and according to his devoted friend and biographer, the lord of Joinville, went out of his way to teach them to his courtiers from his throne. Louis believed that to be known as a *preudomme* was great and good, and the most pleasant thing any man could hear of himself. A *preudomme* was a great and seasoned warrior whose opinion was to be heeded, and he characterised the opposite of a *preudomme* to be a fickle young knight. But principally Louis's court believed that the *preudomme* established himself by his moral probity and religious devotion as much as by his valour (*preu*). Valour was a quality which Joinville reflected could be found amongst Saracens and unbelievers as much as good Christians, so the heart of nobility must lie elsewhere. Joinville, like the author of the *Song of Roland*, made the distinction that there were many *preuz hommes* (brave men), but few *preudommes*.[17] Two-and-a-half centuries after the *Song of Roland* was written down, Joinville's grandson, Geoffrey de Charny, in his great *Book of Chivalry* (*c.*1352), was still just as likely as the *Song* and Joinville to use the word *preudoms* to denote a man of surpassing worth.

Courtliness and the Court before 1170

Preudommie is clearly linked to courtliness. Courtly conduct is believed by recent commentators to have become a fashion in noble behaviour in France and England at the end of the twelfth century. But the *preudomme*,

[15] *Dits et contes de Baudouin de Condé et de son fils Jean de Condé*, ed. A. Scheler (3 vols., Brussels, 1866-7) i, 95–105.

[16] *Oeuvres complètes de Rutebeuf*, ed. E. Faral and J. Bastin (2 vols, Paris, 1959–60) i, 455.

[17] Joinville, *Vie de Saint Louis*, ed. J. Monfrin (Paris, 1995), 12, 16, 76, 278. See for comments on this, M. Aurell, *La noblesse en Occident, v^e^-xve siècle* (Paris, 1996), 104.

as we have seen, was a restrained and courtly man at the time of the *Song of Roland*. By my reasoning, the antiquity of *preudommie* betrays the antiquity of courtliness. How far back did the idea and ideal of the *preudomme* stretch before the *Song of Roland*? As we have seen, a theme in the writings of John Gillingham is that lay 'courtliness' and 'chivalry' developed far earlier in secular culture than Stephen Jaeger's model would allow (see p. 27). Although Gillingham uses the anachronistic label of 'chivalry' for the period before the 1180s, idealised aristocratic behaviour, in the form of the *preudomme* certainly already existed. But tracking it back into the tenth and eleventh centuries is not easy. A useful but difficult source is the Latin hagiographical essay by clerics on lay folk who were regarded as exemplary laymen, or who turned to the cloister after long careers in the world. Three particular examples are Herluin, son of Ansgot, the founder of Bec-Hellouin, and Count Simon of Amiens, Valois and the Vexin, both men of affairs who had a distinguished career in the world before their conversion to monasticism. A further example is Count Bouchard of Corbeil or Vendôme, who also became a monk, although only in his last illness. The problem with this sort of source is that the authors of these *vitae* idealise their subjects' lay lives so that they can be seen to have been exceptionally religious or on the road to sanctity even before they converted. But in so far as the *vitae* do portray lay virtues, we find in them the following indications of the proto-*preudomme*.

One of the best examples is Herluin, son of Ansgot. He was the son of a landowner of Viking extraction settled in central Normandy in the late tenth century. Herluin was born around the year 996, the eldest of several brothers. His father fostered him into the household of Count Godfrey of Eu and Brionne, the brother of Duke Richard II, and he was brought up in company with Godfrey's son, Count Gilbert of Brionne, with whom he struck up a companionship which was later portrayed as not unlike that between Roland and Oliver: like Roland, the young Count Gilbert was aggressive and hot-headed, he was also fiercely acquisitive. Herluin, by the 1030s a leading member of Gilbert's military household, was praised by all the magnates of Normandy as a prudent and skilled knight, and even came to the attention of Duke Robert (1027–35). He was welcomed and talked of at the courts of the princes beyond the Norman frontier. Herluin became wealthy enough to support his own military household, but fell out with his master over some imagined slight, the implication being that the argument was linked to the count's envy of his knight's growing fame. Yet even though he had been insulted by Count Gilbert, Herluin still thought sufficiently little of his own dignity to rally to the count when he went to war with a rival, despite there having been no reconciliation between them. Gilbert, 'marvelling that such great service should be rendered in return for his injuries, at once granted Herluin access to his court again'.[18] Herluin seems, in his earlier career, to have been the model *preudomme*, as our later sources define the term: a practised soldier; a loyal but outspoken counsellor and courtier; a reasonable and upstanding man, recognised by his social superiors as deserving of their patronage. It could be argued that Herluin had to be portrayed that way for the hagiographical purposes of the monk who wrote his life a decade or so after his death. But in answer to that it could be replied that the eleventh-century author must himself have had an ideal of a lay aristocrat on which to build his picture. That author, Gilbert Crispin, later abbot of Westminster (died *c.*1117), was himself from a magnate family of the Norman march, and brought up in the 1060s in an environment in which the ideal of the *preudomme* would be very well-known.

For other, and more exalted, examples we have two eleventh-century counts. The first is Count Bouchard I of Vendôme (died *c.*1005). His memory was venerated at the abbey of St-Maur-des-Fosses in the valley of the Marne, east of Paris, and his life was described some five decades after his death by Eudes, a monk of the house, drawing on the abbey's records and the memories of its older inhabitants. Whether or not Eudes portrayed anything other than an idealised vision of the late count is unlikely, but the author did provide us with a catalogue of desirable tenth-century lay conduct. According to him Bouchard was a young man of noble origins, but he has nothing to say about any land Bouchard might have inherited. For Eudes, Bouchard was a soldier and counsellor who rose high at the court of Hugh Capet by his talents, and earned his wealth and his county by the marriage which was his reward for his loyalty. He resembled William Marshal, but was a prototype who lived two centuries earlier. Like any rightful lord, Count Bouchard was the protector of the weak, the clergy especially. In common with the successful courtiers of later centuries, Bouchard, as he rose through the ranks, had to deal with envious enemies at court. For all his 'modest manner of behaviour and speech' he could not avoid conspiracy against him, his particular enemy being Count Odo of Blois. But he stood up to Odo and overthrew him by his military

[18] *Vita beati Herluini*, in, *Patrologiae cursus completus: series Latina*, ed. J-P. Migne (221 vols., Paris, 1847–67) 150, cols. 695–6; trans. P. Fisher, in, S.N. Vaughn, *The Abbey of Bec and the Anglo-Norman State, 1034–1136* (Woodbridge, 1981), 67–86, quotation from p. 69.

skill. Yet, though ready for war, Bouchard was also a fluent and indomitable ambassador for peace and a great benefactor of the poor. He took to the cloister in his final illness and died at St-Maur.[19]

Count Simon of Amiens, Valois and the Vexin (1074–78) was a magnate of higher birth than Bouchard. His lineage stretched back to the Frankish Carolingian empire, and he ruled a complex of counties north of the Seine valley between the power of Paris and Rouen. He was the son of Count Ralph IV and had been brought up as a youth at the royal court in Normandy, probably in the period 1069–1074. There, according to his hagiographer, he had been tutored in an exceptionally religious environment, under the eye of the pious Queen Mathilda. When his father died, Simon was thrown into affairs of state, still a young man. As with Roland and Oliver, Count Bouchard and Count Odo, and Herluin and Count Gilbert, Simon's hagiographer gives us a foil to show up Simon's virtues, which were said to be exceptional. In this case the foil was his father, Count Ralph. Ralph was an accomplished warrior, but acquisitive and greedy, ready to use violence to take what he wanted. His son was also a tireless warrior, but fought instead to preserve his people from the rapacity of King Philip, not for his own advantage. Like Queen Mathilda and William the Conqueror, Simon regularly heard mass and divine office; as a righteous lord should, he protected and fed the poor, the orphan and the widow; honoured the humblest of monks, clerks and pilgrims, and gave alms handsomely.[20] He therefore, like Bouchard and Herluin, betrayed some expectations of ideal conduct amongst eleventh-century noblemen. Leaving aside the matters of piety and birth, there are expectations common to the later period: successful and admirable nobles should be accomplished and loyal soldiers, but not quick to violence; they should be useful and wise advisers; they should be mindful of the weak and defenceless and not proud in speech and conduct. Such at least was the ideal.

Something that resembled the *preudomme* as an ideal of lay behaviour seems therefore to have been as well-known in the century before the *Song of Roland* was written down, as he was in the century afterwards. That is perhaps as far as we can go in antedating his appearance as an ideal social type in French lay culture, although historians of Carolingian culture

[19] Eudes de St-Maur, *Vie de Bouchard le Vénérable*, ed. C. Bourel de la Roncière (Paris, 1892), and for the description that he was 'dictis factisque modestus', see p.30 (part of his epitaph). For the not inconsiderable amount which can otherwise be known about the man, see D. Barthélemy, *La société dans la comté de Vendôme de l'an mil au xive siècle* (Paris, 1993), 279–90.

[20] *Vita beati Simonis comitis Crespeiensis*, in, *PL* 156, cols. 1211–23.

might have an opinion on this. Sufficient has been said to confirm what some writers on courtliness have suggested. An ideal of noble conduct was in existence long before Chrétien de Troyes wrote, and it arose out of a secular milieu where the princely court modified lay behaviour. It had nothing to do with Classical humanism. It was a pragmatic response to a society where success depended on patronage. It was a modification of behaviour adopted by intelligent warriors which was calculated to improve their chances of gaining position and reward. Whether or not it was entirely a secular ideal is a further question, which will be addressed later on. At this point, I would only say that I believe Sainte-Palaye was right in believing that it owed a fair amount to the moral rationalisation of clerics.

We must stay for the moment in the civil field in which the *preudomme* operated. What were the modifications that made the courtly *preudomme*? The sources for the early twelfth century are sufficient to tell us how the early courtier behaved. For the ambitious and accomplished lay person, as much as for the clerk, the principal test of the man was how he conducted himself at the courts of the great princes and kings. There is no doubt that the virtue of the *preudomme* was recognised there, for in the 1170s Walter of Arras looked upon such a man as belonging to the higher echelon of the court: ‘An envious man shoulders a great weight when he sees a *preudomme* come to court’.[21] The culture of the twelfth-century court has recently received much attention, although largely from the perspective of the courtly clerk. Can we say anything as persuasive about the lay courtier, his conduct and aspirations? Since the court has been regarded for some generations now as the engine of the supposed civilising process in medieval society, this is an important area of enquiry.

In the Anglo-Norman realm in the first half of the twelfth century, we can glimpse several instances of the way the court shaped the behaviour of its inhabitants. The court of Henry I of England (1100–35) gives us a number of instances. It was a court rich in opportunities for the talented layperson. The king himself was a man willing to assist the fortunes of men who had administrative and legal talent, whatever their lack of lineage. We have an insight into the complex of offices and opportunities of the Anglo-Norman court in the *Constitutio*, a register of court appointments and allowances drawn up for the information of King Stephen in 1135–6, just after he had succeeded his uncle. There were already established and

[21] *Eracle*, ed. G. Raynaud de Lage (Classiques français du moyen âge, 1976) ll. 1069–70.

salaried departments: the chamber, the constabulary, the marshalsea, and the hall, with its groups of dispensers, butlers, pantlers, ushers and janitors under the supervision of the domestic steward. There was an element of hierarchy established within the departments, for instance, the ushers of the rank of knight were distinguished from the lesser ushers. Such men formed a permanent cadre of courtiers, augmented by a more diffuse group of other laymen who came into proximity of the king, men called by the general word 'justice', meaning that they had sufficient status of their own, and closeness to the king, to do justice and fulfil other commissions in his name. It is amongst these crowded and competing men that we would expect to find idealised courtly culture in the early part of the twelfth century.

One early and rather good example of the *preudomme* of the Norman court was Gilbert, sheriff of Surrey. Gilbert was apparently the heir and successor of Roger, sheriff of Cambridge and Huntingdon, and succeeded him around 1107; he may already have been presiding over Surrey by then. He died in 1125. The memorial of his life compiled soon after his death at his foundation of Merton priory described him as a well-born *miles*, an accomplished knight who had fought bravely in Normandy during his younger years before he took up public office. He is said to have had a considerable ability to engage the affections of his social superiors and inferiors alike. He was a man particularly in the favour of Queen Mathilda II, who took a personal interest in his career and most especially in his love of the advanced piety she too pursued. He is said to have had high standards of probity and an ability to discern falsity in people he met. King Henry was always deeply and publicly suspicious of his sheriffs, but never, we are told, did he treat Gilbert any way other than honourably and affectionately. His relationship with the royal court is described in telling terms.

Counts and barons held him in the highest regard and they recognised his nobility of mind with great gifts. He also had the respect of the lesser attendants of the royal household to the extent that he was treated by them all as if they were his own servants. He was served by them all as well as if he were the king. You might frequently see many bishops and other people of the highest distinction hanging around the door of the royal chamber for long periods, begging to go in, but quite unable to get a hearing. But if Gilbert happened to appear the doors were flung open to admit him, as soon as the ushers knew who it was. He was admitted to the royal presence as often as he wanted. When the sheriffs of England assembled at the exchequer and were all agitated and apprehensive,

Gilbert was the only man who turned up unperturbed and cheerful. As soon as he was summoned by the receivers of money, he sent the cash in and he promptly sat among them, quite at his ease, as if he were one of them himself. As everyone who knew him would confirm, it is impossible to underestimate the respect in which he was held, so much was he loved, esteemed and praised.[22]

This work, it should be remembered, is not hagiography, even though Gilbert's pious relationship with his mother is elsewhere portrayed much like that of St Augustine of Hippo with Monica. It is an attempt to picture a monastery's founder as the summit of lay excellence and virtue. Gilbert is therefore portrayed as the definitive *preudomme*, and it is significant that among the adverbs which the canon of Merton who wrote his memorial deployed about his demeanour and speech was that he was *curialius* (most courtly).

Successful lay courtiers were being ascribed particular virtues by the 1130s. They were talented soldiers and honest administrators. They were affable to all alike, and universally respected by all, from the king down to the palace servants. In their modesty they solicited no favours, but favours were rained upon them nonetheless. They lived amply but remembered the poor and their own undeserving humanity. Such men had a recognised label: they were *preudomme* in the vernacular and *curialius* in Latin. Count Stephen of Mortain was another recognised practitioner of curial virtue at the same court. The terms in which his courtly success is described echo those applied to Gilbert of Surrey. Both his friends and enemies agreed that he was *affabilis* (easy-going) in personal relations with all sorts of people, and *audax* or *impiger* (dashing) in war.[23] His friends and supporters praised him for being of high birth and great wealth, yet also *humilis* (humble). Like Gilbert of Surrey, he was also outstandingly pious; the epithet *piissimus* is the one most frequently given to him by medieval historians after he became king.

It is Stephen who leads us to the *preudomme* of whom we can know most in the twelfth and early thirteenth centuries. William Marshal was born around 1147 in Wiltshire in the latter years of the reign of Stephen to

[22] Translated from, M.L. Colker, 'Latin Texts concerning Gilbert, founder of Merton Priory', *Studia Monastica*, 12 (1970), 260–1.

[23] See the complementary and contrasting judgements of the *Gesta Stephani*, ed. and trans. K.R. Potter and R.H.C. Davis (Oxford, 1976), 4–6 (*c.*1147) and William of Malmesbury, *Historia Novella*, ed. and trans. K.R. Potter rev'd E. King (London, 1998), 16 (*c.*1143).

a father who was one of the king's opponents. In 1152 the boy William was handed over to the king by his father, John Marshal, as a hostage, so that he could trick the king into allowing him to reprovision his besieged castle at Newbury in Berkshire. The king was at liberty to mutilate or kill the captive boy, and indeed attempted to persuade the garrison of Newbury that he would do so; they apparently knew his reputation for being 'mild' (*lenis*) to his enemies and ignored his threats to their lord's son. Stephen finally gave up, and took on the little boy as his page for the next year or so. William, when he was an adult, talking to his own sons, recalled with affectionate astonishment that the bearded, venerable king and he at one time sat on the floor of the flower-strewn royal pavilion, playing knights with little men made of straw. Courtly men were already comprehending women and children within their gracious affability before the middle of the twelfth century. Stephen is particularly known for his refusal to make war on women; he would not besiege Sibyl de Lacy in Ludlow in 1138 and his rival, the Empress, at Arundel the next year.

The boy whom King Stephen entertained in his tent was to become the next in the apostolic succession of twelfth-century *preudommie*, and, we are told by his biographer, its greatest practitioner. As a young knight, William Marshal attracted royal attention and was retained in a succession of English royal households: that of Queen Eleanor, *c.*1168–70; the Young King Henry, 1170–83; and King Henry II himself, *c.*1185–89. He was given possession of a major baronial honor in 1189 by Richard the Lionheart and promoted to the earldom of Pembroke in 1199 by King John. He died in 1219 just after resigning as regent and protector of the boy Henry III. He had been a courtier for the best part of five decades. Since he was the subject of a rare medieval biography, written at his sons' commission in 1224–26, the Marshal should be the defining instance of a *preudomme* of the court. The adjectives applied to him by his biographer are a list of the ideal *preudomme*'s qualities: he was (of course) *pruz*, but also *leials* (loyal) *senés* (shrewd) and *vasauls* (manly).

Although the Marshal was the only *preudomme* of his day and age to have been memorialised by a biography, he was not the only one to have been memorialised. There is therefore a chance to compare the qualities (*taches*) for which the Marshal was praised with those praised by other writers. Between 1188 and 1189 the royal clerk, Gerald of Wales, wrote a history of the Anglo-Norman conquest of Ireland, in which his family had played a leading part two decades previously. In his narrative he incorporated sketches – in the measured manner of Suetonius – of the personalities and physical characteristics of several noblemen who had been known to him as a boy. We hear of Gerald's uncle, Maurice fitz Gerald (d.1176), a modest (*verecundus*) and distinguished (*venerabilis*) man who was naturally good and who eschewed arrogance.

It was his rule to observe restraint in all things, so that his life may be regarded as an implicit criticism of the manners of his country and of his times, but equally as an outstanding example of polished manners. A man of few words, he said little, but that little was well phrased, for he had a greater fund of sincere feeling than he had of words ... Yet when circumstances demanded that he speak, he was knowledgeable as he was slow to give his opinion. In war he was courageous and second to none in the valour he displayed. But he was neither headstrong nor impetuous in courting danger, though as unyielding when himself attacked as he was careful in mounting an attack. He was sober (sobrius), *temperate* (modestus) *and continent* (castus), *reliable* (stabilis), *steadfast* (firmus) *and loyal* (fidelis). *He was indeed not without his faults, but he was devoid of all great or extraordinary vices.*[24]

Gerald also gave a memoir of his recently-deceased elder first cousin, Raymond le Gros (d.c.1188) a man of vivacity and fine intelligence (*animi virtus*).

He was fortunate in this respect that never, or very rarely, did any body of men of which he had command come to grief through carelessness or enterprises rashly undertaken. He was a modest and thoughtful man, who was not fastidious in matters of food and dress. He had an equal capacity for putting up with heat or cold, and could endure anger and drudgery alike. He always preferred to help those under him, rather than to command them, to seem their servant rather than their master. To sum up the character, disposition and virtues of the man in a few words, he was generous (liberalis) *and lenient* (lenis), *careful* (providus) *and thoughtful* (prudens), *and although a man of very great courage and skilled in the use of arms, in war it was his sound judgement* (prudencia) *and foresight* (providencia) *which marked him out.*[25]

We hear something of the academic and archdeacon in these descriptions of men from the lay world: their chastity and temperance are praised, and Raymond, more keen to serve than be served, shares one of the defining

[24] *Expugnatio Hibernica*, ed. and trans. A.B. Scott and F.X. Martin (Royal Irish Academy, Dublin, 1978), 120–22.

[25] Ibid., 154.

qualities of Christ. Yet the lay world was also Gerald's world, for he was a determined frequenter of the court, so his witness as to what his world thought were desirable qualities in its leading laymen is sound. The virtues were solid ones: reliability, loyalty, good judgement, reticence, generosity, modesty, hardiness, and above all intelligence and restraint in making war.

Creating Chivalry: The Noble Habitus

We know now the qualities of the courtier-*preudomme* as they were recognised before the time of Chrétien de Troyes. We also have a fair idea of the antiquity of each. The question follows as to how *preudommie* became *chevalerie*. How did this conscious but as yet unarticulated set of norms for desirable lay behaviour become something different, a 'code', as writers have long called it? An answer to this lies where Léon Gautier found it in the nineteenth century: in the way that bad and uncourtly behaviour was stigmatised by writers, so as to point out what was good and courtly. *Preudommie* was taught by proverbial sayings, but also by cautionary tales. It was out of this didacticism that eventually arose the handbook on *preudommie*, where the roots of chivalry are to be found. The fact that cautionary tales circulated about uncourtly men and how they were not to be imitated, is very significant for the appearance of chivalry. It is powerful evidence that, although the twelfth and early thirteenth century had no self-conscious codification of noble behaviour, it had something else: a shared expectation of behaviour which operated in much the same way as a code.

Medieval literature thrived on opposites. If there was an Oliver, there was also a Roland, if there was a Lancelot there was a Mordred. Oliver illustrated Roland's rashness, and Lancelot illustrated Mordred's wickedness. For a medieval mind it had to follow that if there was a *preudomme*, there was also its mirror image. Baldwin de Condé in the mid-thirteenth century called the *preudomme*'s antithesis the 'wicked man' (*li mauvais*).[26] Such a contrasting couple in medieval literature is to be found at King Arthur's court where, if there was a courteous and well-spoken Gawain, there was also a sharp, rude and sarcastic Kay.[27] Roland was a *preudomme*

[26] *Dits et contes de Baudouin de Condé* i, 97.

[27] The Arthurian pair are contrasted in just such a way in the early-thirteenth century *Roman de la Rose*, ed. D. Poirion and J. Dufournet (Manchecourt, 1999), ll. 2090–96. Elsewhere, Lancelot and Mordred, *sanz pitié et sanz debonnaireté*, are contrasted in the cyclical Lancelot, *Lancelot: roman en prose du xiii*[e] *siècle*, ed. A. Micha (9 vols., Geneva, 1978–83) v, 221.

who simply judged badly, but there were characters in life and fiction who were thought quite unworthy of the name, anti-*preudommes*. Such men became, in effect, teaching aids: notorious examples of how *not* to behave in courtly society. As such, they actually help to define what a *preudomme* was, by demonstrating what he was not.[28] Twelfth-century literature was happy to give some extreme examples of aristocratic unpleasantness. The earliest portion of the epic *Raoul de Cambrai* (perhaps composed around 1150) features an eponymous and foul-mouthed anti-hero who murdered without compunction, insulted women, alienated his friends, stole the land of others, and reached the nadir of his career by ordering the burning to death of a community of nuns whose abbess was the mother of his best friend. It is unlikely that this Raoul was introduced into the work as an example of upright nobility, but rather as a warning against noble power without civil restraint. We are told of the high hopes that he had raised when he was a bright and talented youth, and how he dashed them. Although it was admitted he was *preus* (valiant) and *senez* (shrewd) and even *cortois* (when he was in a good mood), the epic never calls Count Raoul *preudomme*, that role is given to his companion, the bastard Bernier 'the noble and good', whom Raoul insults and betrays and who describes his friend – even before they fall out with one another – as 'more fell than Judas'.[29]

Raoul is frequently commented on as the unacceptable face of twelfth-century aristocracy, but he is by no means the only literary psychopath to be found. In the *Song of Aspremont*, a work of the time of the Third Crusade, there is a comparable example of a violent and truculent aristocrat in Girart d'Eufrate, the duke of Auvergne and Burgundy, who chooses to ignore the power of Charlemagne. When the emperor needs his help against the Saracens, Archbishop Turpin, Girart's kinsman, goes to him as

[28] This was in fact an idea broached by Léon Gautier, *La chevalerie* (Paris, 1884), 88. The study by C. Stephen Jaeger, 'Courtliness and Social Change', in, *Cultures of Power: Lordship, Status and Process in Twelfth-Century Europe*, ed. T.N. Bisson (Philadelphia, 1995), diagnoses the same process from a literary perspective, analysing the way that clerics constructed social polemic out of contrasting extremes of behaviour. I would point out that the device occurs in other non-clerical contexts, not least in epic, non-courtly narrative where every hero needs a villain to offset his virtue. The fact that 'all things go in pairs, one the counterpart of another' was fixed as a principle for the medieval scholar in Biblical Wisdom literature, Ecclus. 42: 25a (*omnia duplicia, unum contra unum*).

[29] *Raoul de Cambrai*, ed. S. Kay and trans. W. Kibler (Paris, 1996), ll. 340–43, 359, 425, 1204, 1974. The one *preudon* named as such in the work, is Guerri le Roux (*preus et saiges*), Raoul's uncle and gonfanonier (ll. 869–70).

ambassador, though, as he says, 'the old man is violent and fell; if he is annoyed ever such a little by what I say, as like as not he will knife me ... [he] is unsufferably proud, but fell and treacherous though he is, he is my kinsman.' The archbishop's prediction turns out to be true, although he evades the thrust and seizes his cousin's wrist and escapes Girart's castle with his life. Turpin fails in his mission to his hasty (*desree*), crazed (*derver*) and untrustworthy (*desloial*) relative and it is hardly surprising that he accuses Duke Girart of being no *prodom*.[30] But Girart at least made good when he joined the Franks in their fight against the Muslim invasion of Italy.

Early in the thirteenth century, the author of the non-cyclical Prose Lancelot, in one of his several telling critiques of contemporary society, goes one step beyond most medieval authors. He imagines such an 'anti-preudomme' – serene in the conviction of his own virtue – justifying his conduct, and rationalising the qualities (*teches* or *vertus*) he considers essential in public affairs. The anti-hero is King Claudas, the enemy of Arthur. While bewailing the death of his son Dorian, a man after his own cold heart, Claudas says that he displayed the great qualities of *debonairetez*, *largece* and (most of all) *fiertez*. But what he meant by these qualities was not what others understood them to be. Being 'debonaire' was to patronise graciously, but without discrimination, *preudome* and 'bad men' alike, but not to be too generous, and not to give to one sort more than the other. Largesse was to him not unstinting generosity, but giving sufficiently to inferiors to establish their dependency. *Fiertez* (Aggression) was to Claudas the greatest virtue. It meant protecting his friends and working against his enemies without pity or mercy. The author of the Prose Lancelot in this way exposes the manipulation and selfishness which many of the great of his own world displayed, and says in effect that the true *preudomme* had to do more than profess the qualities society admired: he must live them and understand their moral importance. If the reader did not quite get the message of Claudas's selfishness, it was explained later by the Lady of the Lake. Yes, a good knight should be hard towards some and tender towards others, but it is to traitors and evildoers to whom he should be pitiless, and he should be kindly to good and poor people.[31]

The ultimate summing-up of what it mean to be an anti-*preudomme* occurs in the 1230s. Twelfth-century writers invested a lot of thought and

[30] *La Chanson d'Aspremont* i, ll. 1033–5, 1046–7, 1123.
[31] *Lancelot do Lac*, i, 71–2, 145.

care in the crafting of their wicked characters. The traitor Ganelon in the *Song of Roland* provided the ultimate exemplar on which to draw. By 1200, many writers were looking to Ganelon as the *chiés de lignage* of a family whose hereditary characteristics were treachery and violence, and took care to make their wicked characters relatives or descendants of his. Their audience then knew who was going to be the bad man in the unfolding story. The Ganelon lineage was by the 1180s being given the name of Maience, from the rebel character Doon de Maience. In the romance *Gaydon*, written during the 1230s, we find described a creed of wickedness to which members of the family of Maience had to swear when they were knighted. The anonymous author decided that the best way to define wickedness was to see it as the negation of good. His anti-*preudomme* had to blasphemously swear before his wicked uncle – a bishop – to the following articles before God: never to be loyal and faithful to one's lord and to betray those who were, to promote wicked men and overthrow the good, to run down good men behind their backs while flattering them to their faces, to abuse and rob the poor, to make victims of orphans and widows, to retain murderers and thieves, to undermine the Church and not associate with clergy, especially Franciscans and Dominicans, to rob from monks, to murder and abuse children and old people, to burn abbeys and seduce nuns, and to lie and cheat on all occasions wherever he was. As Léon Gautier pointed out in 1884, there never was a better definition of noble conduct than this reversal of expectations in *Gaydon*.[32]

A historical, and not dissimilar, use of the negative features of aristocratic conduct occurs in the account by Henry of Huntingdon of the

32 For the evolution of the wicked lineage of Maience, see M. Ailes, 'Traitors and Rebels: the *Geste de Maience*', in, *Reading Round the Epic: A Festchrift in Honour of Professor Wolfgang van Emden*, ed. M. Ailes, P.E. Bennett and K. Pratt (King's College London Medieval Studies, 14, 1998), 41–68. For the oath, *Gaydon*, ed. M.F. Guessard and S. Luce (Anciens Poètes de la France, Paris, 1862), ll. 6431–69. Something resembling a reverse of the oath of Maience can be found in the early 1190s when Duke Girart of Burgundy is depicted as commending his brother-in-law Florent as new king of Hungary: he should avoid *losengiers*, protect churches and monasteries, refuse bribes and never be loose with promises, he should feed and clothe poor knights, and support poor women and orphans. But as he says, this is *li roial mestier*; 'in such a way ought princes to govern'. He describes a code for rulers, not knights, see *La Chanson d'Aspremont* ii, 11180–98, 11227–54. Pope Innocent II defines good kingship in such general terms in his confirmation of the coronation of Stephen of England in 1136, see D. Crouch 11., *The Reign of King Stephen, 1135–54* (London, 2000), 301.

prologue to the battle of Lincoln (2 February 1141). Before the battle Henry imagines the harangues with which the rival leaders edified their armies. For the rebels, Earl Robert of Gloucester is pictured reflecting complaisantly on the unequalled *probitas* (probably meaning *preuz*) of many of his barons and on the iniquity of their enemies, who were called criminals, evil men and cruel, deceitful tricksters, liars and braggarts, cowards, perjurers and turncoats. His opposite number on the royalist side, Baldwin fitz Gilbert, held forth with a becoming modesty of bearing on the loyalty of his people to their king, on their valour and prowess. Their enemy, Earl Robert, he said, has the mouth of a lion and the heart of a hare; he is idle and all bluster. The rest of his noble followers are no more than vagabonds and deserters.[33] The passage gives in sum a list of all the things that a *preudomme* should not be, and by implication everything that he should be: *preuz*, honest, good, kind, straightforward, truthful, modest, valiant, steadfast, active and respectable. Henry of Huntingdon's view was paralleled by those of other contemporaries – Jean Flori's analysis of the writings of the Anglo-Norman monk, Orderic Vitalis (d.*c.*1142), a man fond of associating with aristocrats, found that Orderic approved in noblemen those qualities which Henry praised as noble: respect for truth, liberality, forbearance, hardiness.[34]

We find the same opposition of good and bad qualities in the next generation, the one that began to define them as 'chivalry'. When Gerald of Wales provided character sketches of his relatives, he had to deal with some who were known to be less than paragons. The most notorious of these was his second cousin and contemporary, Meilyr fitz Henry. Meilyr was notorious for his acquisitiveness and his energy in his own interest. The biography of William Marshal, whose enemy he was, records him as an evildoer, and the opponent of all true *prosdomes*. Meilyr was not loyal to the Marshal – who was technically his lord – he did not keep his word, and plotted behind the backs of his opponents; he was, a *felon* (literally, a 'fell (evil) man').[35] Gerald, his kinsman, was also markedly circumspect about Meilyr. Gerald says that Meilyr, even when he was younger, was violent, impatient and headstrong and too eager for the blood of his enemies. Meilyr lacked restraint in war and peace and neglected his duty to the Church. His great and indomitable courage was praised by Gerald,

[33] *Historia Anglorum*, ed. and trans. D. Greenway (Oxford, 1996), 726–36.

[34] J. Flori, *L'Essor de la Chevalerie, xie-xiie siècles* (Geneva, 1986), 271–4.

[35] *History of William Marshal*, trans. S. Gregory and ed. A.J. Holden and D. Crouch (3 vols, Anglo-Norman Text Society, Occasional Publication Series, 4–6, 2002–6) ii, ll. 13432–9, 13555, 13576–8, 13677 (as *felon*).

but he does not forget the lack of restraint and judgement which turned this quality into a major fault (as with Roland and Raoul de Cambrai).[36]

In the *History of William Marshal*, it is such men – called *felons* and *losengiers* – who are its hero's adversaries and enemies. They plot against him, they misrepresent his innocent actions, they are pocket Iagos. Weary and satirical clergy, such as Peter of Blois, expected little of people at court. Writing around the year 1184, he said that the natural disposition of a courtier was to conspire, to succumb to envy, to accept bribes, and to imagine an insult when none was intended: 'For it is one of the most common vices in courtiers that they deeply resent the smallest offence in another; they cannot live with any patience under resentment, nor do they requite such injuries according to the size of the offence'.[37] Yet, in fact, the anti-*preudomme* was often not so much a conspirator as the very opposite, a man who could not guard his tongue and said the things he had better not have said.

Saying the wrong thing at court could be due to several reasons. It might be lack of education and the wrong social background. In the French romance-epic of the reign of Louis VII, *Garin le Loherenc*, Duke Garin has a great-nephew called Rigaud, born from a liaison of a niece with a worthy and wealthy man who was also a villein. Rigaud grew up in his father's household tall and exceptionally strong, but ignorant of the court. When he was brought to the court, Rigaud amused all his relatives by his lack of cleanliness, ragged attire and rustic directness. When he was properly dressed for court, he slashed off the impractical fur train of his court dress. He swore mightily and drew his sword on his uncle when he was struck on the shoulder with the ritual blow of knighthood.[38] The author of *Fergus*, writing around 1218, described just such another example of a peasant moving out of his proper social milieu and comments that 'foul speech is just what you expect of a peasant'.[39] It may not have been uncommon as

[36] *Expugnatio Hibernica*, 154–6. It has to be said in fairness to Meilyr that the character sketch given of him in the contemporary *Song of Dermot and the Earl* is much more approving than the image of him given by the sources mentioned here.

[37] *PL* 207: *Epistolae*, no. 150, col. 440.

[38] *Garin le Loherenc*, ed. A. Iker-Gittleman (3 vols., Classiques français du moyen âge, 117–19, 1996–7) ii, ll. 8873–915.

[39] *The Romance of Fergus*, ed. W. Frescoln (Philadelphia, 1985), ll. 478–9. It is worth noting that some writers had no difficulty in visualising peasants who were *preu*, *nobile*, *sené* and *gentil*, as did the mid-thirteenth century author of the mystical romance, *Ami et Amile*, when describing Count Ami's loyal and heroic serfs, Garins and Haymmes, see *Ami et Amile*, ed. P.F. Dembowski (Classiques français du moyen âge, 97, 1987), ll. 2473, 2503, 2572. Philip de Remy, in the same period, described

late as the 1220s for some knights of the court to lack the appropriate background; uncultured and untutored youths like Rigaud, Fergus and Perceval might well have been recognisable social types.[40] Sir Richard Siward (died 1248) made a distinguished career in the households of the count of Aumale, William Marshal II and King Henry III despite his apparent humble origins in a Yorkshire smallholding family.[41] But by the 1230s he had a social price to pay. He was known at court as 'Severus', a probable allusion to the courtly and cultured emperor whom he clearly did not in any way resemble.[42]

Such was the uncodified code of noble conduct focussed on the *preudomme* that preceded codified chivalry. I would suggest that what those writers were discussing was not their own individual or idiosyncratic ideas on what was or was not praiseworthy noble conduct. All of them shared a common idea of what made a man a *preudomme*. Before the *Ordene de Chevalerie* there was conduct which was recognised as noble, but it was a matter of norms. The small and intimate noble society – focussed on its common meeting-places of mannered courts, social dinners, church festivals and tournaments – generated and imposed expectations on its members from an early date.

It is time to call this uncodified code the noble 'habitus'. 'Habitus' is an idea that can be found in the work of the leading French sociologist, Pierre Bourdieu, emerging out of his studies of the changing native culture of the Maghreb in the 1950s. A habitus is the environment of behavioural and material expectations (what he called a 'structuring structure') which all societies and classes generate. They do so without the need for any directing individual intelligence (a 'conductor'). Bourdieu's habitus is the all-important explanation of how a mental construct like 'society' can act on the people within it. The expectations the habitus imposed could be

a group of respectable and well-meaning Italian fisherman who, in their conduct towards his heroine as she realises, 'were trying to be *preudomme*'. Only a few lines later Philip talks of the richest and the most noble and courtly senator in Rome as 'plus preudomme qui fust en la vile de Romme', *La Manekine*, ll. 4917–19, 4965–6.

40 For evidence that knighthood in England only became exclusive to the aristocracy in the first or second quarter of the thirteenth century, see P.R. Coss, *The Knight in Medieval England, 1000–1400* (Stroud, 1993), 61–71: K. Faulkner, 'The Transformation of Knighthood in Early Thirteenth-Century England', *English Historical Review*, 111 (1996), 1–23.

41 For Richard Siward, D. Crouch, 'The Last Adventure of Richard Siward', *Morgannwg: The Journal of Glamorgan History*, xxxv (1991), 7–30.

42 M.L. Colker, 'The "Margam Chronicle" in a Dublin Manuscript', *Haskins Society Journal*, 4 (1992), 137.

very powerful, and in the Maghreb (just like in the middle ages) defying or misunderstanding the habitus could be fatal. But the habitus is not written down. Its members acquire their understanding of it through their upbringing and social contacts. They may or may not abide by the norms of the habitus, and the norms can themselves slowly or abruptly shift. Some members also fail to understand the social nuances by which they are supposed to live, yet are tolerated within it. Nonetheless, although only easily perceived when it is affronted, the habitus is still there, and is used as a measure for each person's behaviour and aspirations.[43] Codified medieval noble conduct, as Sainte-Palaye understood it, began between 1170 and 1220. But the habitus on which the superstructure of chivalry was built, and of which the *preudomme* was a part, was there long before 1100.

People in the twelfth century were half-aware that they occupied a habitus. Social norms flickered on the edge of becoming more self-conscious. So those who conformed to it were praised as 'de bon aire' and those who did not or who could not understand them were condemned as 'de mal aire'. So in 1200 Alexander Neckam perceived aristocratic behaviour as a distinct pattern of conduct involving choices. To God, he said, everyone was equal. But, he adds, 'men of social distinction are urged to acquire the further distinction of noble conduct (*illustrium morum insignia*)'. When he talked of knights, he talked of some who try to do just that, but get it wrong, because they do not understand the habitus: some of them swagger arrogantly around, trying to *seem* like noblemen (*ut generosi videantur*).[44] A century earlier Guibert de Nogent had given a strikingly similar social comment. He talked of an impostor who walked, or rather swaggered, about northern France pretending to be the noble count, Everard de Breteuil (died *c.*1095). He adopted what he thought was noble conduct: excesses of dress and fashion, and a haughty and reserved demeanour. He was detected when he had the misfortune to introduce himself to the real Everard (a modest and serious nobleman of the stamp of Simon de Crépy).[45]

[43] The concept of the habitus first appeared in, P. Bourdieu, *L'amour de l'art* (Paris, 1966). For his full explanation of 'habitus' – which is a mechanism to explain how society acts on the individual, as Durkheim said it did – P. Bourdieu, *Outline of a Theory of Practice*, trans. R. Nice (Cambridge, 1977), 78–86; expanded in, idem, *Distinction: A Social Critique of the Judgement of Taste*, trans. R. Nice (London, 1984), 169–225.

[44] Alexander Neckam, *De Naturis Rerum Libri Duo*, ed. T. Wright (Rolls Series, 1863), 244, 312.

[45] *De vita sua*, ed. E.R. Labande (Paris, 1981), 54–6.

By 1200 the noble habitus was appearing over the horizon of self-consciousness. Andrew the Chaplain, writing in the 1180s, comes closest to providing the earliest self-conscious list of aristocratic norms of behaviour in the first book of his *Tractatus de amore*. The book is overtly about love and seduction, but a seductive man or woman had to have attractive traits of character. Besides, Andrew was keen to describe what made a man or woman 'noble' and engaged directly therefore with what was noble in behaviour. At one point he even presented a list of twelve rules for the model lover: they include precepts such as being honest, modest, decent in speech, urbane and courtly. This was to be expected of any noble knight. Elsewhere in the book, Andrew has much to say of what it is that made behaviour noble, even amongst the 'lower orders', as he called the urban merchants. The qualities are given as generosity, humility, affability, confrontation of wickedness, peaceability, piety, mercy and restraint in language and dress. A noble knight certainly had to fight well, but he must also study the arts and history, so that he was a proper associate for princes and magnates. Other twelfth-century writers tell us that there was a recognisable way that true nobles behaved and other writers of the period tell us how: humbly and affably but still with a supreme confidence of their own consequence in any assembly; it could all be summed up by the phrase *de bon aire*, already a word of praise in the mid twelfth-century vocabulary of Wace of Bayeux, Henry II's court historian.[46]

It is clear that Andrew was talking in his tract of love in terms of the *preudomme* not of the *chevaler*, because he explicitly associated the quality of *probitas* (preuz) with good conduct.[47] But he was writing in the generation that was beginning to call noble conduct – the conduct that was expected of the *preudomme* – 'chivalry' . With Andrew and Chrétien de Troyes we begin to see the emergence out of habitus of a self-conscious and codified idea of noble conduct. When self-conscious chivalry emerges, the habitus retreats. Habitus can exist in corners of a self-conscious analytical

[46] *De Naturis Rerum Libri Duo*, 312. For *debonaireté* as an aristocratic quality, P. Hyams, 'What did Henry III of England think in bed and in French about Kingship and Anger', in, *Anger's Past: The Social Uses of an Emotion in the Middle Ages*, ed. B.H. Rosenwein (Ithaca NY, 1998), 113–16. The opposite quality – *de mal aire* – also appears in twelfth-century literature and relates to presumption, rudeness, arrogance and malignity. Philip de Novara said that the great lord in particular should behave 'debonairement et humblement' as his social elevation put him on constant display; no one noticed the same qualities in a poor man, Philip de Novara, *Les Quatre Ages de l'Homme*, ed. M. de Freville (Société des anciens textes français, 1888), c. 130.

[47] Andrew the Chaplain, *On Love*, 82–4, 116.

modern society, but once an aspect of social behaviour becomes codified then, as Bourdieu says, it has acquired a conductor who can structure it. It was no long a self-conducting structure which itself structures behaviour. Chivalry could be taught from books, criticised in tracts, could be revived and could eventually fall into decline. The habitus had moved elsewhere.

As well as men who were in tune with their habitus and so were *de bon aire*, there were some who disappointed expectations by being *de mal aire*, our anti-*preudommes*. It is this element of failing to live up to expectations which gives us a very early glimpse of the norms of noble conduct. The 'Conventum' drawn up by Hugh de Lusignan around the year 1030 to list what he had suffered at the hands of his lord, William, count of Poitou, tells us something of how aristocrats were supposed to behave. Count William should have been honest, loyal and trustworthy, he should have freely rewarded the good service of his men. According to Hugh – a model of loyalty by his own account – the count did none of these things. It was the outrage done to his expectations of his lord that inspired Hugh's need to get the count's iniquities immortalised in writing. About the only thing Count William could be relied on to do, was to dauntlessly seek his own interests over those of others; he was at least brave and enterprising in that. As an aside, and incidental to Hugh's woes with the count, the 'Conventum' also says that a nobleman was expected to treat captured knights in a certain way: they should be ransomed rather than murdered or executed.[48]

It is by no means impossible to analyse the norms of the noble habitus before chivalry, despite basing the analysis on the works of authors with different priorities and concerns. They did at least occupy the same habitus. To take a didactic example: the analysis of the habitus of middle-class behaviour in North London and New York in the last quarter of the twentieth century will not be too difficult for future historians, such is the quantity of the literature of manners both cities generated during that period. Twelfth-century northern France is the same. What is more, the traditional method of social analysis is in this case the right one. The epistemological route followed by Charles Mills and Léon Gautier, was to generate lists of qualities which they had found in their sources to be desirable qualities in noble conduct. The method is a sound one because it identifies conscious but uncodified norms living in the medieval mind. Working independently, both Mills and Gautier discovered similar sets of

[48] *Le Conventum (vers 1030): un précurseur aquitain des premières épopées*, ed. G. Beech, Y. Chauvin and G. Pon (Geneva, 1995), 123–53.

knightly virtues, which perhaps tells us that attempting to reconstruct the pre-chivalric noble habitus is not a vain endeavour, even though it can only be a reconstruction.

1. Loyalty and its Limits

The first of the expectations of noble conduct identified by Mills and Gautier that we turn to are the ones which had an obvious practical utility in a warrior nobility. Of these, as Richard Kaeuper has said, loyalty is one of the most important. Kaeuper associates it closely with prowess, indeed, he points out that prowess without the rudder of loyalty might as well simply be undirected violence.[49] Medieval people were themselves well aware of this. Count Theobald II of Bar, in prison around the year 1253, wrote a song appealing to his relations and friends for aid. He addressed also the people of Bar in Lorraine, urging them to stand by him, telling them that 'it is their loyalty that gives many *preudomes* their reputation'.[50] The count was putting the point of view of the lord, and a lord in great need. It was their reputation for loyalty which recommended courtiers to a prince, and it was their unimpeached loyalty which courtiers offered as an inducement for employment. The same sentiment was earlier expanded on in proverbial style in the 1170s by Jordan Fantosme: 'He who acts falsely towards his rightful lord or does any wrong which causes him annoyance can be sure of getting his merited punishment; and he who serves him loyally is greatly to be esteemed'.[51]

Medieval sources continually stress that loyalty to lords by their soldiers is all-important, and reckon that obedience was the great quality of the Roman soldier of the Ancient World, which they so admired.[52] An English legal tract of around 1116 talks in horrified terms of what deep treachery it is to kill one's lord. No amends were possible to make up for it, and the person who committed the offence was promised punishments of particular squalidity and barbarity, 'so that he may declare, if it were possible, that he had found more mercy in hell than had been shown to him on earth'. Its author despised treason to one's lord as something contrary to God and to Christianity, indeed it was like apostasy. Geoffrey

[49] R.W. Kaeuper, *Chivalry and Violence in Medieval Europe* (Oxford, 1999), 185.

[50] *Chansons des Trouvères*, ed. S.N. Rosenberg, H. Tischler and M-G. Grossel (Paris, 1995), 806–8.

[51] *Jordan Fantosme's Chronicle*, ed. R.C. Johnston (Oxford, 1981), ll. 845–8.

[52] See the Classically inspired treatment in, *Ioannis Saresberiensis Policraticus*, ed. C.C.I. Webb (2 vols, Oxford, 1909) ii, 20–1.

Gaimar put the same sentiment more economically a couple of decades later: 'There is no law for the traitor'. The author of *The Song of Roland* told his audience that 'a man should be willing to suffer no end of trials for the sake of his lord', trials such as numbing cold and searing heat, wounds and loss of blood. This is a sentiment precisely echoed a century later in the non-cyclical Prose Lancelot where the noble knights of the realm of Gaunes encourage each other in adversity, saying: 'he who wants to save the life of his liege lord must put his own body in peril without complaint'.[53]

The reason why such a stern ethic of loyalty should be so central a component of the medieval noble habitus is perhaps self-evident, but it needs examination, simply because there were times when noblemen did not adhere to it. The principal Latin word for what we are talking about in the sources is *fidelitas*, with its twelfth-century vernacular equivalents *leiauté* and *feauté*, the last of which has produced in English the antiquated pseudo-technical term, 'fealty'. Alan of Lille in the 1180s gave a good, if idealised, definition of the faithful warrior, a man who avoided deceit and fraud, kept pacts of friendship and was true to his real friends, while avoiding fairweather flatterers, 'the footmen of Fortune'.[54] Alan pinpointed the characteristics that brought loyalty to the fore as a noble virtue. It encouraged men to keep to agreements that they had made, to avoid known fraudsters and to stand by their friends. The analysis of the qualities and the complications of the relationship of loyalty between lord and man were a frequent theme in eleventh- and twelfth-century sources, by which we may assume that they were echoing a vigorous and long-running contemporary debate.

How far did the ethic of loyalty bind a man? This was already an ancient question when Alan wrote. Around the year 1020, in response to a query from Duke William V of Aquitaine (993–1030), the respected scholar, Bishop Fulbert of Chartres (1006–1028), did his best to set out a rationale concerning the 'nature of loyalty' (*forma fidelitatis*).[55] Fulbert's

[53] *Leges Henrici Primi*, ed. L.J. Downer (Oxford, 1972), 174, 232; *La Chanson de Roland*, ed. F. Whitehead (2nd edn., Oxford, 1946) ll. 1117–19; *L'Estoire des Engleis*, ed. A. Bell (Anglo-Norman Text Society, 1960), l. 3717; *Lancelot do Lac* i, 73.

[54] Alan of Lille, *Anticlaudianus*, trans. J.J. Sheridan (Pontifical Institute of Medieval Studies, Toronto, 1973), 184–5.

[55] *The Letters and Poems of Fulbert of Chartres*, ed. and trans. F. Behrends (Oxford, 1976), 90–2. The translation of *forma fidelitatis* offered there is 'the oath of fidelity', but the Latin is not so precise and the translator was working in the light of the work of feudal theorists, for whom Fulbert's letter was of course a key document.

answer dwelt on the obligations of men to their lord, but said rather less about what the lord owed to his men; he was, after, all writing to a duke much troubled by his rebellious aristocracy. Fulbert stressed that a faithful man must safeguard his lord's fortresses and interests, and not hinder his ambitions. The faithful man must give honest advice and whole-hearted assistance in all his lord's plans. If he did that, he was worthy of the *beneficium*, his reward from his lord (which Fulbert does not specify as being land, privilege or money). On the other side of the coin, Fulbert only said that in return for faithful service, the lord should be faithful in the same matters to his man. Over a century later the same concerns still preoccupied noble society. In the *Roman de Thèbes*, a work of the 1150s or early 1160s, we are given a household debate between two knights about loyalty between lord and man. Echoing Fulbert, although probably not directly, one knight, Alys, says that a man owes his lord military aid and all other assistance he can give in pursuit of his interests, and in return the lord 'has to look after my interests as if they were his own'. But the debate here goes a further step, and considers what should be done if the lord did not honour his obligations. Alys responds sharply: 'Do you think I would keep faith with someone who did not keep faith with me? To the Devil with a man who trifles with me, who will not keep to his promises'.[56]

The question of loyal service is nowhere more prominent than in the biography of that loyal servant, William Marshal (*c.*1146–1219). William occupied a truly Anglo-French world, living and fighting during his long life in a great arena: from south-east Ireland, through Wales, England, Normandy, Picardy and Paris, south to Poitou and Burgundy, and venturing as far as Jerusalem. William did not hold an acre of land until he was over forty, and until then he existed on food, board, and salaries from his employers. His reputation for loyal service was literally his bread and butter. He had enemies, and when they wanted to undermine him, they did so by attacking his loyalty. One of his chief tasks as the leader of the Young King Henry's military household in the 1170s and early 1180s was to stay by his lord's side in tournaments, and prevent him being captured. Marshal's enemies alleged he was often not to be found there, but instead he rode off on his account after ransoms. After one such adventure the king himself is depicted as rebuking William:

I really think it's about time you came back, Marshal. Any man who leaves his lord in such a situation behaves very badly. You saw fit to do

[56] *Le Roman de Thèbes*, ed. F. Mora-Lebrun (Paris, 1995), ll. 9981–10064.

that just now, and I am not the one to teach you in these matters, but this much I do wish to tax you with, that you did not behave in a rightful manner when you left me at such a time. It was not right, indeed it was wrong.

William turned the rebuke with a courtly excuse, that he was wrong to go, but on the other hand he had not thought that his young master had ambitions to be quite so forward in the field as to put himself in danger, but now he saw that Henry was going to rival his royal ancestors in valour, he would take more care.[57]

Later in life, William Marshal was again accused of disloyalty, and again sought to justify himself. In 1205 he had crossed to France in the aftermath of the French conquest of Normandy to attempt to negotiate a peace settlement between King John and King Philip. The negotiations failed, but during them Marshal made an act of homage to King Philip for his Norman lands, so as to keep them from confiscation. When he returned to the English court, he found that King John was very angry, and had taken his pragmatism as treachery. The Marshal protested vociferously that the instructions King John had given him before he left had allowed him the latitude to save his French lands. The king for his part utterly denied it. Marshal continued to stonewall:

Sire, I was never disloyal (fals). *There is no* prodome *in this land of yours against whom, if he wished to prove and establish that my intent was to do you wrong I would not defend myself in combat. I have never committed treason or any evil deed that would make me hide my head in shame, nor will I as long as I live.*[58]

Marshal was in the end driven to demand that anyone who wished to maintain the charges of disloyalty against him should fight a duel. No-one was willing to do this, given William Marshal's military reputation, and so the charge lapsed. However such charges rankled with the next generation of the Marshal family. After the old Marshal was dead, his biographer was careful to note that King Philip of France, on hearing the news, had remarked in condolence to Richard Marshal, his younger son, that William Marshal had been the most loyal man (*li plus leials*) he had ever met.[59]

[57] *History of William Marshal* i, ll. 2541–62; the text later stresses the Marshal's assiduous protection of the young king, ibid., ll. 3612–37.

[58] *History of William Marshal* ii, ll.13149–57.

[59] *History of William Marshal* ii, ll. 19150–1.

The importance of a reputation for loyalty in noble conduct is amply demonstrated by the Marshal biography, as is also its fragility. There are many other contemporary medieval agonisings over what was or was not good faith. A particularly early and instructive example is the mutual reproaches of the two parties in the civil war in the Anglo-Norman realm of 1139 to 1147. These focussed on which had demonstrated the most integrity in the matter of the oaths sworn to support the candidature of the Empress Mathilda for the English throne in 1127. Here the crucial point occurred in 1138 when Earl Robert of Gloucester (died 1147), the late King Henry's eldest illegitimate son and the Empress's half-brother, decided no longer to support King Stephen (1135–54) but to embrace his sister's cause. So conscious was Earl Robert of his reputation for loyalty, that he commissioned the historian William of Malmesbury to write a sympathetic account of the events which followed from the reappearance of Mathilda in England in 1127 and the swearing of the oaths. When he came to 1138, William took care to make a delicate and not entirely convincing justification of the reason why Earl Robert had not in fact embraced his sister's cause on their father's death in 1135, but supported Stephen for nearly three years.[60]

The key point for us is what happened in the early summer of 1138 when Earl Robert chose to withdraw his allegiance from King Stephen. William of Malmesbury says that:

... immediately after Whitsuntide the earl sent representatives from Normandy and abandoned friendship and faith with the king in the traditional way, also renouncing his homage, giving as his reason that he did it justly, because the king had both unlawfully claimed the throne and disregarded, not to say belied, all the faith he had sworn to him[61]

[60] For studies of the relationship between Earl Robert and King Stephen, R.B. Patterson, 'William of Malmesbury's Robert of Gloucester: a re-evaluation of the *Historia Novella*', *American Historical Review*, 70 (1965), 983–97; D. Crouch, 'Robert of Gloucester and the daughter of Zelophehad', *Journal of Medieval History*, 11 (1985), 227–43.

[61] *Historia Novella*, pp. 42–3. An interesting literary comparison is the defiance of King Porrus towards his lord Alexander. He sent messengers to withdraw his friendship (*amisté*) and refused his greeting (*saluz*). He accused Alexander of taking his lands, killing his men and behaving badly. They formally defied Alexander as Porrus did not want to be accused of being a *traitre* or *felon*; he returned his oath and used the symbol of a glove to enact his defiance, see Thomas of Kent, *Le Roman de Toute Chevalerie*, ed. B. Foster (2 vols., Anglo-Norman Text Society, 1976–7) i, ll. 7303–16.

Earl Robert had found, for whatever reason, the limits of his loyalty and signalled it to his lord in the 'traditional way' (in Latin, *more majorum*). We have a substantial amount of information on what that 'accustomed' or 'traditional' way was. Just as the delivery of arms, the handing over of a glove, the joining of hands or an oath of fidelity were ways that lords and dependents inaugurated a relationship, so 'defiance' (literally 'un-faithing') ended it. In Earl Robert's case it was done by an emissary who delivered to the king a (probably written) statement of the reasons why the earl and he has reached the end of the road. According to William of Malmesbury, part of the reason was that King Stephen had committed the ultimate offence a lord could impose on one of his men, and had attempted to procure Earl Robert's assassination in Normandy in the summer of 1137. At much the same time that this was happening, the Lincolnshire clergyman Geoffrey Gaimar was coincidentally imagining just such a scene, a mythical confrontation between a dissident earl and an unworthy king. Accompanied by his kinsfolk, Buern Buccecarl confronted King Osfrith at his court. Buern accused the king of raping his wife and 'defied him on the spot' (*iloches le desfiad*). He proclaimed: 'I defy you and give you everything back, for I don't want to hold anything of yours. I give you back your homage here and now. I want nothing at all of yours.'[62] Here, unlike in the case of the historical Earl Robert, Buern severed the link completely by returning the lands that went with the act of homage. Earl Robert seems to have concluded that he could keep his estates, perhaps because he thought he held them now from the rightful heir to England, the Empress Mathilda.

These examples of the limits of loyalty come from the heights of society, but there exist other examples from lower down the slopes. At much the same time as William of Malmesbury and Geoffrey Gaimar wrote, the French author of the *Couronnement de Louis* depicted the guard keeping the gate of the city of Tours defying his lord, the duke of Normandy. Deciding to switch sides to the more honourable Count William of Orange, the knight symbolically took off his glove and shouted to the duke in his hall: 'I defy you, Richard ... I have no further wish to serve you'. He then rode off to serve Count William with exemplary loyalty.[63] This imagined

[62] *Estoire des Engleis*, ll. 2675–82. The personal element in return of homage is demonstrated in an example of 1256 when, during the course of an argument, Fulk fitz Warin's lord called Fulk's late father a 'traitor'. This was enough for Fulk to declare that 'on account of so deep an offence imputed against him and his father' he would return his homage and would hold no more land of him, National Archives (formerly PRO) JUST1/734, m. 15.

[63] *Le Couronnement de Louis*, ll. 1600–08.

incident is matched a generation later by the real-life behaviour of the retained knights in Thomas Becket's household. When it became clear to the archbishop's household that its master was about to be forced into exile by his confrontation with King Henry II, the knights decided as a body that they had reached the limits that could be expected of their loyalty. On 13 October 1164 they went to Becket at the priory of St Andrew at Northampton and, in tears, they renounced their homage to him and quit his service.[64] Becket's knights' behaviour indicates that there were pragmatic limits to the ideal of loyalty, but that knights who heeded the limits were still not happy to behave counter to that ideal, such was the power of habitus. The mid-twelfth-century epic *Raoul de Cambrai* illustrates this bloodily, in its colourful way. Despite his waywardness, sadistic violence and foul mouth, Count Raoul retained the loyalty of his protégé, the noble bastard Bernier. It took the murder of Bernier's mother by Raoul's men and a heavy blow from a stick wielded by Raoul before he finally renounced his loyalty (*fiance*) to the count. Yet even so, the barons standing around thought that the breach (*deseverance*) might be made good if Bernier accepted Raoul's ritual humiliation as compensation.[65]

No wonder then that Geoffrey de Charny in 1352 should say that those who lived loyally and honestly were *preudomme*. He rated loyalty higher than cleverness in a nobleman, because cleverness could become cunning and calculation. If the native disposition (*sens naturel*) of a man were sound, that was more important than intelligence, which could be perverted into malice.[66] He also unconsciously echoed King Henry of England's clerk, and said that loyalty was bound up with faithfulness towards God. A man's loyalty or disloyalty enacted in this world the cosmic decisions of the angels, and disloyalty was the way of Satan. In an age when oaths were taken upon relics, which were intrusions of the holy into the secular world, then such a parallel was to be expected. What it also did was to apotheosise loyalty in a way that did not happen to other such virtues like hardiness, liberality and honour. It would seem to affirm that, in the pre-chivalric mind, loyalty was the principal warrior virtue and thus the principal noble virtue.

[64] Herbert of Bosham, *Vita S. Thomae*, in, *Materials for the History of Thomas Becket, archbishop of Canterbury*, ed. J.C. Robertson and J.B. Sheppard (7 vols, Rolls Series, 1875–85) iii, 323–5.

[65] *Raoul de Cambrai*, ll. 1517–1619.

[66] *The Book of Chivalry of Geoffroi de Charny*, ed. and trans. R.W. Kaeuper and E. Kennedy (Philadelphia, 1996), 148, 154.

2. Forbearance

Forbearance and loyalty form a pair of warrior virtues; both can be said to have arisen amongst a military nobility in response to their particular circumstances. Forbearance and loyalty were good survival characteristics in a warrior's world. As we have seen, a lot of the recent debate about noble, as opposed to knightly, conduct concerns self-control, but this would be the self-control that was imposed on any would-be courtier. Warrior forbearance and noble reticence were qualities which arose out of different social circumstances, and we have already looked at the latter in the previous chapter under the heading of courtliness. It is however easy to get them mixed up. Eighteenth and nineteenth-century writers did not in general make that confusion. They assumed as a matter of course that restrained and 'chivalric' conduct was imposed by the Church on the native brutality and aggression of the early medieval warrior. Stephen Jaeger, for instance, assumed that knights acquired self-control at a late stage in their historical development, as better to advance their careers at the courts of their lords, but the sources indicate that self-control had long been part of their world.[67]

Forbearance towards other warriors was a part of the early noble habitus, or at least it was thought by them to be a good thing. We have early evidence of this in the 1020s in the 'Conventum' of Hugh de Lusignan. He tells us that Josfred, viscount of Thouars, outraged accepted norms by refusing to take ransom for Hugh's captured knights, and mutilating them instead.[68] Elsewhere in France in the eleventh century, we find the same idea that capture and prompt ransom, rather than slaughter and mutilation, was the preferred option for defeated opponents in noble warrior conduct. Guibert de Nogent criticised William of Normandy in the 1050s for keeping knights he captured in a war with King Henry of France in prison for long terms, rather than allowing them to be ransomed (but, as William de Poitiers argues, he eventually did release them).[69] Andrew of Fleury, between 1043 and 1056, depicted the treatment of a knight of the

[67] C.S. Jaeger, *The Origins of Courtliness: Civilizing Trends and the Formation of Courtly Ideals, 939–1210* (Philadelphia, 1985), 242–3, makes a contrast between the archaic warrior values of 'unrestrained manhood, violence, vengeance and self-assertiveness' and the new knighthood of the thirteenth-century romance.

[68] *Le Conventum*, 126.

[69] *Self and Society in Medieval France*, trans. J.F. Benton (Toronto, 1985) 69 and n; *The Gesta Guillelmi of William of Poitiers*, ed. and trans. R.H.C. Davis and M. Chibnall (Oxford, 1998), 50.

Gâtinais called Erbert as 'cruel' and 'inhuman': he was kept in chains for a long time after his capture and not allowed to be ransomed, but starved and kept in squalor at the castle of Montreuil. Writing in the 1070s, William de Poitiers – once himself a knight – had much to say about inhumane treatment of prisoners. He berated the count of Ponthieu and other contemporaries for their unscrupulous capture and maltreatment of wealthy nobles who passed through their lands. William clearly saw a decline in the noble ethics of his own day, although among the French, not the Normans.[70]

Further and similar evidence of the dominant noble ethic of mercy in eleventh-century France can be found in the shocked comments of Anglo-French writers on the ruthless ways of foreigners. John Gillingham has pointed to the perception of Henry of Huntingdon in Henry I's reign that the Norman treatment of the English aristocracy in the conquest of 1066–70 had been merciful compared to the bloodbath of the Danish conquest of 1016-17.[71] That, at least, was the perception. The lack of prisoners taken at Hastings may indicate otherwise, although it could be pointed out in defence of the Normans that the English ethos of warfare dictated that their defeated army should fight to the death around their king. Vikings and pre-Conquest English did not themselves spare their defeated enemies, and Harold of Wessex had been delighted to receive as a gift in 1063 the decapitated head of his arch-enemy, Gruffudd ap Llywelyn. The Normans professed to be equally shocked by contemporary Welsh warriors, who were brutal and merciless and lived outside their accepted conventions. A Norman clerical poet of the 1140s called the Welsh 'savages'; Richard of Devizes said in the 1190s that they were 'prodigal of the lives of others' and a decade earlier William de Briouze told Walter Map that there was no act so fiendish in war that a Welsh warrior would not commit. Peter of Blois used the conduct of Welshmen and Scots as a simile for unrestrained behaviour.[72] It is implicit in all this

[70] *Gesta Guillelmi*, 68; *Les miracles de Saint-Benoît*, ed. E. de Certain (Paris, 1858), Bk 7, p. 266.

[71] See generally, M. Strickland. 'Slaughter, Slavery or Ransom: the Impact of the Conquest on Conduct in Warfare', in, *England in the Eleventh Century*, ed. C. Hicks (Stamford, 1992), 41–60. J. Gillingham, 'Thegns and Knights in Eleventh-Century England', *TRHS*, 6th ser., 5 (1995), 150–1.

[72] C.H. Haskins, *Norman Institutions* (New York, 1918) 144n; Richard of Devizes, *Chronicon*, ed. and trans. J.T. Appleby (London, 1963), 66; Walter Map, *De Nugis Curialium*, trans. M.R. James, rev'd edn C.N.L. Brooke and R.A.B. Mynors (Oxford, 1983), 146; *The Later Letters of Peter of Blois*, ed. E. Revell (Auctores Britannici Medii Aevi, xiii, 1993), 26.

that Anglo-French warrior behaviour by contrast was neither irrational nor unrestrained.

Such at least was the perception. Whether it was universally true is another matter. Richard Kaeuper has demonstrated at length quite how violent Anglo-French society could be in the twelfth and thirteenth century, and it is not too difficult to find examples of erratic and ruthless violence in western knightly society, even after the appearance of chivalry as a code of knightly conduct. Joinville's graphic and affecting description of warfare in the Nile delta and Palestine in the 1250s reveals the courage and fear, the panic and the conscienceless aggression of the western knight in his noble heyday. But saying that the knight was violent is a different matter from saying that he was heedlessly and needlessly violent. Knights liked to believe that they knew also how to forbear. In 1174 Jordan Fantosme repeated the view of Henry II's court that Earl Robert of Leicester's ruthless pillaging of districts of England in his rebellion during the previous year had been the act of a man who was no more than a child in terms of morality.[73] Whether knights had been taught this forbearance ultimately by the social pressure of the Peace movement of the early eleventh century or by a pragmatic sense of the need to contain the effect of long-term warfare in France is not now possible to say. But since ecclesiastical teaching did succeed in instilling consciousness of ethical behaviour in the higher nobility (see below), it is at least possible that the Church did have some effect on the behaviour of early knights too.

The nobility of mercy and forbearance was well established by the second half of the twelfth century long before there was any 'code' of chivalry. It may be that knightly practice on the tournament field had played a part in this. It was the established custom at the tournament by the mid-twelfth century that defeated knights should pledge their faith to pay a ransom to their captors. When they did this, they might be freed to try to find better luck on the field. Such is the practice we find described in William Marshal's early career. He made his career and his fortune in the 1160s and 1170s by offering advantageous terms to defeated opponents. He was so undemanding in the matter of ransoms, that knights on one occasion queued up to surrender to him. Tournament morality and restraint seems to have permeated society to such an extent that mercy to the fallen became the normal expectation of the good knight. This was graphically demonstrated in the mid-twelfth-century moral epic, *Raoul de Cambrai*. Count Raoul severed his enemy Ernaut de Douai's hand and

[73] *Jordan Fantosme's Chronicle*, 74.

hunted him remorselessly across a battlefield, and, when he finally cornered him, he turned a deaf ear to Ernaut's pathetic pleas for his life. Raoul swore that God and his saints could not save Ernaut and so butchered him. The episode was introduced to demonstrate that failure to listen to pleas for mercy was an offence to God, and Raoul's own hideous end followed soon after as a consequence. The moral hero of the epic, the bastard Bernier, when he had an enemy at his mercy bathing in a roadside pool, sheathed his sword and said: 'an unarmed man has nothing to fear from me'.[74] At much the same time Wace of Bayeux wrote aphoristically that 'mercy is more befitting to a lord than any other virtue' and his King Arthur on conquering Flanders and Boulogne demonstrated this quality by refusing to allow his troops to pillage the land, and insisting that they buy their supplies.[75]

The reticence at court of the *preudomme* in time of peace, and the forbearance of the good knight in war naturally moved into alignment as knighthood became noble in the late twelfth century. Both became chivalric, and it did not matter in the end that they were in origin different qualities. It is certainly true that this expectation was not adhered to in any way consistently. Forbearance might suit the purposes of the knight, but not necessarily suit the magnate. William Marshal may have been a merciful knight, but, as an earl, he was anything but forgiving to those Irish tenants who rebelled against him in 1208, once he had them at his mercy. Geoffrey of Monmouth in 1136 gave it as his belief that a good lord should be an unrelenting terror to his enemies, and over two centuries later, Geoffrey de Charny said much the same. But although there is plenty of evidence of remorselessness in twelfth and thirteenth century warfare and politics, not least in the brutal treatment of Simon de Montfort and his household on the field of Evesham in 1265, there was still a powerful expectation that a true knight should withhold his hand from his brother.

[74] *Raoul de Cambrai*, ll. 2832–44. A similar view was expressed around 1190 when Charlemagne was imagined as finding a Saracen king unarmed as he drank from a spring. Charlemagne stood by as the emir armed himself and mounted, saying: 'I shall never be condemned for attacking an unprepared man', *La Chanson d'Aspremont* i, ll. 5796–5905.

[75] *Le Roman de Brut*, ed. I. Arnold (2 vols., Société des anciens textes français, 1938–40) i, ll. 4781–2; ii, ll. 9897–904.

3. Hardihood

To be a useful soldier it was necessary for a man to be hardy. This quality therefore aligns itself with forbearance and loyalty in being one of the military virtues of the *preudomme*. Hardiness is not a quality that struggles for a definition. To be physically tough and undaunted is what the word evokes now in English, and it meant the same to the Francophone author of the *Song of Roland*. The Saracens quailed at the bravery and toughness of the French; they had never fought a people so *hardi*, who were so fierce and who cared nothing for their lives. *Hardiz* was a stock item in the description of noble men, from Count Rabel in the *Song*, to Lancelot of the Lake.[76] This is not to say that the quality had no moral dimension, although it was not until the mid-thirteenth century that this was fully explained.

Philip de Novara had much to say about hardiness in his reflections on the moral virtues which a mature nobleman should have acquired. Being hardy, he said, was 'haute chose et honorable' (a pressing matter of nobility and honour). He linked it with the quality of discretion (*sens*) because true hardiness led men into situations where they might acquire honour, and also demonstrate their sense. 'Rashness' he said, 'is not hardiness', so a man should not leap into life and death situations without first assessing the consequences. The honour of an enterprise should balance its risks. But if the worst came to the worst, and things went wrong, a hardy man could at least be counted on to sell his life dearly and think nothing of the danger or of flight.[77]

Geoffrey de Charny also emphasised the masculine admirability of hardiness, but interpreted it more broadly in the light of the religious feeling of the *contemptus mundi*. He believed that noble men should despise the flesh. They should rise early and work hard all day long, they should spurn indulgence and luxurious living. The should endure cold and heat with equal indifference; they should care little for the fear of death; they should strive hard and ignore discomfort and wounds. Geoffrey was writing in an ascetic spirit, the same that sent the Templars to the Holy Land and the Cistercians into the wildernesses of Europe. For him, the body is of little consequence in the face of the honour that an undaunted spirit can earn. Geoffrey was not perhaps the first to teach this (see below for the views of

[76] *Chanson de Roland*, ll. 2603–4, 3352; *Lancelot do Lac*, 142.

[77] *Les Quatre Ages de l'Homme*, cc. 133–4.

Raoul de Houdenc over a century earlier) but he offered the most detailed rationale.[78]

4. Largesse or Liberality

So far we have been looking at internally-generated masculine expectations of a warrior aristocracy. But the habitus also included distinct moral qualities, which had roots independent of practical utility, and which had to be intellectually justified. Largesse would seem at first sight to be an utilitarian quality. So Philip de Novara in the 1260s put the case for liberality amongst the wealthy of his days succinctly:

... rich people should spend if they wish to earn the affection of their retainers, and keep in their minds the words that a king of Jerusalem said to one of his wealthy magnates who refused a gift that the king wished to make him saying: 'My lord, you have been generous enough to me, give this to someone else.' The king replied: 'Take what I have given, for it seems to me that a fresh gift produces renewed love.[79]

In the same generation, Baldwin de Condé repeated the proverb that a *preudomme* gains approval by giving, for gifts wipe out bad will.[80] Gifts created bonds as well as approval, and a man was all the stronger the more people were indebted to him.[81] Generosity was therefore a social necessity as much as a noble quantity. An expectation was laid upon the great of the world that they should live large. But Philip de Novara believed that the generous magnates of his day trod a fine line. Some were rather more miserly than he thought did them credit, and others gave without discretion.

Everyone should be as generous as his ability and circumstances permit, firstly for the sake of his soul and then for his honour in the world. No one should indulge in the sort of generosity that fools praise, for profligacy (gas) *is not generosity. A man should give judiciously, and if he has not the means to be liberal, then who will miss the sort of gifts he could afford! But none should abandon the idea of generosity. Avarice is a very sordid vice and Envy is even worse.*[82]

[78] *The Book of Chivalry of Geoffrey de Charny*, 122–8.
[79] *Les Quatre Ages de l'Homme*, c. 71.
[80] *Dits et contes de Baudouin de Condé* i, 96.
[81] A view to be found in *Lancelot do Lac*, 287–8.
[82] *Les Quatre Ages de l'Homme*, c. 132.

Philip was in a long line of critics of the miserliness of the rich. It is an opinion that we find much earlier. Around 1200 Alexander Neckam mocked the hypocrisy of the magnates of his day and the paltry rewards they offered their harassed and exploited followers: 'Miserliness enforced away from the public gaze. Generosity which never gets beyond giving absolute necessities'.[83]

However, there was more to generosity than simple gift exchange. Philip de Novara rated it as a virtue to set against the mortal sins of Avarice and Envy. A generation before Neckam, several writers had stressed the importance of Largesse for sublime reasons. Stephen de Rouen, monk of Bec-Hellouin, wrote a lament on the death of Waleran II, count of Meulan and Worcester, in 1166. He expounded on the count's generosity in this way:

Wealth melts away, honour is trodden down, and the world's glory is one day remembered, the next forgotten, and once forgotten is gone for ever. Count Waleran himself saw that he would be earth, worms and dust: he dreaded eternal punishment and he strove to enter heaven. He gave away, dispersed and thought little of his belongings, and he took the easy yoke of Christ upon his body with a pious heart.[84]

Stephen linked liberality and indifference to possessions. He made it into a religious frame of mind, a dualistic one that prioritised spiritual concerns over the material. It was for this reason that Chrétien de Troyes said that Largesse was the queen of the virtues and that of itself Largesse made a man a *prodome*.[85] When he did, so he was not necessarily being self-interested, although he did represent the group which expected to benefit from noble generosity. Like Stephen de Rouen, his was a religious understanding of Largesse.

Chrétien's contemporary, Alan of Lille, drew out a further moral understanding of Largesse. He explained in more detail what sort of nobility lay in the concept of Largesse. It was not just a simple matter of giving away what he had: *Largitas* in a man caused him to set no store on

[83] *De magnatibus*, in, *De naturis rerum libri duo*, ed. T. Wright (Rolls Series, 1863), 314. Kaeuper, *Chivalry and Violence*, 193–6, suggests that Largesse was emphasised in noble culture in order to distance the nobility from equally rich but grasping townsfolk, but clearly there were also rich and grasping nobles to contend with.

[84] *Carmen elegiacum de Waleranno comite Mellenti*, in, *Chronicles of the Reigns of Stephen, Henry II and Richard*, ed. R. Howlett (4 vols, Rolls Series, 1886–89) ii, 768.

[85] *Cligés*, ll. 188–213.

greed or gifts, and to have nothing but contempt for bribes.[86] Walter Map, at much the same time, had his own contribution to make about what made Largesse moral and noble. He reports a conversation he claims that he had with the most famously generous nobleman of his age, Count Henry the Liberal of Champagne (1152–81). When Map queried him on the great gifts of which he was notoriously prodigal, Count Henry smiled and said that even he drew a line: 'Where there remains no more to be given there is the limit; for it is not *largitas* to procure by base means what you can give away'.[87] This makes clear the meaning of the passage of the Marshal biography which reflected on Largesse. Like Chrétien, the author made it the principal noble virtue, indeed he said that Nobility (*gentilesce*) was raised in the household of Largesse. Largesse was a symptom of a 'good heart', and therefore was a defining moral quality.[88]

For all these twelfth-century writers, writing just as noble conduct was on the verge of reaching codification, Largesse was an elevating moral and religious quality. As early as 1118 we find a clerk of the count of Anjou itemising the virtues to which his master aspired, and these included the emulation of the patience and generosity (*largitas*) of the patriarch Job, regarded as one of the patrons of all ascetics.[89] It was for this reason that Count Henry the Liberal's epitaph proclaimed on his part, '*Largus eram, multis dederam*' (I was generous; to many I gave).[90] Largesse was the symptom of a Christ-like mind which set little store by material things, and rejected the sin of greed and the corruption that flowed from it. This was why Chrétien regarded it as the defining feature of a *preudomme*: Largesse was true nobility.[91] Raoul de Houdenc said much the same in the next generation. He taught that *Larguece* was in fact one of the two key qualities in noble conduct, the other being courtliness. Raoul argued that when true knights exhibit Largesse, they were showing above all the courage to do without material possessions. Unlike Walter Map, he was quite happy to

86 Alan of Lille, *Anticlaudianus*, 185.

87 *De Nugis Curialium*, 452.

88 *History of William Marshal* i, ll. 5060–6.

89 *L'abbaye Toussaint d'Angers des origines à 1330. Étude historique et cartulaire*, ed. F. Comte (Société des Études Angevines, 1985), 148.

90 H. d'Arbois de Jubainville, *Histoire des ducs et des comtes de Champagne* iii (Paris, 1861), 312.

91 Kaeuper, *Chivalry and Violence*, 198, points out the link between Largesse and Prowess as noble virtues, the latter enabling the former, and therefore finds Chrétien's comments unconvincing because he regards Prowess as the principal chivalric quality. But his comments rely on an interpretation of medieval society as being materialist; sometimes however its outlook was ideological.

see a nobleman give more than his income, as it attested to his bravery. Raoul believed that a truly generous man gave without a second thought, without calculation or desire for a return, and that he entertained generally and lavishly. It is no surprise, therefore, to find that Raoul considered that Largesse arose not out of Prowess, but out of Hardihood (*Hardement*), because as he interpreted their significance, both derived from a commendable contempt for the things of the world, the same contempt recommended to noblemen by Stephen de Rouen in the late 1160s.[92]

5. The Davidic Ethic

The moral justification for the privilege of the nobleman was always at the forefront of the twelfth-century mind as it approached the verge of codification of noble conduct. When the Burgundian author of the Prose Lancelot constructed his explanation for the appearance of noble knights in the distant past, he explained that it was their exceptional morality that led to the selection of the first noblemen. They were selected for their strength and goodness so as to defend the weak from the wicked and false who wanted to prey on them. When he said this, in the first decade of the thirteenth century, he was saying nothing new, in fact he was repeating what was by then the oldest justification for nobility and the oldest quality that defined it: its moral leadership. This quality was evident to the earliest writers on chivalry, although they articulated it in roundabout ways. Mills and Gautier in their day both identified it as a core Christian ethic that underpinned all noble conduct. To Mills in 1825 it was 'the duty of the cavalier to peril himself in the cause of the afflicted and of the Church'. To Gautier in 1884 it was commanded of a knight that 'tu auras le respect de toutes les faiblesses, et t'en constitueras le défenseur'.[93]

It is the strongest and most frequently cited of the qualities of a *preudomme*, and almost amounts to a sub-code in its own right. I will call it here the 'Davidic ethic', and for good reason. It was generated by clerics and drew on Biblical tradition. Gautier wove it into several of his 'ten commandments of chivalry'. But it was in origin a set of expectations of good rulership, and is first found fully articulated in the canons of eighth-century councils of the Frankish church, and later in the 'mirrors of

[92] Raoul de Houdenc, *Le Roman des Eles*, ed. and trans. K. Busby (Utrecht Publications in General and Comparative Literature, 17, Amsterdam, 1983), ll. 144–266, esp. ll. 154–7.

[93] Mills, *The History of Chivalry*, 56; Gautier, *La Chevalerie*, 33.

princes' composed by ninth-century clerics at the Carolingian courts. A concise example is the harangue delivered by Archbishop Hincmar of Reims to the lay powers of his province in 881, instructing them on their duty under God:

No consideration should cause them to stray from righteousness. They should be impartial judges between neighbours. They should protect and assist orphans and widows and other poor folk, and they should hold the Church and its servants in respectful deference, as far as they are capable. By constant effort and repression they should restrain those who, in their arrogance and violence, seek to undermine the common peace of the people by theft and brigandage.

The obligations involved in the ethic can be reduced to something brief and simple. Rightful authority was based on protection for the weak and helpless, especially the Church; respect for widows and orphans; and opposition to the cruel and unjust. It is an ethic which is ancient and Biblical in inspiration, describing the righteous power of the Lord: 'the Lord loves the righteous and protects the stranger in the land; the Lord gives support to the fatherless and the widow, but thwarts the course of the wicked.' (Vulgate: Ps. 145: 8b–9). This key passage occurs in one of the more frequently-said and heard psalms of the office; the five great praise psalms at the end of the psalter. It echoes several similar moral injunctions found in the Pentateuch and the Prophets.[94]

As a manifesto for good lordship this ethic had great authority, since it was believed in the middle ages that the psalms were composed by David of Israel, the pattern of the good king. The antiquity of the practice of using this ethic to criticise the lay aristocracy long precedes Hincmar.[95] Hincmar in fact tells us this when he marshalled a similar text in his more substantial essay on kingship, *De regis persona et ministerio*, which he addressed to Charles the Bald (838–77). Quoting Psalm 145 in part, he says what a king should do was: 'to judge justly between neighbours, to be a protector of the stranger and of the fatherless and the widow, to restrain theft, to punish adultery, to repress the wicked and to deprive the impostor and the shameless of support.'[96] But Hincmar in this case adds that the words were not his own. He was quoting an earlier writer, the one known

[94] For the relevant texts, J. Flori, *L'idéologie du glaive: préhistoire de la chevalerie* (Geneva, 1983), 66–8.

[95] Flori, *L'idéologie du glaive*, 68-73 gives a comprehensive survey of the early history of what he too calls an 'éthique'.

[96] *De regis persona et ministerio*, in, *PL* 125, col. 835.

as the Pseudo-Cyprian, author of a tract called the 'Twelve Abuses current in the World'. The Pseudo-Cyprian was an early writer on kingship and law, working apparently in eighth-century Ireland, and it was he who first used the ethic as a reproach to a 'wicked king'. In Hincmar, we see that the ethic was assimilated by the Carolingians into the rhetoric of just kingship and transmitted onward to the Capetian world. The message was received clearly, and, according to Abbot Suger in the mid twelfth century, the sceptre and rod used in the coronation were regalia which signified just this: the defence of churches and the poor.[97]

However, Hincmar used the ethic to criticise aristocrats as well as kings, as is apparent in his statement of 881, which was directed as much at the counts as the king who was their master. It had by then long been a theme in Carolingian capitularies that the counts and bishops had an obligation to respect the ethic by which their master the king was bound.[98] Hincmar is clear that they, too, were bound by it as lesser rulers. This practice of applying the ethic to all men of power continued into the sub-Carolingian world. When Witgar of Compiègne composed a eulogy for Count Arnulf I of Flanders in the 950s he praised him as 'the assiduous restorer of God's churches, the pious support of the fatherless, dependents and widows, the merciful source of aid to all in need who turn to him'.[99] When an anonymous cleric composed a lament for William Longsword, count of Rouen (murdered in 942, incidentally, by the pious and merciful Count Arnulf) he bewailed a man who was: 'maker and lover of peace; comforter and defender of the poor; maintainer of widows and orphans'. This for a man who had been born overseas as the son of a pagan Viking jarl.[100] Two or three generations after this, the programme for the Peace of God movement in France was in part the fulfilment of those very ethical requirements: the protection of the poor and the defenceless, although, of course, for its ecclesiastical promoters, they themselves were the poor and defenceless whose protection they had in mind.[101] Nevertheless, the

97 *De duodecim abusionibus saeculi*, in, *PL* 4, cols. 156–7; Suger, *Vita Ludovici Grossi regis*, ed. H. Waquet (Paris, 1964), 86.

98 Flori, *L'idéologie du glaive*, 80–1.

99 *Genealogiae comitum Flandriae*, ed. L.C. Bethmann, in *Monumenta Historicae Germanniae: Scriptores* ix, 303: 'ecclesiarum dei perfectissimus reparator, viduarum orfanorum ac pupillorum piisimus consolator, omnibus in necessitate auxilium ab eo petentibus clementissimus dispensator'.

100 J. Lair, *Étude sur la vie et la mort de Guillaume Longue-épée duc de Normandie* (Paris, 1893), 61–70 (v. 3).

101 R.I. Moore, 'The Peace of God and the Social Revolution', in, *The Peace of God: Social Violence and Religious Response in France around the year 1000*, ed. T. Head and R. Landes (Ithaca NY, 1992), 318.

Peace itself is some evidence that the ethic had deeply penetrated the lay habitus by 1000, for this was the ethic being appealed to by the peace legislators.[102]

The invocation of the Davidic ethic speaks generally of God's view of the legitimate and rightful use of power, which was why it featured in the rituals blessing swords, royal or princely. It also appeared in chronicles and in the prologues (*arengae*) to solemn acts issued by princes and noblemen. When William de Poitiers was looking for ways to eulogise the rule of Normandy by Duke William II in the 1050s he could do no better than to say that: 'He listened to the cause of widows, orphans and the poor, acting with mercy and judging most justly. Since his fairmindedness restrained other people's greed, no one, however powerful or close to him, dared to move the boundary of a weaker neighbour's field or take anything from him'.[103] In 1118 a clerk of Count Fulk V of Anjou, in an act of his master to the abbey of All Saints at Angers, itemised the ideal qualities of the godly prince that Fulk was. These included the support of the poor and the destitute, charity to the downtrodden and desperate, and the overthrowing of the proud and ambitious.[104] It was by adherence to the Davidic ethic that the Church, at least, assessed a ruler's reputation. So, in a funeral sermon of 1152 quoted by Arnold of Bonneval, Count Theobald IV of Blois and Champagne was commemorated thus: 'He trained his secular power towards the high duties incumbent on a prince: to bear down on the oppressors of the poor, to defend widows and orphans, to be merciful and to serve, to arrange his words so that justice should be done, and to maintain the peace of the Church. This is what is required of a prince, that he should apply himself to earning the praise of good men and to punishing the wicked'.[105]

As early as the end of the eleventh century, the scope of the Davidic ethic had broadened out to embrace all warriors of good will. The well-connected but untitled Norman marcher lord, Robert of Rhuddlan, was the subject of an epitaph composed in 1102 by no less a person than Orderic Vitalis. Robert was praised in stone because, 'all priests, monks, orphans and homeless men, held in honour by him, received his gifts'. Orderic's eulogy is intended to portray Robert as a 'true knight', therefore the inclusion of the Davidic ethic in his description can only be significant

102 Flori, *L'idéologie du glaive*, 137–57.

103 *Gesta Guillelmi*, 80.

104 *L'abbaye Toussaint d'Angers*, 147–8.

105 *Sancti Bernardi Vita Prima auctore Ernaldo*, in *PL*, 185.1, col. 299.

for our understanding of the moral idealisation of the eleventh-century warrior by the clergy. Vernacular epic writers of the mid-twelfth century resorted to the same definition of lawful power. The *Couronnement de Louis* in the 1130s contains the advice to all lords that they should maintain orphans and widows, serve the Church and be considerate to their knights.[106] By the last quarter of the twelfth century Stephen de Fougères believed that, ideally, 'a knight must draw his sword to do justice and to defend those who cannot implead others for themselves: he should suppress violence and theft' and also of course, defend the Church. In the same decade Alan of Lille considered that for all knights who were pious it was necessary (amongst other things) to defend widows, console the unhappy, support the needy, feed the destitute and befriend orphans. It is no surprise therefore to find that William Marshal in his day ostentatiously respected the ethic. In the retreat from the city of Le Mans in 1189 he found time to direct his squires to assist an old lady to retrieve her goods from her house in the burning city, and hauled out her smoking mattress himself.[107]

There are several reasons why this transference should have happened. The first is the way that the Church had deliberately preached the ethic to knights, as well as princes. This had been going on since at least the late eleventh century, when knights had been recruited to go to the aid of Christendom against the Turks. Pope Urban II is credited as having preached to the assembled lay magnates and knights in 1095 that if up till then they had oppressed orphans, robbed widows, killed, robbed and desecrated churches, they could now leave behind their bad ways, and go to fight for the Church in the East.[108] He used the alleged failure of the armed laity to respect the Davidic ethic as an incentive to get them to do at least one thing right, and seek salvation by fighting for God's church. We find continuing echoes of this preaching in the first half of the twelfth century. In the aftermath of the Crusades, an English clergyman composed an entire tract of moral instruction taking the equipment of the knight as the basis

[106] Orderic Vitalis, *The Ecclesiastical History*, ed. M. Chibnall (6 vols, Oxford, 1969–80) iv, 143; *Le Couronnement de Louis*, ll. 152–9. There is a possibility that Robert may have held the rank of constable of Chester, see D. Crouch, The Administration of the Norman Earldom', in, *The Earldom of Chester and its Charters*, ed. A. Thacker (Cheshire and Lancashire Record Society, 71, 1991), 74–6.

[107] *Le Livre de Manières,* c. 135: 'Chevalier deit espee prendre por justisier et por defendre cels qui d'els funt les autres pleindre: force et ravine deit esteindre', see also cc. 155, 159, 162; Alan of Lille, *Anticlaudianus*, in, *Satirical Poets of the Twelfth Century*, ed. T. Wright (2 vols, Rolls Series, 1872) i, 393. For the Marshal's act of charity, *History of William Marshal* i, ll. 8753–72.

[108] Baudrey de Bourgeuil, *Historia Hierosolymitina*, in, *PL*, 154, col. 568.

for his exposition, and the letter to the Ephesians as his inspiration. Although the tract is not explicitly addressed to knights, but to all laymen, it leaves the impression that a knight could be a model of Christian virtue if only he would love justice, protect the Church and embrace continence.[109]

In the later 1120s Bernard of Cluny was much more pointed, and much more concerned with the ethical conduct of knights in particular, not the armed laity in general: he berated ruthless knights who plundered the people they should by rights be defending, and who dishonoured their own lineage by their violent and dissolute behaviour.[110] We are clearly here in the world of moral instruction based on the sermon 'to various conditions of men'. Clergy who were dissatisfied with the norms of conduct amongst contemporary nobles and knights had decided to intervene and change them. In the language of theology, they countered social habitus with Biblical hermeneutic. We catch glimpses of the process at work. A solemn act of around the year 1166 issued by the great nobleman, Count Ralph II of Vermandois, opened with this prologue (or *arenga*):

Since, as we have heard that the apostle Paul once said that we all will one day be brought to judgement and will there receive the reward for the good or ill we did in life, we ought to heed this solemn warning, while we still may, and work for the good of all people, but particularly for the servants of the Church.[111]

We can only assume that this reflection – which is not a standard one – was the fruit of meditation on a particularly pointed sermon 'ad status' which the count had heard on the text of the Second Letter to Timothy.

Another contemporary clerical Bernard made further reforming use of the Davidic ethic in relation to knights: this was Bernard of Clairvaux. The very reason that he sponsored the foundation of the Knights Templar was to propagate a 'new knighthood' which would reform the old knighthood: luxurious, violent and heedless of its salvation. The new knighthood would protect the Church and direct its swords only against the enemies of peace. Bernard returned to this theme again and again during his lifetime, which is evidence of his discernment of an ethical void at the heart of con-

[109] *De similitudine temporalis et spiritualis militis*, in, *Memorials of St Anselm*, ed. R.W. Southern and F.S. Schmitt (London, 1969), 97–102.

[110] Bernard of Cluny, *De Contemptu Mundi*, ed. and trans. R.E. Pepin (East Lansing MI, 1991), 94.

[111] *Cartulaire de l'abbaye de Notre-Dame de Ourscamp*, ed. M. Peigné-Delacourt (Amiens, 1865), 176.

temporary aristocracy. There is some reason to think that the talk of an 'order' of knighthood later in the century was a consequence of the concerns of Bernard and his generation about the lack of ethical restraint amongst the rising social group of knights in their own day.[112]

Bernard of Clairvaux could not have so readily preached a new knighthood at the military aristocracy of his day had the Davidic ethic not been part of the clerical armoury against the aristocracy for so very long. As the *Couronnement de Louis* proves, by the 1130s the lay world had itself long absorbed it by means of sermons and investiture rituals. We find that, in due course, Sir Geoffrey de Charny would use the Davidic ethic around 1350 as an argument for just warfare, and as the way that his violence might in fact aid a knight's salvation:

> ... *if some people wanted to seize the land and inheritance of defenceless maidens or widows and could not be dissuaded from this except by war or combat, one ought to embark on this confidently in regard to one's personal reputation and the saving of one's soul, and the same is true in relation to the defence of orphans.*[113]

In this ethical template we find the central core of the idea of praiseworthy noble conduct: the later heart of chivalry. It was not internally generated, so much is clear. But it had been accepted by the aristocracy from the hands of the Church at least as early as 1000, both for idealistic and pragmatic reasons. Thirteenth-century laymen wholeheartedly consented to it, because it summed up a programme by which they could live Christian lives in a society where violence was endemic. They also accepted it because it gave nobles and knights a solid and Biblical justification for the power which they assumed and exerted. If their power was exercised in a righteous and ethical way, then those who resisted it were clearly in the wrong, and at odds with the expectations of their society.

It is under this heading that we should consider the knight's famous obligation to honour and assist *all* women, not just widows, that begins to appear in the literature of the late twelfth century. The logic would seem to be that women, as much as the clergy, were the weak in society and needed the protection of their swords. The best, and one of the earliest, statements of this occurs in Chrétien de Troyes's *Conte de Graal* (*c.*1170). When young Perceval's mother reluctantly lets him go to seek knighthood

[112] *De laude novae militiae*, in *PL* 182, cos. 923–7. For Bernard's views on the reform of knighthood and rightful force, see Flori, *L'Essor de Chevalerie*, 209–19.

[113] *Book of Chivalry of Geoffroi de Charny*, 164.

she urges on him the necessity of assisting any lady (*dame*) or young woman (*pucele*) whom he finds needs help, 'for that is a matter of the highest honour'. He is warned that when a man fails to behave honourably to women, his own honour is plainly dead. She tells her son that if he was of service to women, then he would be honoured wherever he went.[114] Wace of Bayeux expresses a similar sentiment at much the same time. He has the good Duke Richard I of Normandy overwhelmed by horror at the murder in his presence of a woman by her lover, 'For shame! Wickedly done! A woman is more deserving of peace than any other.'[115] The same sentiment turns up once again in the same generation in dialogues between various conditions of men and women in Andrew the Chaplain's tract on Love, although here already there is a deliberate hypocrisy being unmasked, for the man wants not to honour the woman, but sexually exploit her.[116] But hypocritical or not, there is some evidence of this feeling penetrating real life. In 1183, William Marshal apprehended a disguised runaway monk and his lover on the road because he at first believed that she was being taken by the monk under compulsion, and wished to prevent it.[117]

This is not that form of noble behaviour which has been called 'courtly love'. It is a more general and disinterested benevolence of the strong toward the weak, which is the core of the Davidic ethic. But the fact that this benevolence has become focussed so powerfully on women in the last quarter of the twelfth century cannot be other than significant. What precisely it signifies is not at all easy to say. However, one deduction might be that, by 1170, the Church's preaching of the ethic had been so integrated into expectations of noble conduct, that the nobility had now made the ethic its own, and in its assemblies and courts was reshaping it into something that reflected its own powerful concerns, not least the continually changing and always sexually-charged relationship between women and men. Such a reinterpretation of the ethic allowed men to follow their instincts to approach closer to women, but in the sexually neutral role of

[114] *Le Conte de Graal*, ed. F. Lecoy (2 vols, Classiques français du moyen âge, 1972–5) i, lines 531–54.

[115] *Le Roman de Rou*, ed. A.J. Holden (3 vols, Société des anciens textes français, 1970–3) I, pt 3, ll. 531–5.

[116] As for instance the desire the count evinces as to it being the highest happiness to serve a woman of knightly class, so as to charm her into complaisance; her clever riposte is that a man of his rank should be eager to serve all women, not just her, *On Love*, ed. and trans. P.G. Walsh (London, 1982), 132, 134.

[117] *History of William Marshal* i, ll. 6683–716.

honourable protector. No wonder that Andrew the Chaplain saw this interpretation of the ethic simply as an excuse to flirt. Contemporary knights might have thought him jaundiced.

6. Honour

In terms of the pre-chivalric noble habitus, the feeling of being honourable was a defining emotion, as it was desire for honour and fear of shame that policed the whole system. Writers on chivalry have tended to include honour amongst their categories of chivalric virtues. But honour was not itself a moral quality, simply part of a social mechanism to impose morality. Medieval people themselves knew this. In the romance of the *Castelain de Couci*, written in the last third of the thirteenth century, the hero Reginald is described as a man who '. . . wanted constantly to achieve *honnour*, to be generous, courtly and upright, to be cheerful, lively and worthy of love'.[118] From this brief but telling aside we can see that honour was what was achieved by living up to the ideal of the *preudomme* and pursuing the qualities and behaviour we have already listed above. Since no outside agency conferred certificates of honour, and it could only be experienced as a sense of the general approval of one's peers; the only way to achieve honour was to try fully to live up to the expectations of society, whether expressed through habitus or chivalric code.

Twelfth- and thirteenth-century vernacular texts are full of honour and its desirability. But they say little more than what the *Song of Roland* said as early as *c.*1100. In the *Song* honour is the reputation and self-respect which men have; it is the quality of which a man would wish to deprive his enemy; it is what a man acquires when he does a brave deed and protects the Church; and it is what a man gets when he does a thing in good order and appropriately. In every case honour is about appearance and reputation. The loss of honour is a blow to a man's standing, and it is something which is received and lost in a public forum. Loss of honour is a disaster worse than death. To lose one's head is better than to lose honour and the dignity (*deintét*) that goes with it.[119] Bertran de Born, the mouthpiece of the magnates of Aquitaine in the 1180s had, as usual, a strong opinion on the subject: 'For myself I prefer to hold a little piece of land in *onor*, than to hold a great empire with dishonour'.[120]

[118] Jakemes, *Le Roman du Castelain de Couci et de la Dame de Fayel*, ed. M. Delbouille (Société des anciens textes français, 1936), ll. 869–71.

[119] *Chanson de Roland*, ll. 45, 1223, 2507, 2960.

[120] *Poésies complètes de Bertran de Born*, ed. A. Thomas (Toulouse, 1888), 13.

Dishonoured men were made the object of public humiliation, often in as gross a way as possible, even if they were not executed. When Henry of Essex abandoned the royal banner on campaign in Wales in 1163, he first tried to exculpate himself by fighting his chief accuser, and, when that failed, took refuge from his shame as a monk in Reading abbey.[121] His dishonour had to be acknowledged and acted out in as public a way as possible because the habitus would collapse if there were no sanctions to maintain it.

The Appearance of the Code of Chivalry, 1170–1220

Having established the existence of ethical norms before 1180, and having identified an avatar of early noble behaviour in the *preudomme*, we need to conclude by looking at how these came together into a self-conscious code of aristocratic conduct, or chivalry. At what point did the middle ages recognise a formal code of conduct for noblemen? It would certainly be easy to sustain this argument for the fourteenth century. The statutes of the chivalric orders provide one source. An even better and more detailed source is the cultured and popular essay by Geoffrey de Charny (died 1356), the *Livre de chevalerie*, probably addressed to his fellow companions in King John II of France's Company of the Star in or just before 1352.[122] If we move back to the thirteenth century, we could still sustain the view that writers were propagating a coherent code of ethical noble conduct. In the second half of the century two Mediterranean aristocrats and men-of-affairs, Ramon Llull (1232–1316) of the kingdom of Majorca and Philip de Novara (d.*c.*1264) of the kingdom of Cyprus, both wrote books intended for the instruction of noblemen in what noble conduct was, and both had a wide circulation across Europe. Llull's *Libre que es de l'ordre de cavalleria* (1279 x 83) presents all that an aspirant to knighthood needed to know about the ethos and honour of his order. Philip de Novara's *Des Quatre Tenz d'Aage d'Ome* (*c.*1260) was not specifically directed at knights but at males and females alike, and refers to what is proper conduct at each stage of life. But since the people Philip addressed were those of his own class, his book naturally became a book of noble

[121] *Radulfi de Diceto decani Lundoniensis Opera Historica*, ed. W. Stubbs (2 vols., Rolls Series, 1876) i, 310; Robert de Torigny, *Chronica*, in, *Chronicles of the Reigns of Stephen, Henry II and Richard I*, ed. R. Howlett (4 vols., Rolls Series, 1885–9) iv, 218.

[122] *Book of Chivalry of Geoffroi de Charny*, esp. pp. 18–21.

conduct.[123] Both writers were literate laymen of wide political experience who chose to present a code of moral secular behaviour heavily overlaid and informed by religious expectations. Apart from their own pronounced piety, the reason they did so was that there was already a tradition of writers dealing with chivalry in that way. Both books were widely read in their day; Llull's became an abiding favourite for centuries, being translated into several languages in the middle ages, including English. It was a direct inspiration to Charny in his generation.

It is best if we pursue the idea of a code backward through time. Llull and Novara had acknowledged predecessors, which allows us to project back the idea of a prescribed and self-conscious code for nobles to yet an earlier generation. Both men, for instance, drew on the *Lancelot*, an inspired work whose first (non-cyclical) version was probably composed in Burgundy and may well have been in circulation before 1210. Part of the *Lancelot* deals with the instruction in knighthood of the young Galaaz (Lancelot) by the Lady of the Lake. Llull copied the Lancelot in its ideas of the origins of knighthood and also in its idea of taking items of the knight's equipment as a way of explaining the qualities of an ideal knight. Novara, for his part, copied the Lancelot in its ideas of proper conduct of young knights in the presence of elders. There was therefore a prior discourse on noble conduct that they themselves had tapped. Novara was an adult in Outremer by 1218, and that is where he would have acquired his ideas of what he called *droiture*, or 'proper order'.[124] So we are drawn to that particular time when looking for the emergence of a self-conscious code of chivalry. The two decades after 1200 show in fact much activity in the attempt to define what proper social order actually was.

I would suggest that it is to the generation in which the non-cyclical Prose Lancelot was first composed that we can date the appearance of a self-conscious and didactic code called 'chivalry'. Other significant works appeared at this time. The most significant and influential was the *Ordene de Chevalerie*, a work composed probably by a cleric around the year 1220. It is important in several respects. It opens by announcing that 'it is a good thing to talk of *preudomme*, for one can learn much by doing so'. The word 'preudomme' occurs in it several times in the sense of a man worthy of respect and reverence, such as Hugh de Tabarie, its hero 'qui molt fu sages et preudom'. But it is a book which assumes that the

123 Ramon Llull, *Libre que es de l'ordre de cavalleria, Obres essencials*, i, ed. P. Bohigas (Barcelona, 1957).

124 *Les Quatre Ages*, 36.

preudomme is also a *chevaler*. *Chevalerie* is a word that occurs in the *Ordene* numerous times. When it does, the word means a social code as much as the art of horse management in battle.[125] The most significant thing about the *Ordene* is its title. Although the word 'order' had been applied by ecclesiastical writers to warriors and nobles for over a century, they had only meant it in the sense of an epistemological division of society, a line drawn for the convenience of analysis.[126] But the *Ordene* could be intended to mean 'The Ordinal of *Chevalerie*', in the sense that deacons and priests were admitted to their orders by use of a book called an ordinal which instructed them liturgically and symbolically in their duties. To use the word 'ordinal' implies that knighthood was a recognised and sanctioned rank within society, a rank which bestowed a recognisable quality on those who enjoyed it and which demanded also certain moral duties.

The idea had in fact been openly discussed in society and influential writings from the first half of the twelfth century. The first glimpse we have of it is in 1146, when a clerk of Count Ralph I of Vermandois commenced a solemn act in the name of his master in favour of one of his abbeys by reflecting on how important it was that 'those in priestly or knightly orders' should attend to what scripture says, because it was their particular responsibility to govern others in the light of it. Knights, he said, ought particularly to attend to written instruments issued in the past because it was by their swords that peace and peaceful possession of goods was maintained.[127] This intriguing little passage, emanating from the household of a distinguished northern French statesman and colleague of Abbot Suger, is interesting for a number of reasons. It unapologetically equates priestly orders with the state of being a knight, and calls them both *ordines*. It is clearly drawing this idea from the ancient social theory of the three orders (see pp. 226–8). But it is going a step further in equating the orders as equal by divine appointment and describing their social roles.

125 In the *Ordene de Chevalerie*, the word *chevalerie* is used as follows: Hugh de Tabarie is said to be a man of physical toughness and *grant chevalerie* (p. 106); *chevalerie* is said to be a *sainte ordre* (p. 107); *chevalerie* is said to be a concept imbued with honesty, courtliness and goodwill (p. 108); *chevalerie* is that by which a knight wins his way to Paradise (ibid.); if it were not for *chevalerie* lordship would amount to very little (p. 117). Two of these five instances are purely ideological statements, and do not reflect the military and physical sense of the word.

126 Flori, *Chevaliers et chevalerie*, 204–6.

127 *The Cartulary and Charters of Notre Dame of Homblières*, ed. W.M. Newman, revised T. Evergates and G. Constable (Cambridge, Mass., 1990), 120–1, '. . . qui in ordine sacerdotali sive militari'.

Count Ralph was a close counsellor of Louis VI and Louis VII, and we are getting a glimpse in 1146 of the views on knighthood current at the Capetian court.

We next glimpse this self-same rationale in England, in John of Salisbury's great essay on social philosophy, the *Policraticus*. It has an instructive digression on the profession of arms. Its relative lack of learned allusions to obscure Classical writers perhaps indicates that it was a subject in which John of Salisbury felt a considerable interest; enough to speak clearly rather than through the veil of Classical allusions he usually employs. It was written in 1159, at a time when there was war brewing in France after the best part of a decade of peace. As a youth being educated in Chartres and Paris, John had lived through a period of great princely wars in northern France. It is hardly surprising therefore that in 1159, as secretary to Archbishop Theobald of Canterbury, he should repeat the ideology of knighthood we find in the circle of Count Ralph of Vermandois in the 1140s. John equates the oath of good faith taken by knights to their lords with the promises deacons and priests made at ordination.[128] 'Milites' were, like clergy, 'ordained' (*ordinatus*). Men who had taken the oath were an honourable profession with duties to their prince and to his people. Those who had taken up the sword without that sanction were no more knights than unordained laypeople with a missal were priests. When he elaborates the duties laid on knights, he also discusses the proper use of the sword to keep civil peace. He repeats the Davidic ethic that knights should attend to the protection of the poor, and makes strong statements of the knights' duties to support the Church and the faith (see pp. 71ff).[129]

Following on from John, we can see why his colleague Bishop Stephen de Fougères famously suggested around 1170 that you could equate the

[128] The content of the military oath John describes has not survived, but it clearly is to a contemporary oath he is alluding. Flori doesn't find any evidence of it in surviving liturgies of the blessing of military arms, Flori, *L'Essor de la Chevalerie*, 288 and n. However, there is a reference in 1220 to the oath of loyalty English knights customarily took to their lords to report any treason against them, *Curia Regis Rolls* viii, 365.

[129] *Ioannis Saresberiensis Policraticus* ii, 21–3. See the comprehensive study in Flori, *L'Essor de la Chevalerie*, 280-9, who makes the argument that it is the knight that John was describing, not a Roman legionary. He finds some elements of the moral teaching of William of Conches, his master at Chartres in the 1140s, in John's views. But clearly, in the light of the Vermandisien charter, Flori is incorrect in thinking John to be the first author to define the knight's role in society (p. 281): he was echoing an earlier debate.

taking-up of knighthood with the taking-up of ecclesiastical orders. Like John, he did so to criticise his irresponsible contemporaries in the Angevin world; he was urging on them the view that '*chevalerie* was once a high order (*haute ordre*)'.[130] Although a man of the Plantagenet court, his argument follows what was clearly being discussed in Capetian circles in the 1140s and 1150s. Firstly, he was openly saying that if you took up knighthood, you were ontologically changed by grace, and by new expectations and privileges, just as was a new deacon or priest. In the *Ordene de Chevalerie* this was even more explicit: when a young man was *adoubé* ('equipped') and *ordené* ('instituted' or 'ordained') as a knight, he had entered upon a new social level which had strict requirements of ethical conduct.[131] But there was more to Bishop Stephen's words than this. There had been a number of earlier writers who thought that knighthood was morally corrupt and needed reforming by a programme for elevating it. But Stephen put it the other way around. Knighthood had for him once been a 'high order', but now it was in a state of decline and was in need of reform to get it back to what it had been. Such an assumption tells us that noble conduct was emerging from the habitus. Once it was perceived as a body of ethics which could be listed, comprehended and criticised because of its decline, noble conduct had lost ability to structurise independently, and was capable of being structured by individuals, as Stephen was trying to do. In the 1170s Bishop Stephen perceived *chevalerie* as a code.

Why did 'chivalry' become the label for the aristocratic code of conduct? It is possible to argue from the *Ordene* that the noble code of conduct borrowed the existing label of 'chivalry' at much the same time as it became established that the *chevaler* was a nobleman: namely in the years at the end of the twelfth century. The earlier twelfth century had equated noble conduct with the conduct of the *preudomme*, but this would not do for the new social world of the thirteenth century. If anyone had ever suggested in 1200 that *preudommie* was a better word for a social

130 *Le Livre des Manières*, l. 585. The bishop offers numerous observations to support the analogy of the ordained knight: salvation was to be found by living *en son ordre*; failure to live as a true knight could incur expulsion from his order (*sil deit l'en bien desordener*); knightly ordination and degradation had to take place before an altar, see ibid., ll. 621–36.

131 The same ontology is found in the contemporary Prose Lancelot, where Lancelot received *l'ordre de chevalerie*, *Lancelot do Lac* i, p. 139. It is also found explicitly in the 'Romance of the Wings' where Ralph de Houdenc says that *chevalerie* came from God and the *chevalier* possessed it by God's grace, *Le Roman des Eles*, ll. 11–15. For a reflection on the application of the sacramental term to the secular rank, Duby, *The Three Orders*, 295.

code than *chevalerie*, it would have been immediately obvious that it was an idea which could not work.[132] Everyone knew that not all knights had ever been *preudommes*. The word signified an advanced state of recognised public virtue which had to be laboured at, so *preudommie* would never have done as a name for noble conduct appropriate to all noble knights. Young knights were not *preudommes*, they were men who were only setting off on the path to *preudommie*; if they were bound by ethical norms, the norms could only be described as *chevalerie*. This change in meaning did not happen abruptly and at the whim of the author of the *Ordene*. The generation before 1200 was already assessing the social application of the world *chevalerie*. I would suggest that the decade which commenced *chevalerie*'s transformation into something new was the 1170s. We have seen Bishop Stephen de Fougères' contribution, but in the same decade Chrétien de Troyes famously talked of the *chevalerie* in which Greece once led the world in ages gone by, which had passed to Rome and was in his day exemplified in France, from where, he prayed, it would never depart.[133] Chrétien certainly meant the word to signify deeds of war, but he also meant it to refer to the dignity and public virtue of the aristocracy of his day.

In that final respect, it is important to note what Stephen Jaeger has said about *clergie* and *chevalerie*. The upbringing of the ideal courtly knight of the late twelfth and early thirteenth century included learning his letters. Literate and culturally ambitious noblemen had been visible in French society since the eleventh century, although they were not then common. By 1170 they were no longer quite so uncommon. Noblemen and knights with ambitions to be considered *preudomme* might include in their aspirations the seeking of fame as a composer and vernacular poet, like Huon d'Oisy, castellan of Cambrai, or as a collector of Latin and French books, like Gilbert of Monmouth. It was in this decade that the seneschal of Normandy read, analysed and detected a forged charter presented in his court, a skill which his contemporary Wace of Bayeux said that he thought the ideal aristocrat should possess.[134] It was in this generation that romance writers assumed as a matter of merit that their heroes were put to learn their letters when they were children.[135] Philip of

[132] The word *preudommie* is used c.1350 by Geoffrey de Charny to describe the highest standard of conduct attainable by a knight, *Book of Chivalry of Geoffroi de Charny*, 134.

[133] *Cligés*, ll. 28–42.

[134] National Archives (formerly PRO), 31/8/140B (D'Anisy's transcripts), pt 2, p. 42; *Roman de Rou* i, pt 2, ll. 1765–6.

[135] *Eracle*, ll. 252–8; *Garin le Loherenc* i, ll. 3143–9; ii, ll. 10821–3

Harvengt, abbot of Bonne Espérance, admitted to being embarrassed at this very time by the literacy and poetic accomplishments of the knights of Flanders, when their abilities were compared to the poor standards of education amongst the lower clergy.[136]

It may not be entirely a matter of coincidence that chivalry emerged as a self-conscious code of noble conduct in the generation that the aristocracy became noticeably literate. It is not so much that the aristocrats themselves wrote treatises on chivalry and conduct, or even that they were able to read such treatises as came their way. The very fact that a significant number of leaders amongst the nobility of England and France were literate encouraged them to take the same historical perspective as Chrétien de Troyes and Stephen de Fougères in relation to *clergie* and *chevalerie*. Both writers addressed the nobility directly in the vernacular and told them that their 'order' had a moral responsibility, and that it was their task to maintain and improve the standards of conduct which they had acquired. In such an environment it is hardly to be wondered at that writers responded within a generation by publishing ethical treatises such as the *Roman des Eles* and the *Ordene de Chevalerie*. These were works which plucked out themes which had previously existed only in the habitus, listed, assessed and defined them, and suggested ways that they could be refined further. This was the way that the code of chivalry appeared.

[136] *De institutione clericorum* in, *PL*, 203, col. 816.

CHAPTER 3

Out of the Iron Age

An old theme in medieval studies is the idea of 'taming'. The view of previous generations of writers was that a number of things were 'tamed' in the middle ages; not least death, although according to Philippe Ariès it got loose again. But the wildest thing of all to be tamed was the human heart. It was taken for granted by nineteenth-century historians that early medieval society was composed of violent and uncontained children, capable of savage outbursts of temper and violence. Medieval warriors have long had the reputation of being unrestrained in their appetites for sex and violence, and if you view medieval society through particular sources it can look that way. When Marc Bloch chose to use the epic, *Raoul de Cambrai*, as one of his principal sources in his reconstruction of feudal society, it had to follow that its irrational and vengeful hero would inevitably colour Bloch's view of medieval society in a deep and reeking blood-red. There was indeed violence and unrestrained sexuality in medieval society. The open question is whether it was any more or less violent than that of later societies; say, that of the sixteenth century. The personalities and reigns of Henry I and Henry VIII of England make an interesting comparison in that regard. As we will see in the following chapter, the view of early medieval people as unrestrained and morally childish depends rather too much on the presuppositions of nineteenth-century anthropologists about undeveloped societies. In fact, as the sources tell us, even eleventh-century society and behaviour was far too complex to be readily dismissed as made up of simple and childlike souls.

In considering medieval noble conduct we lie between two traps. As I have just said, the one is an ancient pit of old assumptions about the unsophistication of past societies, out of which a superior modernity evolved. The other is a more modern noose, which lassoes us to ideas of continuity in society, saying that little in fact changed. In considering the past historiography of noble conduct, and in surveying the sources, it is clear that things really did change between 1000 and 1300. A code of chivalry did emerge as the self-conscious moral guide to a nobleman, which he could be taught. To that extent, the fourteenth-century nobleman was a different, and – if you like – more modern creature than his twelfth-century predecessor. He had handbooks of etiquette and conduct to give him a new level of self-assurance. But the twelfth-century nobleman nonetheless occupied a world where there was an ideal of noble conduct. It was not to be found described in books, and it was not called chivalry, but it was nonetheless a powerful governor of his actions. And it can be legitimately suggested that the same was as true of the eleventh-century nobleman, not least because of the social truism that noblemen of all periods need some moral justification for their power and privilege, if only to give reasons why they should be obeyed. This earlier noble conduct was embedded in the shifting social habitus of society. It was to be found in proverbs, anecdotes and principally in the existence of the ideal type of the *preudomme*, against which any man wishing to be thought noble had to measure himself.

For historians, the task is to explain how this change happened. It is reassuring to look back over three centuries of historical debate on this particular subject and discover that historians have in the end actually got somewhere. It reassures you that the study of history is ultimately something more than a debating society. Eighteenth-century social philosophers identified 'chivalry' as a social phenomenon specific to a particular time before they lived, and they constructed a line of historical development for it. Nineteenth-century social commentators and political idealists picked up on their work. Unfortunately for us, they found that chivalry was not quite as spent a social force as their predecessors had thought. Since chivalry then became appropriated by them for their various contemporary purposes, most serious nineteenth-century historians rode off the field. Nonetheless the work of the analysis and compilation of sources on chivalry continued, and Gautier in particular was able to identify the twelfth and early thirteenth centuries as the period when society developed a self-consciousness of chivalry. For much of the twentieth century the eighteenth-century model of chivalry, as elaborated by Gautier, held the lists. Then, as in other historical debates, the 1980s produced major new ideas.

In Britain, Maurice Keen (implicitly) and John Gillingham (explicitly) challenged the eighteenth century's assumption that chivalry necessarily arose from the progressive christianisation of noble conduct. A secular idea of warrior freemasonry was substituted. In America, Stephen Jaeger suggested a renewed emphasis on the demands of the princely court as the engine for social transformation. Courtliness was recognised as a phenomenon acting on noble behaviour. Jaeger kept the clergy in the centre of the debate, as educators of the laity in modified conduct, although their ends were in this case secular, not evangelical. In France, Jean Flori retained and refined the eighteenth-century model of chivalry, emphasising the place of peace legislation and the preaching of the Crusade in offering knights a critique of their unrestrained behaviour. But, most importantly, Flori was the first historian to note the significance of what had been often overlooked, that *chevalerie* did not become the word for noble conduct until the end of the twelfth century. This matched well with what he also knew, that knights did not become unequivocally noble by being knights until the generation after 1200.

What a difference a decade makes. As we have seen, there is something to be said for all these late twentieth-century theories. Clergy did articulate, live and teach ideals whose origins can be traced back to Cicero and the social ethics of the late Roman Republic. Also, as early as the eighth century the clergy found in the Davidic ethic an effective Biblical hermeneutic for noble conduct. In the twelfth century, the sermon and tract, and the imperative of the Crusade gave a new model for a self-consciously Christian knighthood. But, as we have seen, there is more to say. If you accept the validity of all these varied observations, then what is needed is a synthesis. I would suggest once again that its focus can be found in the fact that, in and before 1100, there was an engine which processed all these new social influences. It lay in the ideal type of the moral nobleman, the *preudomme*. The *preudomme* was created by a variety of social and intellectual pressures. Since a nobleman had to be a warrior, there were expectations of him to be tough, brave and uncomplaining. Since a nobleman had to be a courtier, then he had to be amiable to his equals, sound in his advice and also loyal to his prince, but not unreasonably so, for his honour and dignity as a warrior and as a lord of lesser men demanded he preserve a certain autonomy. Noblemen were insecure as to their moral position as regards their inferiors. But ecclesiastical intellectuals had long ago discovered a moral justification that made their authority rightful. If lords protected the weak and the Church and resisted the wicked and violent, then God sanctioned their authority. All these social and moral pressures formed the noble habitus of the eleventh century. In due course the habitus was itself hardened by the pressures of a literate and self-conscious twelfth-century society which was creating internal hierarchies. So *chevalerie* appeared in the years after 1170, as an increasingly self-conscious code, and by 1220 it was codified. Habitus became 'chivalry' because the chevalier was the rising aristocrat around whom it formed, not the *preudomme*.

It would not do to overemphasise the originality of the basis of the synthesis I have proposed. The intellectual kernel of it can be found as far back as the eighteenth century. The man who first articulated it was Adam Smith, in a work he called *The Theory of Moral Sentiments* (1759), which in turn influenced Marx's social thinking. Smith proposed that social conduct is formed and transformed when the individual holds up his own modes of behaviour to his own internal criticism. A man looks for behaviour which is rewarded by approval and takes his example of conduct from others, modifying his behaviour accordingly. Social codes form out of this individualistic reflex: and the code is the 'concord' and mutual 'sympathy' between individuals in the social context in which they find themselves.[1] Apart from the emphasis on self-conscious 'codes' of behaviour, Smith's work was a remarkably prescient heralding of some aspects of Bourdieu's social engine of habitus. We have seen how the *preudomme* was the basic pattern of social concord on which aristocrats had agreed as early as the eleventh century. Behave like a 'preudomme' and you were approved of. The 'anti-*preudomme*' was held up to display the sort of behaviour which might well happen in society, but which gained you no credit and no long-term advantage. The late twelfth-century romances and tracts simply elaborated and adjusted this pattern, restating it and thus slightly altering it.[2]

The recent debate on courtliness has tended to question the tradition that the Church played a crucial part in the formulation of chivalry. French scholarship going back to the eighteenth century tended to see conflict between Church and aristocracy in the eleventh and twelfth centuries: the Church labouring through teaching, through the Peace movement and through excommunication, if necessary, to restrain a violent, competitive but superstitious aristocracy from undermining all public order. It followed for Sainte-Palaye and his successors that the teaching of ethical conduct by clergy was a way to curb that innate anarchic tendency in the noble warrior caste. But modern scholarship points out quite reasonably that there were essentially secular noble ethics which owed little in origin

[1] This connection is signalled by G. Welty, 'Social Antagonism: the General and Specific Theory', *Revue Internationale de Sociologie*, 20 (1984), 100–18.

[2] There is a resemblance here to the structurist social theory of Anthony Giddens. He proposed that society evolves by progressively restating accepted norms in every generation, and in restating them, subtly modifying them.

to the Church's teaching: in particular, generosity, loyalty, good faith and hardiness. To admit that, however, is not to admit that clerical influences were of no moment. There is every reason to agree with Jean Flori's analysis that Church authorities made a conscious and long-lasting effort from the 1020s onwards to contain and direct knightly aggression.

To begin with, the relationship of the warrior aristocracy to the church and its pronouncements was not necessarily conflictual, as the historical tradition generally assumes. It could be consensual: one thinks here of Orderic Vitalis's charming portrayal of the knights of the castle of Maule in the Vexin resorting to the cloister garth of its priory to converse on serious subjects with the monks on warm afternoons, and also the way that Gerold the chaplain of Earl Hugh of Chester enthused his master's military household in matters of religion, and indeed turned three of his knights to the cloister.[3] Henry I's minister, Nigel d'Aubigny – languishing and near death around the year 1109 – was so vulnerable to the Church's correction not because he feared its lightnings but because he fully shared its ideals and lived in a society which engaged in the constant dialectic between gospel ideal and worldly weakness which is the process of auricular confession. Recent work has tended to the conclusion that there was an introspective confessional culture already well established amongst the Anglo-French lay aristocracy by the mid-twelfth century.[4] We can see in it evidence of that internal criticism that was for Adam Smith one of the motives in individuals adopting acceptable social conduct.

But there has nonetheless been a fitful new emphasis since the 1980s on the secularity of the thinking of the twelfth- and thirteenth-century knight. We are asked to look at the evidence for antagonism between the knight and the cleric in society: and hence the rejection of their teaching and their household influence. Peter Noble has suggested that the twelfth-century epic reflected a secular thought-world where the clergy was of 'little importance', a thought-world where the Church was the victim of the knight and his lord, and where it is of consequence only when it appears in

[3] Orderic Vitalis, *The Ecclesiastical History*, ed. M. Chibnall (6 vols, Oxford, 1969–80), iii, 182–4, 226–8.

[4] For recent studies, A. Murray, 'Confession before 1215', *Transactions of the Royal Historical Society*, 6th ser., 3 (1993), 51–82; M. McLaughlin, *Consorting with Saints: prayer for the dead in medieval France* (Ithaca NY, 1994), 219–27; P. Biller, 'Confession in the Middle Ages', in, *Handling Sin: Confession in the Middle Ages*, ed. P. Biller and A.J. Minnis (York Studies in Medieval Theology, 2, 1998); D. Crouch, 'The Troubled Deathbeds of Henry I's Servants: Death, Confession and Secular Conduct in the Twelfth Century', *Albion*, 34 (2002), 24–36.

its subordinate role as landowner and lord. He suggested that the contempt he detected in writers' depictions of their knightly heroes' attitudes towards the clerical caste had a basis in mutual competition for limited favour at the courts of lords. Monks in particular come in for knightly disapproval, being seen as lazy and useless occupiers of land that could be better used to support them.[5]

It is worth noting that all of Noble's selected texts were drawn from the Carolingian epics, which tend to depict more rivalry between clergy and lay nobility than the Arthurian, Saxon and Alexandrine romances. Any work which trawls the age of Charles Martel will find anticlerical material, because Charles was a notorious despoiler of Church property in contemporary history.[6] This is not to say that there was not a critical and hostile sentiment towards the clergy in the air in the twelfth and thirteenth centuries, even if we mostly hear of them in somewhat artificial clerical sources, such as the scoffers in sermon *exempla*. A fair number of well-known instances can be cited. The canons of Laon in 1114 encountered three delinquent teenagers in Totnes in Devon, who brazenly questioned the authenticity of their relics and then stole money from the offerings placed around their reliquary. William Marshal famously had a few sharp things to say on clerical teaching about salvation on his deathbed in 1219 when, after his confession, it was foolishly suggested (by a household knight, not a cleric) that he should make a gesture of monetary restitution to atone for his sins.[7] But, intriguing though these isolated examples are, the critical and sceptical spirit they represent was not by any means the dominant sentiment of their times. In the intellectual ferment of any human society, it would be surprising were there not such examples, however notionally pious the age.

Richard Kaeuper takes a different approach to the idea of medieval secularity. He certainly does not ignore ecclesiastical influence on knights, but

[5] P. Noble, 'Anti-clericalism in the Feudal Epic', in, *The Medieval Alexander Legend and Romance Epic: Essays in Honour of David J.A. Ross*, ed. P. Noble, L. Polak and C. Isoz (Nendeln, 1982), 149–58.

[6] For instance, the opening of the romance 'Garin le Loherenc', written in the third quarter of the twelfth century, also gives some material to conclude that the historical tradition of the time concerning the Carolingian period helped push writers towards an anticlerical stance. It depicts the protracted debate when the Church resisted giving land to help fight the pagans. *Garin le Loherenc*, ed. A. Iker-Gittleman (3 vols, Classiques français du moyen âge, 117–19, 1996–7) i, ll. 14–125.

[7] Hermann of Laon, *De miraculis sanctae Mariae Laudunensis*, in, *PL*, 156, col. 985; *History of William Marshal*, trans. S. Gregory and ed. A.J. Holden and D. Crouch (3 vols, Anglo-Norman Text Society, Occasional Publication Series, 4–6, 2002–6).ii, ll. 18468–96.

interprets knightly society as principally fixated on masculine competition and the demonstration of Prowess (meaning deeds of physical excellence). As a result his interpretation can tend to discount the moral striving within the noble habitus in favour of physical conflict. We see an example of this in his interpretation of Largesse within the knightly ethic (see above). Twelfth- and thirteenth-century emphasis on Largesse as a noble virtue is by this interpretation meant to demonstrate the unsuitability of merchants who wish to act the noble, but who are by nature avaricious and miserly. Largesse is also a symptom of the cult of material success on the tournament and battlefield, as it shows the wealthy nobleman what he should do with his winnings to be considered noble. Yet, as I have demonstrated, a number of contemporary lay and clerical writers say quite a different thing, that Largesse was good because it demonstrates how little store those who embraced it set by material things. It was a sign of moral excellence that those who have money can give it freely, and that its pursuit meant nothing to them.

Is there a destabilising bias in late twentieth-century historical work towards materialistic explanations of medieval conduct? The nature of historians is to be wary of single, simple causes. Peter Noble's essay on twelfth-century anticlericalism is the nearest to a secularist analysis of medieval aristocratic conduct. But he nonetheless notes an overmastering sacramental need amongst knights, from baptism to funeral: they tend to bewail the absence of priests at the point where they are most needed, to confess and give viaticum to those in imminent expectation of death. This too is an aspect of medieval life to which Kaeuper in fact also does full justice.[8] Noble and Kaeuper are simply attempting to adjust the past tendency to analyse the moral values of the laity through clerical sources. Another parallel readjustment in interpretation is represented by the work on courtliness of Stephen Jaeger, who sought to track the self-conscious development of the courtly ethic from Cicero through a tenth-century Ottonian renaissance to the courts of eleventh and twelfth-century France. Here he emphasised that there was secular calculation in clerical behaviour too; there was purely humanistic thinking in medieval society ultimately drawn from pagan Classical antecedents.[9] The Ottonian bishops and the northern French nobles he described were students of Cicero; they were

[8] Kaeuper, R.W. *Chivalry and Violence in Medieval Europe* (Oxford, 1999), 45–62.

[9] For observations on the secularity and idiosyncrasy of Jaeger's analysis, see P. Hyams, 'What did Henry III of England think in bed and in French about Kingship and Anger?', in, *Anger's Past: the Social Uses of an Emotion in the Middle Ages*, ed. B.H. Rosenwein (Ithaca, NY, 1998), 105–7.

careerists and their behaviour was consciously modulated to that end. Their aim was self-promotion, not self-examination. The moderating influences in their courtly conduct were for him ambition and the presence of women, and he makes the abrupt observation that 'the feudal nobility was a distinct class; the monasteries and the church under the reform were distinct spheres'.[10]

A move to bring forward material and secular explanations of noble conduct is certainly characteristic of work on chivalry since 1980, but it does not amount to a denial of ecclesiastical and spiritual aspirations and explanations. There are still authors able convincingly to assert the importance of their faith to some medieval aristocrats, and their desire to live that faith in their daily lives.[11] The future direction of the study of the phenomenon of noble conduct is likely to be more subtle than the results won by the empirical methods of the scholars of the eighteenth and nineteenth century. Their work is now complete and the parameters that they worked to establish have been established. The epistemology of chivalry that Gautier worked out in the 1880s was improved and broadly validated over a century by Painter and Keen. We now know what chivalry was and when it came to be. Debate since the 1980s has focussed more on *how* it came to be, and what it tells us about the society in which it grew to self-consciousness. In a sense we need to return with a vengeance to Sidney Painter's religious chivalry, and to analyse complicated thirteenth-century noblemen such as Philip de Remy: corrupt Capetian bureaucrat, poet, novelist, aficionado of the tournament and devotee of Marian spirituality. Chivalry was propagated by complicated minds like his, and it must therefore have been a very complex moral code.

A final observation needs to be made to assert what the study of chivalry has established in terms of society. I have argued that between 1170 and 1220 noble conduct became self-conscious and codified around the idea of *chevalerie*. It was used alongside the status of knight to help define a class, as Flori and Duby have demonstrated. The fact that writers produced handbooks and tracts to educate aspirants as to what noble conduct ought to be tells us a number of things. It tells us, with other things (see Chapter 2) that there was an impulse to create a hierarchy of social groups in society. But it tells us more. A self-conscious and codified ideal

[10] C.S. Jaeger, *The Origins of Courtliness: Civilizing Trends and the Formation of Courtly Ideals, 939–1210* (Philadelphia, 1985), esp. pp.xii, 257–72.

[11] For a rather different view of the place of religion in eleventh and twelfth-century secular conduct, see M. Chibnall, *The World of Orderic Vitalis* (Oxford, 1984), esp. 15–16, 52–5.

of noble conduct divided French-influenced societies of the late twelfth century radically from earlier and peripheral societies. It was not since the Classical period that there had been quite so structured and introspective an ideal of noble conduct. French society in the twelfth century had left behind the Iron Age societies of pre-Conquest England, Wales and Ireland, as Strickland and Gillingham have said each in their ways. For all the sophisticated literary culture that Anglo-Saxon England and twelfth-century Wales enjoyed, their aristocratic habitus was harsh, unreflective, unforgiving and violent compared to the contemporary world of French *preudommie*. It is not unsurprising that the Anglo-French after 1066 found the English and Welsh difficult to understand, and indeed went so far as to label them barbaric. The emergence of chivalry after 1170 made that cultural chasm all the more evident, for French society had mutated into something modern and self-conscious, and left behind a more ancient social world.

PART TWO

NOBLE DESCENT

CHAPTER 4

Constructing Families

Family (expressed as '*lin*', or lineage, and '*sang*', or blood) is one of the concepts closest to the heart of the idea of aristocracy. Indeed, you might even say– considering its association with blood – that it *is* the heart of aristocracy. Aristocrats inherited their power and position. Every generation of aristocrats included newcomers, it is true. But these newcomers generally married into a powerful group of families, which already existed. The family was the heart that pumped blue blood around society. No study of aristocracy is possible without coming to terms with what family meant to claims to social eminence. If we use the modern English word 'lineage' for 'family', the concept takes on a seductive aura of glamour and history. Lineage is what aristocrats have. Peasants and smallholders did not have a lineage. The line that connected them to past generations brought them nothing except obligation and servitude. No-one was interested in their forbears, unless, that is, peasants were trying to argue that their forbears were free and so escape their servitude. For nobles, of course, it was different. They were well aware that past generations of their family brought them an inheritance of prestige and aspiration, as much as land. As we will see in the next chapter, nobles were well aware of the importance of their forbears. They were perfectly capable of rationalising for their contemporaries what it was that made them different from and superior to others in their society, and family was at the core of their explanation. Manners might have given the semblance of nobility to a man; his blood gave him an unanswerable reason why his nobility demanded deference and respect.

The academic study of noble families began in an era when noble privilege was still a reality in western societies. In those days – not yet long gone – historians and genealogists were happy to be auxiliaries in the constant campaign of aristocrats as individuals and as a group to establish their superiority in society. Some of the earliest efforts of scholars of the family were deployed to produce lavish volumes on the histories of powerful and long-lived noble houses, such as the magnificent French seventeenth-century histories of the Harcourts and Montmorencies. In the eighteenth and nineteenth centuries, European scholars beavered away to create almanacks, directories and handbooks of national peerages. In Britain, where there remained to this generation a noble and hereditary legislative chamber, the collaboration of scholarship and aristocracy lasted longer than anywhere else. The genealogical master-project to produce a *Complete Peerage* of Great Britain continued its authoritative work into the 1950s. And all of these stock books of aristocracy go into great detail on the ancestry of each of its illustrious families, because ancestry unarguably established nobility. The longer the lineage how much greater was the nobility. In 1857 Trollope smiled at this attitude in his sketch of Mr Thorne of Ullathorne, proud but gentle descendant of Cedric the Saxon:

Were you in your ignorance to surmise that such a one was of good family because the head of his family was a baronet of old date, he would open his eyes with a delightful look of affected surprise, and modestly remind you that baronetcies only dated from James I. He would gently sigh if you spoke of the blood of the Fitzgeralds and De Burghs; would hardly allow the claims of the Howards and Lowthers; and has before now alluded to the Talbots as a family who had hardly yet achieved the full honours of a pedigree.[1]

Yet the glamour of antiquity was turning men's heads already in the twelfth century, as we shall see in the next chapter.

While antiquaries and genealogists were still compiling elaborate family trees to bolster their noble patrons' pride, the academic study of the family began. Its concerns were very different from those of the genealogists. Early sociologists studied families as a clue to finding general rules about the way societies, like organisms, evolved. This broader debate was not unconnected to the history of the noble family, as a lot of it revolved around what earlier genealogists had discovered about succession customs in past societies. Some of the models of family structure scholars produced owed a lot in fact to the early study of noble families. But we are interested here in general rules of family development and their influence on historians of the nobility. So we must begin our study not with the great genealogists but with the pioneering nineteenth-century scholars of the

[1] *Barchester Towers* (repr. Oxford, 1980), 212.

family. They have provided us with many presuppositions about families, presuppositions so deep rooted that historians generally forget where they have come from.

The Age of Durkheim: The 'Law' of Family Contraction

The conscious historical debate on family and lineage has been going on for a century-and-a-half. Its origins, though complicated, need to be briefly sketched for reasons that were just mentioned.[2] It begins in the 1860s, a decade which saw the establishment of the intellectual dominance of Darwinian 'evolution' as a master-theory amongst natural philosophers, including those who set themselves to the study of the family and society. Categorisation (or taxonomy) in the manner of the Swedish naturalist Linnaeus, and Darwinian evolution, were the intellectual fashions of the mid-nineteenth century. They were enthusiastically applied by French, American and British scholars to a whole range of fields, one among them being the study of humanity and its institutions.[3] Family was one of the first areas of social anthropology to be subjected to concentrated academic study. It was believed at that time that the family preceded any other form of social organisation, and that the complex structures of law and national government were all founded upon the primitive family. So it was not surprising that the scholars who looked at family naturally did so as social evolutionists.

First – as was scientifically appropriate – there had to come the great pioneer and taxonomist. He was the eminent French senator and academician, Frédéric Le Play (1806–82).[4] Le Play's masterwork, *L'organisation de la famille (selon le vrai modèle signalé par l'histoire de toutes les races*

[2] Some elements of this chapter were published earlier in D. Crouch, 'The Historian, Lineage and Heraldry', in, *Social Display and Status in the Middle Ages*, ed. P.R. Coss and M. Keen (Woodbridge, 2002), 17–37, and, D. Crouch and C. de Trafford, 'The Forgotten Family in Twelfth-Century England', *Haskins Society Journal*, 13 (2004), 41–52.

[3] Note Conan Doyle's impish reference in 1887 to 'the Darwinian Theory' in his pastiche of a *Daily Telegraph* story condemning subversive social influences, 'A Study in Scarlet' in, *Sherlock Holmes: Long Stories* (London, 1929), 52–3.

[4] For Le Play's importance in historiography see, P. Burke, *History and Social Theory* (Cambridge, 1992), 53–4, giving a succinct and brilliant sketch of these developments, following on from P. Laslett, 'The History of the Family', in, *Household and Family in Past Time*, ed. P. Laslett and R. Wall (Cambridge, 1972), 16–21. See also on this D. Herlihy, *Medieval Households* (London, 1985), 136–8.

et tous les temps), was first published in 1871 (although he had been writing about the diverse nature of family structures since 1864). Le Play was very much a creature of his own political age. He wanted to prove that Napoleon's Code Civil was dangerous to modern French society. The Code allowed partible inheritance (that is, for sons to split the paternal property), which to him was a danger to the social fabric. He was a great admirer of the Anglo-Saxon democracies, and his idea was that contemporary British and American industrial pre-eminence was based on a different system of inheritance: primogeniture, where the eldest son was the sole or chief heir to his father. As a result, he preached the superiority of what he called the 'stem family', or in the terms we will be discussing, the narrow agnatic (male-dominated) family.[5] To do this, of course, he had to work out all the permutations of family, to demonstrate just that. It was on the basis of Le Play's categories that an evolutionary model of family development was worked out.

Hot on the heels of the sociological categoriser came the true sociological evolutionists. Perhaps the most famous ultimately was the American scholar Lewis Henry Morgan (1818–1881), who, like Le Play, was a senator of his native republic. He considered and discussed the subject of family for over a decade, and eventually, in 1877, published his masterwork, *Ancient Society*. It was a deeply influential book, and much admired by Marx and Engels.[6] Morgan was an evolutionist. His models of social development were meant to be universal. All societies began, he believed, with a basic primitive family dominated by matriarchs (trading on their sexual predominance). Loose kin-groups, such as these were supposed to be, naturally fragmented under the economic pressures of growing civilisation and property-owning. They evolved first into patriarchy, and then into monogamy, and eventually into what we today would call nuclear families. Morgan's ideas were duplicated independently by other scholars. In Britain, Sir Henry Maine, who found the material for his

[5] For Le Play's first essays, F. Le Play, *La réforme sociale en France deduite de l'observation comparée des peuples européens* (2 vols, Paris, 1864) i, 167, cited in A. Pitt, 'Frédéric Le Play and the Family: Paternalism and Freedom in the French Debates of the 1870s', *French History*, 12 (1998), 78–9, 79n. Pitt points out that before Le Play primogeniture was established as a nostrum amongst French social commentators for the ills of their society; Balzac and Maurras wrote on the subject, ibid., 77 and n.

[6] To be found in, F. Engels, *The Origin of the Family, Private Property and the State* (London, 1884). For studies touching on Morgan's wider importance, T.R. Trautman, *Lewis Henry Morgan and the Invention of Kinship* (Berkeley, 1987); A. Kuper, *The Invention of Primitive Society: Transformations and Illusions* (London, 1988).

social analysis in the study of the law, the Bible and the ancient classics, proposed his own evolutionary model of social organisation in his *Ancient Law* (1861). For Maine, in contrast to Morgan, it all started with Abrahamic patriarchy, not matriarchy.[7] Then there was the Scottish scholar John Fergus McLellan (1827–81). He independently duplicated Morgan's scheme in his *Primitive Marriage* (1865). He too saw matriarchy and extended kinship groups as the earliest form of social organisation. By the end of the nineteenth century, every British and French scholar knew that Western European societies had all experienced a slow change from an original social structure based on the primitive kin group towards smaller social units. They knew too what had caused the change. Monarchy and law courts and ideals of public order had dispelled the repressive solidarity of those Dark Age kindreds which had once held land in common and protected their members by feud and weregild.[8]

A key (if unoriginal) figure in publicising the nineteenth-century model of social evolution was the populist and polymath, Herbert Spencer (1820–1903). He brought this fertile seedbed of sociological ideas and analysis to the forefront of popular attention in his best-selling *Principles of Sociology* (first volume published 1876): a standard work in all Working Men's Institutes and on Victorian thinking-men's bookshelves, and available in French before the end of the century.[9] Between them McLellan, Morgan, Maine and Spencer (who were all dining companions together in the London of 1871) provided the material for the first master-model of family development, proposed by Emile Durkheim (1858–1917).[10] Durkheim never actually published a complete study of the family, but expounded the subject for two decades in his university teaching in Bordeaux and at the élite École Normale Supérieure between

[7] Published in French as, *L'ancien droit considéré dans ses rapports avec l'histoire de la société primitive et avec les idées modernes*, trans. J.G. Courcelle Seneuil (Paris, 1874).

[8] This is the basic tenet of the prolonged comparative history of feud and kindred by Bertha Phillpotts, *Kindred and Clan in the Middle Ages and After: A Study in the Sociology of the Teutonic Races* (Cambridge, 1913). Miss Phillpotts principally quoted Maitland and Vinogradoff as the sources of her views.

[9] Eventually published in French as *Principes de sociologie*, trans. M.E. Cazelle (4 vols., Paris, 1899–1904).

[10] For some penetrating observations on the basis of this evolutionist school of family in Anglo-American circles and its colonisation of the historical mind, A.C. Murray, 'Theories of Germanic Kinship Structure in Antiquity and the Early Middle Ages', in *Germanic Kinship Structure: Studies in Law and Society in Antiquity and the Early Middle Ages* (Toronto, 1983), 11–32.

1888 and 1908. His teaching was, however, reconstructed by his pupil, Marcel Mauss. From Mauss we find that Durkheim proposed a universal 'law of contraction' by which the family had evolved through several stages. Its earliest manifestation was as a diffuse nomadic tribe, which, when it settled down to agrarianism, tightened into a clan more narrowly defined on blood kinship. In turn the clan narrowed to an agnate or cognate kinship group, and then from there into a narrower patriarchy, out of which emerged the nuclear family.[11] In all this we see Durkheim borrowing and reorganising the models proposed by Morgan and McLellan. But his model is more important for historians than the works of his predecessors. This is because one of the eager students sitting in front of Durkheim at the ENS between the years 1904 and 1908 was the young man who would become France's greatest historian of the middle ages, Marc Bloch (1886–1944). It is because of Bloch that Durkheim's 'law of contraction' has become so familiar to historians looking at the medieval family.

Bloch's classic work on feudal society reproduced a scheme of family development which is unmistakably Durkheim's.[12] In his Durkheimian way, Bloch saw 'family' as a social entity with a real existence subject to evolution due to the pressure of social and economic forces. The 'loi de contraction' is one of Bloch's conscious social principles, and it was neatly identified in his work, and tagged and translated by the American historian, David Herlihy, as the 'theory of progressive nuclearisation'.[13] As Peter Laslett has pointed out, the generation of French historians which succeeded Bloch, including Emmanuel Le Roy Ladurie, in his study of the peasantry of Languedoc, and Philippe Ariès in his study of childhood, make the same basic assumption about family evolution as Bloch. Indeed,

[11] This model, along with the phrase 'loi de contraction' is expressed in the essay 'La famille conjugale', *Revue Philosophique*, 91 (1901), 1–14, published in conjunction with his student, Mauss. For a reconstruction and analysis of Durkheim's thought on the family, E. Wallwork, *Durkheim: Morality and Milieu* (Cambridge, Mass., 1972), 88–98.

[12] M. Bloch, *Feudal Society*, trans. L.A. Manyon (2nd edn, 2 vols, London, 1962) i, 139 '... it looks as if from the thirteenth century onwards a sort of contraction was in process. The vast kindreds of not so long before were slowly being replaced by groups much more like our small families of today', see also, idem, *Les caractères originaux de l'histoire rurale française* (Oslo, 1931), 170. For Durkheim's influence on Bloch and on the early Annales school, C. Fink, *Marc Bloch: A Life in History* (Cambridge, 1989), 34–8.

[13] D. Herlihy, 'Family Solidarity in Medieval Italian History', in, *The Social History of Italy and Western Europe* (London, 1978), 174.

because of his work it seems to be have been a commonly accepted idea after the Second World War, so much so that its origin was usually forgotten by the writers who expressed it.[14] Not surprisingly, the 'loi de contraction' surfaced in the work of the undoubted star of the post-war generation of French medieval historians, Georges Michel Claude Duby (1919–96). Indeed, since its adaptation by Duby, it has remained an important idea in the study of medieval society.

We have already met Georges Duby in previous chapters, and will meet him again and again. He needs some formal introduction for British readers. As a boy, Duby was brought up in the historic Burgundian city of Mâcon and graduated from the university of Lyon. He began his distinguished academic career as a young scholar in post-war Burgundy, studying the local society of the Mâconnais for his doctorate, which he completed in 1949. The publication of his thesis in 1953 drew immediate attention in France, and was noticed even in Britain (eventually). His brilliant social studies of the middle ages brought him to a Chair in the Collège de France in 1970. There he presided as something of a modern Michelet until his retirement in 1992. Like Michelet, his public lectures drew great audiences and his books gained widespread acclaim beyond the profession. He was himself aware of the parallel, and even deliberately echoed Michelet in the choice of a title for one of his greater works: *The Knight, the Lady and the Priest*. Duby's field was medieval social history, and he didn't have Michelet's exalted idea of his own contemporary importance. But what they did share was a deep consciousness of the place of style and method in historical writing.

Duby's ideas of family in his great master-thesis on the society of the Mâconnais did not at first echo Bloch's idea of progressive nuclearisation. This is not surprising as in the late 1940s, the young Duby was an empiricist working from his own observations, not necessarily from what sociological models told him should be there. His study of the early charters and diplomas of the Mâconnais led him to believe that the family there did not so much narrow, as adjust to political circumstances. Whenever royal or princely authority was weak, the family turned in on itself for protection, and brothers banded together to defend the patrimony. When

[14] P. Ariès, *Centuries of Childhood: a Social History of Family Life*, trans. R. Baldick (New York, 1962). Le Roy Ladurie's work on the family of the Languedoc (like Duby's initial work on the Mâconnais) was more nuanced than Bloch's, Le Roy Ladurie allows (for instance) that the fraternal kin-group (in French, the *frèréche*) might resurface in times of economic stress, such as the late fourteenth century, *Les paysans de Languedoc* (2 vols., Paris, 1966) i, 162, 167.

society was peaceful and royal authority strong, then the nuclear units could look after themselves, and siblings went their own way.[15] By the 1970s, however, his views had changed, method and theory had taken over his mind, and he had adopted 'progressive nuclearisation' with a vengeance. This was in part the result of his reading of the work of a German contemporary, Karl Schmid, who worked within a parallel German tradition of Durkheimian thinking initiated by Otto Hintze in the 1920s.[16] In the 1950s, Schmid was a member of the great prosopographical investigation into German aristocratic society in the earlier middle ages known now as the 'Münster-Freiburg school'. Looking at the Rhineland, Schmid found, like Bloch, a shift away from a horizontal, kin-based family to a society of vertically-organised lineages. For Schmid and his colleagues, working from the evidence of *libri memoriales* and the study of aristocratic names and surnames, the eleventh century saw a transition from a society made up of influential kin-groups of undifferentiated cousins (the *Sippe*, or clan) into a society based around lineages (the *Geschlecht*).[17] The mature Duby was more accepting of grand theories. He and others amongst French historians of his generation seized on Schmid's

[15] G. Duby, *La société au xie et xiie siècles dans la région mâconnaise* (repr. Paris, 1971), ch.5, esp. 225–6.

[16] Evolutionary social thinking passed into German historiography by a parallel route, for in one version of German national myth the nation rose out of the free barbarian clans or tribes of the early middle ages, which in breaking down into lineages allegedly produced the familiar pattern of duchies, marches and counties of medieval Germany (*Markgenossenschaft*), see Murray, 'Theories of Germanic Kinship Structure', 30–1. Note the views on the 'collapse of clan institutions', which was placed at the centre of the formation of ninth-century feudal society in the evolutionist overview by Otto Hintze, 'Wesen and Verbreitung des Feudalismus', *Sitzungsberichte der Preussischen Akademie der Wissenschaften, phil.-hist Klasse*, 20 (Berlin, 1929), 321–30, translated as 'The Nature of Feudalism', in, *Lordship and Community in Medieval Europe: Selected Readings*, ed. F.L. Cheyette (Huntington, NY, 1975), 22–31, at p. 27.

[17] K. Schmid, 'Zur Problematik von Familie, Sippe und Geschlecht, Haus und Dynastie beim mittelalterlichen Adel: Vortragen zum Thema "Adel und Herrschaft in Mittelalter"', *Zeitschrift für die Geschichte des Oberrheins,* 105 (1957), 1–62. See for a general overview, idem, 'The Structure of the Nobility in the earlier Middle Ages', in, *The Medieval Nobility*, ed. and trans. T. Reuter (Amsterdam, 1978), first published as 'Über die Struktur des Adels im früheren Mittelalter', *Jahrbuch für fränkische Landesforschung*, 19 (1959), 1–23. For an accessible and informative critique of the German thought-world which produced Schmid's work, J.B. Freed, 'Reflections on the Medieval German Nobility', *American Historical Review*, xci (1986), 553–75. See also now, M. Aurell, 'La parenté en l'an mil', *Cahiers de civilisation médiévale: x^e^-xiie siècle*, 43 (2000), 128–9.

works and by the 1970s he had worked the German scholar's ideas of name-giving within families into his own master-thesis.[18]

Duby was a systematic thinker, one of the greatest of the *Annales* tradition; he always took ideas to their logical conclusion. His historical thinking is unusual and remarkable for the way that he interwove his ideas into a unified theory of social development. The idea of lineage became very much one of the golden threads in his tapestry. If you suggest, as he suggested, that there was a fundamental crisis in family identity in medieval society, you might well want to relate it to other perceived crises. The historiography of the twentieth century has been very keen to explain political and religious movements in earlier times as symptoms of social and economic change. If Europe was flooded by rootless younger sons in the late eleventh century, newly excluded from their kin-groups, isn't it remarkable that the Crusades happened at just that time?[19] Isn't it remarkable also that the same period saw the emergence of the knightly order founded on the rootless bachelor seeking service with a lord. Equally, did not that knightly order by its mercenary violence precipitate the rise of the principalities in medieval France?[20] It is all just too neat, and Duby for one had no intention of resisting the seductions of that neatness; it would be asking too much of that rare creature, a systematic historian.

Between them, Duby and Schmid, their pupils and colleagues, created a dominant school of thinking in Franco-German medieval history which maintained itself into the 1990s and also colonised part of the Anglo-American medieval community.[21] Other crises could be explained by the

[18] G. Duby, 'Lignage, noblesse et chevalerie au xiie siècle dans la région mâconnaise: une révision', in, *Hommes et structures du moyen âge* (Paris, 1973), 395–422, repr. in English, *The Chivalrous Society*, trans. C. Postan (London, 1977), 59–87, esp. 67–75. In 1964, Jacques Le Goff employed a kinship scheme deriving from the Münster–Freiburg model, *La civilisation de l'Occident médiévale* (Paris, 1964), translated by J. Barrow as, *Medieval Civilisation, 400–1500* (Oxford, 1988), 280–85.

[19] G. Duby. 'Au xiie siècle: les "jeunes" dans la société aristocratique dans la France du nord-ouest', in, *Hommes et structures du moyen âge* (Paris, 1973), 213–25, repr. in English, *The Chivalrous Society*, trans. C. Postan (London, 1977), 112–22, see esp. p. 120: 'It is obvious that it was the bands of 'youths' excluded by so many social prohibitions from the main body of settled men, fathers of families and heads of houses, with their prolonged spells of turbulent behaviour making them an unstable fringe of society, who created and sustained the crusades'.

[20] G. Duby, *Les trois ordres ou l'imaginaire du féodalisme* (Paris, 1978), repr. in English as *The Three Orders: Feudal Society Imagined*, trans. A. Goldhammer (Chicago, 1980), 98.

[21] For a recent example of the application of this theoretical model to a historical case, see M.T. Clanchy, *Abelard: a medieval life* (Oxford, 1997), 137, whose reconstruc-

theory of progressive nuclearisation of families. Since the famous work of Jakob Burckhardt in the 1860s, or even indeed since Jules Michelet in the 1840s, there has been a deep-rooted perception that the understanding of what it meant to be an individual underwent a shift in the middle ages. If kin-group corporate solidarity broke up in the middle ages, could not the two developments be related? Robert Fossier (despite being no advocate of steady and regular nuclearisation of the family) suggested as much in his study of medieval Picardy.[22] It fell to Fossier to sum up the whole thesis succinctly in 1986 in what was intended to be an authoritative French pronouncement on the family in history, 'it does seem that between 1000 and 1300 the family passed a point of no return: the nuclear family . . . crystallised as an individual unit, from the clan, the lineage, the kindred': not strictly evolutionist, this, but certainly Durkheimian.[23]

Some recent Anglo-American interpretations of early French society are written in the same tradition.[24] A basic assumption of both David Bates's *Normandy Before 1066* and Eleanor Searle's *Predatory Kinship* – although in many ways very different books – is that the late eleventh-century Norman aristocracy arose out of earlier Franco-Scandinavian kin-groups (although Searle didn't believe that the narrowing process had gone far by 1100).[25] In 1990 it might have seemed that 'progressive nuclearisation' was an unchallenged and unchallengeable socio-historical orthodoxy, in Britain and America as much as in France. The only serious

tion of the succession of the lordship of Le Pallet depends entirely on the theory that restriction of inheritance to one son was practised in Abelard's family lordship (despite Abelard himself telling us that his younger brother was married with children, a fact which hardly fits that model).

22 R. Fossier, *La terre et les hommes en Picardie jusqu'à la fin du xiii*[e] *siècle* (2 vols., Paris, 1968) i, 266–7.

23 R. Fossier, 'The Feudal Era (Eleventh-Thirteenth Century)', in, *A History of the Family*, trans. S.H. Tenison and others (2 vols., Cambridge, 1996), 407, originally published as, *Histoire de la famille*, ed. A. Burguière and others (Paris, 1986).

24 One may cite here the study by T.N. Bisson, 'Nobility and Family in Medieval France', *French Historical Studies*, 16 (1990), 597–613. Others who have looked at it remain sceptical, note particularly the resumé and critique in, R. Bartlett, *The Making of Europe: Conquest, Colonization and Cultural Change, 950–1350* (London, 1994), 43–51.

25 D.R. Bates, *Normandy before 1066* (London, 1982), 34–5, 111–16, 134–5; E. Searle, *Predatory Kinship and the Creation of Norman Power, 840–1066* (Berkeley, 1988), esp. chs. 14, 22. Searle provides in ch. 14 a valuable, nuanced and subtle contextualisation of the understanding of kinship in various northern European societies, including England. Bates' work emphasises the Frankish influence on Norman family structures, Searle prefers to look to northern Celtic-Scandinavian influences.

difference would seem then to have been whether, like Bloch and the later Duby, you saw the crisis as a step in an evolutionary development of family, or whether, like most of the rest of his contemporaries, you saw it as part of a broad socio-economic transformation, a mutation, in medieval society.

The idea of the evolution of family structures inevitably got tied into other social evolutions. French ideas of social history were particularly vulnerable to evolutionism. Underlying the whole narrative of French history was the idea that it had been transformed from one state into another by feudalism. The idea of a social 'mutation' which supposedly happened in medieval French society is an ancient one. It is tied up with eighteenth-century ideas of 'feudal society', and we will be looking at it in Chapter 7 in greater detail. Nineteenth and early twentieth-century writers on feudalism treat it as an unusual form of government, a transitional one, a sort of social chrysalis. Western society had slid into feudalism while still recognisably Roman, unified and imperial; it emerged from feudalism as a complex of national monarchies. In between there had been a crisis. The 'law of progressive nuclearisation' of families matched the crisis theory of a feudal mutation beautifully. No wonder Marc Bloch made so much of families, and that later writers worked family change into their own favoured feudal theories. Not everybody dealt with it in the same way. For Bloch there was an abrupt and single crisis that hit France in the tenth century. To other writers in the later twentieth century, there was a rolling crisis that affected different levels of the aristocracy at progressively later times, and affected different regions at different times. But it nevertheless remained a crisis which channelled family into lineage and carved off social casualties.[26]

In the 1980s the idea of family change and the rise of lineage was still one of the great pillars of the idea of a feudal mutation. Those writers who strayed from the evolutionist view of family, on empirical grounds, were not in the mainstream of historical thinking on family. Not everybody had ever been convinced by it. Long ago, Sir Henry Maine's early version of social evolution had been comprehensively refuted by no less an historian than Frederic William Maitland. But his ironic tone and the greater authority of the likes of Herbert Spencer defeated him. His attempt to criticise

[26] Aurell, 'La parenté en l'an mil', 128–39, gives a wide-ranging, comprehensive and orthodox mutationist overview of the subject of kinship and lineage, published in the autumn of 2000, orthodox especially in his irrepressibly Annales-like wish to see mutationism integrated into a world view on family development (p. 142).

the theory by empirical reasoning was long forgotten.[27] Yet within a decade this all-powerful model of 'family mutation' has dissipated. It is no longer a core concept in medieval French historiography, and indeed it had begun to erode in the late 1980s.

The Age of Lévi-Strauss: Unstructuring Families

The collapse of the old idea of lineage formation as founded by Bloch and elaborated by Georges Duby was a major historiographical shift in the 1990s. As we have seen, the French school of regional medieval history, dominant in France from the 1950s to the 1980s, had taken lineage to be a key component of its ideas of social transformation. The regionalist school depended on a view of medieval social history as undergoing – at some point – a major crisis, and the principal aspect of this great crisis was the notion that family changed and narrowed. It was a major part of the 'mutation' or 'transformation' which was at the core of what made society feudal for Bloch and Duby. Duby's modification of the crisis-theory was related to the Carolingians and their problems. In the power vacuum of the struggle between the last Carolingians and the first Capetians, he saw lesser men, princes and magnates, seizing power and assuming a quasi-regal authority over the regions where they were powerful. In the course of this, these families reinvented themselves along the lines of a royal dynasty. This is where change in family structure comes in. To continue their local dominance, these new princely families limited inheritance to only a few heirs, or even one heir.[28] So the line, the lineage, would perpetuate its wealth and influence vertically through time. This crisis was placed by Duby – based on his study of the Mâconnais – in the early eleventh century. Then from Duby's idea stems the master-theory adopted and elaborated by many other French historians, the idea of a social or feudal '*mutation*' ('transformation') around the magical year, 1000.[29] The idea of

[27] S.D. White, 'Maitland on Family and Kinship', *Proceedings of the British Academy*, 89 (1996), 91–113, looking at the way Maitland particularly responded to the evolutionary model of Sir Henry Maine. Maitland's laudable independence of mind was noted earlier, in Murray, 'Theories of Germanic Kinship Structure', 27–8.

[28] See the summary of this development in, D.R. Bates, 'West Francia: the Northern Principalities', in, *The New Cambridge Medieval History* iii, c.*900*–c.*1024*, ed. T. Reuter (Cambridge, 1999), 398–419, esp. p. 414.

[29] Duby referred to a wide-ranging eleventh-century social '*mutation*' or '*bouleversement*' as far back as 1966 in his three classic essays on medieval art and society republished as, *Le temps des cathédrales: l'art et la société, 980–1420* (Paris, 1976), see esp. p. 45. Duby's name is usually associated with that of Pierre Bonnassie in the

the feudal mutation is a broad one, and the appearance of lineage is only one part of it, although an important part. Mutation affected many areas of society, but the strand that concerns us here is its alleged effect on family (*la mutation familiale*). The other major component of the theory – the 'descent of the ban' – is dealt with in Chapter 7.

But, as we have seen, the 'mutation familiale' was based on the antiquated sociology of the nineteenth century. None of the Annales historians who used it seem to have thought to check whether sociologists were still sure about it. As it happened, they had moved on. Yet only a few amongst the historical community had noticed that the sociological ground has been cut from under the basic assumption that family structure evolved.[30] In fact, as early as 1923, the American sociologist William Fielding Ogburn was attacking the application of Darwin's biological model of natural selection to disciplines that dealt with human cultures. He argued that social change did not happen in response to environmental changes.[31] Not only that, but any ideas of progressive structural change in families over time were being rejected even as Duby concluded his doctoral studies. It was in 1949 that Claude Lévi-Strauss published his sophisticated reassessment of the sociology of marriage and kinship, *Les structures élémentaires de la parenté,* translated as *The Elementary Structures of Kinship*. He dedicated it, without irony, to the memory of Lewis Henry Morgan. In it, he urged that families can only be understood from within, not by the models and presuppositions of outside categorisers. Evolutionary thinking on social structures is significantly absent from his work: he was a structuralist. It is from Lévi-Strauss, not from the nineteenth-century thinkers who inspired Durkheim, that modern sociology draws its intellectual inspiration. Yet historians – still working on the questions Durkheim threw out – unconsciously remained till the 1990s trapped with the Marxists in the head of Lewis Henry Morgan.

Over the decades since Ogburn wrote, it has been established by social anthropologists that the nuclear (or conjugal) family can be found in all

framing through regional studies of the period of mutation between 980 and 1030, *La Catalogne du milieu du xe à la fin du xie siècle* (2 vols., Toulouse, 1975-6). A convenient summation of the whole mutationist thesis can be found in, J-P. Poly and E. Bournazel, *La mutation féodale, x^e^-xiie siècles* (Paris, 1980), esp. ch. 4; revised by the authors in 1991 and translated by C. Higgitt as, *The Feudal Transformation, 900–1200* (London, 1991).

30 One of the first mainstream notices of this was by David Herlihy, *The History of Feudalism* (London, 1971), 67–8.

31 W.F. Ogburn, *Social Change with respect to Culture and Original Nature* (London, 1923), 56–7.

contemporary human cultures, even in the remote and undeveloped ones which were once assumed to resemble earlier forms of western society. There is every reason to believe that family typology within any culture is much more complex than the interpreters of Le Play had assumed. Different types of family occur within the same cultures, and it is no longer believed, as Engels, Weber and Durkheim believed – and the underlying philosophy of historical materialism dictated – that changes in family structure played a part in the creation of the modern industrial West. So, in sociological thought, changes in family structure have been uncoupled from association with broad social change; something approaching a cataclysmic change for social history.[32] Where then does this leave the concept of the evolution of medieval lineage? The answer is that it doesn't affect the idea of lineage at all, but what it does affect is the general theory that lineages evolved out of the narrowing of earlier patriarchal family structures, and the particular idea that agnatic (that is, male-dominated) lineage was the characteristic perception of family by the twelfth century.

The Duby-Schmid thesis has been found by historians to perform badly under testing in northern Europe. Some of the main critics came from the Anglophone world, which is not surprising considering that criticism of a dominant historical school within the French historical establishment cannot be easy. There is also the point that British and many American historical schools remain tied to the limiting but discriminating empirical method, which tests comprehensive schemes of history against observed facts. Criticism of mutationism – or, to be more specific to the material of this chapter, 'family mutation' (*la mutation familiale*) – has been widespread but uncoordinated. One of Schmid's principal contentions was that the leading members of his perceived lineages took the name of their principal castle or estate as a surname. They thus identified their family's line with the source of their power – their land and dominion. John Freed's 1984 case study of the German counts of Falkenstein noted major inconsistencies in the identification of castle, surname and lineage in the Rhineland heartland of Schmid's thesis.[33] Stephen

[32] For a summary, see T.K. Hareven, 'The History of the Family and the Complexity of Social Change', *American Historical Review*, 96 (1991), 95–124, repr. and revised as 'Recent Research on the History of Family', in, *Time, Family and Community: Perspectives on Family and Community History*, ed. M. Drake (Oxford, 1994), 13–43.

[33] J.B. Freed, *The Counts of Falkenstein: Noble Self-Consciousness in Twelfth-Century Germany* (Transactions of the American Philosophical Society, 74, pt 6, 1984), 52–7. The earliest criticism on the same point seems to have been, K. Leyser, 'The German Aristocracy from the Ninth to the Early Twelfth Century: A Historical and Cultural Sketch', *Past and Present*, no. 41 (1968), 32–4.

D. White's careful studies of of family relationships as they appear in the charters and diplomas of western France between 1050 and 1150 have been particularly revealing. In a study informed by current sociological thinking, and without claiming too much for the evidence, he has nonetheless been able to conclude that ideas of family over that time and in that place were complex, and give no real support for the line of development as Duby and Schmid predicted. The idea of family *where it related to property* (note the emphasis) was generally limited, and rarely extended to first cousins. It might occasionally include maternal connections throughout the period under examination. The one developmental model that White could detect was a generational one. The legal family was broader at the beginning of a marriage, but narrowed as soon as children were born to a couple. But this was a cyclical change within the lifetime of a particular generation, not a long-term change within society. The birth of children caused their parents to modify and narrow their own view of what their family was. White was reluctant to reflect on the wider implications of his evidence, but was willing enough to conclude that ideas of family and kin in his chosen period of study were complex and clearly changed according to need.[34]

The main Anglophone critic of the lineage aspect of the mutationist thesis has so far been Constance Brittain Bouchard. This American scholar was presenting a view of family radically different to that of the mutationists as early as 1981, well before any criticism was to be heard in France or Germany. She constructed two powerful empirical contradictions to the mutationist view of family. The first concerned names. Mutationists thought that when lineages formed they liked to identify themselves by taking the name of the castle which they had adopted as their base. Bouchard demonstrated that the appearance of the toponym in France had less to do with the appearance of lineages than the fact that the stock of Christian names was dwindling in the eleventh century. Too many people were sharing the same name, so some other form of supplementary identification became necessary. Also on the subject of naming patterns, she has pointed out forcibly the methodological void at the heart of Schmid's belief that lineages can be reconstructed from the recurrence of Christian names in the generations of powerful men in a particular locality. The second contradiction lies in her unanswerable argument that patrilineal sensibilities can be found in Carolingian society long before the supposed mutation in family structures around

[34] S.D. White, *Custom, Kinship and Gifts to Saints: the* Laudatio Parentum *in Western France, 1050–1150* (Chapel Hill, 1988), ch. 4.

1000.[35] In her most recent work, Bouchard has undertaken a pragmatic reevaluation of the French evidence on which so much of mutationist scholarship depends, and interpreted it very differently. In her opinion, there is not much difference between the ninth and the eleventh centuries in family structures. The eleventh century was simply more peaceful and is better documented than the two previous centuries, so it might give the impression of the appearance of regular successions occurring and new lineages being founded, but if so, that is but an impression.[36] In this she agrees with the anti-mutationist French scholar, Dominique Barthélemy, who talks of the 'realignment' of society in the year 1000, and of a 'documentary mutation' as lying at the root of all the changes previous historians have imagined.[37]

A further critic of the 'mutation familiale' (or 'mutation lignagère' as Barthélemy calls it) also comes from outside France. The British scholar Pauline Stafford has offered a critical study from the perspective of the history of women.[38] Self-evidently, considering that its roots are in nineteenth-century anthropology the mutationist view of lineage presumes a deteriorating social position for women. The argument goes that when inheritance began to focus on a single male heir around 1000, sisters, as much as younger brothers, were squeezed. The mutationist argument found apparent confirmation of this in a unique run of documents dealing

[35] C.B. Bouchard, 'Family Structure and Family Consciousness among the Aristocracy in the Ninth to Eleventh Centuries', *Francia*, 14 (1986), 639–58. Her doubts about the origins of the new lineages were earlier aired in, eadem, 'The Origins of the French Nobility: A Reassessment', *American Historical Review*, 86 (1981), 501–32, esp. 527–8. From this it seems that while she accepts that perceptions of families were complex, she subscribes still to a limited evolutionary theory of family, in the sense that she is willing to see the eleventh century giving rise to customs of unigeniture amongst the French aristocracy: a narrowing of the those qualified to inherit (p. 69). Her earlier attacks were based on her analysis of family structure in the ninth-century pious work by the princess Dhuoda, *Liber manualis*, ed. and trans. M. Thiebaux (Cambridge, 1998).

[36] Bouchard gives a characteristically lucid summary of her thinking in, *Strong of Body, Brave and Noble: Chivalry and Society in Medieval France* (Ithaca NY, 1998), ch. 3., but has since published a major study on patrilinearity, *Those of My Blood: Constructing noble families in Medieval Francia* (Philadelphia, 2001), which expands on her already stated views.

[37] *La mutation de l'an mil a-t-elle eu lieu? Servage et chevalerie dans la France des xe et xie siècles* (Paris, 1997), 13–27.

[38] P. Stafford, 'La Mutation Familiale: A Suitable Case for Caution', in, *The Community, the Family and the Saint: Patterns of Power in Early Medieval Europe*, ed. J. Hill and M. Swan (Turnhout, 1998), 103–25.

with grants from dower lands found in the archives of the abbey of Cluny. They seemed at first sight to show that women had free use of the lands granted them on marriage in the tenth century. But in the next century they held their land on less generous terms. The land might only come from the marginal interests of the family. Also women apparently had limited rights over the dower, which were compromised by the husband's ultimate control over his wife. So alienation from the dower by the woman was made more difficult.[39] Along the lines of Barthélemy's documentary mutation, Stafford's point is that this apparent change in inheritance customs may be no more than the growing tendency of the monks of Cluny to try to head off challenges to their acquisitions by seeking written consent for potential rivals to the land in an increasingly competitive environment.[40] She also points to the evidence, not of evolution in the landholding position of women, but of a simultaneous variety of different possibilities in landholding, none being dominant at any particular time.

It is because of this, and other challenges to the Duby-Schmid theory, that the current generation of post-Annales French scholars has developed a moderately revisionist version of it. 'Progressive nuclearisation' is still accepted as having happened (although it is now called by some *l'essor de topolignages*, 'the rise of dominant local lineages') and younger children are still supposed to have been excluded from succession as the allocation of property within a family narrowed. To fit the evidence empiricists continually throw up, the new version teaches that nuclearisation happened earlier, a century earlier than Duby suggested. It sees the cognatic kindred as a power base for the master lineage, rather than as something it cannibalised, and as such the kin-group, by this interpretation, remained a powerful fact into the eleventh century, when 'secondary lineages' breaking off the master lineage became a threat to its integrity, and so in

[39] For a summary of the mutationist view, see G. Duby, *Le Chevalier, la Femme et le Prêtre* (Paris, 1981), published in English as, *The Knight, the Lady and the Priest: the Making of Modern Marriage in Medieval France*, trans. B. Bray (London, 1983), 95–104. This evolutionism is just as evident in more recent work on marriage, female inheritance and power in Catalonia, the best-documented area of early medieval Europe: see the comprehensive study by M. Aurell, *Les noces du comte: mariage et pouvoir en Catalogne (785–1213)* (Paris, 1994), 137–8. Incidences of female free will over property that Aurell finds in the eleventh century are ascribed not to individual variations but to the persistence of the forms (if not the spirit) of Roman law in the south, ibid., p. 140.

[40] The influence here is the *mutation documentaire* of Dominique Barthélemy, first tentatively proposed (on the basis of Duby's own cautious qualifications) in his, *La société dans le comté de Vendôme de l'an mil au xive siècle* (Paris, 1993), esp. p. 514.

the end the revisionist interpretation reunites itself with the Duby-Schmid scheme.[41] Very recently indeed, this tinkering with mutationism has not seemed enough to some French historians, and a major defector has emerged in the thoroughly revisionist work of Dominique Barthélemy (for which see Chapter 7). As other major components of mutationist theory have been rejected, the French 'mutation familiale' would seem at last to be destined for the same treatment.

Noble Primogeniture and Lineage in England

This brings us at last to England and its place in the debate. Studies of lineage and kinship for a comparable period (and to the standard of) those studies we have already looked at for France and the Empire barely exist in Britain.[42] The reasons are several, but the principal one is the perceived lack of continuity within the English aristocracy as a result of the Norman Conquest of 1066–70. For most of the twentieth century, Franco-German scholarship was proclaiming that Continental family structure was evolving by stages from the ninth through to the thirteenth century. From the continental perspective it would therefore seem that England – which was colonised abruptly by French lineages at the end of the eleventh century – had little independent contribution to make to the debate. Its own indigenous structures would then have been more or less eliminated at a stroke, so there was no English continuity comparable to that of the Continental kingdoms and regions. In any case the sort of evidence used so profitably by German and French historians to reconstruct family structure barely exists for pre-1066 England, where private charters and diplomas are rarities.

The rights and wrongs of this particular argument need not concern us here, although it should be said that, even at the very least, English social history should be useful for comparative purposes. This is certainly true in one particular area: the growth of the agnatic or patrilineal family. A rejection of progressive nuclearisation should be difficult to go along with for

41 This is the scheme to be found in, R. Le Jan, *Famille et pouvoir dans le monde franc (viie-xe siècle): Essai d'anthropologie sociale* (Paris, 1995), 414–27. For an English summary, eadem, 'Continuity and Change in the Tenth-Century Nobility', trans. J. Nelson, in, *Nobles and Nobility in Medieval Europe: Concepts, Origins, Transformations*, ed. A.J. Duggan (Woodbridge, 2000), 58–61.

42 The survey 'Kinship, marriage and family', by J.A. Green, *The Aristocracy of Norman England* (Cambridge, 1997), ch. 10, is exceptional here in the degree to which it synthesises Continental scholarship and offers comparative observations.

anyone brought up on medieval English history. Le Play looked to England to find his stem-family, and the way that the Common Law of inheritance developed in these islands meant that he had no difficulty finding it. The Common Law – from the writer known as 'Glanvill' (active in the 1180s) onwards – preached primogeniture in strong terms, as if it were the desirable norm in the later twelfth century that younger sons of knights be disinherited so as to favour the eldest.[43] England should be the very heart and centre of lineage formation, by that belief. Although, as we have seen, Maitland did not subscribe in his day to any theory of agnatic lineage formation, primogeniture in medieval England was for him nonetheless an empirical reality. Although he did not find primogeniture in eleventh-century England or Normandy, he had to account for its appearance a century later. His suggestion was that it was a natural consequence of hereditary knights' fees. Lords preferred to deal with one heir, not several, and so, Maitland suggested, a principle of primogeniture was set up against the natural tendency of fathers to share their possessions between all their children. He did not, however, explain how precisely this might have been accomplished. Maitland had to assume that Henry II simply made it clear to one and all that primogeniture was what a strong realm required, and that was Glanvill's ultimate authority for his statement.[44]

We are in as much of a fog as Maitland when it comes to accounting for the decided preference in royal circles for primogeniture in England at the end of Henry II's reign. Since Maitland wrote, we have got no closer to why exclusive inheritance by the eldest son was urged as a desirable norm in England, when (with a few exceptions) it was not in France.[45] What has become clearer in the century since Maitland is that primogeniture was not in fact the norm in England when Glanvill wrote, and did not became the

[43] Glanvill in fact portrays a world where multiple heirs within a generation are not unusual, but stated (on unknown authority) that the *ius regni Anglie* was that his eldest son should succeed a man holding by knight's tenure, *The Treatise on the Law and Customs of the Realm of England commonly called Glanvill*, ed. G.D.G. Hall (London, 1965), 75. The *Leges Henrici*, a work of the first half of the reign of Henry I, preach a form of priority for the eldest son in any division, see Green, *Aristocracy of Norman England*, 337. However, if Glanvill is not quoting this work, he may simply be citing a common viewpoint on succession to military tenures amongst royal justices which goes back at least to Henry I's reign.

[44] F. Pollock and F.W. Maitland, *The History of English Law* (2 vols, 2nd edn, Cambridge, 1898) ii, 262–78. It might be noted that since Glanvill urged primogeniture in the inheritance of knights' fees and not in other holdings, Maitland's deduction as to the process by which it happened was perfectly reasonable.

[45] Green, *Aristocracy of Norman England*, 339, simply repeats Maitland's reasoning.

norm until after he (whoever he was) died. The most important contribution after Maitland's was the study on Anglo-Norman aristocratic inheritance practices published by Sir James Holt in 1972. Professor Holt's reconstruction and analysis of actual, rather than rhetorical, successions in England and Normandy in the eleventh and twelfth centuries uncovered a world where partition of the family lands in each generation might very well happen. True, inheritance of land was restricted, but it was not restricted to one son. When there was a multiplicity of sons, an Anglo-Norman landholder might try to accommodate several with lands.[46] The eldest two were generally always favoured, but there are instances of a share-out between three, four or even five sons. The eldest would usually, but not invariably, get the most, and where there was a title to be inherited, he got it. Holt did not consider that multiple divisions of discrete feudal baronies were common after the Conquest (indeed he thought them 'unusual') and they were certainly moderated sometimes by reservation of the patrimony to the eldest child and acquisitions to the younger.[47] But subsequent studies have tended to find that substantial provision in land for younger children from patrimony was by no means uncommon or unusual in the twelfth century. More and more such divisions are being reconstructed for the eleventh and twelfth centuries, and not just at the highest level of the barony, but even at the level of the county knight.[48]

It may be that English and northern French society was moving towards a stricter primogeniture, but it had not reached it by Glanvill's time.[49] Glanvill and his legal circle certainly had an influence. In 1206 two agnatic cousins of English descent were arguing in the royal court over the right of one of them to a large estate near Ilford which had been parti-

[46] J.C. Holt, 'Politics and Property in Early Medieval England', *Past and Present*, no. 57 (1972) 3–52.

[47] Ibid., 10–15, a point supported for baronies-in-chief by Green, *Aristocracy of Norman England*, 338. Holt's careful position is over-asserted in, J. Hudson, *Land, Law and Lordship in Anglo-Norman England* (Oxford, 1994), 109–10, who seems to imply that all divisions of patrimonial inheritance were therefore rare.

[48] For some late-eleventh- and twelfth-century Anglo-Norman non-baronial examples, D. Crouch, *The Beaumont Twins: the Roots and Branches of Power in the Twelfth Century* (Cambridge, 1986), 120–27 (Harcourt), 127–29 (Burdet), 117–18 (Tourville). For an example of the reign of Henry I at a knightly level (the Gay family), idem, 'Robert, earl of Gloucester's mother and sexual politics in Norman Oxfordshire', *Historical Research*, lxxii (1999), 323–33.

[49] J. Goody, *The Development of the Family and Marriage in Europe* (Cambridge, 1983), 118–23, considers that moves to unigeniture to be a general twelfth-century European characteristic, although his work relies ultimately on that of Schmid.

tioned before 1100. The cousin who was seeking to acquire the estate attempted to appeal to the justices by claiming that he and his cousin 'were of one lineage, but that he was descended from the eldest brother', and so the land should be his. Perhaps significantly, the jurors summoned to elucidate this gave him short shrift, saying that they knew nothing of the family descent.[50] The succession in 1219 to William Marshal, earl of Pembroke, three decades after Glanvill was written, is good evidence that primogeniture was still not a priority in families in the early thirteenth century. We know this succession was arranged by William himself, for the discussion of it by his council around his deathbed and its commitment to writing in a sealed testament is attested by his biography. His eldest son and namesake got the earldom and the small patrimony, but mostly he inherited his mother's lands in Wales and Ireland. A second son, Richard, obtained the Norman lands, but also lands in England, all by right of his mother. The third son, Walter, was given a sizeable inheritance from amongst his father's acquisitions. A fourth son was a clerk, and a fifth gained a large annual rent from his brothers' lands. Since the old Marshal's daughters had all benefited in marriage portions, all but his clerical child gained some share of their father's wealth, and the three elder boys each did very well for themselves in land.[51] The Marshal succession was not exceptional: the two sons of Earl Saher de Quincy, Roger and Robert, also partitioned their lands in 1217, although the longevity of their mother meant that the partition did not come into effect, as she kept her inheritance in her own hand. In the very heartland of theoretical Common Law primogeniture, what we actually see is many families planning to distribute their landed endowment amongst their offspring – male and female – well into the thirteenth century.

That this had changed by 1300 has also long been obvious. Maitland knew that primogeniture had established itself as the norm by the end of Edward I's reign. That it was being argued to be the norm with increasing insistence is clear from the following example. In 1263 Thomas, Simon

[50] *Curia Regis Rolls* iv, 301.

[51] D. Crouch, *William Marshal: Knighthood, War and Chivalry, 1147–1219* (2nd edn, London, 2002), 139–40. Similar deathbed debates can be found in literary sources: around 1170 Wace describes Richard II of Normandy and his council discussing the post mortem disposition of his estates between his sons, *Le Roman de Rou*, ed. A.J. Holden (3 vols., Société des anciens textes français, 1970–3) i, pt 3, ll. 2221–31. Another from around 1240 can be found in Philip de Remy, *Jehan et Blonde*, ed. S. Lécuyer (Classiques français du moyen âge, 1984), ll. 2087–9, where Jehan urges the interest of his younger brothers while his father makes his testament.

and William, the three younger sons of Andrew of Braunston, Rutland, went to law against their eldest brother, Gilbert. They each sought three-quarters virgate as their reasonable right of inheritance from their father against their brother:

Gilbert came and said that Thomas and the others could not claim any part of the inheritance, for he says that all his predecessors from the time of the Conquest and time beyond memory held the land without it ever being partitioned.[52]

The appeal to a non-existent past of primogeniture and lineage to be found in this passage is revealing. Clearly the men of law had got through to the English landowner by then. But nevertheless, the younger Braunston brothers were still willing to argue otherwise, and indeed divided successions between sons can still be found in the later thirteenth century, even if they are cloaked as paternal grants before death, or enfeoffments by elder brothers. By then also the lawyers were finding ways to circumvent the norm of primogeniture that their predecessors had worked so hard to establish. The last testament of a landlord was increasingly used to make post mortem gifts and entail away estates on to a younger son and his descendants, so much so as to make the practice a matter of concern to Edward I's council by 1285.[53] By the mid-fourteenth century in England, divisions of estates between multiple sons were again the norm, but now they were executed by probate, and not by custom.

It should follow from the legal theory of primogeniture that the idea of noble lineage ought to be particularly prominent in England. But in the next chapter we will find no observable difference between attitudes in France and England as to the meaning and importance of lineage. Both countries had the same contrasting horizontal and vertical views of family, and lineage 'markers' like heraldry and surnames developed and progressed in much the same way in both. This unity could have had much to do with the long-standing family and social links between the English and French aristocracies, which continued into the thirteenth century. For instance, as late as the reign of Edward I (1272–1307) scores of English bannerets (or magnate-knights) and knights were still regularly making tours of the great tournament grounds of northern France, as they had

[52] National Archives (formerly, PRO), JUST1/721, m 5d.

[53] S.L. Waugh, *The Lordship of England: Royal Wardships and Marriages in English Society and Politics* (Princeton, 1988), 15–16; K.B. McFarlane, *The Nobility of Later Medieval England* (Oxford, 1973), 61–3.

been doing since the reign of Henry I (1100–1135).[54] This social mixing reinforced the linguistic unity of both aristocracies. French remained self-consciously the language of the aristocrat in England well into the fourteenth century.[55] In the end, the English divergence from the French in the matter of primogeniture may simply reflect the different ambitions and capacities of the English and French monarchies to control the societies dependent on them in the twelfth century. Indeed, to take a reductionist view, Common Law primogeniture could be described as no more than a variation amongst the diverse customary laws of the Francophone lands of north-west Europe, although that would be to ignore the implications of the fact that England was an ancient nation in European terms.

New Models of Noble Lineage

Despite the bold heading, it has to be said that there is a distinct lack of any new model of noble lineage being proposed by the historical community at this time. We have seen from the recent work of Stephen D. White and Pauline Stafford that, among Anglophone historians, the present stress is on family as being a complex and shifting concept within each generation in the middle ages. As soon as there were children of a marriage, families tended naturally to be understood as the unit represented by parents and children, the nuclear family. As the parents aged and the children matured, that basic unit would fragment and reform. The belief has grown that the affective family was never large in the middle ages. Wider inclusion of cousins, agnatic and cognate, as of any affective importance was rare. The central importance of 'kin groups' in historical understanding of noble lineage has declined. Its real importance, as we will see in the next chapter, may be more to do with individual opportunity and honour. Kin might be inclined for reasons of blood to offer employment and assistance to a

[54] On the English contingent at Philip III's great tournament at Compiègne in May 1279, A. de Behault de Dornon, 'La noblesse hennuyère au tournoi de Compiègne de 1238', *Annales du cercle archéologique de Mons*, xxii (1890), 87–8 (comprising two earls and ten English bannerets with their households). For Osbert of Arden's tourneying tours in France in the 1120s or 1130s, J.R.V. Barker, *The Tournament in England, 1100-1400* (Woodbridge, 1986), 7.

[55] On the aristocratic use of French in England, M.T. Clanchy, *From Memory to Written Record* (2nd edn., Oxford, 1993), 198–200; R. Bartlett, *England under the Norman and Angevin Kings, 1075–1225* (Oxford, 2000), 486–90. It might be noted that young male au pairs crossing the Channel to teach French to English noble households are mentioned in the 1170s and 1230s, as in ibid., p. 490; Philip de Remy, *Jehan et Blonde*, ll. 127–395.

relative and to have rich and noble cousins gave a man a degree of honour, especially if they acknowledged him. But kin did not have any active role in transmitting and disposing of property amongst its group.

French and British historians agree on some things. As far as inheritance within families was concerned, the steady impulse throughout the middle ages was for fathers to divide their inheritance amongst their several children (male and female) if they had a multiplicity of heirs. There is a growing understanding that in England as well as France the natural tendency was for family estates slowly to fragment if each generation produced several sons and daughters. This has consequences for our view of the mobility of medieval noble society. As we will see in Chapter 7 there are indications that twelfth-century urban elites were closely interlinked with the landed aristocracy. This may have been not so much because landless and impoverished younger sons were forced to find livings in towns by the demands of harsh primogeniture. It may be that younger sons used their share of the family lands to capitalise their mercantile projects. Another impulse towards social mobility, especially in the thirteenth century, may have been the existence of cadet lines of noble houses whose small inheritances might be acquired by rising men through marriage and through purchase as the building blocks of new magnate estates. Since thirteenth-century English noble society is accepted to have been a mobile one – with slowly rising and slowly declining families – the prevalence of fragmentation of inheritance rather than concentration by primogeniture is more convincing as a model of family and property. Fragmentation of an estate between sons, marriage portions of daughters and alienation of property in one family allowed growth in others.[56]

The place of women in family structures is also being reassessed in the current historiography of medieval families. The patrilineal emphasis of the Duby-Schmid model of family change necessarily suggested that women became less and less important after the year 1000. As we have seen, Pauline Stafford and Constance Bouchard have argued in their different ways that things were more complicated than such a simple model implies. Women were not often dominant within medieval families, but the blood, honour and connections that they brought with their marriage were highly prized. Twelfth- and thirteenth-century men were not at all reluc-

[56] See particularly the summation of his thinking on the economic standing of thirteenth-century knightly families by Peter Coss, *The Origins of the English Gentry* (Cambridge, 2003), 69–108. The degree to which divisions of estates between sons influenced the fortunes of knightly families of the thirteenth century has yet to gain much academic attention, although the evidence certainly exists.

tant to claim lineage through their mothers, and they rejoiced in the family connections of their wives. Honour and not gender was their overmastering concern so far as lineage was concerned. Their hopes for the future were centred on their sons, as Bouchard says, but their present status was as often as not drawn from women.

There is no new model of changing family structures emerging in present scholarship, and that may well be because historians are reverting to the alternative, seeing continuity instead of change. The future view may well be that there was a plurality of structures in medieval families within every generation. Therefore, the generation of the early eleventh century resembled in its structures the generation of the early thirteenth century. As we will see in the next chapter, resorting to a model of continuity may yet mislead us. The perceptions of lineage, at least, were different in the thirteenth century from what they had been two centuries earlier. The change in levels of literacy and symbolism meant that the noble man and noble woman of 1300 were much more self-conscious in their search for individual distinction; the means to express their aspirations were more diverse; their understanding of their place within their class was much more acute; and the means they had to draw connections of parage and lineage were considerably more sophisticated than they had been in 1000. The idea and consciousness of being a member of a noble house was asserted at a lower social level in 1300 than it had been in 1000. Moreover, the apparent solidity and permanence of a noble house was more firmly set in memory. In the fourteenth century, quarterings on arms advertised that every strand in the weave of lineage was being closely woven into the assertion of an individual's nobility. A family may have been defunct, but its heraldry continued to feature in the arms of later generations who had inherited its time-hallowed blood.

CHAPTER 5

The Power of Lineage

The historical study of families has recently lost the Victorian master-thesis that stood once at its heart. Although this is hardly before time, it has left historians of family and lineage without a point of focus at the moment. They are now emphasising the complexity and shifting nature of families in the middle ages and have stopped looking for single characteristic medieval family structures. This is good, and an improvement on the former state of affairs. However, if the study of family structure has not been all that helpful to historians so far, it is worth asking if there are not other ways to understand medieval families. Perhaps the importance of family in history is a question that should have been posed another way. This chapter looks at a different range of evidence: not so much as at how medieval people understood families, but how they used them. This is to go with the evidence. Medieval writers do not speculate much, if at all, on the nature of family other than the duties of one family member to another. They talk a great deal, however, about the use that can be made of the family and kinship, and the honour that can be drawn from it. Sometimes they approve of it, and sometimes they don't. But if the weight of evidence is any indication, it is here that medieval concerns about family rested.

Lineage and the Search for Distinction

The key word for us continues to be lineage, as it has always been in the study of medieval families. In the past, lineage has been used in a structural way by historians. Its 'appearance' has been said to reveal deep changes in medieval society. But it never in fact 'appeared', as we have seen. It is a constant in most societies, Biblical, Classical, Anglo-Saxon, Frankish and Celtic, literate and non-literate. Lineage is simply the way that families develop an image of their generations being on a track through time. It is a simple idea, whatever complex theories have been built upon it. Some of those theories have suggested that lineage was an idea newly conceived in Franco-German society in the early eleventh century as a symptom of sweeping changes in contemporary noble family structure. In the last chapter I gave my reasons for disagreeing with such theories, but that does not deny the fact that lineage was an important concept in the eleventh-century view of nobility. It is a measure of its importance for medieval people that vernacular works make so much of 'lineage': *lignage* and *ligniee*. When contemporaries used these words, they meant them to be understood in the way we use lineage now, as the vertical dimension of family.[1]

Writers in the middle of the twelfth century used the word frequently and unequivocally to refer to people vertically linked by common ancestry. One of the best instances of this is when Wace portrays Julius Caesar at Boulogne, surveying the distant cliffs of Britain and learning that its people were descended from Brutus, exclaiming, 'Indeed I know of this Brutus! He and we Romans are of one ancestry (*fumes d'un lignage*), the common source (*chiés*) of our relationship began in the city of Troy'.[2] In that respect the word 'lignage' can approximate to the word *parents*, or *parenz* (meaning 'kinsfolk' or 'relations'), in that what defines kinsfolk is some sort of common descent.[3] The concept is universal in medieval literature.

[1] Philip de Beaumanoir, in his treatise on the customs of the Beauvaisis in the 1270s, defined *lignage* vertically as either ascending back to one's forbears or descending to one's issue, *Coutumes de Beauvaisis*, ed. A. Salmon (3 vols, Paris, 1970–4) i, 298, c. 604. Dominique Barthélemy has attempted to make a distinction between *lignage* and *ligniee*, suggesting that *ligniee* signifies what we call lineage nowadays, and *lignage* means simply 'family', D. Barthélemy, 'Kinship', in, *A History of Private Life* ii, *Revelations of the Medieval World*, ed. P. Ariès and G. Duby and trans. A. Goldhammer (London, 1988), 90.

[2] Wace, *Le Roman de Brut*, ed. I. Arnold (2 vols, Société des anciens textes français, 1938–40) i, ll. 3870–73.

[3] See Geoffrey Gaimar, *L'Estoire des Engleis*, ed. A. Bell (Anglo-Norman Text Society, 1960), ll. 2693–4, where the Northumbrian nobleman Buern Buccecarl takes counsel with his *lignage*, who in the same passage are also called as a synonym, his *parenz*. Dominique Barthélemy on similar grounds chooses to translate the medieval term *lignage* as 'parenté cognatique', that is, in the widest possible sense of 'kin', see, *La société dans le comté de Vendôme de l'an mil au xive siècle* (Paris, 1993), 517–18. This may reasonably reflect some medieval usage, but I have noted an instance in a late twelfth-century romance where *lignage* and the term *germains cosins* (that is the sons of the uncles of a person) are used as synonymous, see *Garin le Loherenc*, ed. A. Iker-Gittelman (3 vols, Classiques français du moyen âge, 1996–97) i, l. 570. I stay with the lineage concept here, both for this reason and because of the historiography of the term.

The word 'lineage' is to be found in French literature's earliest surviving work, the *Life of St Alexis* (*c*.1070 × 90) and in every work of importance afterwards. By the time the French vernacular matured as a literary medium in the romances of Chrétien de Troyes (*c*.1170–80) we find a strong consciousness of the *lign*, *lin*, or *franc lin*, as the family descent which distinguishes a man or woman.

The search for distinction – that all-purpose medieval word 'honour' – was one source of motivation for people to seek out and make the most of their lineage. There was little to be gained in recalling ancestors who were undistinguished, although the point has been made that a certain amount of medieval 'reverse snobbery' could be drawn from an ancestor who had made it big from nothing. But more to be desired were acknowledged links of descent to the great departed. Mid-twelfth-century literary flatterers like Geoffrey of Monmouth and Guy de Bazoches alluded to descent from the Emperor Charlemagne when they wished to secure the good will and patronage of (respectively) Count Waleran II of Meulan and Worcester (died 1166), and Count Henry of Champagne (died 1181). Guy packed as many royal connections into his genealogy of Count Henry as he could, tracing the count's Frankish royal connections as far back as Clovis (taking in the sainted Frankish queens on the way), and he traced the count's English royal connections to Edward the Elder and the Conqueror. But Guy also reminded us that there were moral consequences which followed from the possession of a magnificent lineage. It was not just a matter of antiquity, quantity and sanctity.

Guy de Bazoches, noble but impoverished graduate of the Paris schools and self-made scholar as he was, was conscious of his own very distinguished lineage, which he too traced back to Clovis. He vigorously lectured his nephew on the moral demands required of the shoots from such a seed:

Ponder on what sort of man should you be when you have such great forefathers. What is more befitting to such as you than that, while not ruling nations, you are at least able to govern your own impulses, and while not possessing the great lands they did, you can at least display their virtues?[4]

[4] For Geoffrey and Waleran, D. Crouch, *The Beaumont Twins: the Roots and Branches of Power in the Twelfth Century* (Cambridge, 1986), 11–12.; for Guy de Bazoches and Count Henry, M. Bur, 'L'image de la parenté chez les comtes de Champagne', *Annales*, 38 (1983), 1016–39. For Guy's lineage of Henry of Champagne, *Liber Epistularum Guidonis de Basochis*, ed. H. Adolfsson (Acta Universitatis Stockholmensis, Studia Latina Stockholmensia, 18, 1969), 58–60, for his own lineage, 141–2 (quotation p. 142).

Alas for the demands of blood. Guy's belief was widely shared. His English contemporary, Daniel of Beccles, had similar things to say to the readers of his book on courteous conduct for clerics, the *Urbanus Magnus*.

The idea that a child of corrupt blood could be born to a noble line seems absurd. A noble line brings forth only the best qualities and conducts itself generously. It is the corrupt and idle line that spews out wastrels and deals out bitterness. The finest fruit are produced from the finest tree. Noble heir, if your father is distinguished, wealthy, generous and upstanding, take care not to disgrace his blood! It is a dreadful disgrace to discredit noble birth, because of the distinction which comes with it. It is your prime concern never to fall from the highest standards of behaviour. Never do anything dishonourable. Since you are a nobleman, pursue noble behaviour; haughtiness has no place in courtly conduct.'[5]

The fact that Daniel and others used blood as a physical metaphor for lineage often passes without comment, but the metaphor echoed medieval beliefs about descent. The middle ages called a man's relatives (in Latin) his *consanguinei*, 'the people who share his blood'. Those medieval people who studied the subject knew that the humours carried in the blood were the arbiters of the emotions and spirits of the one through whose veins and arteries it coursed. Medieval scholars acquired the view from Classical medical texts that blood was a vital element in the process of human genesis. The embryo grew out of the commixture of menstrual blood and sperm (the purest distillation of male blood – and the source of the idea of 'blue blood'); the menses provided the matter from which the child grew and the sperm gave it its shape and soul. Since blood was directly associated with the process of reproduction, it carried the dispositions and characteristics of the parent to the child, not least of course, his nobility.[6]

So it was that people expected to see an ancestor's qualities reproduced in his descendants, through the medium of his blood. They expected to see

[5] *Urbanus Magnus Danielis Becclesiensis*, ed. J.G. Smyly (Dublin, 1939), 6–7.

[6] For medieval views on blood and lineage see generally, R. Carron, *Enfant et parenté dans la France médiévale, x^{e}–xiiie siècles* (Geneva, 1989), 21–2, and in more detail, M-C. Pouchelle, 'Le sang et ses pouvoirs en moyen âge', in, *Affaires du sang*, ed. A. Farge (Paris, 1988), 17–41; M. van Proeyen, 'Sang et hérédité: à la croissée des imaginaires médicaux et sociaux', in, *Le sang au moyen âge (Actes du quatrième colloque internationale de Montpellier, Université Paul-Valéry (27–29 novembre 1997)*, ed. M. Faure (Montpellier, 1999), 69–85. I must gratefully acknowledge the assistance here of Professor Nicholas Vincent.

it, but of course an individual's choices might disappoint them and produce something unnatural, an immoral nobleman. Ailred of Rievaulx, a Cistercian ascetic who as a young man had moved in the highest circles, was well aware of the way of the world in the matter of descent. Writing early in 1154, he put the matter of family and privilege delicately, and deployed the gospels as weighty backup.

It is the greatest incentive to acquire superior conduct by keeping in mind that one has noble blood of the highest sort, since it would be an eternal disgrace to a noble spirit to be found unworthy of a glorious ancestry (progenies), *and it is against the nature of things for a good root to produce bad fruit.'*[7]

This particular gospel view (Matt. 7:17 or Luke 7: 44) is also cited as a justification for believing that noble conduct and nobility of soul should be reproduced in every generation of a noble house. The passages are obliquely cited by Daniel of Beccles (see above) and also by the layman who was the biographer of William Marshal. In the 1220s he praised the younger William Marshal for fulfilling the expectations which his father's blood laid on him: '. . . William, renowned for his great deeds, as everyone knows, for good trees bear good fruit'. A contemporary Cistercian abbot, Peter of Celle, cited just the same passages when praising the continuing distinction of the lineage of the counts of Blois.[8] In twelfth-century eyes, to disgrace your lineage (your ancestors and your present relatives) was unforgivable, and Bishop Stephen de Fougères sermonised on the rich and promiscuous women who slept with servant men, indifferent to 'what sort of lineage (*tal lineie*)' they were from.[9] The valiant deeds and prowess of

[7] Ailred of Rievaulx, *Genealogia regum Anglorum*, in, *PL* 195, cols. 716. If that was not enough to keep it in people's consciousness, it was a text also cited to confute the Albigensian belief that the Creator demiurge was evil, Gervase of Tilbury, *Otia imperialia: Recreation for an Emperor*, ed. and trans. S.E. Banks and J.W. Binns (Oxford, 2002), 30–2.

[8] *History of William Marshal*, ed. A. Holden, S. Gregory and D. Crouch (3 vols, Anglo-Norman Text Society, 2002–6) ii, ll. 19178–80; *The Letters of Peter of Celle*, ed. J. Haseldine (Oxford, 2001), 11–12, no. 4 (1154 × 56).

[9] *Le livre des manières*, ed. R.A. Lodge (Geneva, 1979), p. 97. Galiene, maddened by her love for Fergus, contemplates suicide but then comes to herself realising it would be an outrage, 'never had any woman of her *lingnage* killed herself for love!', *The Romance of Fergus*, ed. W. Frescoln (Philadelphia, 1983), ll. 2003–5. Bertan de Born attacked Alfonso II of Aragon in 1184, saying his misdeeds had disgraced his *linhatges*, *Poésies complètes de Bertran de Born*, ed. A. Thomas (Toulouse, 1888), 47. This bespeaks a common attitude on this aspect of lineage from Occitania to Anglo-Norman Scotland.

their *lignages* was the reason why a romance character of the 1150s, Galeran de Sypont, urged his company to engage in a suicidal battle: 'they would have rather died than be cowards', he said.[10]

There was, therefore, a widespread medieval belief that a father's qualities should be replicated in each generation through lineage. Stephen de Rouen, in one of his poems, dwelt on the extent to which the physical and moral qualities of a father reappear in his sons and daughters, who are all his 'living image'.[11] In the Prose Lancelot the author comments that Merlin: 'had his father's nature, deceitful and wayward', since his father was an aerial spirit. In the 'Romance of Thebes', the character Salin of Pontus was very wise 'and this was only right for he had forefathers whose wisdom was remarkable'. Richard Kaeuper has recently demonstrated how widespread was this assumption in early thirteenth-century Arthurian literature. It even explained Kay's legendary rudeness by the fact that, although of good parentage, the mistake had been made of putting him to nurse with a peasant girl.[12] This was the case with appearance and morality, and was so equally with nobility.

The nobility of ancestors was physically present in their descendants, and it was a moral requirement on descendants to behave as if it were, and to live up to it. Orderic Vitalis in 1141 reported the prodigious valour of King Stephen on the field of Lincoln as the king being inspired by the deeds of his *antecessores*.[13] Early literature is full of the concern to draw distinction and moral strength from forbears. The dying Roland reflected on the 'humes de sun lign', his heroic forbears, when he chose to recall those things which had given dignity to his life (along with his beloved France, his own exploits and his duty to his emperor).[14] The author of the

10 *Le Roman de Thèbes*, ed. and trans. F. Mora-Lebrun (Paris, 1995), l. 1851–55. In the epic story of Vivien, nephew of William of Orange (*c.*1200), the young hero at the battle of Aliscans declared that he would rather die than survive the battle by flight in the face of the pagans, for it would disgrace his kinsfolk, *La Chevalerie Vivien*, ed. A-L. Terracher (Paris, 1909), ll. 409–16.

11 *Carmen elegiacum de Waleranno comite Mellenti*, in, *Chronicles of the Reigns of Stephen, Henry II and Richard*, ed. R. Howlett (4 vols., Rolls Series, 1886–9) ii, 767.

12 R.W. Kaeuper, *Chivalry and Violence in Medieval Europe* (Oxford, 1999), 190–1.

13 William of Poitiers, *Gesta Guillelmi*, ed. and trans. R.H.C. Davis and M. Chibnall (Oxford, 1998), 92; *Lancelot do Lac*, ed. E. Kennedy (2 vols, Oxford, 1980) i, p. 23, ll. 7–8; *Le Roman de Thèbes*, ll. 9771–3. For a similar instance (*c.*1240), where a devious count flatters a servant into a difficult mission, by implying that the servant had inherited the quality of being a *preudom* from his father, *Gaydon*, ed. F Guessard and S. Luce (Anciens Poètes de la France, Paris, 1862), l. 146.

14 *La Chanson de Roland*, ed. F. Whitehead (2nd edn, repr. 1985), l. 2379. The translation of the term *lin/lign* as 'line' might be contested. It might well have been used in

Coronation of Louis, a romance epic written in Northern France around 1130, suggested a number of ways that distinction may be found in lineage. Principally it was in providing good examples, and stiffening the moral backbone of the latest members of the family. It was brought to the attention of Count William of Orange, its hero, that his lineage was one that had never been backward in war. His *lignages* was of 'high birth' and he must act accordingly. The same work also used lineage in its broader, family sense: Count William prayed to the Virgin that he might not be found faint-hearted, and so become a reproach to his *lignage*; he was also upset by the suggestion that injuries might reduce him to poverty and dependence on charity, and so also make him (again) a reproach to his *lignages*.[15]

When a man claimed noble lineage he had to demonstrate the qualities which he claimed ran in his blood. The distinction of blood, and the wealth and prowess of ancestors, were very important to the perception of status in the world, and the claims to deference from those around an individual.[16] Hugh, bishop of Lisieux (1049–77) 'was never heard to boast of his ancient lineage (*stemma*)', but that did not stop people being aware of the fact that he was a grandson of Richard I of Normandy, and treating him accordingly.[17] This search for lineage was not confined to the medieval aristocracy. Students of hagiography have long appreciated that the distinction and antiquity of a saint's family and descent was in the

a sense nearer the Latin *gens* (family), as seems to be the case in the Anglo-Norman poem on the voyage of St Brendan, which dates to the first half of the reign of Henry I of England: it says that Brendan 'fud de regal lin', Benedeit, *The Anglo-Norman Voyage of St Brendan*, ed. I Short and B. Merrilees (Manchester, 1979), l. 22. Similarly, a generation later, Wace portrays Edward the Confessor considering William of Normandy to be his best potential successor (*qui ert le mielz de son lignage*) meaning he was the best amongst those who shared his ancestry, *Le Roman de Rou*, ed. A.J. Holden (3 vols., Société des anciens textes français, 1970–73) ii, pt 3, ll. 5552–3. Nonetheless, the Latin antecedent term *linea* could not have been understood otherwise than in the modern English sense of a 'line', and is found in that sense in written genealogies (see below).

15 *Le Couronnement de Louis*, ed. E. Langlois (Classiques français du moyen âge, 1984), ll. 787–9, 855–60, 1100–4, 1573.

16 For an extended treatment, M. Keen, *Chivalry* (London, 1984), ch. 7. See also, for some insights into the relationship in later literature between lineage and individual status, E. Kennedy, 'The Quest for Identity and the Importance of Lineage in Thirteenth-Century French Prose Romance', in, *The Ideals and Practice of Medieval Knighthood*, ii, ed. C. Harper-Bill and R. Harvey (Woodbridge, 1988), 70–86.

17 *The Ecclesiastical History*, ed. M. Chibnall (6 vols., Oxford, 1969–80) vi, 544.

eleventh century an almost inevitable prologue to his or her *vita*; a point made ironically as early as the 1190s by Alexander Neckam.[18]

The heroic past, blood and noble forbears were the means by which lineage gained power as a concept. When a family saw itself as the latest generation of a sequence of noble generations, then lineage itself informed the way its individual members behaved. Lineage, forged in the past, became a machete to clear the way through the tangled present and into a future. Present members of the lineage had a duty not just to live up to the dignity of its past but to hand on a notable example and improved fortunes to future generations. We see this concern for the future of the line quite early. In a supernatural tale of the first half of the twelfth century, which comes from the monastery of Sélestat in Alsace, the ghost of Count Conrad of Swabia (d.1094) was depicted as appearing to a former vassal soon after his death. The dead count was eager to pass on to his living brothers through his vassal several pieces of critical advice. For our purpose, it is only necessary to reflect on what Count Conrad wanted to pass on to his younger brother, Duke Frederick I of Swabia: that his *progenies* was destined for imperial glory, that future generations of their family through him would become kings of the Romans and emperors (his grandson was in fact the Emperor Frederick Barbarossa). To make sure of this, the monastic writer says, Frederick's descendants would have to honour the monastery of Sélestat. In crediting Conrad with a passionate concern for his dynasty's future which could transcend physical death, the writer betrays a fourth dimension of lineage: its projection into the future.[19]

The medieval mind put great importance on securing future generations of a family. In the 1260s Philip de Novara reflected that one of the most important things about marriage was to secure an heir 'who has his father's surname, and through whom the memory of himself and his ancestors will last longer in this world'.[20] The lack of such an heir was supposed to be a great sadness to a nobleman. On the death of his only son, the fic-

[18] *De Naturis Rerum Libri Duo*, ed. T. Wright (Rolls Series, London, 1863), 244. See on this, Carron, *Enfant et parenté*, 24.

[19] The story is to be found in *De fundatione monasterii sancte Fidis Sletstatensis*, ed. O. Holder-Egger, in *MGH, Scriptores*, xv, pt 2 (Hanover, 1888), 996–1000. See the commentary on it in J-C. Schmitt, *Ghosts in the Middle Ages: the Living and the Dead in medieval society*, trans. T.L. Fagan (Chicago, 1998), 103–5.

[20] Philip de Novara, *Les Quatre Ages de l'Homme*, ed. M. de Fréville (Société des anciens textes français, 1888), 45–6: 'mais por les maus ne doit demorer que l'an n'ait fame espousée por avoir hoirs qui puet; car por les hoirs, qui ont les sornons dou pere, dure en cest siecle plus longuement la memoire de lui et de ces ancestres.'

titious Count Florentin of Brabant in the romance of *Gui de Warewic* (*c.*1200) lamented: 'Who now will rule my lands and great honors after I am dead?'. His lack of a son after three marriages was reputed to have clouded the last years of Earl Roger de Quincy of Winchester (died 1264).[21] There is little doubt that kings and princes might well be obsessive about their immediate heirs. The mental agonies of Henry I of England on the death of his only legitimate son, William atheling, in 1120 are very well known, as are the protracted labours that he made to secure first another son and then his daughter's succession. Equally well known is the relief of Louis VII of France on the birth of a male heir, Philip 'the God-given' in 1165. But this has to be balanced with indications that such concerns remained limited in the twelfth and thirteenth centuries. This can be seen most clearly not so much in births, but in deaths. Henry I of England – although he built his own mausoleum at Reading – showed some consciousness that there might be a dynastic imperative in burial. In 1134 he argued with his seriously-ill daughter, Mathilda, who wanted to be buried at the distinguished Norman Benedictine house of Le Bec-Hellouin. Henry is said to have expressed a preference that she should lie in the cathedral of Rouen where the founders of their lineage lay. But the fact that he gave in to her shows that this sort of argument was not then too strong at the time.[22]

Despite the physicians' belief that the father's qualities alone were reproduced in his children, society in general was willing enough to believe that distinction could be drawn from the mother's lineage (certainly Ailred thought so).[23] The romance hero Fergus (*c.*1218) had a wealthy peasant for a father but a noble woman for a mother. It was his mother's family's qualities that emerged when he became an adult: he was noble in form and lusted to become a knight. His mother was not surprised, and commented with a certain amount of satisfaction: 'Well, he does have many fine knights in his lineage on my side'.[24] Sometimes, the distaff side had to be

[21] *Gui de Warewic: roman du xiiie siècle*, ed. A. Ewert (2 vols, Classiques français du moyen âge, 1932) ii, 7039–40; Matthew Paris, *Chronica Majora*, ed. H.R. Luard (7 vols., Rolls Series, 1872–84) v, 341.

[22] William de Jumièges, *Gesta Normannorum Ducum*, ed. and trans. E.M.C. van Houts (2 vols., Oxford, 1992–95) ii, 246.

[23] Barthélemy, 'Kinship', 87, points out how this lack of preference to male over female lineage was commented on by Marc Bloch in his *Feudal Society*, trans. L.A. Manyon (2 vols., London, 1962) i, 138, but that the implication of Bloch's conclusions were ignored by later commentators.

[24] 'Car il a maint bon chevalier en son lignage de par moi', *Fergus,* ll. 499–500.

more important. When around 1220 a French clerk wrote about the earls of Gloucester, he could not see that the first earl, Robert, had any status, being a bastard. So for him the source of the status of the Gloucesters lay with the heiress Earl Robert married, Sibyl, daughter of Robert fitz Hamo, whose 'chiés de linage' – the fount of her nobility – was Robert (*rectius* Roger) de Montgommery, her maternal grandfather.[25] The concept of bastardy, propagated by the Gregorian church in the eleventh century was indeed a particular problem for the social world of the nobility. Since nobility and lineage was commonly believed to be transmitted by the father's blood, the bastard son of great man could claim his father's lineage. The Church however argued that the sin of extramarital sex tainted that blood. The fact that society in general believed otherwise is still clear in the late twelfth century.[26] Fictional bastards such as Bernier in *Raoul de Cambrai* can be portrayed as truly noble and generous, as indeed could also be the upright and truthful Morgan Bloet in the Durham Annals, an historical royal bastard who, in 1213, would not tell a lie, even though a lie would have made him a bishop.

Lineage helped to support a man or woman who wished to lay claim to a status above that of others. For instance, Wace depicted Alan III of Brittany as being of such *parage*, *haltesce* and *lignage*, that he did not care to serve Duke Robert I of Normandy, as his ancestors had, and opposed him instead.[27] By the twelfth century, humility and circumspection was indeed expected to be shown to people who were acknowledged to be of great *parage* and *haut lignage*.[28] But of course, those who were all too conscious of what was due to them, risked going over the edge of public respect, and laid themselves open to charges of unreasonable pride and arrogance. Around 1073, William de Poitiers could write of the late kinsmen of William the Conqueror (his uncle, Count William of Arques, and his first cousin, Guy of Burgundy): 'The fame of their high birth,

[25] *Histoire des ducs de Normandie et des rois d'Angleterre*, ed. F. Michel (Société de l'histoire de France, 1840), 69.

[26] A point made recently in J-P. Poly, *Le chemin des amours barbares: génèse médiévale de la sexualité européenne* (Paris, 2003), 350–1.

[27] *Le Roman de Rou*, i, pt 3, ll. 2599–602. This vignette can be paralleled in contemporary history, for William of Malmesbury talks of Hervey the Breton, vicomte of Léon, as 'of such distinction and so proud' (*tantae nobilitatis, tanti supercilii*) that he disdained Henry I's invitation to come to England, *Historia Novella*, ed. and trans. K.R. Potter, rev'd E. King (Oxford, 1998), 54 (my translation). Potter translated *nobilitas* as 'high-born' but the word is not that specific in contemporary use.

[28] *Le Roman de Thèbes*, ll. 8426–8, speaking of the dangerous ill-nature of King Etiocles, who did not extend respect even to people with such claims.

which ought to inspire noble hearts to perform praiseworthy deeds, led them both into excessive and overweening arrogance, and brought both to ruin. For both knew, to their undoing, that they were counted among the progeny of the dukes of Normandy . . .'.[29]

Lineage could bring more material advantages than honour. There was also the fact that lands and rights descended with blood. It is this aspect of lineage which has to date most concerned historians, particularly since one school of Anglo-American legal historians has suggested an evolutionary shift in ideas of property in the middle ages. The suggestion was made by Samuel Thorne in the 1950s that ideas of automatic hereditary succession to property did not exist in the earlier middle ages, and did not come about in England until the legal reforms of King Henry II. The historian R.H.C. Davis went so far as to suggest that the struggle by barons in England to secure automatic heredity to their honors was what ultimately caused the civil war of King Stephen's reign (1135–54).[30] This radical view is not now popular, especially as it has been pointed out that the Latin phrase *iure hereditario*, or some variant of it, meaning 'by hereditary right', was already well-established in the early eleventh century as the reason why people acquire property. Ralph Glaber, writing in the 1040s, wrote of princely characters in the previous century claiming territories and realms 'by hereditary right' (on one occasion, the hereditary right was a wife's), and of noblemen whose lands were 'patrimonies'.[31]

In twelfth-century legal cases, the 'right' (*ius*) by which a man or woman claimed land as theirs was almost invariably their descent. We see this in the eleventh-century documentation for Normandy. We see this frequently enough in twelfth-century literary sources too. It was because he was of the *lignage* of Hengist that the Saxon, Cedric, claimed the land from Humber to Caithness as his inheritance, according to Geoffrey Gaimar in the 1140s. It was because 'my *lignages*, my *encestres*' had held Soissons that Duke Beugon took such exception to the counterclaims of his enemy Fromond, in the later twelfth-century romance, *Garin*.[32] The honourable Saracen king, Galafre, moved his armies against Rome because he considered it his 'dreit heritage'. It was his inheritance because he considered

[29] *Gesta Guillelmi*, ed. and trans. R.H.C. Davis and M. Chibnall (Oxford, 1998), 32–4.

[30] S.E. Thorne, 'English Feudalism and Estates in Land', *Cambridge Law Journal* (1959), 193–209; R.H.C. Davis, 'What happened in Stephen's Reign, 1135–54', *History*, xlix (1964), 1–12.

[31] Ralph Glaber, *Historiarum Libri Quinque*, ed. and trans. J. France (Oxford, 1989), 17, 25, 67, 279.

[32] Gaimar, *L'Estoire des Engleis*, ll. 13–14; *Garin le Loherenc* i, ll. 5286–90.

it a pagan city, and in his pagan lineage were Romulus and Julius Caesar, his 'ancestors and forbears'.[33]

This is ground that the previous chapter has already travelled, but it is worth visiting again here briefly. As we have seen, the models of family structures of the nineteenth century insist on the growing importance of male-dominated or 'agnatic' lineage. They do not necessarily insist on one exclusive idea of the agnatic linear family. You might have brothers dividing the family property or even holding it in common (which latter model is technically called 'parage'), and at its most liberal such an agnatic linear family might even have all male cousins sharing the family property (in which case it is hardly distinguishable from the undifferentiated 'kin group', the clan). But the narrowest form, and the agnatic ideal, would be *uni-geniture*, where one male in every generation succeeded exclusively to the estates of his father. This brings us back to primogeniture, the succession of the eldest surviving son: the model of succession prevalent amongst royal and princely families at the end of the eleventh century. What needs to be emphasised here is that medieval sources, other than some tracts on customary law, do not regard primogeniture as at all automatic or desirable, although they assume that males will succeed before females.

Parage and the Search for Security

Such was the vertical nature of medieval thinking on family, and there is no doubt of the considerable impact that the idea of lineage had on the conduct and expectations of individuals, lay and clerical alike. What is less well-known is that there was another vernacular term of the time which offered a contrasting view on family. The word was *parage*. 'Parage' had a rather different impact on social conduct than 'lineage'. It did not so much affect individual conduct, as group behaviour. It is more difficult to define than *lignage*, and relates to the noun *per* or *par* (which we translate as 'peer' or 'equal'). There are plenty of instances when *parage*, like *lignage*, is meant to signify 'family', and it is also translated as 'birth'. But a strand of its meaning centres around the idea of status and dignity, the status of one man measured against another: status in birth, wealth and power.[34]

[33] *Le Couronnement de Louis*, ll. 463–6, they were his 'ancestre et mes aves'. In a romance epic of the next generation King Agolant of the Saracens was said to desire to conquer all that Alexander had once held because it was his *iretage*, and he was of royal *linage*, *La Chanson d'Aspremont* i, ll. 458–60.

[34] See for instance the scornful dismissal by King Nicholas of Elim faced with the young Alexander of Macedon: 'Boy, you're a fool! You have no idea who I am! You have

The concept can be found in vernacular sources as early as the last quarter of the eleventh century. In the French *Life of St Alexis* the author contrasts the 'great poverty' of Alexis with his 'great *parage*'. As a saint, 'he loved God better than all his *linage*', but at the same time, he kept the knowledge of his circumstances from his mother, who did not share the low value he put on his connections and who presumably would have told him so in the way peculiar to concerned mothers down the ages.[35] Wace of Bayeux had a lot to say about *parage* as a concept. When, in the *Roman de Brut*, Cassibelan, king of Britain, refused to pay tribute to Caesar and Rome, it was because they descended from one *lignage*; this meant that the Britons stood in a relationship of *parage* to the Romans, they were equals in status (as drawn from birth), and it was arrogance (*hunte*) in Caesar to presume otherwise.[36] In the same work, the brothers Belin and Brennius fell out. Brennius was goaded to defy his elder by a false friend who asked him scornfully why he should accept dependence on his brother: 'Are you not of a *parage*? The one who bore him, bore you also. You had the same father. You are brothers born of the same father and mother. How does Belin outrank you and take precedence in the inheritance?'[37] So if 'lignage' is a twelfth-century word that usually indicates vertical perceptions of family tracked back through time, 'parage' is a word which usually talks of a different perspective on family, betraying horizontal ideas; seeing an individual and his connections (*liens*) focussed in the present moment.[38]

It was the horizontal dimension of family – the family as it was understood at a point in time – that had a cash value. An individual drew status and honour from his bloodline, but in addition he might acquire opportunities for personal advancement through those who shared his blood, his

no conception of my rank (*parage*)! I'm king of this realm, and others beside owe me tribute!', Thomas of Kent, *Le Roman de Toute Chevalerie*, ed. B. Foster (2 vols., Anglo-Norman Text Society, 29–31, 1976–77) i, ll. 577–9.

35 *La Vie de Saint Alexis*, ed. M. Perugi (Geneva, 2000), ll. 246–50.

36 *Roman de Brut* i, ll. 3927–8: 'Ki sumes de vostre parage; per as Romains estre devum, ki d'un lingnage descendom'. The Latin term *paragium* (as found in Domesday Book and later Norman custom) relates to the vernacular *parage* in the sense that it indicates brothers holding shares in an undivided estate, but *paragium* lacks the wider application of the vernacular term, F. Pollock and F.W. Maitland, *The History of English Law* (2 vols, Cambridge, 2nd edn, 1898) ii, 263–4, 276; J.C. Holt, 'Politics and Property in Early Medieval England', *Past and Present*, no. 57 (1972), 44–5.

37 *Roman de Brut* i, ll. 2349–60.

38 This simultaneously horizontal and vertical view is apparent in a customary of Lille dated to *c.*1290, when it defines family relationships, as cited in, Carron, *Enfant et parenté*, 15–16

consanguinei. In a society without professions, CVs and interviews, it was only kith who could be expected to provide protection and opportunities for kin.[39] The writer Hermann of Laon provides one of the best examples of this. When he wished to demonstrate the status of his hero, Bartholomew, canon and treasurer of Reims, who was elected bishop of Laon in 1113, he went into elaborate detail about the 'notability of his family' and the 'excellence of his cousins', distinguished people spread across France, Spain, Burgundy and Lorraine. Bishop Bartholomew's father was Falkes of Jura, count of Burgundy, but great man though Count Falkes was, Hermann attributed the bishop's progress in life to Bartholomew's collection of distinguished relatives on the side of his mother, Adelaide, daughter of Count Hilduin of Roucy. Through Adelaide, Bartholomew could claim six counts and a king of Aragon as uncles and the archbishop of Reims as his great-uncle. His cousins included bishops of Chalons and Verdun, a queen of Navarre and Countess Margaret of Flanders. Bartholomew made the most of these grand maternal connections. As a boy he was sent to his uncle, Eblé count of Roucy, whose family then dominated the see of Reims. Letters of Count Eblé to his own uncle, Archbishop Mannasses, secured Bartholomew a canonry of Reims, and eventually the treasurership of the cathedral. To these offices Bartholomew added the treasurership of the church of St-Quentin in Vermandois, a gift he obtained from Countess Adelaide of Vermandois, who had taken as her second husband Bartholomew's first cousin, Count Reginald of Clermont 'and knew him to be a cousin of her husband, so for love of him made Bartholomew treasurer'. Finally, impressed perhaps as much by his connections as his learning, Archbishop Ralph of Reims nominated Bartholomew to the see of Laon in 1113.[40]

Bartholomew is an excellent study of the way the horizontal links of 'parage' worked in a man's favour in medieval society, and it is worth noting how it was his maternal family that provided him with the most opportunities. But if his biographer had done further research he would have found that Bartholomew's paternal grandmother, Adeliza countess of Burgundy, was no less than an aunt of William the Conqueror, king of England, and through her he could have claimed kinship with most of the earls and counts of the Anglo-Norman realm. The boughs of the family

[39] Carron, *Enfant et parenté*, 27.

[40] Hermann of Laon, *De miraculis sanctae Mariae Laudunensis*, in, *PL* 156, cols. 965–7. Hermann also notes that King Alfonso I of Aragon, son of Bartholomew's aunt Felicia, presented him with relics of St Vincent the Martyr and a chasuble, once the property of St Alfonso, archbishop of Toledo, ibid., col. 961.

tree were heavy with fruit for some men. This was so much so that Bishop Bartholomew simply chose the branch that it suited him to rest upon. This mechanism is most obvious in looking at the Church, where there was a clear hierarchy and a multitude of offices through which a young nobleman might seek advancement. Indeed, the opinion was occasionally given in the late twelfth century that only young men of noble families had any business being ordained and that measures should be taken to exclude ordinands not born of noble and free families. People of peasant stock should be excluded, it was said, as their coarse and grasping nature would soon come out and be a disgrace to their orders. England and France provide innumerable examples from the eleventh to the fourteenth century where noble or episcopal kinship made a young man's career for him in the ecclesiastical hierarchy.[41]

So universal was this mechanism, and so unmeritocratic even to medieval sensibilities, that senior clergy were embarrassed into justifying it. Bishop Stephen de Fougères was one such apologist. Since he thought it necessary to justify it (including a reference to the Biblical authority of the book of Numbers) he obviously realised that it was a practice which had incurred, and was always likely to incur, criticism; criticism based on grounds of pragmatism and natural justice (or equal rights, as we would call it today):

If a bishop gives to his relations, this is but following human nature, and it is no more than Scripture advocates; but it should be done with moderation, to support them and not to enrich them. If indeed they are of good character, the bishop does well to bring them into his household, for the more of his people who are of good counsel, the more he knows from them how to do good. He does well to associate himself with his own family – so, should anyone wish to attack him, to strike at him or to ill-use him, such followers cannot let him down.[42]

[41] For studies of ecclesiastical dynasties in action, C.N.L. Brooke, 'The composition of the chapter of St Paul's, 1086–1163', *Cambridge Historical Journal*, × (1951), 111–32 (the Beaumeis family); *The Letters of Arnulf of Lisieux*, ed. F. Barlow (Camden Society, 3rd ser., lxi, 1939), pp. xi–xxv (the dynasty of Norman the dean, at Lisieux and Séez). For statements arguing against peasant clerics see Walter Map, *De Nugis Curialium or Courtiers' Trifles*, ed. and trans. M.R. James, C.N.L. Brooke and R.A.B. Mynors (Oxford, 1983), 12; *Chanson d'Aspremont*, ii, 11214–26, 11306–23, which advocates a board of enquiry and a jury of inquest before each ordination to establish that a candidate is 'de jentil feme, de franc ome engenré' (l. 11322).

[42] *Le Livre des Manières*, p. 74, ll. 361–72.

We can only think that the bishop had encountered the same petitions from kinsfolk as did Abbot Samson of Bury St Edmunds in 1182, who on his return from the royal court after his election was met by 'a multitude of new kinsmen ... desiring to be taken into his service'. Samson took the same line as Bishop Stephen, retaining only one of this crowd as a knight and this man 'not so much because he was a relative, but because he was a man of some usefulness, skilled in worldly business.' In the mid 1170s Philip, the new prior of St Frideswide in Oxford, was similarly embarrassed into taking into his household a young cousin called Robert, after the boy besieged him relentlessly.[43] It is clear that, by the end of the twelfth century, clergy were beginning to be apologetic about such nepotism. The commentator and clerk, Walter of Arras, described their quandary with proverbial economy between 1176 and 1184: 'The more your wealth and treasure, the more numerous your kinsfolk!'[44] By the thirteenth century, such behaviour was no longer tolerated, at least in abbots. Abbot William of Peterborough was forced to resign by Bishop Robert Grosseteste in 1249, because of his monks' complaints that he was pillaging the abbey's estates to endow his numerous kinsmen.[45]

The same mechanism was there in lay life too. The mesnie of Raymond le Gros in Ireland in the 1170s was made up of thirty or so men described by Gerald of Wales as all his 'kin'.[46] Raymond had clearly been besieged

[43] *Chronicle of Jocelin of Brakelond*, ed. H.E. Butler (London, 1949), 24. Abbot Samson was accounted by his biographer as a man with less love for his kin than other men, acknowledging only those who had acknowledged him when a poor, young monk, and employing few as reeves, ibid. 43. For Prior Philip and Robert, *consanguinitate sibi conjunctum*, see *De miraculis sanctae Frideswidae*, in, *Acta Sanctorum*, Oct. 8, p. 569. Complaints of the dispersal of monastic resources by abbots to relations occur early, and in 1125, King Henry I laid down at his foundation of Reading Abbey that when an abbot was elected he should not honour his 'worldly kinsfolk' or bestow the abbey's alms on others who would waste it, but use its wealth to care for the poor, pilgrims and guests, *Reading Abbey Cartularies*, ed. B. Kemp (2 vols, Camden Society, 4th ser., 31, 33, 1986–7) i, 34. In 1177 a similar restriction was laid on the abbot of Waltham by Henry II, that no *consanguineus* of his should hold the stewardship or any other secular *ministratio* of the abbey estates, *Cartae Antique Rolls, 11–20*, ed. J. Conway Davies (Pipe Roll Society, 1960), 44.

[44] 'Car cascuns a grant parenté quant il a riqueche et plenté', *Eracle*, ed. G. Raynaud de Lage (Classiques français du moyen âge, 102, 1976), ll. 2797–8.

[45] Matthew Paris, *Chronica Majora*, ed. H.R. Luard (7 vols., Rolls Series, 1872–84) v, 84.

[46] Gerald of Wales, *Expugnatio Hibernica*, ed. A.B. Scott and F.X. Martin (Dublin, 1978), 168, Gerald uses the word *nepotes* (usually meaning 'nephews), but since one of them was Meilyr fitz Henry (actually Raymond's first cousin) the meaning of 'kin' is preferred. For the ten knights of the household of Geoffrey of Malaterra, abbot of Burton (1085–94), who were all his *parentes*, see Geoffrey of Burton, *The Life and Miracles of St Modwenna*, ed. R. Bartlett (Oxford, 2002), 192.

by family for places in his entourage. A well-known individual example of creating a career by means of kinship is the great William Marshal, whose father used his wife's kinship with the Tancarville family to secure William a place as squire in the household of the chamberlain of Normandy until he came of age *c.*1166. After a brief period as a retained knight with William de Tancarville, Marshal crossed over to England and sought out a household position with his mother's brother, Earl Patrick of Salisbury, in 1168. By some convoluted and tragic accidents he then made the transition to the royal household. Once he had made his fortune there, he was in a position to further his own siblings and younger relatives. He exerted himself at court to further his brothers, John and Henry Marshal, and John's namesake and illegitimate son, his nephew; his patronage also brought his nephews from his sister's marriage to the Gloucestershire knight, William le Gros, into his household and into royal notice.[47] A comparable but less well-known example can be found in the family of the earls of Arundel. Around 1138, William d'Aubigny obtained the marriage of the dowager queen Adeliza, widowed on the death of King Henry I of England in 1135, bringing to him the castle and lordship of Arundel in Sussex. She also brought him a distinguished lineage, for she was daughter of Duke Godfrey I of Brabant and related not only to the counts of Flanders and Hainault, but also to the imperial family. The marriage produced several sons, and it is perhaps no surprise to find three years after Earl William's death, at the head of a list of the *familiares* of Duke Godfrey III of Brabant at Wavre in 1173, 'Godfrey the Englishman, the duke's cousin' (that is Godfrey d'Aubigny, son of Earl William of Arundel). Like William Marshal, young Godfrey had been sent overseas to his distinguished relatives to find his fortune.[48]

This feeling for kin was a universal political and social mechanism, but its effects can be overestimated, and it was not always regarded with favour in the middle ages. The fact that kin could be an obstacle to ambition is implicit in the succession struggles of so many medieval European princely houses, and it appears at lower levels too. The sort of situation

[47] D. Crouch, *William Marshal: Court, Career and Chivalry in the Angevin Empire* (London, 1990), 19–25, 34–7, 67–9, 73, 143, 166 and n, 199. For the Le Gros connection, see N. Vincent, 'The borough of Chipping Sodbury and the fat men of France', *Transactions of the Bristol and Gloucestershire Archaeological Society*, 116 (1998), 141–59.

[48] *Cartulaire d'Afflighem*, ed. E. de Marneffe, in, *Analectes pour servir à l'histoire ecclésiastique de la Belgique*, iie section, *Série des cartulaires et des documents étendus* i, pt 1 (Louvain, 1894), 218.

portrayed in the *Roman de Thèbes*, where Polyneices finds his first cousin defending a castle against him had many real-life echoes in times of civil strife: 'Surrender in good faith . . . or no consideration of kinship, friendship or family will prevent me from hanging you and your men at the gates!'.[49] Similarly, there were medieval people who were quite eager to throw off relatives when to acknowledge them would be to incur trouble. Matthew Paris talks of the greater citizens of Genoa denying their kinship with the city's famous son, Pope Innocent IV (1243–54), when he sought refuge there in his flight from the emperor. They feared imperial retribution if they helped their cousin.[50]

But it was nonetheless an important social fact of life in the middle ages that your kinsfolk were more likely to be your patrons and protectors and were more likely to advance you than anyone else. It was kin who were traditionally supposed to take responsibility for a murder of one of their own, and be the *mortels enemis* of the murderer. In England in the reign of Henry I (1100–35) both the maternal and paternal kin of a man accused of murder were expected to assist in clearing his name and making compensation.[51] Finding examples before 1300 of the kin of a victim taking vengeance on the criminal is not as frequent as one might suppose in England or France. In fact it is much easier to find examples before 1100, due to the nature of the evidence. Monks in the eleventh century did not just record property settlements, but often the circumstances that led up to the settlement, which might have been the consequence of a feud. The eleventh century was maybe no more violent and feud-ridden than the twelfth, but its documents talk more openly about private hostilities.[52]

A study by Stephen D. White of eleventh and early twelfth century feuding in the Touraine based on such sources has very revealing things to say of the place of kin in the process of feud. In the seven feuds White analyses, the desire to avenge the death of kinsfolk features very strongly, as in the case of the pursuit of Achard of Marmande by the men of Les Puys, whose women and children became collateral casualties in his war against other local lords. But the case is also revealing about the place of family during feuds, in that Achard was driven to make a settlement with

[49] *Le Roman de Thèbes*, ll. 3051–7. It was his *consanguineus*, Robert de Montfort, who engineered the treason trial in 1163 which overthrew Henry of Essex, *Chronicle of Jocelin of Brakelond*, 69–70.

[50] *Chronica Majora*, iv, 355.

[51] *Leges Henrici Primi*, ed. L.J. Downer (Oxford, 1972), 204, 276.

[52] S.D. White, 'Feuding and Peace-Making in the Touraine around the Year 1000', *Traditio*, 42 (1986), 205–6.

the villagers because his own nephew had undermined his position, turned against him and had taken him captive. In other cases, brothers seem, not surprisingly, particularly keen to avenge a sibling's death. They were the closest kin and most physically able to seek vengeance. But kin might well mobilise friends so as to expand the group seeking to prosecute the feud: the more powerful the man they were pursuing, the bigger the 'vengeance group' needed, as White says. But a powerful kin group would be dangerous to antagonise. In the case of the death during a local war of a noble young knight, Philip son of Geoffrey son of Savaric, his powerful relatives raised the entire country against the killer. In this case, the peace involved the killer meeting Philip's mother and receiving her forgiveness with a kiss. When a settlement was eventually reached – if there was to be one – it was to the kinsfolk of the victim that the instigator invariably had to humble himself. White's examples also reveal that during a feud, the vengeance group was likely to include kinsfolk both from the mother's and father's side. Not every case White analyses involved a death. Bartholomew, lord of L'Isle-Bouchard, antagonised Garnier son of Maingod, a knight of one of his rivals, by ordering one of his squires to humiliate him after he had been captured. Garnier swore to kill the squire (perhaps Bartholomew himself was too intimidating a lord to dare to resent), and it took the intervention of the squire's father and brothers to broker a deal by which Garnier forswore his feud.[53]

Whatever the Touraingeau examples might tell us about the volatility of eleventh-century French society, they provide some fine insights into the place of kinship in a man's life at the time. A rich and powerful kin might encourage a man who had one to prosecute a feud, or it might cause a man who was faced by such a group to seek peace. Kin was perhaps therefore a neutral factor in the way feud might destabilise society, although it might be a factor in the decision of a man not to let an injury pass. Kin were certainly necessary in order to end feuds. It was their intercession, and sometimes their resources, that were deployed in order to pacify the vengeance group. But kin groups were not predictable or necessarily cooperative. They did not act in any programmed way.

The twelfth century produces limited examples of kin feud. But one of them is very revealing of how kin could wish to settle feud. Before 1162 a nephew of the Norman magnate, Philip de Colombières, killed the niece of the bishop of Bayeux. Philip repudiated the boy's action and swore peace with the bishop's *cognatio*, his kin, and offered compensation. This was

[53] Ibid., 213–46.

not because he preferred to keep out of it, he was simply settling the dispute as quickly as he could and avoiding a private war he did not want.[54] There are some other well-known twelfth-century stories. Roger of Howden reported as fact the execution in 1175 by Count Philip of Flanders of the knight Walter de Fontaines for adultery with his wife, following which Walter's *parentes* allied with the lord of Guise and devastated the count's lands in retaliation, until Philip paid them compensation. Although the facts of Howden's story have recently come under some suspicion, he clearly expected kin in foreign parts to take vengeance for what amounted to a murder of one of their own.[55] Not every story of feud arose from a death. Fulbert, dean of Paris, got his kin to swear to take a grim revenge on Abelard for his illicit relationship with Heloise, his niece.

Was feud any less common in twelfth-century France than earlier? It was not uncommon to profess hatred of a man to the point where he was a 'mortal enemy' (*inimicus mortalis* or *mortel enemi*), an enemy till death. Such enmity was real, but was it carried as far as the killing of such a man? When, in the 1120s, Orderic Vitalis portrayed eleventh-century Normans as prone to kin violence, was he implying that this was in the less civilised past? He gives examples of how the killing of Roger de Tosny by Robert fitz Humphrey was avenged by Robert's murder by a Tosny vassal; the killing of Osbern fitz Herfast of Breteuil by a member of the Montgomery family, was avenged by his steward, Bjarni de Glos, on another Montgomery.[56] It may be that he believed his contemporaries in the 1120s

[54] For this case see *Antiquus cartularius ecclesiae Baiocensis*, ed. V. Bourienne (2 vols., Société des historiens de Normandie, 1902–3) i, 39–40, noted in Carron, *Enfant et parenté*, 28. The peace legislation of 1200 for the county of Hainault describes exactly this situation: the close kinsfolk of a murderer should forswear his deed to the kin of the victim, or be subject to retribution, *MGH Scriptores* xxi, 619. See also the *exemplum* of James de Vitry concerning a brigand who confessed his sins, but whose enemies killed him because of their *consanguinei* he had killed, *The Exempla of Jacques de Vitry*, ed. T.F. Crane (New York, 1890), 32.

[55] For a full analysis of Abelard's castration, M.T. Clanchy, *Abelard: A Medieval Life* (Oxford, 1997), 195–200. Roger of Howden, *Chronica*, ed. W. Stubbs (4 vols., Rolls Series, 1868–71) ii, 82–3. For a critical assessment of the anecdote, R.E. Harvey, 'Cross-Channel Gossip in the Twelfth Century', in *England and the Continent in the Middle Ages: Studies in Memory of Andrew Martindale*, ed. J. Mitchell (Harlaxton Medieval Studies, viii, Stamford, 2000), 48–59.

[56] Orderic Vitalis, *The Ecclesiastical History*, ed. and trans. M. Chibnall (6 vols, Oxford, 1969–80) iii, 88; *The Gesta Normannorum Ducum of William of Jumièges, Orderic Vitalis and Robert of Torigni*, ed. and trans. E.M.C. van Houts (2 vols., Oxford, 1992–95) ii, 94.

under the iron rule of Henry I were less given to slaking their blood lust.[57] In the twelfth century, a homicide did not necessarily lead to kin strife. Earl Patrick of Salisbury was assassinated by members of the Lusignan family in Poitou in 1168. His nephew, William Marshal, who was present at the deed, was certainly unhappy with the Lusignans thereafter, and did not cease from accusing them of murder, but he did not retaliate in kind, and the most he got in apparent acknowledgement from them were protestations from Geoffrey de Lusignan that it had all been a tragic accident.[58]

In the case of England, blood feud was probably exceptional by the twelfth century. The reason was simply that homicide had been defined nationally as an offence against the king's peace. It may even be that this was the case before the Conquest, for the frankpledge (which predated 1066) made a community, not a kin group, responsible for homicides and other crimes within them. In the reign of William the Conqueror the murdrum fine – imposed on villages, towns and districts – extended this idea, at least for the killing of Frenchmen. Royal coroners, sheriffs and justices took responsibility for hunting down and punishing murderers; the role of the victim's kin was to petition for justice. Twelfth-century Englishmen seem to have believed they were above the blood feud, and looked down on societies where they believed blood feud was a reality – like the contemporary Welsh – as primitive and anarchic.[59]

It was expected in medieval literature that the 'parage' or 'cosinage' – the current members of the lineage – would stick together in adversity, in good times and bad.[60] This was not always a moral stand: blood was thicker than water, but not so thick as always to be able to keep morality

[57] See the stern declaration of Norman custom on public order and the ducal peace, supported by a writ from the time of Henry I in, *Coutumiers de Normandie*, ed. E-J Tardif, i (Rouen, 1881), 64–8.

[58] Crouch, *William Marshal*, 37–9; *History of William Marshal* i, ll. 6420–58.

[59] See J. Hudson, *The Formation of the English Common Law* (London, 1996), 29–31, 61–9. On the characterisation of the Welsh as murderous see the comment that 'they are prodigal of the lives of others', *The Chronicle of Richard of Devizes of the Time of King Richard the First*, ed. and trans. J.T. Appleby (London, 1963), 66. In fact the evidence for blood feud in Wales is limited, Welsh society (like Anglo-Saxon society) was also geared to the compensation of kin for lives lost, see W. Davies, *Wales in the Early Middle Ages* (Leicester, 1982), 79–81. Ironically, the violent age of kin-strife in Wales might have been initiated by catastrophic Anglo-Norman intrusions in the late eleventh-century. See generally, R.R. Davies, *The Age of Conquest: Wales, 1063–1415* (Oxford, 1991), 123–5.

[60] Philip de Beaumanoir said it was important for a man to know who was in his *lignage*, 'because then he can ask them to support him in time of conflict', *Coutumes de Beauvaisis* i, 298.

floating on the surface. Roland Carron gives the example of some officers of the count of Flanders who in 1280 assisted a rapist to escape justice. When asked why, they replied that they were close kin of the criminal and could not refuse to help him when he asked. It is from this thought-world that Walter of Arras comments, a century earlier: 'People prefer a crook who is a kinsman to a decent fellow from another family'.[61] When he had been newly knighted in 1168, the young and energetic Baldwin V of Hainault devoted his time to exterminating the infestation of armed robbers by which his father's realm was disturbed, 'who had no fears of carrying on in their wicked ways because of the support of a the numbers of noblemen to whom they were related by blood'. Baldwin spared none of them for the sake of their grand kinsfolk, however.[62]

The vernacular chronicler, Jordan Fantosme, clearly shared the same assumption of 'kin solidarity'. In describing events in East Anglia in 1173, Jordan notes the defection to the rebels of the Essex baron and royal forester, Gilbert de Montfichet. He records a messenger announcing to Henry II that Gilbert had garrisoned his castle in Essex 'and he said that *les Clarreaux* had allied with him'. *Les Clarreaux* refers to Gilbert's cousins, the earls of Hertford and the lords of Dunmow, and their auxiliaries.[63] The use of that one significant phrase indicates a contemporary perception in the 1170s that the various families in the Clare lineage formed a kin-group capable of common political purpose. Jordan Fantosme was not the only writer to notice the power of these families. His contemporary at the cathedral priory of Ely who compiled the *Liber Eliensis* wrote of Abbot Richard fitz Richard (1100-1107) – the great uncle of Gilbert de Montfichet:

When he went to the king's court, he was feared second only to the king, for he was walled around by a great crowd of relatives, who, as the whole of England knew and recognised, were of the descent of the Ricardi *and* Gifardi. *The* Ricardi *(the family of Richard fitz Gilbert de Clare) and the* Gifardi *(the family of Walter Giffard, earl of Buckingham)*

[61] Carron, *Enfant et parenté*, 21–2. 'Mix aiment lor felon parent c'un bien preudome d'autre gent', *Ille et Galeron*, ed. Y. Lefèvre (Classiques français du moyen âge, 109, 1988), ll. 852–3. Compare the earlier comment of William de Poitiers, writing in the 1070s: 'Many good people, misled by carnal affection, spare the crimes of those who are their blood relatives', *Gesta Guillelmi*, 86,

[62] *La Chronique de Gislebert de Mons*, ed. L. Vanderkindere (Brussels, 1904), 97.

[63] *Jordan Fantosme's Chronicle*, ed. R.C. Johnston (Oxford, 1981), 120. There is a reference to Earl Roger de Clare of Hertford leading his 'Clarenses' to the aid of Henry II in the battle of Coleshill in 1157, although here the 'men of the honor of Clare' may be indicated, *Chronicle of Jocelin of Brakelond*, 70.

are two related families, who have made their members (natales) *illustrious by their reputation for power and the size of their family. They dominate every assembly of nobles by their magnificence and numbers. It was then no safe thing for any nobleman to openly oppose them either in sheltering their enemies or in pursuing law suits.'*[64]

The Clares – the descendants of Count Gilbert of Eu-Brionne, the grandson of Duke Ricard I of Normandy – and the Giffards had formed a close political and marital alliance at the court of the Conqueror. From the mid-eleventh century to the late twelfth century, they were recognised as a formidable and large group of kinsfolk, who worked together. If that was true in the 1170s, it had certainly been even more true in the 1140s when we know that the solidarity of the Clares and Giffards in the period of the civil war was notorious to several writers.[65] It is worthwhile noting that the Clare-Giffard lineage had its impact on the development of heraldry: the particular Clare device of a chevron (an inverted 'V') appears on the mid-twelfth century seals of the principal Clare lines, and is to be found on the shields of all of them (Montfichets, Monmouths and fitz Walters) and of their chief tenants in the early thirteenth century.[66] The chevron is a device derived from the rafters of a baronial hall: the implication it carries of a kinship group sheltered together under the common protection of their house's lineage may not be accidental.

The Clares and the Giffards were a particularly effective and close kinship group, whose alliance for mutual protection and promotion can be plotted for over a century. It is probable that it was exceptional in its longevity, in the distinction and the uninterrupted power it enjoyed, but it was certainly not unprecedented. The resort to an adjectival noun in describing such families is an intriguing insight into contemporary perceptions of family. What it implies is an almost clan-like allusion to 'those Clare people' or 'those Giffards' as an interest group of relatives who

[64] *Liber Eliensis*, ed. E.O. Blake (Camden Society, 3rd ser., xcii, 1962), 71, with acknowledgement of the useful translation of the bulk of this passage by R. Bartlett, *England under the Norman and Angevin Kings, 1075–1225* (Oxford, 2000), 230, although I have differed from its emphases in places, principally the phrase *ex propinquo*, which Blake interpreted as meaning the Clares and Giffards had adjoining Norman honors, which was simply not so.

[65] See now, D. Crouch, *The Reign of King Stephen, 1135–54* (London, 2000), 127–32.

[66] See the diagram in D. Crouch, *The Image of Aristocracy in Britain, 1000–1300* (London, 1992), 234, and also now, idem, 'The Historian, Lineage and Heraldry', in *Heraldry, Pageantry and Social Display in Medieval England*, ed. M. Keen and P.R. Coss (Woodbridge, 2002).

worked together. Another, less exalted, example is an off-hand allusion in an 1153 charter of Duke Henry of Normandy to the relatives of a minor southern English baron, Henry Hose, in which he devised upon him the lands of his kinsman Walter and also made him heir of the members of his prolific family who had fought against the duke's party (*omnium parentum suorum Hosatorum*, which could be translated 'of all his relatives, the Hose-ites'). The *Hosatenses* or *Hosati* were recognisable to contemporaries in the south of England in the mid-twelfth century as a 'parage'.[67] Matthew Paris accords the allied English courtier families of Sandford and Basset of Wycombe the same treatment a century later. In 1251 he refers to Aline, the wife of the justice, Henry of Bath, as being far too conscious of her connection with the wealthy *Bassatenses* and *Sandfordenses*, and urging her husband on in his greedy extortions. When Henry eventually found himself in trouble it was to the Sandfords and Bassets that he sent his wife to get help, and it was Bishop Fulk Basset of London and Philip Basset who eventually secured for him a reconciliation with the king.[68]

We can look to France to find much the same perception. In the court of Philip I and Louis VI of France, a similarly formidable group to the Clares was represented by the Garlande family. One of its clerical leaders, Stephen the chancellor (d.*c.*1148) was (like Abbot Richard of Ely) described as 'second only to the king' at the royal court. The *Garlandenses*, as Abbot Suger of St-Denis called them, were given a group name, like the Anglo-Norman *Clarenses*, because contemporaries realised they were a force at the court of France.[69] The group's strength was in the close relationship between four of the brothers: Stephen, Anselm, William and Payn. They were not men of distinguished lineage (unlike the Clares and Giffards) being a lesser branch of the family of the hereditary royal butlers. But it was kinship that brought them access to royal favour, and it was as a lineage that they promoted themselves. The family was still recognised as a group close to the king as late as the 1180s.[70] If we look to Flanders, we

[67] N. Vincent, 'Sixteen New Charters of Henry Plantagenet as Duke of Normandy, 1150–1154', *Historical Research*, forthcoming. The *Hosati* were not a cannibalistic group of kinsfolk, as first appearances might imply: Henry Hose may well have been working hard to protect his extended family's interests rather than use their political mistake to exalt himself. By becoming the universal Hose heir, he preserved the family's landed interests in himself, which was better than that they be confiscated. There are several other such examples from the period, see Crouch, *Reign of King Stephen*, 128–32.

[68] *Chronica Majora* v, 213–15.

[69] Suger, *Vita Ludovici Grossi*, ed. and trans. H. Waquet (Paris, 1964), 42, 70.

[70] '*cels de Garlanda*' were characterised by Bertran de Born in a sirvente of 1182 as those closest to King Philip II, see *Poésies complètes,* 18.

find a similar group at the comital (or count's) court in the 1120s, the lineage of Erembald, castellan of Bruges. His sons occupied a similar place at the court of Count Charles of Flanders as the Garlandes did at Paris. It was the attempt to discredit and overthrow them by their rivals that led to the shocking murder of Count Charles in 1127, and the subsequent root and branch extermination of the kinship group.

Defending Lineage and Parage

Between them, the concepts of lineage and parage dominated medieval lives. They could be the making of a man, however undeserving. Naturally enough, those who did not possess either and had great ambition and talent were likely to resent the way of their world. So alongside the literature in praise of nobility there existed critiques of the idea of nobility by birth, whose roots are equally ancient. In William Peyraut's *Summa* of Vices and Virtues (*c.*1240) appears the theological view that all the sons of Adam were essentially equal. Yet in stating this to be so, Peyraut was doing no more than theologising Juvenal's ancient humanist aphorism that 'true nobility is virtue'.[71] The criticism of nobility in medieval society was directly connected with the meritocratic sentiments of Ancient Rome, where noble descent was also everything to a man's success. It was Boethius, declaiming from the ruins of the Antique world, who brought this criticism to medieval attention in his perpetually influential work, *The Consolation of Philosophy*:

> *All humankind on earth arises from the same origin; there is one Father of all things ... He locked into limbs spirits brought down from their high abode. So did a noble seed produce all mortals. Why shout about your lineage* (genus) *or your forbears* (proavos)*? If you consider your beginnings and God your author, no man is now degenerate save who, embracing baser things in vice, forsakes his proper origin.*[72]

Boethius was by no means the only late Roman thinker to broadcast ideas of equality to posterity. Gregory the Great stated with powerful economy that 'Nature makes all men equal'. Unlike Boethius, Gregory was not offering any social teaching in that statement, it was a theological state-

[71] A. Murray, *Reason and Society in the Middle Ages* (Oxford, 1978), 274–5.
[72] *De Philosophiae Consolationis*, Book 3, c. 6. As pointed out in Murray, *Reason and Society*, 272.

ment of equality before Death and Judgement, but social teaching might eventually be drawn from it, as Peyraut did.[73]

This sort of criticism of lineage, and the privilege it brought to a few, can be found several generations before Peyraut. It is sometimes forthright, and more often implicit, but is not at all uncommon in the sources between 1120 and 1220. One example of the subtlety of the criticism can be seen in the popular *Roman des Eles*. It was written by a Picard clerk called Raoul de Hodenc around the end of the first decade of the thirteenth century, and is a high-flown catalogue of the virtues appropriate to a true knight, gathered around the defining concepts of *cortoisie* and *larguece*. Nothing demeans a knight as much as parsimony, says Raoul; meanness, boastfulness, envy and pride all come in for criticism. But, strangely, Raoul fails to say anything about lack of lineage. The reason is that, for him, *chevalerie* is acquired, not innate, behaviour; it is taught, and not a genetic gift. Raoul wished to define the qualities of *chevalerie* so his readers would recognise a true knight when they saw one; and they would not have to pick up the message just from his appearance.[74] For Raoul, like the allegorist Alan of Lille in the generation before he wrote, noble birth was a random piece of luck: Alan said that *Nobilitas* was the child of *Fortuna* and the sister of Chance (*Sors*); she had no independent existence outside her mother.[75] For these writers, therefore, noble lineage was only one factor in achieving true nobility.

A different sort of criticism of lineage can be found in the genealogical tract which Peter of Cornwall, prior of Holy Trinity, composed while he was dying in 1220. Peter, an eminent scholar of his day, decided to tell the story of his family, which was composed of landowners long established in the neighbourhood of Launceston. Although his known lineage went back to one Theodulf, a native Cornishman who inherited or acquired several estates in the area at the time of William the Conqueror, it was not his family's noble lineage Peter claimed as its source of distinction, but the curious strand of supernatural visitation which surfaced in each generation, and which was particularly strong in that 'holy man of God', his grandfather Aethelsige (or 'Ailsi'), who was in fact a layman. Aethelsige

[73] As noted by J. Huizinga, *The Waning of the Middle Ages*, trans. F. Hopman (repr. Harmondsworth, 1990), 61–2.

[74] Raoul de Hodenc, *Le Roman des Eles*, ed. and trans. K. Busby (Utrecht Publications in General and Comparative Literature, vol. 17, 1983).

[75] Alan of Lille, *Anticlaudianus*, in, *Satirical Poets of the Twelfth Century*, ed. T. Wright (2 vols, Rolls Series, 1872) ii, 396, trans. J.J. Sheridan (Pontifical Institute of Medieval Studies, Toronto, 1973), 46, 184–6, 193 (dated c.1181 × 1184).

was deliberately portrayed by his grandson as the antithesis of a nobleman: for all his personal dignity and rectitude, he was *simplex*. His father Jordan too was a visionary, and distinguished in his case by many of the personal qualities ascribed to the nobility – he was just, modest, reasonable, cultivated and affable and he was venerated by the entire county – but no reference is made to his blood or descent. Even in dealing with his uncle Bernard, a royal chaplain, Peter is reticent about his courtly connections, and prefers to dwell on the miraculous signs of God's grace in his life. Yet Peter allows himself in the end to slip in modestly that he was a *cognatus* of Earl Reginald of Cornwall, presumably through a late eleventh-century marital connection with the earl's wife's family, the lords of Cardinan. Why did Peter adopt this outlook? For him, an Augustinian of an ascetic London house at the end of his life, true distinction lay not in blood but in the justified faith of his parents, kin and grandparents: *semen sanctum sunt vocati* ('they are reputed to be a holy line').[76] Much the same logic lies behind Stephen of Rouen's elegy for Count Waleran II of Meulan (died 1166): 'arisen from the root of counts, cousin of kings'. It was not lineage that gave Waleran distinction, Stephen said, but that at the end of his life he had spurned the joys of this world, rejected his worldly glory, and become a monk.[77]

Other writers were perfectly direct about their meritocratic agenda. The earliest version of the Prose Lancelot (*c.*1210 x 20), written in Burgundy by a highly-educated lay person, has much to say on the subject of knighthood and lineage. Its author – through the mouth of the Lady of the Lake, his heroine – reflected that immediately after the Creation none was any more noble or of any higher lineage than any other: 'for everybody was descended from the same mother and father'. But – in case she appeared too democratic – the Lady said that the fact that mankind had fallen meant that knighthood had to be founded and located in certain high lineages, more resistant to the corrosive effect of original sin; which admittedly tainted everyone. By the efforts of these lineages the violent and predatory might be restrained. The highest and most noble was the lineage

[76] Peter of Cornwall, 'The Visions of Ailsi and his Sons', ed. R. Sharpe and R. Eastrey, in, *Mediaevistik: Internationale Zeitschrift für interdisziplinäre Mittelalterforschung*, i (1988), 222–34, for the cousinship with Earl Reginald, see p.225. Another such reference to a 'holy line' (*sancta genealogia*) occurs in Osbert de Clare's petition (1140–48) to Abbot Anselm of Bury St Edmunds, nephew of St Anselm of Canterbury, *The Letters of Osbert de Clare, prior of Westminster*, ed. E.W. Williamson (Oxford, 1929), 98.

[77] *Carmen elegiacum de Waleranno comite Mellenti*, ii, 766–70.

of Joseph of Arimathea, through his son Galahaz, which was the fount of knightly Christian kingship. Yet, despite these high claims for lineage, another of the author's mouthpieces, the holy man who acts as father confessor to King Arthur counsels the king that he should not exclude from patronage worthy poor folk just because of their poverty and 'low lineage': beneath their unprepossessing exteriors may be *richece de cuer*. Arthur was to go so far as to get his local justices to inform him of such poor folk worthy of raising to knighthood.[78]

The Prose Lancelot is eloquent about tensions within a society where the lack of lineage was an obstacle to the advancement of capable and honourable men.[79] But the meritocratic views with which it juggles appeared much earlier. Early in the reign of Richard I of England, a writer under his patronage praised the legendary court of Charlemagne because: 'sons of poor vavassors' could arrive at the court as humble men and leave it as dukes or counts.[80] We find such egalitarianism particularly in the literature of love of the mid-twelfth century, and very close to the hearts of its humble clerical authors. Walter of Arras, writing between 1167 and 1178, has one of his characters, the daughter of an emperor, express meritocratic statements, deriding the idea that the man she loved must be of equal status to her, she asks 'what do I care about your ancestors?': such a concern was not 'cortois', 'It rests within the heart of each, whether he be reviled or respected!' (*A cascun en son cuer demore por coi on l'aville u honore*).[81] His contemporary, Andrew the Chaplain – a member of the same court of Champagne with which Walter wished also to be associated – made points which parallel Walter's:

> *Honesty of character alone truly enriches a man with nobility, and makes him thrive with glowing beauty. Since all of us are descended originally from one stock and have all taken the same origin in nature's way, it was not beauty or bodily adornment or even material wealth but only honesty of character which originally brought distinction of nobility and introduced difference of class.*[82]

The Lady of the Lake had said the same. In a Christian society, morality had to refer back to Scripture, and Theology had for centuries provided a

[78] *Lancelot do Lac*, i, pp. 142, 146, 287.

[79] M. Keen, *Chivalry* (London, 1984), 156–7.

[80] *La Chanson d'Aspremont* i, ll. 101–2, and for similar sentiments about the importance of noticing and furthering poor *prodome*, see ibid. i, ll. 1572–4.

[81] *Ille et Galeron*, ll. 4711–20.

[82] *Andreas Capellanus on Love*, ed. and trans. P.G. Walsh (London, 1982), 45.

powerful social critique of hereditary privilege. The fact that all descend from 'one stock' was a Biblical truth which had disturbing implications for the great of the earth and Boethius, as we have seen, said as much in *The Consolation of Philosophy*. The flatterers of kings themselves inadvertently brought this critique of lineage to public attention, and in due course may have wished that they hadn't. If a writer wanted to praise a king, one elaborate way to do it was to catalogue the length of generations that stood behind him; the more the better. But if he went too far, he ended up with Adam 'the father of all mortal lineages' as Ailred of Rievaulx had to acknowledge in the ambitious genealogical tract he presented to Duke Henry fitz Empress of Normandy early in 1154. A critical mind, like Andrew the Chaplain's, might well then echo Boethius and ask why nobility lay in one lineage rather than another, since everyone went back to Adam. Andrew had an answer and it repeats Boethius: nobility lay not in the lineage but in the conduct of individuals.[83]

Alexander Neckam, son of a lowly citizen of St Albans, said much the same at much the same time as Andrew wrote. He subtly theologised his reply to Boethius by saying that nobility derived both from virtue and descent. When a man chose to behave nobly he was following the example of God, source of all nobility and creator of Adam. When a man behaved ignobly, he was following the earth that was Adam's mother. For Neckam, distinguished birth was peripheral to nobility, a mere adjunct.[84] Ailred's answer – by contrast – prefigured that of the author of the Prose Lancelot. He fled the implications of the argument that nobility lay elsewhere than in descent, and said that nobility lay in the special, Messianic nature which descended in the highest lineage. Descendants of Seth son of Adam shared the Easter quality of 'resurrection' of which Seth – who had replaced the dead Abel – was the prototype. He also worked into his royal lineage of Duke Henry, Melchizedek, the priest and king who prefigured Christ.[85]

83 *Andreas Capellanus on Love*, 49: 'Originally one and the same nature brought forth all mankind, and all would have remained equal up to our own day had not greatness of soul or honesty of character begun to mark men out at different levels of nobility'.

84 Neckam, *De Naturis Rerum*, 244.

85 Ailred of Rievaulx, *Genealogia regum Anglorum*, in, *PL* 195, cols. 716–17. For other twelfth-century royal genealogies which terminated with Adam, or at least with the sons of Noah, see the *genealogia* of King Edward the Confessor compiled at St-Evroult around 1120 from English sources, Orderic Vitalis, *The Ecclesiastical History*, iv, appendix I, p. 352; see also that of King William of Scotland compiled by Ralph de Diceto, *Radulfi de Diceto decani Lundoniensis Opera Historica*, ed. W. Stubbs (2 vols., Rolls Series, 1876) ii, 35; and see that of Gruffudd ap Cynan (d.1137), in, *A Medieval Prince of Wales: the Life of Gruffudd ap Cynan*, ed. and trans. D. Simon Evans (Llanerch, 1990) 23–4, 53–4.

And so thanks to Ailred (and happily for the flatterers) kings and the most noble could truly be said to be marked out by birth, and lineage had hereditary qualities to give it meaning.

The disagreement all too evident in these twelfth-century views of the worth of lineage must echo contemporary tensions. Some writers fulminated against men of no birth who were raised by princes to power over men of great lineage. Orderic Vitalis in the 1130s delivers the loudest broadside, disapproving of Henry I of England for raising up men of 'base stock' (*ignobilis stirps*) who had proved their worth to him, and loading them with favours, while overthrowing and disinheriting the more eminent. Orderic – the Anglo-Norman monk of no notable birth – was not speaking for himself. He was a man of his age, enamoured of high birth, who was reporting the ill-feeling of the higher aristocracy of his generation. Geoffrey of Monmouth was a man of the same age who did exactly the same. He created a felon-king, Argal, whom he criticised because he overthrew men who were *nobiles* and raised up in their place men who were *ignobiles*. A century and more later Matthew Paris described the hostility amongst the court nobility when Henry III created his clerk John of Gatesden a knight in 1244, and gave him a noblewoman as wife, 'and so he rose to the status of a great nobleman'. He also hinted at the subsequent conspiracies to overthrow John amongst those of the nobility who were offended by the elevation.[86]

This criticism was not only generated within the area of the oppressive Norman-Angevin monarchy. The earlier (mid-twelfth century) portion of the epic, *Raoul de Cambrai*, portrays the Emperor Louis outrageously raising up from nothing a stipendiary knight, Giboin of Maine, by disinheriting the noble Raoul.[87] From about the same time and also from north-eastern France comes a powerful satire which drips with venom for the wealthy parvenu, reversing with rhetorical panache the social theology of the Magnificat:

Throughout the whole world, kings and princes
offer lordship over the poor to these usurers;
they esteem them and elevate them
and respect them as much as if they were their own sort.
Behold what miracle Mammon has accomplished,

[86] *Chronica Majora*, iv, 403.

[87] Orderic Vitalis, *The Ecclesiastical History*, vi, 17; Geoffrey of Monmouth, *Historia Regum Britanniae* i, *Bern Burgerbibliothek, MS 568*, ed. N. Wright (Cambridge, 1984), 32: *Raoul de Cambrai*, ed. W. Kibler and S. Kay (Paris, 1996), ll. 535–63.

raising the proud and overthrowing the humble!
Wonder at such sovereignty, that God may lay it low!
Stand aghast at this irony, so may God destroy it![88]

So it seems that the Capetian lands experienced the same tension, which was a consequence of the ability of the king to control marriages, and marry off noble women to men of no lineage, if he chose. These men were voicing the disgruntlement of established lineages about the rise of men of less lineage, or none at all. But those established twelfth-century lineages had to take some blame. One or two of them found it irresistible to exalt their own ideas of their virtue by creating genealogies that traced their fortunes to a remote and obscure ancestor who rose from poverty to great power, as the counts of Anjou did, claiming the ultimate founder of their dynasty as a simple forester.[89]

The 'new men' would have considered their social aspirations as being perfectly respectable, and the Boethian arguments about meritocracy and innate nobility either come from them, or pander to them. Between them, these opposing groups of advantaged and disadvantaged men created a social debate. The debate confused the thinkers of the twelfth and thirteenth century. Anyone who reads the contradictory views on nobility collected by Daniel of Beccles can see this. Daniel apparently loved a lord, or at least he believed in being respectful and circumspect towards one. But at the same time he made a number of sarcastic comments concerning love of lineage and high birth: 'Soon enough the names of grandfather and forbears are blown away in the wind; do what deeds you may, worms will be your next heir.'[90] It may not have been their intention – their intention was to further their fortunes – but in debating the value of established lineage, these writers were sharpening a critique of medieval society which could be employed by those who wished to change and overthrow it. When he considered the consequences of common descent, Ailred of Rievaulx was visiting the same dangerous territory as John Ball, the radical mendicant preacher, over two centuries later, who was reported by Froissart as asking: 'If we all spring from a single father and mother, Adam and Eve,

[88] *Poésies Inédites du moyen âge*, ed. M. Édélestand du Méril (Paris, 1854), 315.

[89] For this, C.B. Bouchard, *Those of my Blood: Constructing Noble Families in Medieval Francia* (Philadelphia, 2001), 14. For a convenient survey of this topic, see R.V. Turner, *Men Raised from the Dust* (Philadelphia, 1988), 1–15. Contemporary curial commentators on the phenomenon include John of Salisbury, Walter Map, Peter of Blois and Gerald of Wales.

[90] *Urbanus Magnus*, 10.

how can they claim or prove that they are lords more than us?' This was by then an old question. Alexander Neckam, a man of greater intellectual courage than his fellow-abbot, Ailred, had not been afraid to ask a similar question two hundred years earlier: 'Why are the present generation of noblemen asserted to be noble from their birth, when their predecessors were of the most debased life?'[91]

The fact that lineage and parage could be criticised in such a lively and ascerbic manner in sources between 1100 and 1300 is testimony enough that they and their consequences – rather than the idea of family structure – were the concepts which stood at the heart of medieval nobility. Because they drew the fire of commentators, they were clearly big and recognisable targets. Perhaps it is just as telling that the practice of primogeniture did not get such attention in literary sources and social tracts. If primogeniture was transforming medieval society it was not something of which medieval people were conscious. As individuals, they were more conscious of the need to assert their own honour and distinction by praising their ancestors and numbering their kinsmen. If they had no ancestors and kinsmen to boast of, they were equally as keen to argue that honour and distinction could nonetheless be found in their own personal nobility of conduct. The fact that they were willing to argue against the importance of lineage was just as important as the fact that others were arguing in its favour. It was not a simple matter of social snobbery. In medieval society there were more material advantages to gain from belonging to a distinguished lineage than in contemporary societies, where boasting of lineage would be simple snobbery. From medieval lineage came self-confidence, recognition, respect and deference, even when it did not bring land or possessions by inheritance. From parage came connections, patronage, protection and a whole world of possibilities.

[91] Neckam, *De Naturis Rerum*, 244.

CHAPTER 6

Inventing Snobbery

In the last chapter I came close to describing a universal mechanism of the use and abuse of noble descent, from Ancient Rome to the France of St Louis and the England of Henry III. But in the chapter before that I warned solemnly about how ideas of continuity in family structures may mislead us. So now comes the corrective. Something undoubtedly did change in ideas of nobility and descent between 1100 and 1300. It was perhaps a consequence of what is called the 'twelfth-century renaissance', the increase in levels of literacy and education which led to a more self-conscious society. Educated clerics discussed and put forward social concepts, and disinterred in their support the views of the humanist writers of Greece and Rome. They did not keep the arguments to themselves. The debate embraced the educated and aspirational amongst the lay nobility. One thing they debated, as we have seen, was the mismatch between blood and merit. But there was a much more pressing reason why the idea of lineage, which was already old, should suddenly become more important and self-conscious an idea in the later twelfth century. The perception of injustice about the abuse of parage, the disadvantages to which lineage and parage put the talented nobody, tell us that barriers raised by the concept of lineage were beginning to be resented. These barriers were being erected because nobility was becoming more than just a matter of descent, but a matter of what step you stood on in society.

The Evidence of Heraldry

There are some 'lineage markers' which help us plot the change. The one that has recently begun to engage the attention of academic historians is heraldry. Something resembling heraldry begins to be noticeable soon after 1100. We can observe the great nobles of England and north-east France beginning to take coloured and symbolic devices which identified them on their military equipment, on banner, surcoat and shield. There are a number of theories why this should have happened. The oldest one, and the one most likely to be true, is the problems caused by the anonymity of a fully armoured knight under his hauberk, ventail and helmet.[1] In battle and tournament, where capture meant ransom, it was very necessary to know who were your friends and enemies. The most likely direct stimulus for heraldry was the tournament. This is because the earliest heraldry is that associated with the persons of counts and other great magnates. The way that the tournament developed in the eleventh century was that great magnates led teams of knights on to the field. The task for a count's team was to safeguard their lord and employer from capture, so it was most important to know who and where he was. Heraldry assisted in identifying him and rallying to him. This theory of the tournament origin of heraldry is supported by the fact that in the middle of the twelfth century, the lord was made even more conspicuous by hanging heraldic covers on his horse. Although heraldry was useful too in the circumstances of battle, its early development was clearly more geared to the circumstances of the tournaments (which were in any case far more frequent than military campaigns). Although we glimpse common knights carrying uniform equipment that identified them as belonging to a lord's company in the 1150s and 1160s, the only individuals early heraldry identified were the lords themselves.[2]

What is highly significant for changing ideas of lineage in the Anglo-French aristocracy is the correspondence between the devices which early twelfth-century magnates took. The first identifiable armorial devices linked to lineage are those of the great families allied to the northern French house of Vermandois, which boasted of imperial descent. This symbol (a chequy pattern) appear on seals of the counts of Vermandois and Meulan in the 1120s and 1130s. Retrospective evidence finds the same symbol employed by the related comital houses of Leicester, Warwick and Warenne before the 1180s. In the 1140s and 1150s seals also reveal another lineage-based device used by the houses linked to the earls of Hertford and Pembroke (the *Clarenses*) who boasted of Norman ducal descent. The device in this case was of chevrons (inverted 'V's), a pattern derived from the rafters of the noble hall. It may have been selected

[1] See on this A. Ailes, 'The Knight, Heraldry and Armour: the Role of Recognition and the Origins of Heraldry' in, *Medieval Knighthood*, iv, ed. C. Harper-Bill and R. Harvey (Woodbridge, 1992), 1–21

[2] For the model of early tournament development given here, see D. Crouch, *The Tournament: An Aristocratic Way of life* (London, 2005), chs. 2, 9.

deliberately to allude to the great hall under whose roof the lineage was all gathered. These early examples of lineage-based heraldry straddle the Channel, and reveal of a common perception of what lineage was in the lands between Paris and York. It also tells us that noble lineage was not perceived as needing to be agnatic or patrilineal. The Vermandois check alludes to Carolingian imperial descent, but that descent for the Meulans and Warennes was through two female heirs. For the Warwicks it was through three women. The Vermandois check talks as much of perceptions of parage, as we examined them in the last chapter, as it does of lineage. Everyone wanted to be tied vertically into the imperial descent of the Vermandois, but the allied comital houses were equally keen to refer to each other. So much so that if the count of Meulan, the earl of Warenne and the count of Vermandois ever rode out on the same tournament field, there was some risk of confusion as to who was who.[3]

Heraldry started as a matter for the elite in society. The very fact of its exclusiveness made heraldry very attractive. In the thirteenth century, knights, too, aspired to such symbolic declarations of nobility, although the earliest knightly heraldry tends to copy that of the great houses to which the knights were allied by service, as if pretending that they also shared their lineage. This tendency of symbols of nobility to travel down the social scale is something we will be dealing with in Chapter 7 in greater detail. What we need to look at here is something different. This is the other tendency in heraldry as the twelfth century passed, which was to focus closer on lineage than parage. Early heraldry is something of symbolic minefield. It had no rules, other than social imperatives. It was not by any means unknown for great noblemen to use multiple devices, and apparently to change them at a whim. For instance, Ranulf III, earl of Chester (died 1232) features on his seal of *c.*1199 a rampant lion. But on his seal in use after 1217 he features the more familiar device historically associated with Chester, wheatsheafs, in a group of three.[4] We can only

[3] I have argued this elsewhere in, 'The Historian, Lineage and Heraldry', in, *Social Display and Status in the Middle Ages*, ed. P.R. Coss and M. Keen (Woodbridge, 2002), 17–37.

[4] *The Charters of the Anglo-Norman Earls of Chester, c.1071–1237*, ed. G. Barraclough (Record Society of Lancashire and Cheshire, cxxvi, 1988), for descriptions of seals see nos. 209, 211–13, 233, 248, 253, 272, 281, 282, 285, 294, 297, 300, 301, 303, 308, 311, 320, 334, 351, 352, 372, 379, (lion) 273, 274, 310, 386, 387, 392, 402, 410, 413, 425, 432, 436 (three wheatsheafs) 409 (six wheatsheafs). For comments and illustrations, T.A. Heslop, 'The Seals of the Twelfth-Century Earls of Chester' in, *The Earldom of Chester and its Charters*, ed. A.T. Thacker (Journal of the Chester Archeological Society, 71, 1991), 179–97, esp. 193–5. Smith Ellis, the

speculate why he did this, but it is clear at least that he felt still that his own heraldry was under his control, to change at his will. The heroic crusading earl of Leicester, Robert IV de Breteuil (died 1204) is another example. Before he became earl in 1190, his counterseal showed the Vermandois check, which advertised the distinguished royal parage to which he belonged. After 1190 he took up a different device, a five-leaved flower (cinquefoil).[5] This individualistic gesture may have been an allusion to the flower name of his famous mother, Petronilla (Pernel) de Grandmesnil, but what it also did was to redefine the family of Leicester as a lineage apart from others. We know this, because his sister, Countess Margaret of Winchester, and his nephew, Robert de Quincy, both later used the same device on their seals.[6]

Another example of this concern to emphasise lineage can be seen in the practice which heralds call 'differencing'. At its full development in the fifteenth century, the system of differencing elaborately ensured that every coat of arms was different one from the other. Brothers might take the same basic arms as their father, but each placed marks of 'cadency' on his shield to show how far removed from the fount of lineage he was. Only the eldest son in the end took his father's arms undifferenced after he had died. In the twelfth and early thirteenth century this system was unknown. Brothers and cousins might carry the same arms, for part of the purpose of arms was to advertise parage. The shift towards emphasising lineage becomes evident in the growth of primitive and ad hoc differencing. Some of this process is perhaps hidden from us. In the case of the Vermandois check, for instance, it could be suggested that the branches of the parage subtly differentiated their device by means of colour in early days; the Clare chevrons tend to be different in number on each early depiction.[7] But the appearance of differencing within both these heraldic families in the thirteenth century tends to indicate that there had been no differencing in earlier generations. To encourage differencing there was also the prag-

inspired Victorian writer on heraldry, made the point that Ranulf's grandfather married a daughter of Robert Earl of Gloucester, whose 1140s coinage (as we now know) featured a single lion, as did his son's seal, so Ranulf III's lion arms may be a parage emblem, see, W.S. Ellis, *The Antiquities of Heraldry* (London, 1869), 181–2.

[5] D. Crouch, *The Beaumont Twins: the Roots and Branches of Power in the Twelfth Century* (Cambridge, 1986), 212.

[6] *Age of Chivalry: Art in Plantagenet England, 1200–1400*, ed. J. Alexander and P. Binski (London, 1987), no. 141.

[7] It is worth noting here that when coloured depictions of the arms of the Vermandois parage appear in the thirteenth century, the shields of the Meulan, Warwick and Warenne descendants are all blue and yellow.

matic fact that tourneying could become confusing if several participants carried the same heraldry. A good example of the change can be found in the way that the Clare and Vermandois group fragmented symbolically. The Warwick arms was by the 1230s differenced either by a diagonal stripe (a 'bend') or a chevron superimposed on the blue and yellow check. In the 1230s the Monmouth and Montfichet members of the Clare parage used bends and labels to personalise their own lineage's heraldry.[8]

The appearance of specialist heralds during the thirteenth century no doubt assisted the fragmentation of the older parage-based heraldry into more individualised and narrower lineages of shields. Heralds, working to begin with in tournaments, and later nationally, compiled directories of arms, which must have generally demonstrated the bad practice of sharing arms. As knights began to be allowed the privilege of arms in the mid-thirteenth century, the capacity for confusion on the fields of honour must have become an irritant to these emerging professionals. By the mid fourteenth century the court of the Earl Marshal of England was adjudicating between knights who claimed the right to the same arms. The assumption by then was that a coat of arms must be specific to one individual and his direct heir.[9] Yet even so, despite the new concentration on lineage, heraldry did not ever become strictly patrilineal. As early as the first decade of the thirteenth century, according to Matthew Paris, Otto of Brunswick, king of Germany, was 'impaling' (dividing a shield vertically in half to display two shields) his imperial arms with those of his uncle King John of England, as a symbol of kinship and alliance. In the late thirteenth and fourteenth centuries, new practices of marshalling and 'quartering' arms (subdividing the shield vertically and horizontally into four sections) allowed a man to incorporate the heraldry of his mother's family in his arms, if she was its last heir. So Hugh de Balliol, son of Devorguilla, lady and heir of Galloway, incorporated his mother's arms in an interior escutcheon on his paternal Balliol shield in the 1290s.[10] Even later heraldry, it seems, was not exclusively agnatic.

[8] D. Crouch, *The Image of Aristocracy in Britain, 1000–1300* (London, 1992), Figs. 9 a–b.

[9] Henry of Grosmont's argument that he had a right to his father's arms was contested by the Crown in 1325, but conceded by default, see A. Ailes, 'Heraldry in Medieval England: Symbols of Politics and Propaganda', in, *Social Display and Status in the Middle Ages*, ed. P.R. Coss and M. Keen (Woodbridge, 2002), 87–8. In the 1340s it is clear that noblemen claimed a right to inherited arms as a matter of property, and would implead other nobles who used the same arms, see A.R. Wagner, *Heralds and Heraldry* (Oxford, 1939), 20–4.

[10] G. Henderson, 'Romance and Politics on Some Medieval English Seals', *Art History*, i (1980), 36–7; A. Murray, 'The Arms of Emperor Otto IV: English Influence on German Heraldry', *The Coat of Arms*, new ser., 11 (1995), 75–81.

Heraldry tells us a good deal about the slowly elaborating views of family. What it reveals is that twelfth- and thirteenth-century society was not moving decisively towards patrilineal, agnatic lineages, so much as narrowing the concept of lineage more tightly on its antiquity. Aristocratic society was in love with the glamour of noble descent, too much so to worry whether it came from mothers or fathers. It used heraldry indiscriminately. So William, son of Ela, the last countess of Warenne of the old line, called himself 'William de Warenne' and used the Vermandois check to link himself to the parage of his mother, rather than allude to his father, Hamelin. His father was the bastard brother of King Henry II, but even so it would not have been a dishonourable or impossible option for William to link himself into the royal house of Anjou, which included kings of Jerusalem as well as England. He chose not to do so. William's bastard nephew, Richard, the illegitimate son of King John, acted differently. Richard had been born from a liaison between John and William's sister, and indeed he called himself in his seal 'Richard de Warenne', but he took his heraldry from his father, and his seal features two Angevin lions passant.[11]

This indiscrimate tendency in early heraldry can best be interpreted as a consequence of the overmastering power of the idea of the antiquity of lineage.[12] I started Chapter 4 by saying how family and the antiquity of lineage was at the heart of the idea of nobility. If there was ever a way of making such a power tangible, it was heraldry. A coat of arms deliberately evoked the inheritance of privilege and wealth that descended with the lineage. Not suprising therefore that its reference to horizontal links between great lineages had weakened by 1230. Not surprising also that representing female lineage was quite as important in heraldry as representing male descent. By 1300 this glamour of antiquity and nobility was proclaiming itself everywhere. Monastic gatehouses and stained glass featured not just with the arms of their patrons, but also those of neighbouring magnates, as at the Augustinian priory of Kirkham. As you

[11] For a representation of Richard's seal, Oxford, Bodleian Library, ms Dugdale 21, fo. 36r. The charter was issued in the name, *Ricardus filius regis Iohannis*, but the seal legend reads + SIGILLUM RICARDI DE WAREN... For his father's heraldry, A. Ailes, 'The Seal of John. Lord of Ireland and Count of Mortain', *The Coat of Arms*, new ser., 4 (1981), 341–50.

[12] I differ here from the view in, P.R. Coss, 'Knighthood, Heraldry and Social Exclusion', in, *Social Display and Status in the Middle Ages*, ed. P.R. Coss and M. Keen (Woodbridge, 2002), 56, who puts the indiscriminate use of arms down to kinship, but see the urban and abbatial examples below.

approached its gates, you knew it had powerful friends. When Edmund, earl of Cornwall, financed the rebuilding of the choir of Hailes abbey between 1270 and 1277, heraldic tiles bearing his arms covered the floor, and not just his arms, but those of his cousin the king, his father's former wives and the greater magnate houses of England.[13] Furniture, stonework, floors and ceilings, glass, utensils and horse harness blossomed with heraldry in the thirteenth century.[14] Even towns and abbeys, which had no lineage and rode in no tournaments, adopted shields of arms. When they did so, it was not kinship or descent that made them do it, but the power of the past and its association with nobility.

The Evidence of Death

Death was a constant challenge to the concept of lineage, in a way that it was not to concepts of parage. Death could extinguish a lineage, but not a parage. Theorists of death culture argue that the death of a nobleman was a particular challenge to the whole concept of nobility. In the face of the challenge of mortality, enormous expense and efforts were undertaken to manage the whole social trauma. One of those efforts involved the appropriate commemoration of the departed nobleman in an appropriate setting.[15] Medieval people did not go so far in this as those of the post-Reformation period, nonetheless there was an astonishingly rapid development in the practice of erecting individualised tombs in recognisably exclusive locations within churches during the later twelfth century. Since this was precisely the period when the idea of lineage was gaining ground against parage, we might be tempted to link the two developments.

Whether or not the sociologists and anthropologists of death are correct in their theories, death culture does reveal some telling indications of attitudes to lineage between 1100 and 1300. Burial and commemora-

[13] *Age of Chivalry*, no. 131. Edmund's stepmother, Beatrice of Falkenburg, as well as featuring armorially on the Hailes tiles, is depicted in glass with the heraldry of the queen of the Romans in a window deriving from her burial church of the Franciscans in Oxford, P.R. Coss, *The Lady in Medieval England, 1000–1500* (Stroud, 1998), pl. 1.

[14] J. Cherry, 'Heraldry as Decoration in the Thirteenth Century' in, *England in the Thirteenth Century*, ed. W.M. Ormrod (Stamford, 1991), 123–34.

[15] For an overview of sociological and anthropological ideas on elite deaths, which originate from Durkheim's ideas that society is an entity which can be damaged by the loss of one of its members, D.J. Davies, *Death, Ritual and Belief* (London, 1997), 11–19. For ideas about the replacement of the deceased with a constructed and commemorative 'social body', N. Llewellyn, *The Art of Death* (London, 1991), 46–53.

tion practices are the obvious first place to look, and many historians have done so, although it is an area which presents problems. The mausoleum church is frequently cited as an important dynastic marker. The abbey church of St-Denis, near Paris, is an important, but perhaps misleading example of this. Various Merovingian, Carolingian and Capetian kings had found their last resting place in its crypt, but even so it was by no means the invariable burial place of first choice for the eleventh- and twelfth-century kings of France. Louis VI (1109–37) was buried at St-Denis, but his son Louis VII (1137–80) intended from the first to be buried at the Cistercian abbey he had founded at Barbeau near his palace of Fontainebleau. Subsequent royal burials occurred at St-Denis, but the foundation of the magnificent Cistercian house at Royaumont by Blanche of Castile in memory of Louis VIII (1223–28) attracted the burials of lesser Capetians. It was not perhaps till Louis IX comprehensively refashioned the burials at the abbey in 1263 that St-Denis became the great dynastic mausoleum and monument to French kingship that it remains.[16]

England, by comparison, had nothing resembling such a dynastic mausoleum for its kings. Royal Westminster before 1272 had only Edward the Confessor and his great-niece Queen Mathilda II in residence. Of the Normans, the Conqueror and his queen lay at Caen in separate abbeys; William Rufus at Winchester; Henry I and his second queen at Reading; Stephen, his queen and eldest son at Faversham in Kent; and the Empress Mathilda at Bec-Hellouin in Normandy. The Angevin dynasty before Henry III was buried variously at Rouen, Fontevraud in Anjou and Worcester. Each generation of English kings from 1066 to 1272 planned its own personal burial church. Between them the history of the burials of French and English royal families caution us that lineage did not necessarily require generations to lie together in a prestigious church awaiting the end of the world.

Nonetheless, the idea of lineage could still impinge on burial practices. Churches could attract patronage and interest because they contained the remains of members of a lineage. King Henry I of England built Reading abbey as a personal project in the 1120s, deliberately choosing the the Cluniac order because of the magnificent scale of the liturgy of commemoration it offered. His body was buried there in January 1136 in front of the high altar, and his second wife joined him in 1151. The fact that King

[16] E.A.R. Brown, 'Burying and Unburying the Kings of France' in, *Persons in Groups: Social Behaviour as Identity Formation in Medieval and Renaissance Europe*, ed. R.C. Trexler (Binghamton NY, 1985), 241–66.

Henry was buried at Reading encouraged further related burials. His great-grandson, William, son of Henry II, died an infant and was buried at the feet of his ancestor in 1156. Henry I's illegitimate son, Earl Reginald of Cornwall, chose Reading for his last resting place in 1175. The abbey did not give up hope of future royal patronage, and the abbot wrote in 1160 to Queen Eleanor, little William's mother, and tried to interest her in the spiritual benefits that the commemoration of his house could offer her. The queen seems not to have taken up the offer. The link between Reading and royalty was by no means ended however. In 1397, King Richard II wrote to the abbot urging him to have the tomb of his remote ancestor put in good repair, as he had apparently seen how dilapidated it had got. He refused to renew the abbey's privileges until the repairs were done.[17]

Aristocratic examples parallel what we know about royal lineages and death culture. The counts of Eu in Normandy, as much as any other noble family, were buried in a variety of places. Count Robert (died *c.*1093) rested at the family's earliest monastic foundation of Le Tréport, on the Channel coast. His son William (died *c.*1096) was buried in England, at the collegiate church of Hastings. The next two counts, Henry I (died 1140) and John (died 1170), were buried side-by-side in the chapter house of the Augustinian abbey of Eu as canons, 'and thus father and son became brothers' (as their elegy noted). Count Henry II (died *c.*1191), by contrast, was buried in the relatively new Cluniac abbey of Foucarmont, in the south of his county. What is significant about this is the way we know about it. The reason is that the resting places of all the counts of Eu were noted down and inserted in a chronicle for the benefit of later members of their lineage. The family may have been dispersed in death, but the lineage nonetheless kept track of where they all were, not just the counts, but also their wives and other children. From this we discover that the lesser members of the lineage in the twelfth century, about a dozen of them, were customarily laid before the roods of the abbey churches of Foucarmont and Eu.[18]

[17] For royal burials at Reading, *The Chronicle of John of Worcester* iii, *The Annals from 1067 to 1140*, ed. P. McGurk (Oxford, 1998), 214–16; Robert de Torigny, *Chronica*, in, *Chronicles of the Reigns of Stephen, Henry II and Richard I*, ed. R. Howlett (4 vols., Rolls Series, 1885–9) iv, 189, 268. See also, C.R. Cheney, 'A monastic letter of fraternity to Eleanor of Aquitaine', *English Historical Review*, li (1936), 490; *Reading Abbey Cartularies*, ed. B. Kemp (2 vols., Camden Society, 4th ser., 31, 33, 1986–7) i, 107–8.

[18] *Chroniques des comtes d'Eu* in, *Recueil des historiens des Gaules et de la France,* ed. M. Bouquet and others (24 vols., Paris, 1869–1904) xxiii, 440–1.

The nearest thing surviving to a picture of such a dynastic repository of burials from the twelfth century is a woodcut made for Jean Mabillon by an eighteenth-century Maurist monk of the house of Préaux in Normandy (see plate section). The abbey is long gone beneath the turf, but once it was a church under the advocacy of the Beaumont family, counts of Meulan in France, and earls of Leicester and Warwick in England. Members of four generations of the family were laid to rest in the abbey. The founder, Humphrey de Vieilles, was buried before the high altar, but the next three generations found their final home under the chapter house floor. After the death of Count Waleran II of Meulan, the greatest of them all, in 1166, the five tombs in the chapter house were capped by flat stones, carved in relief with civilian effigies of each of the deceased, all under Romanesque canopies. This is the image which survives, giving us some idea of how they had looked.

It does not seem from the arrangement of the Beaumont effigies that the corpses had been exhumed and reordered after 1166, as had happened when Louis IX tidied up the kings laid at St-Denis. The two eleventh-century brothers, Roger de Beaumont and Robert fitz Humphrey, had been placed side by side. The twelfth-century sculptor indicated their antiquity by depicting them with staffs, and Roger, the *chiés de lignage*, with a patriarchal beard. The next to be laid beneath the floor was Robert, count of Meulan (died 1118), who was placed beside his father, to make a row of three. His younger brother, Earl Henry I of Warwick (died 1119) was placed at the feet of his father and brother, so as to commence a second row, presumably because the restricted width of the Romanesque chapter house would not permit a further addition. The earl's nephew, Count Waleran, was placed beside him in 1166. Count Robert and Earl Henry were carefully distinguished by the sculptor with comital swords, with Robert's image apparently inspired by the portrait on his seal. Waleran's effigy alone lacked any insignia to proclaim his status.[19] Taken together, they make a fine and solemn study in lineage, proclaiming both modest piety and quiet pride, a stone gallery of great noblemen fit to inspire their progeny. That this was their purpose, we know from a story

[19] J. Mabillon, *Annales ordinis sancti Benedicti occidentalium monachorum patriarchae*, v (Paris, 1738), 329. The monk who produced the woodcut clearly knew who was buried in the chapter house, but was guessing at who was below which stone. The identifications I give here are I think more accurate than his on the basis of the imagery and sequence of deaths. Count Robert's effigy at Préaux and on his seal both show him in civilian garb, with the sword held point down in front of him, an unusual pose. An original of his seal is to be found at University of Keele, Robert Richards Collection 72/46/1(1).

recorded in the chronicle-cartulary of Préaux. During the minority of Count Waleran, the abbey was experiencing difficulties with his officers in the nearby town. So the abbot requested the fifteen-year-old boy to come and visit the abbey. When he arrived, the abbot took him into the chapter house and stood him 'before the tomb of his father and his other kinsfolk' and lectured him on his duty to protect the abbey, and with the dead lineage as witnesses, begged him to call off his men. In such company, Waleran had little choice but to intercede for his monks.[20]

Wars, reformations and rebuilding campaigns have left us precious few original dynastic groupings of tombs from the twelfth and thirteenth centuries. For instance, we know that William Marshal and at least two of his sons were buried at the Temple Church in London, and both church and effigies survive. But the Church's choir was rebuilt in the mid-thirteenth century, causing the effigies to be removed from their original site. Victorian restorers moved them again, and German bombs shattered and damaged them in 1941. Apart from William's effigy, because it is so stylistically early, we can never be sure who the others represent. But in England, the suggestive fragments of what was in its day one of the greatest of these dynastic groupings do survive: the tombs of the Clare and Despenser families at Tewkesbury abbey. The abbey's chronicle tells us that, as well as the *chiés de lignage*, Robert fitz Hamon (died 1107), it had a very distinguished collection of thirteenth-century corpses and visceral burials (burials of intestines removed during embalming, ranged in front of and around the high altar. There was quite an impulse in the family to rest at Tewkesbury. Countess Isabel, the remarried widow of Earl Gilbert (died 1230) and mother of Earl Richard, could only send her heart to be buried next to her former husband at the high altar, which caused some conflict on her deathbed in 1239 with her then husband, the earl of Cornwall. He wanted the rest of her body buried at his father's abbey of Beaulieu in Hampshire whereas she had wanted it all to lie at Tewkesbury.[21] The Despenser family, which succeeded the Clares as advocates of Tewkesbury in the fourteenth century, remodelled the great chevet of the abbey. As a symbol of her own view of their lineage, and the abbey's place in embodying it, Eleanor de Clare (died 1337), who had brought Tewkesbury to the Despensers, installed in the clerestory of the chevet a series of family portraits in stained glass, from Robert fitz Hamon, up to her husband

[20] Cartulary of Préaux, Archives départementales de l'Eure, H 711, fo. 115v.

[21] *Annales de Theokesburia*, in, *Annales Monastici*, ed. H.R. Luard (5 vols., Rolls Series, 1864–9) i, 113–14.

Hugh. Any mid-fourteenth-century visitor to Tewkesbury – with its daily chantries for the great thirteenth-century earls of Gloucester, its solemn anniversary masses, its glowing glass portraits and the ubiquitous armorial devices of the chevrons of Clare and frets of Despenser – would have had little doubt that the abbey was as much a powerful expression of lineage as of the worship of God. To consolidate the image of an uninterrupted line, the fourteenth-century artist invented appropriate heraldry for the pre-heraldic lords, Robert fitz Hamon and Earl Robert.[22] We can only guess now at how many of these glorious medieval evocations of family lineage and dignity in art and ordered monuments have been lost in France and England.

The Evidence of Literature

The power of the concept of lineage was impossible to escape in the twelfth and thirteenth centuries. It became more intrusive in society as means were devised to represent it symbolically and ritually, and as the written record was devoted to the exaltation of the pride of great families. The very fabric of churches and halls radiated pride in past generations down upon the lesser folk within. But there were other ways in which the power of lineage could be captured and projected onwards. Lambert of Ardres, a clerk of the county of Guines in Flanders, devoted himself to the composition of an entire tract to memorialise the two lineages of Ardres and Guines, of which he was himself a minor member. Lambert began his research into the family history in 1194 after falling out with his kinsman, Count Baldwin II. His genealogical history was intended to curry favour with the count. In fact he seems to have got interested in the project for its own sake, and finished it after the count's death in 1206. His research method relied very much on the memory of older men, such as Walter du Clud, who, he tells us, delivered to him the history of the lineage of Ardres from oral sources. But Lambert wove his anecdotes into a chronological framework derived from written histories of the region.[23]

The end result of Lambert's work was the creation of an image of two interweaving lineages springing up like Jack's beanstalk – or perhaps Jesse's root – from the remote past. Lambert proudly enumerated the 233

[22] G.McN. Rushforth, 'The Glass in the Quire Clerestory of Tewkesbury Abbey', *Transactions of the Bristol and Gloucestershire Archaeological Society*, xlvi (1924), 289–324.

[23] For the background of the text, Lambert of Ardres, *The History of the Counts of Guines and Lords of Ardres*, trans. L. Shopkow (Philadelphia, 2001), 2–8.

years the lineage of Guines had lasted already when he began his work in 1194, and smugly proclaimed how envious people were of the great antiquity of his line. He took care to make it clear that the *chiés de lignage*, one Siegfried, who settled at Guines in 928, came from a noble and even older comital lineage and that there were earlier links by marriage with the royal family of Denmark.[24] Lambert portrayed his family and its county continuing down the generations and the centuries, erecting symbols of its power, such as the fortress of Guines and the abbeys of Andres, Licques and Guines, all the time allying with neighbouring great families and absorbing the distinction of their lineage. The family of Guines, too, had its mausoleum, the abbey of Andres, whose monks told Lambert that it had been built as the place where all the members of the lineage were supposed to be buried, and that they had to be consulted if the corpses of counts and countesses were to be buried elsewhere.[25]

The *History of the Counts of Guines* is a unique history of a lineage. There is nothing else quite like it from the twelfth and thirteenth centuries. The famous biography of William Marshal has very little to say on the Marshal's ancestors, other than his devious father, John. Indeed, its author and his sources, the Marshal's sons, seemed to know less about the Marshal lineage than we do in the twenty-first century. Twelfth-century Anjou, however, produces two parallels. John of Marmoutier compiled from earlier sources in the 1160s a collection of sketches of successive counts of Anjou. An anonymous clerk, well aware of the genealogical materials compiled concerning the lineage of the counts of Anjou, embarked at the same time on a similar exercise in favour of the lords of Amboise, on the marches between the Touraine and Blesois. These Angevin tracts come closest in intention and detail to Lambert's work, and there are parallels between all three. The authors were intent on proving the antiquity of the lineage back into the tenth century and Carolingian times, and both Lambert and John closely identify the fortunes of county and family. But the Angevin works are far less detailed and varied than Lambert's. Georges Duby was of the opinion that these tracts were once a widespread genre in twelfth-century France, outside Normandy, but have almost all been now lost. This is very unlikely, and his suggestion arises from his belief that lineage formation was a product of 'feudal mutation'. To reduce his argument to its basics, if lineage was a new and overmas-

[24] Ibid., 58–9, 60.
[25] Ibid., 91, 118.

tering concern of the aristocracy of France, then there had to be a massive genealogical literature, even if it does not survive.[26]

In fact the genealogical history was merely an extreme form of that medieval lust to rejoice in ancient lineage, and the superior feeling of nobility which it encouraged, an agreeable feeling which was promoted also by heraldry and burial practices. The *History of the Counts of Guines* is a symptom therefore not of lineage formation – the idea of lineage was already ancient – but of class formation, which is why it appears when it does. The idea of lineage was much older than the idea of hierarchical class. It was while that class consciousness was solidifying in the later twelfth century that lineage took on a new importance, and was brought much more to the fore by writers and the aristocrats they were trying to please. For it was a solid justification for why some families should be superior to others. Not everybody liked it. As we have seen, from the early twelfth century onwards, lay people became acutely aware of the injustice implicit in the use of kinship to advance individual fortunes and to pervert public peace.

But, for all the criticism, the power of lineage had been unleashed in the twelfth century, and it could not be suppressed. Superiority through family antiquity and connections was deeply imprinted on every aspect of thirteenth-century life. There was no escape from it even in the aisles of churches. And it had to be so, because upon it was built the superiority of some social groups over others. Those lesser non-noble groups for the most part consented to the conspiracy of lineage. Indeed, they were still consenting to it in the nineteenth century. It is no surprise to find that such consensual and indulgent attitudes survived to be satirised by Dickens, as in the conversation at the dinner party of the snobbish and middle-class Waterbrooks in *David Copperfield*.

We must have Blood, you know. Some young fellows, you know, may be a little behind their station, perhaps, in point of education and behaviour, and may go a little wrong, you know, and get themselves and other people into a variety of fixes – and all that – but deuce take it, it's delightful to reflect that they've got Blood in 'em! Myself, I'd rather any time be knocked down by a man who had Blood in him, than I'd be picked up by a man who hadn't!

[26] G. Duby, 'Remarques sur la littérature généalogique en France aux xie et xiie siècle', repr. in *La société chevaleresque* (Paris, 1988), 167–80, published in English as, 'French genealogical literature: the eleventh and twelfth centuries', in *The Chivalrous Society*, trans. C. Postan (London, 1977), 149–57, esp. 150, 153–4.

We are looking at the dawn of snobbery as a conscious social mechanism. Adam Smith called it 'emulation' and Max Weber called it 'consensualism', but 'snobbery', the fawning abasement to those with a speck of nobility, is a more accurate word for this aspect of lineage. In the next part of this book we will see how its consequences played out in a true transformation of society into a hierarchy of social classes.

PART THREE

NOBLE CLASS

CHAPTER 7

Historians and Noble Class

The idea that there was a characteristic medieval social order which included social class was established in British historiography well before the end of the nineteenth century, and it had nothing to do with Karl Marx. It was the legal tradition in English history which stands at the root of this perception of class. The key thinker was Sir Henry Maine (1822–1888). In his great work, *Ancient Law* (1861) Maine proposed the idea of a 'social state' which had an evolutionary line of progression out of the 'primitive'. Social evolution was for him revealed by the way a society's legal system developed. Once a society had evolved the idea of a contract, entered into by individuals, then a man's status floated free of family and clan and (amongst other things) social classes might develop. He explored how this would happen in his later work on medieval manors (1869). If, as he believed, the idea of lordship was imposed in the middle ages on what he believed were originally 'free' villages, then this would naturally tend to create social levels. The inferior tenants would have to enter into a contract of dependency on the lord whom the king had imposed on them, who would be their social superior.[1] Maine's work lies at the root of many of the basic questions of the developing discipline of sociology, and the historiography of the ideas of family and of class begin with him and his circle of correspondents (see also Chapter 4). Despite Engels' churlish claim in 1884 that Maine had said nothing that the *Communist Manifesto* had not said in essence twelve

[1] H.J.S. Maine, *Ancient Law* (London, 1861); idem, *Village Communities in East and West* (3rd edn, London, 1876). For a comprehensive, if now dated, survey of Maine's significance, G. Feaver, *From Status to Contract: A Biography of Sir Henry Maine, 1822–1888* (Longman, 1969), chs. 5, 9.

years before *Ancient Law*, Maine provided a mechanism to explain the appearance of social class rather earlier than Marx did.

The British and Class

1. Maitland and the Domesday Bug

In his native Britain the wonder is how Maine's eclectic and visionary approach to basic questions of social history simply evaporated after his death; yet it did. He founded no school, and his successors in the chairs of jurisprudence he had held at Oxford and Cambridge were men of more insular outlook and concerns. The nearest thing to an intellectual heir he had in Britain was Frederic William Maitland (1850–1906). Maitland would have been deeply annoyed at that statement, for he found Maine's tendency to give universal significance to his ideas tiresome and pointless.[2] He was not Maine's pupil; he found his reactionary politics abhorrent, and his generalisations and inaccuracies fruitless and annoying, yet in one important respect they were alike. Both believed a key to understanding societies was the law they generated, and they could both put this forward in a compelling way. But the scope and methodology of each man was very different, and Maitland wrote only about England.

The echoes of Maine are very clear when Maitland talked of class. He believed, or at least assumed, that England in the thirteenth century possessed 'legally constituted classes'. By this Maitland meant that there were different sorts or estates of men, and the distinction between them was that they held land by a variety of tenures. Like Maine, it was tenure, for Maitland, which was the essence of social distinctions, such as those between serf and free tenant. The principal difference between the two men was Maitland's method in exploring medieval society. Trained in documentary criticism of a high order at Cambridge by Henry Sidgwick, and inspired by Paul Vinogradoff (1854–1925), Maitland took to the archives with an energy and discrimination rarely matched since. From his first work on the Gloucestershire plea roll of 1221 Maitland applied himself consciously to the reconstruction of English medieval society from its legal and administrative relics. As Stephen D. White has amply demonstrated, Maitland's methodology preserved him from the unsupported generalisations that go hand-in-hand with ambitious theorising.[3] But, although he could see and tell

[2] F.W. Maitland, *Domesday Book and Beyond,* (repr. London 1960), 398

[3] S.D. White, 'Maitland on Family and Kinship', *Proceedings of the British Academy*, 89 (1996), 91–113.

everyone that the emperor of theory had no clothes, it has to be said that Maitland had few constructive suggestions as to where his imperial majesty might find a pragmatic figleaf to cover his embarrassment.

When it came to ideas of social class and aristocracy, Maitland remained a lawyer. This comes out in his matter-of-fact observation that Common Law recognised no noble or gentle class: 'all free men are in the main equal before the law'. Then, sensing the puzzlement of readers who knew well that there were other views on the subject than those of legal idealism, he hastened to assure them that there were other considerations too. But, as he explained them, these, too, looked constitutional and legalistic. Maitland said that closeness to the king counted and that the king could confer status on those he summoned to court to offer him counsel. In other words, his idea of what barons were was drawn from ideas of peerage law, and of the privileges of the Exchequer bench and *curia regis*. The knights, too, were, for Maitland, defined only against the obligations on them to provide juries in particular cases: they were 'an able, trustworthy class'. For him, the military service and obligations of knights were matters of tenure rather than rank. Determined to pursue the matter of 'knightly class' into the ground, he made the clever, if somewhat obtuse, point that in law the holder of a knight's fee did not in fact need to be a knight. In saying this he demonstrated quite clearly that the study of law was not the best way to approach questions of social class.

But, nonetheless, Maitland made the statement which had the biggest impact on social thinking in England. It is because the social mind of Maitland ran on tenure that he popularised the remarkably influential model of post-Conquest English society as a cone or pyramid of obligation: a construct of medieval social structure which has been regrettably long-lived.[4] Maitland derived the material of his social construct in part from Domesday Book. The enormous mass of evidence that the survey offered was irresistible to him and to many an English medieval historian since: his copy of Farley's edition of the survey was exhibited in his study in the manner of a parish Bible. Social models derived from the Domesday survey dominated and still dominate British social historiography. This

[4] F. Pollock and F.W. Maitland, *The History of English Law* (2 vols., repr. Cambridge, 1968) i, 407–16; for the pyramid image, Maitland, *Domesday Book and Beyond*, 170. Maitland may well have acquired it from Michelet, who referred in 1833 to the ruthless English form of feudalism after 1066 as creating a hierarchy with the king 'solitaire et faible à la pointe de cette pyramide', *Histoire de France* (rev'd edn, 19 vols., Paris, 1879) ii, 266.

was particularly the case with the Domesday tenurial model of social class which Maitland proposed for medieval England. It lives still, although nowadays only as a particularly resistant form of microbe in a hostile ecology. But for well over half a century it dominated social thinking amongst British medievalists. As late as 1969 in his influential *The Normans and the Norman Conquest*, Reginald Allen Brown (1924–1988) talked of 'the social hierarchy of the upper classes' comprehending tenants-in-chief, sub-tenants and knights.[5]

Not every British medieval historian between 1900 and 1970 was in captivity to Maitland by any means, but there was a lack of any alternative model of class structure within British historiography. Maitland had himself discredited the broad approach of Maine, and with it isolated his own pupils and admirers from the growing number of sociologists who were Maine's intellectual successors. Sir Frank Merry Stenton (1880–1967) was a reluctant exception. He managed in 1929 to convey serious unease about any belief in Maitland's hierarchical model of class in eleventh and twelfth century society. But he did so without being so assertive as to oppose its possible existence. He believed with Maitland that there had been rigid status levels in pre-Conquest English society, which were preserved in their law codes, but unlike Maitland he found it different from the less formal and coherent Anglo-Norman world that succeeded it. He noted how confused that society may have been because it drew on immigrants from several regions of France, each with its own tradition. He found post-Conquest social vocabulary to be elusive and unstructured, and believed that this mirrored the Anglo-Norman vagueness about social organisation.[6]

Stenton offered no other principle of social organisation than that of tenure, but his empirical approach to the evidence did at least provoke originality, as empiricism can do when practised by a master of the craft. His post-Conquest English aristocracy was organised around the obligations of tenant to lord for the fee that was given him. So far he followed Maitland. His big step forward was to see that those obligations taken

[5] See on this, D. Crouch, 'From Stenton to McFarlane: Models of Societies of the Twelfth and Thirteenth Centuries', *Transactions of the Royal Historical Society*, 6th ser., 5 (1995), 179–81. For some observations on the hierarchical view of society drawn from the artificial hierarchy of Domesday Book, S. Reynolds, *Fiefs and Vassals: the Medieval Evidence Reinterpreted* (Oxford, 1994), 346–8.

[6] F.M. Stenton, *The First Century of English Feudalism, 1066–1166* (2nd edn, Oxford, 1961), 7–28, note especially his comment on the term *vavassor* in England, 'The term is vague because the structure of society was still indefinite' (p. 23).

together created aristocratic communities of interest, the structures he called 'honors'. Within the honors he found a Maitlandish distinction between the lord of the honor, his greater tenants (the 'honorial barons') and the lesser tenants, organised hierarchically around the holding of property and linked by customary jurisdiction. Even so, the idea that aristocracy could be defined by membership of an exclusive community was novel, and was a step away from Domesday Book. It provided a new way of defining a noble class other than through tenure: in this case by being accepted among the intimates and counsellors of a dominant magnate. Stenton saw the lower reaches of the English aristocracy of the twelfth century as being organised in groups of *compares* (honorial colleagues). For Stenton, aristocracy was about community as much as tenure, and this is his abiding contribution to social history.

2. The New Social History

Surveying medieval social history in the first quarter of the twentieth century in Britain we find either dense and unambitious empiricism on one side, or loose Carlylean 'interpretative studies' on the other. This depressing state of affairs changed in the 1930s. The delicate phrase 'interpretative studies' was crafted in 1933 by Eileen Power, lecturer at Girton College and in 1931 Professor of Economic and Social History at the London School of Economics and described what such historians as George Gordon Coulton or George Macaulay Trevelyan wrote. Power was to some extent a creature of her own age, for her *Medieval People* (1924) was a popular book in the Carlylean mould. Like many of her colleagues she was in no position to do anything other than write to satisfy the popular appetite for medieval social history of the 'Merrie England' sort, a genre so savagely satirised in 1954 by Kingsley Amis.[7] But Eileen Power the teacher was a very different person from Eileen Power the writer. She taught medieval social history with a freedom and openness to theory never before seen in Britain. In the environment of the London School of Economics, with a colleague such as Richard Henry Tawney (1880–1962), socialism, Marx, Sombart and Weber were as much part of the atmosphere as pipe smoke. Although Power found the teleological demands of Marxian thinking unconvincing (she called it 'Hegelian twaddle'), she did subscribe to the idea of social evolution and, like Tawney, believed in the divisive social force of capitalism in western society. For her, therefore,

[7] *Lucky Jim* (London, 1954).

tenure was not the organising principle of class, it was the control of productive labour by a dominant group. It is hardly surprising that Eileen Power found herself so much in tune with Marc Bloch, whose sociological and geographical approach to issues of rural history paralleled her own vision so closely.[8] She invited Bloch to lecture at the LSE in February 1934 and they collaborated in her great projects: the *Economic History Review* and the *Cambridge Economic History of Europe*.[9]

Although she never fulfilled her promise to be to British historiography what Marc Bloch was to French, Eileen Power left one impressive statement of what that historiography might have been, had she lived longer and been more independent of the public appetite for Carlylean 'interpretative studies'. In her inaugural address given in 1933 she mapped out a new sort of social history of the middle ages. It was to be open to insights across the disciplines: anthropology, sociology and economics. It was not to be afraid of conceptualisation and theory; she blithely appealed to Weberian and Marxian ideas. Class was one of the sociological issues she wanted addressed by medieval history, and although she never addressed it, her successors eventually did.[10] Power and her pupil, and later husband, Michael Moissey Postan (1899–1981), formed a new historical school in the 1930s, which, although much declined in influence, still lingers to the present day. Under the leadership of first Power at London and then Postan at Cambridge, social history assumed a new importance, although the influence of Postan tended to make it more an adjunct of the economic and agrarian branch.[11]

Postan and his many pupils and admirers wrote socio-economic history that fulfilled Eileen Power's 1933 agenda. It was a web made up of a variety of strands: agrarian, archeological, demographic, settlement, land-

[8] M. Berg, *A Woman in History: Eileen Power, 1889–1940* (Cambridge, 1996), 208–9, says otherwise, but depends on the unsafe testimony of Postan, who had little sympathy with the preceding generation of English historians.

[9] C. Fink, *Marc Bloch: A Life in History* (Cambridge, 1989), 178–9; Berg, *Eileen Power*, 207–12.

[10] E. Power, 'On Medieval History as a Social Study', in, *The Study of Economic History*, ed. N.B. Harte (London, 1971), 111–22.

[11] A. Wilson, 'A critical portrait of social history', in, *Rethinking Social History*, ed. A. Wilson (Manchester, 1993), 11, presents a fourfold-model of mid-twentieth-century British historiography with 'state' historiography on the right, social history on the left, economic history uneasily in the middle ground, and a continuing strand of literary history. Although debatable, the model does not respect the complications within these groups and traditions, and overestimates the influence of constitutional history outside Oxford.

Plate 1 *Roman de la Rose*. The early 13th-century *Roman de la Rose* was an allegorical exploration of virtue and vice, with each personified. Such exercises encouraged definition in concepts such as Nobility and Courtliness. © Archivo Iconografico, S.A./CORBIS.

Plate 2 Four Cardinal Virtues. Nothing illustrates the success of the Church's moral teaching to the laity than the way the literate laity adopted and explored such images as the theological virtues. Illustration from medieval manuscript by Dominican Friar Laurent. 1279. © Historical Picture Archive/CORBIS.

Plate 3 Tree of Jesse. The Old and New Testaments presented medieval people with many illustrations of vertical perceptions of family. Not least was the Tree of Jesse, illustrating the descent of Christ from King David and Jesse his father. It was being illustrated in stained glass already in the 12th century. It justified theologically the importance of lineage. Stained Glass Window Panel, Canterbury Cathedral. © Angelo Hornak/CORBIS.

Plate 4 Woodcut of the Beaumont family tombs. This woodcut (made by an anonymous Norman monk early in the 18th century) illustrates the layout of the 12th-century Beaumont family tombs in the chapter house of the abbey of St-Pierre-de Préaux (destroyed during the Revolution). It is a rare glimpse of the original ordering of a medieval dynastic mausoleum (see pp. 165–6). From Jean Mabillon, *Annales Ordinis Sancti Benedicti Occidentalium Monachorum Patriarchae*, Volume V (Paris, 1738). Reproduced by permission of the British Library.

Plate 5 St Denis (west front). The great abbey of St Denis, outside medieval Paris, was a focus of Capetian dynastic identity as early as the reign of Louis VI (1108–37). By 1250 it had achieved its status as the mausoleum of the French monarchy. Basilique Saint-Denis, France/www.bridgeman.co.uk.

Plate 6 Charles-Louis de Secondat, Baron de Montesquieu (1689–1755), was one of the founding intellects of the study of western history. He is responsible for first articulating many perceptions of the middle ages, not least 'feudalism' in its characteristic French form. © Archivo Iconografico, S.A./CORBIS.

Plate 7 Sir William Blackstone (1723–80) stands in much the same relation to English perceptions of feudalism as Montesquieu does to French. His influential textbook on English law gave it a legal-tenurial tinge that it still retains. Painting attributed to Sir Joshua Reynolds. © Bettmann/CORBIS.

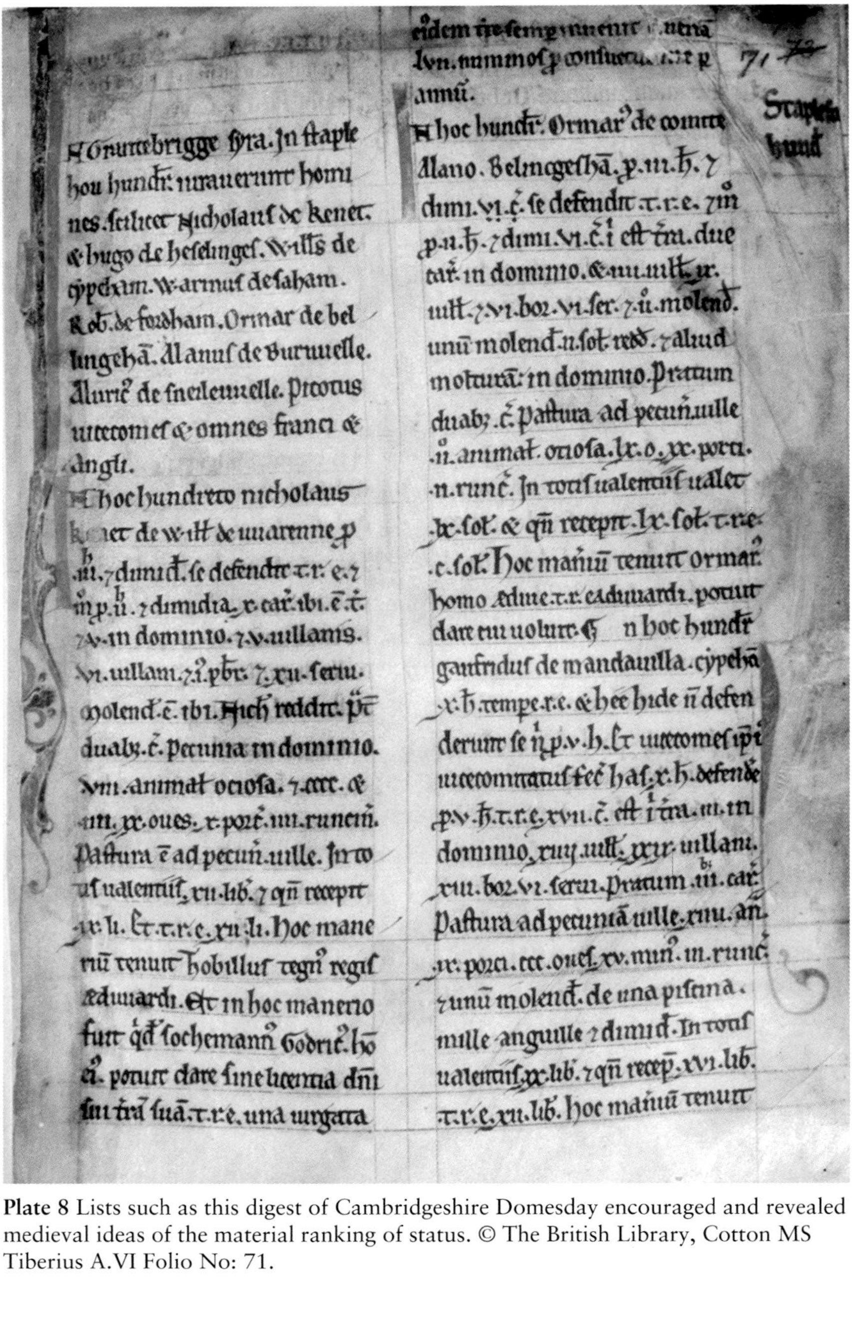

Plate 8 Lists such as this digest of Cambridgeshire Domesday encouraged and revealed medieval ideas of the material ranking of status. © The British Library, Cotton MS Tiberius A.VI Folio No: 71.

Plate 9 Sir Frank Merry Stenton (1880–1967) was arguably the most influential writer on medieval aristocracy in Britain in the 20th century. He discovered a new communitarian focus for study of society in the mechanism of the 'honor' (see pp. 176–7). The Stenton Collection, © University of Reading.

PLATE 10 Women spectating a tournament. Nothing illustrates the importance of women to the tourneying society of the late 12th and 13th century than the invariable depiction of great numbers of them spectating the exploits of their husbands and lovers. Ms 645-647/315-317 t.II f.59 A Tournament (vellum), French School, (15th century). Musee Conde, Chantilly, France. Lauros/Giraudon / www.bridgeman.co.uk.

scape, industrial and urban. It was not the result of any radical change in methodology. The methodology was founded on the same empirical standards of proof that would have satisfied the great Manchester social empiricist, James Tait, but the result was different because of the variety of the stances employed and the great range of evidence. This can be seen in the continuing work of Postan's pupils Richard Britnell, John Hatcher and Edward Miller (1915–2001). But Postan and his pupils and admirers did not write specifically social history. Had they done so they would have soon noticed a major gulf in their project. They continued Maitland and Vinogradoff's great work on villeins, manors and towns, to which a number of scholars, notably Stenton, H.P.R. Finberg (1900–1974), George Caspar Homans (1910–1989), Reginald Vivian Lennard (1885–1967), and Rodney Hilton (1916–2002) had since contributed. But this left an increasingly large gap in the history of medieval society in England, signalled when Postan suddenly noticed with some surprise at the end of his career in 1972 that the English medieval peasant had been far better served by the twentieth-century historian than was his landlord.[12] It is a curious fact that, despite British historiography's supposed fixation on 'feudal society', very little analytical work was written after Stenton on the English medieval aristocracy as a social group.

An early symptom of a realisation that the writing of post-war social history was still inadequate to its potential was the group of social historians who, in 1952, combined to publish a new journal, known by the disconcertingly Carlylean name of *Past and Present*.[13] The opening manifesto of the journal decried the 'new positivism' of the econometricians as producing an inadequate social history, masking jejune analysis with dense jargon; it appealed instead to the inspiration of the Annales group in France. It staked a claim to be continuing the 'scientific approach' handed down by nineteenth-century scholarship, and in that sense it was playing the part of J.B. Bury in its generation to the 'neo-positivists'.[14] The members of the *Past and Present* board did tend to approach social history in broader and more diverse ways than the Cambridge econometrists. It

[12] M.M. Postan, *The Medieval Economy and Society* (repr. Harmondsworth, 1975), 174. For the sudden interest in nobility as a concept after the 1960s in a European context, T. Reuter, 'The Medieval Nobility', in, *Companion to Historiography*, ed. M. Bentley (London, 1998), 177–8.

[13] The journal got its name from a series of wartime worker education historical pamphlets which went by the name of 'Past and Present' published by the Cobbett Press, 'Origins and Early Years', *Past and Present*, no. 100 (1981), 5.

[14] 'Introduction', *Past and Present*, no. 1 (1952/53).

was *Past and Present*, for instance, which first published in 1968 Georges Duby's celebrated essay on cultural diffusion, translated by Rodney Hilton.[15] It was probably the first time Duby's existence was brought to the attention of the majority of British historians, and the first evidence of a rapprochement of methodology between British and French social historiography since the brief intellectual flirtation between Eileen Power and Marc Bloch in the 1930s.[16]

Explaining Class Formation

1. The British and Aristocratic Communities

How did Stenton's great insight about aristocratic class being a product of community flourish in this new climate, to which he himself was not sympathetic? Rodney Hilton's 1966 work, *A Medieval Society: The West Midlands at the End of the Thirteenth Century*, was a deliberate attempt to graft the new social history on to the stock of medieval history. However it ended up by revealing, more clearly than ever before, the importance of the concept of community in noble class formation. Hilton was a product of Oxford and a pre-war student of the agrarian historian, Reginald Lennard, working on Leicestershire manors.[17] Lennard's own work was rooted in Domesday studies and the concerns of Maitland and Vinogradoff, and although an Oxford historian, his methodology had most sympathy with Tait's Manchester. Hilton, on the other hand, developed into a radical Marxist historian with a strong sense of the need for change in the historiography of his own day.[18] His book on the West Midlands was a conscious effort to apply some of the Annalist methodology to English circumstances. He did so by looking at the economy, topography and society of a region, in the same way that Bloch had looked at the Île-de-France in 1913, Boutruche at the Bordelais in 1947 and Duby at the Mâconnais in 1953. The Annalist influence is equally evident in the

[15] G. Duby, 'The Diffusion of Cultural Patterns in Feudal Society', *Past and Present*, no. 39 (1968).

[16] Anglo-French studies were by no means absent in the intervening period however, E. Miller, 'The State and Landed Interests in Thirteenth-Century France and England', *Transactions of the Royal Historical Society*, 5th ser., ii (1952), 109–29, demonstrated the continuing comparative historical strength of the Power-Postan school.

[17] R.H. Hilton, *The Economic Development of some Leicestershire Estates in the Fourteenth and Fifteenth Centuries*. (London, 1947).

[18] See his initial article, 'Capitalism – What's in a Name?', *Past and Present*, no. 1 (1952/53), 32–43.

overlapping of geographical, economic and social analyses. Hilton's Marxism is not particularly evident, although it can be found in some unexamined presuppositions: notably that feudal lay and ecclesiastical landlords occupied a sphere distinct from commercial urban society, and were necessarily a drag on the development of capitalism. In areas where you might expect it – such as in the conflictual nature of social class – you cannot find his Marxism at all, instead you find the consensualism of Weber.[19] Hilton was not following the Duby model in its entirety, for he did not look at the Annalist *longue durée* (the long term): he offered only a study of the final quarter of the thirteenth century. Duby had surveyed his region over three centuries.

Rodney Hilton's study of the West Midlands is not his most satisfying work, largely because it was meant to be the introduction to a second volume which would analyse the same region between 1300 and 1500. Social groups appear within it as misleadingly static. But the book is still important in demonstrating that there had been movement in British social historiography after the Second World War. As Hilton presented it, class structure was hierarchical on the familiar Domesday model, with barons, honorial barons and knights presiding over peasants of varying degree; he employed the vocabulary of Stenton in his description of levels of tenure within the aristocracy. Naturally also, the relationship between the class of landlords and their dependents was portrayed by Hilton in a Marxist way: the peasants owed their lords their labour, and this (rather than legal-tenurial dependence) was what subordinated one class of man to another. Manor, village communities and urban society are treated in ways that Maitland, Vinogradoff and others pioneered. Trade and economy are dealt with as the Postan school would have done. But although it may all seem derivative, Hilton's eclectic approach to the question of social organisation was something new. What was particularly new for medieval studies was his use of the post-medieval work on gentry by R.H. Tawney and Lawrence Stone. The existence of a gentry community was important for Marxist-influenced models of social organisation, because, by their account, it was the gentry who would one day trigger the political revolution of the seventeenth century. But in projecting this community back to the thirteenth century, Hilton was offering a new way of constructing medieval noble identity (and one which was of course satisfying to a scholar with a Marxist world view).

[19] R.H. Hilton, *A Medieval Society: The West Midlands at the End of the Thirteenth Century* (Cambridge, 1966), 176–7, 217–18.

Hilton's *Medieval Society* offered some new thinking on English medieval social structure, but it also showed how the weight of evidence still heavily burdened British historiography, especially when searching for the levels of status within the aristocracy. This remains a problem to this day, although recent contributions have developed ways of containing it. One way is by examining a microcosm of medieval society, and so limiting the evidence which has to be examined. When, in 1991, Peter Coss published (also with the Past and Present Society) a socio-economic study of the Warwickshire town of Coventry and its hinterland between 1180 and 1280 he wrote the book with the same concerns as Rodney Hilton, to whose school he belonged. He also wrote more determinedly in the Annales tradition and, like Duby, endeavoured to employ the totality of available evidence. The evidence is copious, even though the area he surveys is only sixty-four square miles in extent. The result is an insight into a local society to a depth and intimacy beyond anything that could be accomplished in contemporary France. Coss's book reveals the full Namierite complexity of his chosen microcosm, in the interplay of relations between magnates, local landowners and the urban community. Coss proves that the full range of sources for English society simply cannot be easily comprehended, even for the year 1200, but he showed how it could at least be made manageable.

Other than unveiling that complex interplay of communities, Coss has written with the same concerns as Hilton, particularly in his search for 'the gentry'. By 'gentry' Coss means us to understand a local landowning elite with the same aspirations and ethos as the higher baronage, but at a lower gradation in the accepted hierarchy. But local community as it was, the gentry had a wider concern with the realm, and the king recruited his local office-holders from it. For Coss, the thirteenth-century local knights of Warwickshire could be regarded as the first impulse towards gentry formation, although it was not to come fully into effect until the middle of the next century, with its self-conscious hierarchical ranking of knight, squire and the gentleman. The lower gradations of gentry he sees as already present in embryo, in rising families of lesser landholders, men with links to estate administration, or men whose fortunes were based on trade and property in urban Coventry.[20]

[20] P.R. Coss, *Lordship, Knighthood and Locality: A Study in English Society, c.1180–c.1280* (Cambridge, 1991), esp. ch. 9, and see the more detailed treatment now in his, *The Origins of the English Gentry* (Cambridge, 2003), 58–65, app. II–V.

The idea of 'gentry' (unknown to the French[21]), just like Stenton's 'honor', represents a further facet of the English tendency to see class expressed in community, rather than as expressed by noble privilege. It is a concept of social division which chiefly belongs to the historian of the early modern period, and was of particular interest to early twentieth-century Marxist and Marxian historians, for it was a social class which was believed responsible for crisis, and eventual revolution' in the seventeenth century. But the 'origins' of the gentry could be projected back with good reason into the middle ages, and gentry has been for decades a common concept amongst social historians of the fourteenth century. The English word 'gentrye' was in use in that century, although in the sense of 'good birth' rather than as meaning a social group. But common concept or not, it has been notoriously difficult for historians to define what the gentry were in any period, and where membership of it began or ended.[22]

In the period before 1300 the tendency amongst historians has been to relate the 'proto-gentry' to the social group of county knights, recognised as a partner in dialogue with the Crown since the time of King John (1199–1216).[23] A collective local identity, as Peter Coss has said, is one of the principal means of defining a gentry community, and knights were being treated as representatives of their shires in the reigns of the early Angevin kings of England.[24] Coss's verdict is, however, that the gentry did not appear fully formed until the first half of the fourteenth century, and it is a concept of limited use in understanding society before the second half

[21] See the contextualisation offered by, F. Lachaud, 'La "Formation de la *Gentry*", xie-xive siècle: un nouveau concept historiographique?', in, *Histoires d'outre-Manche: tendances récentes de l'historiographie britannique*, ed. F. Lachaud, I. Lescent-Giles and F-J. Ruggiu (Paris, 2001), 13–36, esp. 15–16.

[22] P.R. Coss, 'The Formation of the English Gentry', *Past and Present*, no. 147 (1995), 40–3. Coss has subsequently provided a detailed rationale for the definition of the gentry, *The Origins of the English Gentry,* esp. p.11.

[23] C. Richmond, 'The Rise of the English Gentry, 1150–1350', *The Historian*, no. 26 (1990), 14–17, who uses the term 'proto-gentry' (p. 15); J. Scammell, 'The Formation of the English Social Structure: Freedom, Knights and Gentry, 1066–1300', *Speculum*, 68 (1993), 601–18, operates under this assumption.

[24] Coss, 'The Formation of the English Gentry', 48–9; for the representative function of knights, developing as early as Henry II's reign, see J.C. Holt, 'The Prehistory of Parliament', in, *The English Parliament in the Middle Ages*, ed. R.G. Davies and J.H. Denton (Manchester, 1981), 1–28; J.R. Maddicott, 'Magna Carta and the Local Community, 1215–1259', *Past and Present*, no. 102 (1984), 25–65. See also the comments as to how central authority created local communities in, C. Carpenter, 'Gentry and Community in Medieval England', *Journal of British Studies*, 33 (1994), 375–8.

of the thirteenth century, and, in that, he is in agreement with other historians of the aristocracy of the later middle ages. He also warns that the application of the term 'gentry' to the twelfth century and earlier means applying a broad model of later medieval society to an earlier society which it did not much resemble.[25]

Nonetheless, some early English medievalists have tried to appropriate the term: John Blair used it to comprehend the emerging manorial lords of tenth- and eleventh-century England, a group he also called 'gentleman farmers'. Although his use of terms is loose, he is not alone amongst writers on early medieval society in looking for gradations within the landed elite lower than the tiny group of ealdormen and earls around the king.[26] Coss would deprecate the necessity, as he is working within a late medievalist's idea of what nobility was, and how social hierarchies were formally managed and acknowledged. He may be right in these circumstances to want to restrict the use of the term 'gentry' to the fourteenth century. If so, it would probably be better also not to use the term 'proto-gentry', as that implies that the gentry were the natural end result of an earlier process. But Coss does not dispute that English society before the fourteenth century, and before the twelfth century, was conscious of levels of wealth and influence below the magnates.

As well as the honor and the gentry, British medievalists have offered further notional communities in their search to define the structure of noble class. The late medieval concept of 'gentry' is related to the idea of 'affinity'. An 'affinity' was a social construct formulated by late medievalists and is a construct particularly associated with the Oxford historian, K. Bruce McFarlane (1903–66).[27] Later medieval magnates lived above and beyond localised elites, but they were interested in dominating them so as to dominate certain localities. So they recruited from the gentry communities to enhance their own local power, and they created overlapping

[25] Coss, *Origins of the English Gentry*, 239ff. For later medievalists, see the summary in, C. Given-Wilson, *The English Nobility in the Late Middle Ages* (London, 1987), 14–19, and the comments in N. Saul, *Knights and Esquires: the Gloucestershire Gentry in the Fourteenth Century* (Oxford, 1981), 6–33.

[26] *Early Medieval Surrey: Landholding, Church and Settlement before 1300* (Stroud, 1991), 160–1. For other examples,

[27] In particular see his classic article, 'Bastard Feudalism', published in 1945 and reprinted in, *England in the Fifteenth Century: Collected Essays*, ed. G.L. Harriss (London, 1981), 23–44. So far adrift from each other are English and French historiographies of the late middle ages, that it was not till 2001 that a French historian offered a translation for McFarlane's term 'bastard feudalism' (i.e. 'pseudo-féodalité'), see Lachaud, 'La "Formation de la *Gentry*", xie-xive siècle', 13.

communities which McFarlane called magnate 'affinities'. Affinities were recruited by magnates by the promise of patronage, by gift and indenture, or by simple fear. McFarlane himself regarded them as a symptom of a new ('bastard feudal') social order which evolved in England in the reign of Edward I (1272–1307). You could therefore object to the dating of the existence of 'affinities' before 1250, as affinities were not possible without a gentry to provide the field of recruitment. Some later medieval historians certainly do not see the point in applying the 'bastard feudal' model of society to the centuries before 1300, even if earlier societies possessed some features that resembled those of later medieval society.[28] Yet this objection really depends on seeing society as evolving, as McFarlane did, from one form into another.

The affinity was as much a fact of earlier medieval society as Stenton's honorial community. Before 1250, just as after 1300, the ambition of a great man to subdue a distinct region to his own will could entice or force lesser local noblemen who were not members of his honor to enter into a dependent relationship. They might do so from fear, or from a desire for his protection, or a desire for his patronage, but the effect was the same as when a later medieval magnate attempted to subdue to his will the gentry and officers of his chosen 'country'. In studying the retinues of William Marshal, earl of Pembroke (died 1219) and Henry II, earl of Warwick (died 1229), I found that both these early thirteenth-century magnates had recruited knights from the areas where their landed interests were concentrated, and they were principally (if not exclusively) knights who were not connected with them by any tenurial links. In the case of William Marshal, he made alliances with lesser local barons – the Berkeleys, the Musards and the Earleys – in order to extend his domination in the West Country. In the case of Henry of Warwick, he went out of his way to retain a group of influential county knights with the purpose of building up his power within the Warwickshire shire court and the Avon valley. Earl Henry seems to have offered them household offices in return for their allegiance.[29] The point has been made that William Marshal had to find novel ways of exerting himself as a magnate, since he inherited little in the way

[28] M.A. Hicks, *Bastard Feudalism* (London, 1995), 104–7, sees the twelfth and thirteenth century as being a phase in the development of the affinity, rather than as possessing affinities essentially the same as those of the fourteenth century.

[29] D. Crouch, *William Marshal: Knighthood, War and Chivalry, 1147–1219* (2nd edn, London, 2002), 143–4, 150–1; idem, 'The Local Influence of the Earls of Warwick, 1088–1241: A Study of Decline and Resourcefulness', *Midland History* xxi (1996), 179–200.

of a landed following: he was an 'interloper'.[30] That was not true of Earl Henry, however. He was the heir to five generations of his family's power in Warwickshire, but he needed to erect an affinity to attempt to dominate his county, as the local families attached to him by links of tenure could not – for whatever reason – assist his ambition.[31] How far back can we plot the existence of the affinity as a means of exerting power? Things that look very like affinities can be found much earlier in England, particularly in the reign of Stephen (1135–54) when the king's local position was badly undermined outside the south-east of his realm.[32]

I have suggested we should think of medieval aristocratic society in the twelfth century as an overlapping network of diverse communities – local, tenurial and informal – comprehensible to itself, however hard it is for modern historians to penetrate its complexity.[33] The fact that British historians over the past two decades have begun to identify and classify what these sorts of communities were, and have begun to demonstrate how they interacted with one another is a major advance in the reconstruction of medieval noble society. The fact that it has happened at all is due ironically

[30] P.R. Coss, 'Debate: Bastard Feudalism Revised, *Past and Present*, no. 131 (1991), 200–1.

[31] D.A. Carpenter, 'The Second Century of English Feudalism', *Past and Present*, no. 168 (2000), 30–71, demonstrates the continued importance of the honor court after 1200 in some honors. His key point is that 'fiscal feudalism' (the need for magnates to maximise the revenue from their honorial tenants) kept the idea of honorial communities alive to the end of the thirteenth century. However, as the case of Warwick demonstrates, the continued existence of an honor court did not necessarily mean that the honor was the principal political vehicle for its lord.

[32] D. Crouch, *The Reign of King Stephen, 1135–1154* (London, 2000), 153–5, 166–7, 237–9. For a summary of recent debate, P.R. Coss, 'From Feudalism to Bastard Feudalism', in, *Die Gegenwart des Feudalismus*, ed. N. Fryde, P. Monnet and O.G. Oexle (Veröffentlichungen des Max-Planck-Instituts für Geschichte, 173, 2002), 91–9. It perhaps should be noted that H.G. Richardson and G.O. Sayles, in their idiosyncratic way, applied the bastard feudal label to twelfth-century English society several years before Stenton died, 'The Problem of the Norman Conquest', in, *The Governance of Medieval England: from the Conquest to Magna Carta* (Edinburgh, 1963), 30–1.

[33] D. Crouch, ' 'From Stenton to McFarlane', 195–200. One must also note here the additional communities reconstructed by Judith Green's work on independent aristocratic communities straddling frontiers in Britain and France, see J.A. Green, 'Lords of the Norman Vexin', in, *War and Government in the Middle Ages: Essays in Honour of J.O. Prestwich*, ed. J. Gillingham and J.C. Holt (Woodbridge, 1984), 47–61; eadem, 'Anglo-Scottish Relations, 1066–1174', in, *England and her Neighbours, 1066–1453: Essays in Honour of Pierre Chaplais*, ed. M. Jones and M. Vale (London, 1989), 53–73.

to the same reason that British historians have been so resistant to theoretical models of aristocratic structures: the great mass of evidence that survives in England from the twelfth century. They have had no choice but continually to go back to the quarry and excavate for more evidence to test the theories presented for their endorsement. The more they have quarried, the richer and fuller have been their own reconstructions of past aristocracies.

2. The French and Privilege

The French tradition of writing on noble class in the middle ages is very different from that of the British. The most radical difference is that where the British tradition emphasised tenure as a way of distinguishing aristocrats from others, the French, for even more deep-seated reasons, emphasised privilege. The earliest form of this idea of class distinction was built on a theory of race and conquest. Count Henri de Boulainvilliers (1658–1722) was alienated by the absolutism of Louis XIV's France, and particularly loathed what he believed the king had done to the aristocracy. He saw the nobility of France as the only power – through its status and privileges – able to resist royal oppression. When he was tutor to the king's heir at the end of the seventeenth century he developed the idea that the nobility's power and rights were as old as France, indeed had created France. His origin-myth of the French nobility was that the 'noblesse d'épée' was descended from the free Franks who had conquered and enslaved the Gauls. This was one of the principal theories behind his great work, *L'État de France* (published posthumously 1727).[34]

Although Montesquieu, the dominating intellect of eighteenth-century French political thought, differed politely but firmly from Boulainvilliers's conclusions, the myth of the 'two races' became well established in French historiography. It is a key theme in the work of Claude-Henri de Rouvroy, count of St-Simon (1760–1825) and his friend and follower, the medievalist Augustin Thierry (1795–1856), who both saw the ancient racial division as lying at the root of social conflict in France. Indeed, Thierry tried to import the theory into post-Conquest England, to explain its later development as a liberation from the Norman yoke.[35] It was generally accepted at the beginning of the nineteenth century in France that

[34] See, R. Price, 'Boulainvillier and the Myth of the Frankish Conquest of Gaul', *Studies on Voltaire*, 199 (1981), 155–85.

[35] J. Walch, *Les maîtres de l'histoire, 1815–1850* (Geneva, 1986), 68–70.

inherited privilege was the source of noble power. So when François Guizot (1787–1874) described the generic lord of a medieval fee, he portrayed him sitting in his castle and dominating his serfs in their huts at his gate; the lord had power over his peasants without restraint, and it was the lord's expectation that this power and privilege should continue in his family down the generations. Since this was the supposed feudal order of noble privilege that the Revolution had swept away when he was a boy, it was hardly surprising that Guizot should fix on that as the defining feature of medieval nobility. He spent his mature years fighting the ultra-royalists who wanted to restore just that sort of noble privilege to post-Napoleonic France.[36]

Unlike Boulainvilliers and Saint-Simon, Guizot had no view on the antiquity of this sort of social organisation, but it remains a commonplace among historians of France, from Montesquieu through Alexis de Tocqueville, Paul Guilhiermoz and Fustel de Coulanges to the present day with Karl-Ferdinand Werner, that the power of a privileged aristocracy over the lesser folk on its landed estates was a continuous feature of society, from the villas of Roman Gaul to the manses of the Frankish period and the manors of the later middle ages. French society was divided between lords and dependents and the legal control of the lord over the men of his seigneurial estate was the defining means of social division between classes.[37] This did not of course mean that historians necessarily believed – as Boulainvilliers did – that the aristocracies who lorded it over the common people in Gallo-Roman, Merovingian, Carolingian and Capetian times had inherited their powers and property from their predecessors. French historiography in the early twentieth century generally assumed otherwise. Henri Prentout, for instance, believed in 1911 that Viking colonisation physically replaced the previous Frankish aristocracy of coastal Neustria, and so produced a Normandy ruled by Scandinavian aristocrats.[38] So when Marc Bloch contemplated the shortness of the pedi-

[36] For Guizot's view, *The History of Civilization in Europe*, trans. W. Hazlitt (repr. Harmondsworth, 1997), 68–70; for de Tocqueville, *L'Ancien Régime et la Révolution* (5th edn., Paris, 1866), 41–2, 45. For the rejection of feudal privilege in Europe in the eighteenth century, see the general overview in, M.L. Bush, *Noble Privilege* (Manchester, 1983), 169–85.

[37] It is what Robert Boutruche called the 'théorie domaniale', *Seigneurie et Féodalité* (2 vols., Paris, 1959) i, 115n. For an earlier statement, M. Bloch, *French Rural Society*, trans. J. Sonderheimer (London, 1966), 64ff.

[38] H. Prentout, *Essai sur les origines et la fondation du duché de Normandie* (Paris, 1911), 219–20, cf. C.H. Haskins, *The Normans in European History* (New York, 1915), 50–1.

grees of the tenth-century French nobility, he concluded that it was because they had none, and that an internal social revolution had by 900 swamped the older Carolingian aristocracy of public service with a new military aristocracy which had risen from below and which served only itself.[39]

Since the French explanation of noble class was based on a competition for privilege, some French historians could see no problem in the idea of aristocracy surviving massive social discontinuities; it was just a change of boot in the back of the poor. Unsurprisingly, since its idea of noble class depended on inherited tenure, British historiography, by contrast, stresses the continuing replenishment of the aristocracy over the centuries by new men rising from below by marriage and money.[40] It has even theorised a sort of legal continuity between the English aristocracy before 1066 and the Norman aristocracy that replaced it as a result of conquest, with the concept that the Normans of 1086 had recognisable English *antecessores* from whom they derived some at least of their property rights.[41] This concentration on materialistic explanations for class, curiously, has opened

[39] Bloch, *Feudal Society* ii, 284–5.

[40] For an early recognition of this fundamental difference of approach, unsurprisingly coming from a Frenchman who had studied medieval England, C. Petit-Dutaillis, *Studies and Notes Supplementary to Stubbs' Constitutional History*, trans. W.E. Rhodes and W.T. Waugh (Manchester, 1915), 53–5. Marc Bloch believed he detected a tendency towards hereditary membership of social class in France, but not in England, in 'Pour une histoire comparée des sociétés européenes', *Revue de synthèse historique*, 46 (1925), translated as, 'A Contribution to the Comparative History of European Societies', in, *Land and Work in Medieval Europe: Selected Papers by Marc Bloch*, trans. J.E. Anderson (London, 1967), 64–7. Both noted the absence of noble privilege in England and that social relations there depended above all on tenure. The difference has been more recently registered in passing by J.C. Holt, 'Feudal Society and the Family in Early Medieval England: I. The Revolution of 1066', *Transactions of the Royal Historical Society*, 5th ser., 32 (1982), 208 '... in the end in England, nobility was defined not in terms of blood or lineage, but tenurially and administratively' and latterly also by Susan Reynolds, *Fiefs and Vassals*, 343.

[41] The 'uninterruptedness' of development in English government and society, despite 1066, was a theme of the writing of Sir Maurice Powicke, see his *Medieval England* (London, 1931), 15. In this same vein, Stenton believed that orderliness was a characteristic of the land transfer between English and Normans, *Anglo-Saxon England* (3rd edn., Oxford, 1971), 626. The thesis of extensive continuity of estates constructed on those of *antecessores* is argued in P.H. Sawyer, '1066–1086: A Tenurial Revolution', in, *Domesday Book: A Reassessment*, ed. P.H. Sawyer (London, 1985), 71–85, and affirmed by J.A. Green, *The Aristocracy of Norman England* (Cambridge, 1997), 48–50.

mainstream English medieval history more to classic Marxist social theory than French historiography, despite its love of periodic social crises.

Since French historians talk in terms of privilege when talking of aristocracy it is no surprise to find that many of them prefer to use the word 'noblesse' rather than 'aristocratie' when they talk of European aristocracies. One argument goes that a medieval 'noble' possessed a recognised superiority over the 'non-noble' which became formalised into legal recognition in 1270, when the French king Philip III first issued a patent of nobility.[42] Similarly the French resort easily to concepts which express privilege. The words commonly used to express these are *seigneurie* (lordship) and *ban* (authority). The Frankish term *ban* appears in Latin documents as *bannus*, and although much used in Carolingian capitularies of the ninth century, it is not a word that is by any means common in the sources after 1000. *Ban* appears in the *Song of Roland* as a verb and a past participle, referring to the summoning of an army and an army that had been summoned. This is its principal twelfth-century sense in the vernacular, creating the noun *banier*, for a herald sent to announce something or summon someone. In fact the word *bannus* in later medieval documents usually signifies a lord's rights over his peasants or townspeople, and rarely implies the extent of his whole lordship.[43] It is important principally because of the way historians have made use of it in the twentieth century, as it is defined in a current French textbook: 'the power to command and constrain; the right to judge capital cases and to issue punishments; power which is based on the control of castles'.[44] Most recently, K-F. Werner has offered the Latin word *potestas* (power) as a substitute for *ban* as being a more relevant and contemporary phrase for the earlier period.[45]

[42] Such was Bloch's view of the 'privileged status' of the nobility, founded on a juridical understanding of noble status, which, as K-F. Werner points out, is still important in French thinking, *Naissance de la noblesse: l'essor des élites politiques en Europe* (2nd edn., Paris, 1998), 126, 135. See also, D. Crouch, *The Image of Aristocracy in Britain, 1000–1300* (London, 1992), 2–3.

[43] See the discussion in, D. Barthélemy, *Les deux ages de la seigneurie banale: Coucy xie–xiiie siècle* (Paris, 1984), 32 and n, who notes the anachronism and misapplication of the word, but can only diffidently offer the substitute, 'regalian lordship'.

[44] Y. Sassier, 'De l'ordre seigneuriale à l'époque féodale', in, *Pouvoirs et institutions dans la France médiévale*, ed. O. Guillot, A. Rigaudière and Y. Sassier (2 vols., 3rd edn., Paris, 1999) i, 186.

[45] Werner, *Naissance de la noblesse*, 232ff. Michel Bur made the word *districtio* comparable to *bannus*, and also noted the applicability of *potestas*, *La formation du comté de Champagne, v. 950–v. 1150* (Mémoires des annales de l'Est, no. 54, Nancy, 1977), 333–4.

Transforming Society

1. France and the Descent of the Ban

It was this historiographical lineage which produced the defining French twentieth-century theory of noble class formation: the 'feudal mutation' or 'feudal transformation' of the year 1000. Like all the best theories, it arose from detailed empirical study, in this case a local study of the Burgundian region of the Mâconnais from 900 to 1200, published in 1953 by the then little-known southern French medievalist, Georges Duby (whom we have met in earlier chapters). Rarely can a doctoral thesis in medieval history have had such a long-term impact, not just in France but, as we have already seen, throughout Europe and America. The 'feudal mutation' involved a lot of interrelated components: increasing population, changes in family structure, greater trade and growing towns, but the important component for us is the mechanism it used to account for changes in relations between classes. When Duby did this he talked, as previous generations of French scholars had done, about the 'ban'.[46] Bloch had already defined the ban as 'the right of coercion', which in France had passed out of the control of the weak Carolingian kings after 900 and into the hands of the new nobility. Possessing the ban allowed noblemen to impose their lordship on lesser men and so create social distinctions. Duby, only a couple of years later, said the same, in his initial exploration of the Mâconnais, although he altered Bloch's time scale.[47] But in his thesis of 1953 he took the whole process a significant step further, towards a theory of class formation.

For Duby it was late in the tenth century that the counts of Mâcon began to exercise the power of the ban – of justice and military command – on their own account rather than the king's, and became a hereditary princely dynasty. The leading men of the local assembly recognised the fact, and increasingly after 950 called themselves the count's *fideles* (his sworn and faithful men). But the descent of the ban did not stop there, at the level of the count. Within two generations, the count's faithful men, the half-dozen local lords who had the keeping of fortresses in the Mâconnais,

[46] G. Duby, *La société aux xie et xiie siècles dans la région mâconnaise* (repr. L'École des hautes études en sciences sociales, 1982), 174–86, gives a useful exploration of the early ban from the analysis of monastic immunities.

[47] *Feudal Society* ii, 406; G. Duby, 'Recherches sur l'évolution des institutions judiciaires pendant le xe et le xie siècle dans la sud de la Bourgogne', *Le Moyen Age*, 52 (1946), 149–94; 53 (1947), 15–38.

were being less than faithful adherents of the count. They were found less and less in the count's court, and after 1000 each local lord began to set up his castle in rivalry to Mâcon, imposing his own ban on the surrounding district and taking control of the local judicial office of *vicarius*, by which he dominated the free people of the district. The descent of the ban therefore set up a new social group, the castellans, as miniature local princes. But the descent continued further. The castellans had created a new subordinate level of men below them: those free local landowners (holders of 'allods') who had no choice but to become vassals of the castellans for their own protection. From 1030 this sub-group of vassals were brought into a contractual relationship of dependence on the castellans by which they received back their lands on new terms after doing homage; they were no longer free to dispose of the land as their own.[48]

Here, at the core of Duby's work, we see the precise difference between English and French approaches to the formation of medieval aristocracy. For Duby it was where the privilege of the ban rested that created class divisions: 'from here on this was the point where nobility began'.[49] Noble tenure was just an incidental consequence of class – not the cause of it. In the end, according to Duby, noble status devolved even to the level of the knight. The eleventh-century castellans of the Mâconnais depended on mounted warriors for their ability to impose justice and assert their ban, as well as to defend themselves from rivals. By 1100 these knights had formed themselves into a hereditary and intermarried group, lords of one village for the most part. They were already by then a 'petty nobility' marked off by domination over the peasants of their demesne estate, their horseback lifestyle and the rite of passage of 'adoubement'.[50] The devolution of the ban was not a painless process. Duby was the heir of the long tradition of Montesquieu, which said that the nobility naturally created 'feudal anarchy' whenever it gained power. Feudal anarchy was what the Mâconnais got in the early eleventh century,

Duby's argument convinced most of his generation, and his theory dominated French medieval historiography until the 1990s.[51] The phrase

[48] Duby, *La société dans la région mâconnaise*, chs. 3–4.

[49] 'cette limite est désormais la frontière de la noblesse', Duby, *La société dans la région mâconnaise*, 196. Quite how central is the descent of the ban to mutationist thinking has rarely been explicitly noted, although the late Tim Reuter is a distinguished exception, 'Debate: the "Feudal Revolution" ', *Past and Present*, no. 155 (1997), 195, who also notes the uniqueness of this approach to France.

[50] Duby, *La société dans la région mâconnaise*, 317–36.

[51] G. Duby, 'Lignage, noblesse et chevalerie au xiie siècle dans la région mâconnaise: une révision', *Annales* (1972), 803–23, in fact revises very little of his initial thesis, although

'feudal mutation' became attached to it in the 1970s; Duby himself in 1953 and again in 1966 had referred to the descent of the ban as a social 'bouleversement' (upset) and on at least one occasion even used the word 'révolution' to describe what had happened. He called it that because he saw (like Bloch) the military aristocracy and its knights as a new and socially disruptive force, needing to be restrained by the peace legislation of the Church. But in 1966 he also called what happened around the year 1000 a 'mutation' (transformation), and the word was taken up by his followers and admirers.[52] His study of the Mâconnais began to be taken as a model for further investigation of French medieval society during the 1960s. Several distinguished monographs duplicated his results in viewing the ban descend socially, marking out social groups as it went, and in seeing the whole process as disruptive to a greater or lesser degree, although few if any found the process quite as anarchic as what went on in the Mâconnais. The leading mind here was Robert Fossier, who, in his study of Picardy published in 1968, certainly found that castellans appeared early in the eleventh century, wielding the ban: 'whose infiltration to lower social levels was what made the period "feudal" '. But, unlike in the Mâconnais, some of the castellans in the counties of his region (Amiens, Vermandois, Boulogne and Flanders) did not achieve political independence: they remained *fideles*, tied to the entourage of local princes, whose own public courts remained powerful throughout the period.[53]

he repeats his difference with Bloch about the newness of the eleventh-century nobility, first stated in, idem, 'Une enquête à poursuivre: la noblesse dans la France médiévale', *Revue historique*, 226 (1961), 10–11. Duby here echoes the findings of early regional studies on Hainault and Anjou, see L. Verriest, *Questions d'histoire des institutions médiévale. Noblesse, chevalerie, lignage* (Brussels, 1959), referring back to idem, *Le régime seigneurial dans le comté de Hainaut du xie siècle à la Révolution* (Louvain, 1916/17); J. Boussard, 'L'origine des familles seigneuriales dans la région de la Loire moyenne', *Cahiers de civilisation médiévale*, 5 (1962), 303–22.

[52] G. Duby, *Le temps des cathédrales: l'art et la société, 980–1420* (repr. Paris, 1976), see esp. p. 45.

[53] R. Fossier, *La terre et les hommes en Picardie, jusqu'à la fin du xiiie siècle* (2 vols, Louvain, 1968) ii, 488–518, for quotation, p. 510 ('sa dissémination à un échelon inférieur caractérise l'époque «féodale»'); see also idem, *Histoire sociale de l'occident médiéval* (Paris, 1970), 95, 'La possession de ce droit, dit le ban, ou sa délégation partielle constituent l'un des premiers critères de différenciation sociale'. For a condensed view, idem, 'Land, Castle, Money and Family in the Formation of the Seigneuries', in, *Medieval Settlement: Continuity and Change*, ed. P.H. Sawyer (London, 1976), 159–68. Fossier's view depended ultimately on the idea of the 'rise of the principalities' in tenth-century northern France, as developed by Dhondt and Lemarignier in an earlier generation, which presented the post-Carolingian princes as a new focus of public order.

Fossier's modification of the Duby thesis persuaded the authors of the second generation of French regional studies. In his researches in the later 1960s and early 1970s Pierre Bonnassie found in Catalonia – the Franco-Spanish march – a period of mutation between 1020 and 1060 similar to that which is supposed to have occurred in the Mâconnais between 980 and 1030. But he significantly compared what went on there not with the Mâconnais, but with Normandy between 1025 and 1047, where there was a period of social disruption, but followed by the reassertion of ducal power. Normandy – because it came back from the brink – was a favoured comparison for the later mutationists. In his 1977 study of the county of Champagne Michel Bur also pursued the comparison with the duchy of Normandy, in Champagne's periodic aristocratic crises in the 1040s and 1060s. The fact that the dukes of Normandy had successfully tamed their nobility in the eleventh-century was powerfully asserted in Lucien Musset's 1976 study of the Norman aristocracy of the eleventh century. He portrayed them as in essence a dependent nobility of the court, 'une clièntele' focussed on its duke.[54] Fossier's has become the more popular version of the descent of the ban, since it allows a more nuanced regional approach and since it accounts for the fact that many regional princes survived the growth in power of the castellans of their realms. Nonetheless, whatever standpoint you follow, it is believed by 'mutationistes' that the descent of the ban happened alike in the Mâconnais, Catalonia, Champagne, the Auxerrois, the Chartrain and Picardy and, according to the mutationist thesis, was the essential mechanism for the formation of the supremacy of a social elite over the bulk of the population.[55]

Currently, the theory of a social mutation around the year 1000 is undergoing reassessment within France. It was never wholly accepted outside France, in Germany, North America or Britain. Its critics have generally concentrated on the problems with the mutationist view of family

[54] P. Bonnassie, *La Catalogne du milieu du xe à la fin du xie siècle* (2 vols., Toulouse, 1975–6) ii, 611; Bur, *La formation du comté de Champagne*, 193–4; L. Musset, 'L'aristocratie normande au xie siècle', in, *La noblesse au moyen age xie–xve siècle: essais à la mémoire de Robert Boutruche* (Paris, 1976), 71–96.

[55] For the ban in the mutationist model of medieval society, see J-P. Poly and E. Bournazel, *The Feudal Transformation, 900–1200*, trans. C. Higgitt (New York, 1991), 10ff, originally published as *La mutation féodale, x^e^–xiie siècles* (Paris, 1980). Poly and Bournazel follow Fossier rather than Duby over the ban in this now standard explanation of the thesis. So also do other regional studies published in the 1980s. D.R. Bates, *Normandy before 1066* (London, 1982) 121–2, takes the Fossier line over aristocratic formation in the duchy of Normandy in the early eleventh century.

and lineage (as we have seen in an earlier chapter) or on its chronology. The idea of the descent of the ban, on the other hand, is one component of the thesis that has been left alone by some of the most redoubtable critics of a 'feudal mutation'.[56] However, some are now even willing to challenge that strand. The principal French critic has become Dominique Barthélemy, who has done a rare thing in French historiography, and looked for counter-models to a dominant French paradigm in the Anglophone world. He has found the material for his criticism in the work of non-French legal historians, claiming they have disproved its basic tenets:

It is from America and Britain that new studies on the resolution of conflict and monastic gifts come to us. Their aim is not particularly to prove the mutationist theory to be wrong but – in treating it with such diffidence – that is still what they have ended up doing.[57]

Barthélemy's reference is not, of course, to traditional British legal historiography but to those Anglo-American scholars who have used French legal sources to examine basic questions of conflict resolution in a violent society. He refers particularly to a study of Stephen D. White on monastic narratives dealing with conflicts and their resolutions in tenth and eleventh-century France.[58] The fact that eleventh-century people resorted to discussions concluded by written settlements (*conventiones*) to end disputes means to Barthélemy that they were as interested in order as the people of the century before, and for them order was not 'public order' but a peace for which all were responsible. What changed in 1000 was not the level of violence but only the way the process was recorded. Barthélemy insists on the point that when historians talk of 'public order' as opposed to 'private jurisdiction' they are making assumptions that early medieval people did not share, they are using the 'statist' language of the nineteenth century.

It follows from this radical language that Barthélemy has come to disbelieve in the idea that the power of the ban descended in the eleventh

[56] As for instance, C.B. Bouchard, *Strong of Body, Brave and Noble: Chivalry and Society in Medieval France* (Ithaca, 1998), 58–60, who is highly critical of the 'mutation familiale' but offers a description of the concept of the descent of the ban without comment.

[57] D. Barthélemy, *La mutation de l'an mil a-t-elle eu lieu? Servage et chevalerie dans la France des xe et xie siècles* (Paris, 1997), 24.

[58] S.D. White, '*Pactum legem vincit et amor judicium.* The Settlement of Disputes by Compromise in Eleventh-Century France', *American Journal of Legal History*, 22 (1978), 281–308.

century, an idea to which he still subscribed as late as 1990. If the ban did not descend then it could not, of course, have been a mechanism for class formation in the way that mutationists believed: private violence then was no longer 'the spearhead of social transformation', as he puts it. In Barthélemy's recent work, what distinguished one social group as superior was its means of socio-economic domination. Barthélemy offers instead a recycled Marxism, and in doing so implicitly declares, as Marx did, that class is a constant factor in societies, because social inequality is also a constant factor.[59] A number of scholars have since leapt to defend mutationism, and none have been more eloquent and decided than the American scholar Thomas Bisson, a specialist in Catalan society, who published a strong affirmation of the theory in 1994 in a direct rebuttal to Barthélemy. Bisson's tactic was to emphasise the evidence for a new level of violence in the sources around 1000: violence of lords, knights and provosts against peasants and the unarmed; violence between rival lords, and violence against lords by predatory knights. He reasserted the belief that deep changes were therefore immanent in western society, especially in the newly-feudalised eleventh-century Catalonia he knows best. His chronology of violence and revolution was focussed in time at the end of the tenth century and of course included the symptom of 'the accelerated diffusion of powers of command among more and more lords dispensing knights' fiefs' or 'proliferating dominations under which venerable principles of public order had been deeply compromised' – for which we may read once again the energising principle of the descent of the ban.[60]

Bisson's conservative manifesto provoked several replies which developed further the case against mutationism, although it can hardly yet be said to have been finally relegated to the historiographical lumber room. Since he concentrated on clerical rhetoric about aristocratic violence

[59] Barthélemy, *La mutation de l'an mil a-t-elle eu lieu*, 27–8.

[60] T.N. Bisson, 'The "Feudal Revolution"', *Past and Present*, no. 142 (1994), 6–42, quotations from pp. 28, 39. The paper drifts into many issues, but it does not engage at all with arguments against the 'mutation familiale' which was in Duby's mind so strong an impulse to rootlessness and violence around 1000. Bisson would seem by implication to want to highlight his own idea of predatory lordship as a stimulus for violence instead of the previous concentration on the social disruption produced by new lineage-based families. He reasserts his central point about violent eleventh- and twelfth-century lordship in, 'The "Feudal Revolution": Reply', *Past and Present*, no 155 (1997), 212–17, and argues also for a feudalism which takes more account of power and less of fiefs in, 'Lordship and Tenurial Dependence in Flanders, Provence and Occitania (1050-1200)' in, *Il feudalesimo nell'alto medioevo* (2 vols., Settimane di Studio de centro Italiano di studi sull'alto medioevo, xlvii, 2000) i, 389–439.

around 1000 as a symptom of 'revolution', it was possible for Barthélemy to produce the same rhetoric from the ninth century and ask whether the same revolution did not apply then.[61] Stephen D. White criticised Bisson's argument not for its conservatism, but for its misconceived novelty. He demonstrated that Bisson, in seeking to reestablish the mutationist paradigm, in fact has reinvented it by taking unrestrained violence as the central issue around the year 1000, not the competition for power.[62] But to do that is not to be novel, as White assumed. In stripping away from mutationism the arguments about formation of lineage and the tussle for the power the king had lost, and in focussing on predatory violence, Bisson has inevitably reverted to the foundation of the whole tradition on which the feudal mutation rests. He has unconsciously gone back to the eighteenth century and Montesquieu's original vision of the appearance of a generic medieval feudal anarchy at odds with monarchy. Bisson reminds us unintentionally that the mutationist theories of the late twentieth century were no more than an elaborate superstructure built on a simple eighteenth-century political theory.

White, and Barthélemy after him, have a very different legal-anthropological, interpretation of violence in eleventh-century society. For them, it was not out of control and it was not corrosive to political structures: it was simply an uncomfortable stage in the process of dispute settlement.[63] White's sort of violence was reactive: it occurred as part of a process, so that people became aware that there was a social problem that needed solving. That sort of violence has nothing to do with the question of class formation, unlike the socially-oppressive violence Bisson describes. Bisson's barons and knights used fear and their swords to establish a hegemony over weaker neighbours, whom they forced into a relationship so craven as to approximate slavery. The reformulation of antique models of society such as Bisson proposes tells us more graphically than anything else that anyone who pursues mutationism and the 'descent of the ban' will in the end come up hard against an intellectual dead end. If you look to account principally for the appearance of social class by the idea that

[61] D. Barthélemy, 'Debate: the "Feudal Revolution" ', *Past and Present*, no 152 (1996), 199. As White points out, ibid., 219, Bisson's own arguments tend to concede that society before 980 was routinely violent, even though tenth-century people had an idea that there was an authority in the king who could put it right.

[62] S.D. White, ibid., 207–8.

[63] Ibid., 212–13. White seeks to make Bisson's argument on government parallel with Weber's, but for what purpose is unclear, since Bisson did not cite Weber as his source, and White makes nothing out of the parallel.

medieval lords employed knights to impose their power on others then you have to adopt an unsustainable idea of the innate and anarchic violence of the middle ages. As we will see, the process was more subtle, just as medieval people were more subtle too.

2. A British Model of Localisation

One of Bisson's indirect suggestions in 1994 was that little had yet been done to see if the mutationist paradigm applied to England. For him this is important, as England's high ideal of civil peace under the Normans and Angevins is inconvenient to the whole mutationist thesis. If it was such a key development in western European society, the mutation of the year 1000 must in some way apply to English or Anglo-Norman society. Bisson indeed saw the 'feudal revolution' of around 1000 spreading outwards from France in ripples of space and time, so he was naturally drawn to the one period of English history where 'feudal anarchy', of the sort that Montesquieu had pictured, has long been maintained to have broken out. He focussed particularly on the years of the civil war of Stephen's reign, which he took to be from 1137 to 1145.[64] Here he found the perpetuation of the disorders experienced in France over a century before: the appropriation of Church lands, usurped castle lordships, dispossessions, violence and defiance of royal authority. Bisson was following in an old tradition. Since the time of William Stubbs – who in the 1870s interpreted the reign through the writings of Montesquieu – many historians of Stephen's reign have regarded it as an example of all that was generically violent in aristocratic behaviour.[65]

The concept of an 'anarchy' of Stephen's reign amongst English historians is simply an extension of the eighteenth-century paradigm of feudal government, and is really no more than an historiographical illusion. There are things between 1139 and 1147 in England which look analogous to what happened in the Mâconnais: a multiplication of castles; the appropriation of royal assets; private warfare and private taxation. Many areas

[64] Bisson, 'The "Feudal Revolution"', 28–33. The same suggestion that Stephen's reign had seen a descent of the ban on the Duby model was made independently the same year, see P. Dalton, *Conquest, Anarchy and Lordship: Yorkshire 1066–1154* (Cambridge, 1994), 185–6.

[65] W. Stubbs, *The Constitutional History of England* (3 vols, Oxford, 1874–78) i, 254–5n. For the influence of feudal theorists in forming the prevailing view of the 'anarchy' of Stephen's reign, D. Crouch, *The Reign of King Stephen, 1135–1154* (London, 2000), 2–18.

saw an extensive increase in the power of magnates, and a few areas saw minor lords seizing the same sort of power and jurisdiction of magnates. But before we get carried away with the parallels we need to look more coolly at the evidence. Whatever usurpations of royal rights were being carried out, they were being rapidly reversed even before the end of the reign. Even those great magnates who erected a temporary regional domination in their areas of England, like Earl William of York, Earl Robert of Leicester or Earl Alan of Richmond, continued to receive the king's writs and orders (which makes them more look more like tenth-century *missi dominici* than emerging eleventh-century princes). On the other side of the conflict, magnates like Earl Roger of Hereford or Earl Patrick of Salisbury, answered in their cases to the Empress Mathilda or her son, Henry Plantagenet. Patrick of Salisbury is even found answering to the exchequer of King Stephen in September 1154, a central accounting office which most interpreters see as carrying on throughout the reign in some form, regardless of the war. Intensive castle studies of the reign have found no justification for believing that there was any large expansion of castle building, or that those castles which were built breached any royal prohibition on unlicensed castles. Study of the reign has certainly found that there was damaging warfare in the south west and in the Marches of Wales, but no more than one would expect in what was a war of succession between royal cousins. What is surprising is that we find in the late 1140s that the greater lay magnates on either side were drawing up peace accords to limit what violence there was, and indeed, that they had severely limited the extent of warfare by 1148 without any resort to the French expedient of a Truce or Peace of God.[66]

Stephen's reign saw an outburst of the sort of dynastic warfare which most European monarchies experienced at some time or other, and Germany more than most. The rivals solicited the help of parties of magnates, and those magnates deployed their castles and knights in support of their respective causes, and often they did so ruthlessly. But Stephen's reign is unique in showing us that the magnates felt that they did not do so because they were naturally drawn to violence to promote their own interests. Pamphlets and tracts survive where the rights and wrongs of each

[66] For the views expressed here, Crouch, *Reign of King Stephen*, 121–4, 150–3, 233–9, 320–39; for castles, C. Coulson, 'Castles of the Anarchy', in, *The Anarchy of Stephen's Reign*, ed. E. King (Oxford, 1994), 68–73, 91; for the exchequer and for administrative continuity, G. White, 'Continuity in Government', in *The Anarchy of Stephen's Reign*, 117–44; K. Yoshitake, 'The Exchequer in the Reign of Stephen', *English Historical Review*, 103 (1988), 954–9.

party were argued, and two were written by or on behalf of lay magnates in the thick of the fighting. They show us that the magnates believed that they were fighting in good faith to honour obligations and oaths that they had undertaken. The civil war was fought because some magnates had taken oaths in good faith, and felt strongly enough about it to defy the anointed king. One of them, Brian fitz Count, took to arms knowing that he would be ruined by his stand, as indeed he was. He was no opportunist out to extend his ban, his estates and raise a tax base. It was this same ethical introspection that got the magnates together to reach private treaties between 1148 and 1150, and to band together to impose a negotiated settlement on King Stephen and Duke Henry in 1153.

The current interpretation of Stephen's reign excludes any idea of a 'descent of the ban' or 'feudal revolution' happening in mid-twelfth century England. But that does not mean that the concept does not have some resonances with other models of English society in other periods. In fact there has long been a theory in Britain which developed independently of the French 'feudal mutation' but which parallels it. This is the idea that English economic organisation fragmented between 850 and 1100 and became more local, focussing lordship on smaller units and more individuals. This British theory has its beginnings in the work of the historical geographer, Glanville Jones. Jones suggested in the early 1960s that early Anglo-Saxon landholding was originally organised in large units of many settlements under one lord, dependent on a central settlement; he called them 'multiple' or 'federative' estates. His main argument was that the Anglo-Saxons had acquired these large units from the Britons they displaced, and although this is not really relevant to our purpose, what is relevant is that Jones sketched out a scheme by which these multiple estates eventually disintegrated. He put down the process of 'fission', as he called it, to the increasing prosperity of settlements within the estate, which then broke off to become 'independent unitary manors' and produce the sort of settlement geography we see in Domesday Book.[67]

With certain qualifications, Jones's idea of early Saxon multiple estates breaking down into the manorial map of the twelfth century still com-

[67] G.R.J. Jones, 'Settlement patterns in Anglo-Saxon England', *Antiquity*, 35 (1961), 221–32, develops this model of early English settlement out of his comparative study of northern Welsh sources. The suggestion about 'fission' is found in a more developed study presented at a colloquium in 1969 published as, idem, 'The multiple estate as a model favourable for tracing early stages in the evolution of rural settlement', in, *L'Habitat et les paysages ruraux d'Europe*, ed. F. Dussart (Liège, 1971), 251–67, esp. p. 262. Jones traced his inspiration to an earlier work on early Anglo-Saxon settlement, J.E.A. Jolliffe, *Pre-Feudal England: The Jutes* (Oxford, 1933).

mands the field. The qualifications are that multiple estates were probably themselves created out of block grants from much bigger settlement units, the tribal *regiones* which were the primary units of early Anglo-Saxon political organisation.[68] John Blair, in his intense study of the early history of Surrey, found evidence that multiple estates were not universal, and coexisted with single settlement estates, but nevertheless he still sees a breakdown of the larger earlier units in late Saxon England. His work on the ecclesiastical organisation of Anglo-Saxon England likewise works within a model of big pre-Viking central minster colleges with extensive jurisdictions over multiple settlements – often coterminous with lay multiple estates. He suggests that these lost ground to new local village churches, until, by the end of the twelfth century, the village-based parish system still current in England was established.[69]

Much of this reconstruction of a slowly localising English society after 800 depends on the late evidence of Domesday Book, and the pattern of manorial jurisdictions it reveals. But it becomes very persuasive when combined with similar material from ecclesiastical sources, particularly the large number of surviving agreements by which ancient minster churches came to terms with the growing independence of smaller and more local churches within their former jurisdictions. It seems to be accepted that a similar multiplication of local churches within larger ecclesiastical units took place in the Carolingian Frankish realms. In Carolingian France this localisation – observable in the early ninth century – might well be linked by observers to the descent of the ban in a declining monarchy, but the English situation indicates that this would be an unwarrantable assumption.[70] British historians have not got much further than Glanville Jones in

68 S. Bassett, 'In search of the origins of Anglo-Saxon kingdoms', in, *The Origins of Anglo-Saxon Kingdoms* (Leicester, 1989), 3–27.

69 J. Blair, *Early Medieval Surrey*, 12–27. For his minster model, J. Blair, 'Introduction' in, *Minsters and Parish Churches: The Local Church in Transition, 950–1200* (Oxford University Committee for Archaeology, 1988), 1–19; idem, 'Anglo-Saxon minsters: a topographical review' in, *Pastoral Care before the Parish*, ed. J. Blair and R. Sharpe (Leicester, 1992), 226–66. For some objections to his work on the basis of vocabulary and the early existence of some local churches see, E. Cambridge and D. Rollason, 'Debate: the Pastoral Organization of the Anglo-Saxon Church: a review of the "Minster Hypothesis"', *Early Medieval Europe*, 4 (1995), 87–104.

70 J-F. Lemarignier, 'Quelques remarques sur l'organisation ecclésiastique de la Gaule du viie à la fin du ixe siècle principalement au nord de la Loire', in, *Agricoltura e mondo rurale in occidente nell'alto medioevo* (Settimane di Studio del centro Italiano di studi sull'alto medioevo, xiii, Spoleto, 1966), 451–86, esp. 474–8; for comments, Cambridge and Rollason, 'Debate: the Pastoral Organization of the Anglo-Saxon Church', 97–9

accounting for this slow breakdown of economic organisation. Blair proposed changes in farming patterns as partly to blame. But he also played with the idea that between 900 and 1066 a locally-based group of lesser aristocracy appeared as the landlords of the fragments of the earlier multiple estates. In this he seems to have been influenced both by later English medievalists' romantic search for the 'origins of the gentry' but also the Duby thesis of the descent of the ban.[71] Jones's theory is still worth pursuing as a model of a progressive localisation of jurisdiction and lordship which stands independent from the 'descent of the ban'. The model has the advantage that it is independent of any Montesquieu-based idea that monarchy and feudal aristocracy were in competition. Localisation happened at the grass roots for purely pragmatic economic reasons and slow social change followed on from it. The English evidence might give the appearance of the emergence of a new aristocracy in a new relationship with the rural peasantry in one direction and the king in the other, but in the case of England, it happened when the West Saxon monarchy was at its apogee of power and wealth in the tenth century. In England, the apparently new local aristocracy of around the year 1000 did not rise at the expense of a weak monarchy, but rose instead out of changing economic conditions and settlement patterns.

In the English model of localisation, what was happening to the English aristocracy in the tenth and eleventh centuries becomes a key point of interpretation. Most studies devoted to the pre-Conquest aristocracy focus on the reign of Edward the Confessor (1042–66) for the simple reason that Domesday Book provides an unparalleled insight into landholding in England at the point when King Edward died. Domesday Book is not without problems of interpretation, but even so, French historians would give assorted limbs to have such a source for France in 1066. The other side of the coin is that the sort of sources that French historians can deploy for the tenth and early eleventh century barely exist for England, and extrapolation about the English aristocracy before Edward is based on very slim evidence indeed. Domesday Book demonstrates certain broad points of comparison between England and France before 1066. England possessed a small group of princely figures at the head of its aristocracy, men bearing the English title 'earl', which in Latin was usually translated as *dux*, or 'duke'. The choice of Latin title was deliberate, and French writers in the 1070s fully understood that an English earl before 1066 had been the equivalent of a Frankish or imperial duke, not the lower rank of

[71] Blair, *Early Medieval Surrey*, 84, 160–1.

count.[72] Like a German or a French duke, English earls were military commanders, responsible for the defence of their provinces, commanding personal retinues of warriors and espousing military values. There were major differences, however. These great magnates were drawn from four particular 'earl-worthy' dynasties in Edward's reign, but they did not necessarily inherit their earldoms from their fathers, nor did they necessarily keep them for their political lifetimes. They could be removed, reappointed or transferred, and their earldoms could be adjusted to fit the king's purposes.[73] They therefore had much in common with the counts and marquises of the eighth- and ninth-century Carolingian realms. English earls did not have the sovereign status that French dukes and many counts had attained; they remained recognisably public officers. The king of England had estates throughout his realm, and his power and writ was not excluded from any shire. The king of England was omnipresent in his realm and his earls had to recognise the fact.

Since England had no semi-independent princes monopolising power in their regions, its earls did not accumulate the allegiance of their own dependent, regional aristocracies, who looked to them for leadership, not the king. A far larger proportion of landholders throughout England, the owners of one or several estates, depended directly on the king as their lord. These were the 'king's thegns', so universal in Domesday Book. It is undoubtedly true that the pre-Conquest earls used their powers of patronage and their individual wealth to accumulate groups of men who looked to them for protection and advancement, but the earl of Kent, for instance, did not by virtue of his office command the allegiance of all the people of Kent. What he might do, however, was form links, not based on land and jurisdiction, but on simple clientage, or 'commendation' as Domesday Book calls it. As Susan Reynolds suggests, we seem to glimpse before 1066 in England an aristocratic society running on principles that would later be called 'bastard feudal'.[74] Such an English magnate would have been a powerful man, but not in the way that a count of Perche or Ponthieu would have been. He would not have been a 'banal lord'. This was the inheritance of pre-Conquest England to the succeeding Norman regime, which did not reproduce the

[72] Crouch, *Image of Aristocracy in Britain*, 46–50

[73] C.P. Lewis, 'The Early Earls of Norman England', in, *Anglo-Norman Studies*, xiii, ed. M. Chibnall (Woodbridge, 1990), 208–13.

[74] Reynolds, *Fiefs and Vassals*, 335–42, for the 'bastard feudal' analogy, p. 341.

independence from the king of northern French aristocratic society in England.[75]

3. Castles

These significant differences between the great magnates of England and France argue against anything resembling an eleventh-century 'descent of the ban' in England on the Duby model. However powerful an individual English earl might be, the power he wielded depended not on any inherited principality, but on the office he held at the king's will. While we are pursuing the Duby model of class formation, it is worth repeating the observation made by so many that the mechanism by which a castle might become the base of a lordship for a lesser man did not exist in England before 1066.[76] It was probably the practice for most great earls and other major landholders down to the prosperous ceorl (lesser landowner) to embank and ditch their principal halls in England in the tenth and eleventh century, and even put up characteristic gatehouses, which were a recognised mark of social pretension.[77] This degree of elaboration of their residences certainly would have advertised their personal wealth and status, but the full apparatus of fortification that developed in France in the late tenth century did not happen in pre-Conquest England. There were no masonry great towers, no mural walkways and turrets, and no barbicans. Without robust and sophisticated fortifications at their command, pre-Conquest magnates could not defy the king with any hope of long resistance to a counter-attack. Indeed, if they wanted to defy the king, they did not garrison their private burhs, or fortified sites, but took instead to their private fleets and raided the coasts.[78]

75 There were perhaps some early moves towards it in the Welsh March. This ultimately produced the exceptional earldom of Chester, which stood in relation to the king of England as the county of, say, Clermont, stood in relation to the French royal domain. For the slow development of Chester's semi-independence see, D. Crouch, 'The Administration of the Norman Earldom', in, *The Earldom of Chester and its Charters*, ed. A.T. Thacker (Journal of the Chester Archaeological Society, 71, 1991), 70–3.

76 P.A. Clarke, *The English Nobility under Edward the Confessor* (Oxford, 1994), 150–2.

77 A. Williams, 'A Bell-house and a Burh-geat: Lordly Residences in England before the Norman Conquest' in, *Medieval Knighthood* iv, ed. C. Harper-Bill and R. Harvey (Woodbridge, 1992), 221–40.

78 Williams, 'Bell-house and Burh-geat', 238–9, points out this, and also that King Alfred's laws recognise that a man's enemies might well assault his house, so a siege of a sort could well happen in pre-Conquest England, even if not for long.

Yet nonetheless there was in England a landed aristocracy able to exert power in the localities, even those lower levels of it described as thegns or ceorls. Such men had a local eminence based not on castles but on prestige and on their control of resources. They found ways to express it, not just in material wealth, but in taking a prominent place in the public courts of shire, wapentake and hundred, that were the focus of English political communities both before and after the Conquest. Pre-Conquest England reminds us, in short, that castles were not necessary for class formation within the aristocracy, and that magnates could be powerful without seizing regional domination by military means, and despite being subject to a powerful centralised monarchy. Pre-Conquest England, with its significant absence of castles and knights, provides once again an alternative model to the localisation of power than that suggested by Duby and the mutationists.

But although it is not necessary for the castle to be seen as indispensable to any theory of the localising of power, it certainly might form part of the process. Indeed, it was indubitably and incontestably a major symptom and mechanism in the creation of local lordship in France. It is accepted that there was a move at some time from the embanked residence (the *curtis*) which we find in England too, towards the castle, which we do not find in England before the Conquest (other than in some dubious Herefordshire structures built by immigrant French). But was it part of a 'feudal transformation of the year 1000'? Duby assumed so in relation to the Mâconnais and this assumption has become almost an orthodoxy.[79] But the slow growth of the body of evidence provided by castle archaeologists since 1953 has introduced some cautionary notes. The chief of these is that fact that encastellation was going on quite a long time before 1000 in several places in France. What are we to make of Charles the Bald's well-known mandate in 864 that all *castella*, *firmitates* (strongholds) and *haiae* (banked enclosures) built without his permission were to be dismantled within the month? In his recent authoritative study of the French castle, André Debord deprecates this as a limited measure directed at the castle policy of the emerging great princes of late Carolingian France.[80] But can we be so sure? In various parts of France, private castles were appearing in some numbers well before the end of the Carolingian monarchy. In the

[79] M. Bur, 'Vers l'an mil, la motte, une arme pour une révolution', *L'information historique*, 44 (1982), 101–8.

[80] A. Debord, *Aristocratie et pouvoir: le rôle du château dans la France médiévale* (Paris, 2000), 28–9.

Rémois, princely castles were dominating local politics in the 920s. In Berry, private castles were already a fact of life in the mid tenth century.[81] In the Ardennes the process of building mottes – classic private fortifications – was under way as early as 940. In Lorraine, the count of Bar had built the fortress which was the proclamation and means of his power in 951, but this was in fact the rebuilding of an iron age fort in which his predecessors had resided since at least 828.[82] This chronology makes attempts to tie encastellation into the classic mutation of the year 1000 appear more than a little forced.

It is a valid argument that localisation of power was going on quietly in France, as it was in England, throughout the ninth and tenth century, and for much the same reasons. Economic expansion and rising population made it easier for lords to enrich themselves. In France maybe the fear of continuing incursions from outside forces, like Vikings and Magyars, was a good argument for raising local fortifications. In England this had been done by the West Saxon monarchy, but in France the response was more local, and produced castles. The fact that castles were privatised and built privately throughout the tenth century in France meant that the process of localisation was different there, and politically more fraught for the larger political units, like kingdoms and duchies. Nonetheless, it can be argued that it was still the same process of localisation there as in England. It was more dangerous for the king in France because he did not have the landed and political omnipresence in his realm that the king of England had. It is worth pondering whether, if the pre-Conquest king of England's lands and military influence had been confined to London, Essex and Kent, something like what happened in France would have happened in England in the late tenth century. When the king of England was confined to just that area in Stephen's reign it produced a state of affairs which mutationists instantly recognise as what happened in France a century earlier. This in itself would indicate that England and France were undergoing the same fundamental transformation, but it would better if it were called localisation than feudal transformation.

[81] J. Devailly, *Le Berry du xe siècle au milieu du xiiie siècle: étude politique, religieuse, sociale et économique* (Paris, 1973), 123–35; Barthélemy, *Les deux ages de la seigneurie banale*, 50–1.

[82] G. Guiliato, 'Le château reflet de l'art défensif en Lorraine de xème au début du xiiième siècle', *Annales de l'Est*, 6th ser, 1 (2003), 56–7, despite this however the article argues for castles as the element 'la plus perceptible' of the revolution of the year 1000. The same ideological mutationism is to be found in Debord, *Aristocratie et pouvoir*, 23–4.

A clue to further exploration of this theme of localisation through the phenomenon of castles might very well lie in the study of the *absence*, not the presence, of the noble castle. In England it has been found that great lords did not always feel that they had to build fortifications at the centres of their lordships. Despite the troubled state of England after the Conquest, some magnates built halls and chamber blocks at their central manors rather than raised mottes. The case of Castle Acre in Norfolk is often quoted in this context. The great stone hall and chambers of the Warenne family there was a noble pile, but it was unfortified until the reign of Stephen. For two generations of this great Norman family it was clearly not necessary to build a castle to dominate and awe their neighbours.[83] The continuing importance of the hall, from the tenth century onwards, as well as the fortification, as a symbol of noble power has also been noted in France. The hall was a stage for seigneurial hospitality and patronage, and so it too could express domination, but not necessarily military domination.[84] There is a persistent strand in current literature that the castle, too, may have been part of a wider mechanism to assert status in the eleventh century by magnificent building, as much as to guarantee security and domination.[85] And this brings us to a final theory of class formation: the expression of superior status by the emulation of greater men.

A New Theory of Class Formation: 'Cultural Diffusion'

Georges Duby did not think up just one theory to account for class formation in eleventh-century France. As well as the 'descent of the ban' he came out with a second – and to him complementary – explanation in what he called 'la vulgarisation des modèles culturels', but which has been economically translated into English as 'cultural diffusion'. Since 'cultural diffusion' never became a part of the dogma of the feudal mutation, Duby's work on it has been largely overlooked, but this is to do him a great

[83] J.G. Coad, 'Recent Work at Castle Acre Castle' in, *Château Gaillard: Études de Castellologie médiévale* xi (Caen, 1983), 55–6

[84] A. Renoux, 'Les fondements architectureaux du pouvoir princier en France (fin ixe siècle-début xiiie siècle)' in, *Les princes et le pouvoir au moyen âge* (Paris, 1993), 167–94, esp. 177–80.

[85] C. Coulson, 'Peacable Power in English Castles' in, *Anglo-Norman Studies*, xxiii, ed. J. Gillingham (Woodbridge, 2000), 69–95; and for an extended treatment featuring both English and French examples, idem, *Castles in Medieval Society: Fortresses in England, France and Ireland in the Central Middle Ages* (Oxford, 2003), 66–84.

injustice, for in the long run his idea of 'cultural diffusion' may turn out to be amongst his most lasting work. Another reason it has been overlooked was that he presented this particular study in a roundabout way, initially in the proceedings of a minor conference at the École Normale Supérieure on social division in May 1966, but then chose as his principal forum the British social history journal *Past and Present*, where it appeared in a translation by Rodney Hilton as 'The Diffusion of Cultural Patterns in Feudal Society'.[86] So this brief but powerful paper has somehow stepped outside the main canon of his works.

Was 'cultural diffusion' or 'popularisation' entirely Duby's own idea? He himself said not, and referred to it as '. . . a simple statement of a known fact ... that the cultural patterns of the upper classes in society tend to become popularised, to spread and to move down, step by step, to the most deprived social groups'. So who was the unnamed person or persons who made this social mechanism known? Duby does not tell us, so we have to guess, and guessing takes us back a long way. The lineage of the idea would seem to begin with Adam Smith. In his *Theory of Moral Sentiments* (1759) Smith produced a brilliant analysis of the effect of great wealth on the less wealthy. He identified the idea of 'emulation' as the reason why the poor have a strange sympathy with the rich, even when there is no hope of receiving any material benefit. The poor sympathise with the rich and powerful because they can share their advantages in their imagination. By their deference to the attributes of wealth the poor change their society by affirming levels of status within it.[87] There are some parallels here with Marx's idea of 'fetishism' – the avid pursuit of luxury goods – as an engine for social change and an impulse towards capitalism, although Marx did not see fetishism as a mechanism for class formation. He also saw conflict rather than consent in the relations between classes.[88]

The more likely herald of Duby's 'cultural diffusion' was the eccentric and highly original American sociologist Thorstein Bunde Veblen (1857–1929), the originator of that evocative phrase 'conspicuous con-

86 For the original French text, G. Duby, 'La vulgarisation des modèles culturels dans la société féodale' in, *La société chevaleresque* (repr. Paris, 1988), 194–205. The Hilton translation is republished in *The Chivalrous Society* (London, 1977), 171–7.

87 'Upon this disposition of mankind, to go along with all the passions of the rich and the powerful is founded the distinction of ranks, and the order of society', *The Theory of Moral Sentiments* (London, 1759), 97–114, quotation from p.114.

88 A. Appadurai, 'Commodities and the Politics of Value', in, *The Social Life of Things: Commodities in Cultural Perspective* (Cambridge, 1986), 3–63, esp. 36–8, for a treatment of Sombart and Marx.

sumption'. In his influential and popular book, *The Theory of the Leisure Class* (1899), Veblen pondered at length on what he called the 'Pecuniary Canons of Taste' by which he described the way that the wealthy are tied to higher standards of consumption and manufacture in the goods they have to buy and use. In his study of 'Conspicuous Consumption' he made the social deduction from this that 'since the consumption of these more excellent goods is an evidence of wealth, it becomes honorific; and conversely the failure to consume in due quantity and quality becomes a mark of inferiority and demerit.' Consumption and display was therefore a mechanism in class formation, and within the class that aspired to conspicuous consumption levels of differentiation arose as to what its members could afford, and in this way there evolved a 'system of rank and grades' based on differing status and economic weight. Veblen's views were propagated within Europe by the German sociologist Werner Sombart (1863–1941) who in 1910 made the additional point – since he was a European brought up in the nineteenth century – that royal courts were points from which the propagation of 'pecuniary canons' began, progressively affecting the standards of the aspiring classes beneath them.[89]

In 1968 Duby was quoting Sombart, but perhaps not directly. Sombart's notoriously enthusiastic commitment to National Socialism in later life might in any case be reason enough for a Frenchman of Duby's generation not to refer to him by name. Duby may perhaps have been just as much affected by the rising French thinker Pierre Bourdieu, whose work on refining the concepts of early sociologists like Durkheim, Veblen and Sombart was coming to the attention of the wider world by the mid-1960s. Bourdieu developed an idea of class as derived from material lifestyle and culture, and conditioned into the individual by expectations imposed by the society into which he was born (what he called the 'habitus', for which see also Chapter 2).[90] The debt to Veblen is immediately obvious, as is the approximation to Duby's views derived from his own empirical study. But Bourdieu wrote only about contemporary societies, not medieval ones. Although his theoretical model may have appealed to Duby, there is no

[89] W. Sombart, *Luxury and Capitalism* (Ann Arbor, 1967), esp. ch. 4; originally published as *Luxus und Kapitalismus* (Munich, 1910).

[90] His earliest publication along these lines is, P. Bourdieu, *L'amour de l'art* (Paris, 1966). For an explanation of 'habitus' – which is a mechanism to explain Durkheim's beliefs as to how society acts on the individual – P. Bourdieu, *Outline of a Theory of Practice*, trans. R. Nice (Cambridge, 1977), 78–86; expanded in, idem, *Distinction: A Social Critique of the Judgement of Taste*, trans. R. Nice (London. 1984), 169–225.

trace of Bourdieu's highly technical and allusive vocabulary in Duby's 1966 paper. Duby talks about 'cultural patterns' and not 'habitus', and Bourdieu does not talk about 'diffusion' because he was not a historian. The points of contact seems to be that both Duby and Bourdieu give great weight to social pretension as a mechanism of social mobility, and both are aware that the culture of lower social groups can affect that of social groups above them.

Neither Bourdieu, Veblen nor Sombart were interested in the medieval or any other particular period, and (apart from Sombart's loose allusions to the impact of Louis XIV's court on nobility and bourgeoisie) were not interested in investigating precisely how their scheme of class formation might work out in a historical case study. The achievement of Duby was to do just that. Duby's originality here did not come out of the blue. The idea of 'cultural diffusion' followed on naturally for him from his ideas about the 'political diffusion' which was the essence of the descent of the ban. If power devolved through society down from the king, then so might cultural objects of desire. The neatness of it must have appealed to his unusually systematic mind. One of Duby's more convincing examples was the way that tenth-century modes of royal piety – chapels and chaplains, relics and ornate tombs – had reached the bourgeoisie via the aristocracy by the fourteenth century. But Duby could never be entirely free of the dogma of the feudal mutation. He offered a more contentious example of cultural diffusion in seeing the royal idea of lineage penetrating and defining successive levels of status within society from the princes in the mid tenth century, to the castellans in the eleventh and to the knights in the thirteenth century. This is the 'mutation familiale' criticised in an earlier chapter, and, as we have seen, the evidence simply does not support what he had to say.

Along with the ideologically-charged idea of the diffusion of lineage Duby suggested rather more convincing examples of cultural diffusions. He is clearly right that the progressive diffusion of fortified residences, castles and manor houses of various levels of ambition, defined princes, counts, castellans and knights across the period between 1000 and 1200. Subsequent writers with no connection to his greater project have found a similar chronology. A symptom of the satisfying nature of the theory of cultural diffusion is the way that a variety of historians independently find the process at work in other places and in other times. A good example, divorced from the 'feudal transformation' of France, has been found by Robin Fleming in the way that the English aristocracy a century before

1066 copied royal modes of luxurious living.[91] It might be added that this example demonstrates neatly how continental historians of the middle ages can on occasion find profitable cases for comparison with England.

In 1992 I offered an extended critique of this part of the Duby scheme of cultural diffusion, drawing on British rather than French examples and looking at the use of banners, coronets, swords, heraldry and other insignia, such as seals; castles and halls; the specialised household; the hunting of woodland; and the pattern of piety. The mechanism he proposed certainly worked, not least in the way that characteristically royal trappings and practices travelled down through society, even though I found that there were other avatars of status than the king or emperor, not least the example of Ancient Rome. I also found that some objects of imitation did not travel the whole way down through society, but lodged at a certain point, to mark out status levels. An example of this was the way that the use of the banner stopped as a marker for where baronial status began; the golden spur distinguished knights from squire; and heraldry for a while distinguished the squire from the gentleman.[92] It has to be said that the Sombartian idea of cultural diffusion, or – as Duby more usually called it – 'cultural popularisation', is the most scientifically satisfying mode yet proposed for the formation of class and status levels within medieval societies. It even has the advantage of agreeing with what some contemporary medieval commentators had to say on the subject of the great of their world. We will see later what William of Malmesbury had to say in the 1120s (see below, p. 235). Arnold of Bonneval said much the same in 1152 when talking of the influence of Theobald IV of Blois:

Nothing that was crude was heard, said or done at his court. Those eager to earn his good opinion in this sort of conduct, either because of their natural disposition or because of appearances, increasingly did those things which they saw to be respectable in his domains.[93]

Where Duby was least convincing in 1968 was in his discussion of where the knight fitted into the scheme of cultural diffusion. Duby made the perfectly reasonable point that diffusion could work in reverse, and some social customs and practices associated with more common folk could be

91 R. Fleming, 'The new wealth, the new rich, and the new political style in late Anglo-Saxon England', *Anglo-Norman Studies*, 23, ed. J. Gillingham (Woodbridge, 2000), 1–22.

92 D. Crouch, *The Image of Aristocracy in Britain, 1000–1300* (London, 1992), passim.

93 *Sancti Bernardi Prima Vita auctore Ernaldo*, in, *PL*, 185: 1, col. 299.

adopted by the rich and powerful. One example he had in mind was the religion of the poor, more enthusiastic and passionate than that of the rich, as exemplified by the way that the spirituality of the urban friars conquered the aristocracy in the early thirteenth century. The other example of upward diffusion he offered was the way of life of the knight. He suggested this for two reasons. The first was that his analysis of the language of the documents of the Mâconnais convinced him that the Latin title *dominus* ('lord' or 'messire') had travelled down the social scale in 1000 from count to castellan and by 1200 from castellan down to knight. While *dominus* was travelling down the social scale the description *miles* ('knight') was travelling upwards, originally meaning only a retained warrior, but by 1200 applying to all nobles, however great, who had adopted not just the name but also the ritual the surrounded the act of knighting. Duby's deduction was that the status of the knight rose through the eleventh and twelfth century:

> *... as the values which the title implied – courage, military efficiency, and loyalty – spread and came to occupy for so long such an important place in the aristocratic ethos, so the use of the title itself penetrated into higher and higher social levels. By 1200, the development was complete: the greatest of princes, even kings, were proud to be knights, and the ceremony of the dubbing was one of the most important steps in their lives.*[94]

Duby here echoes another argument he was developing in the 1960s relating to class definition. This was that when admittance into the fellowship of knights, by the ceremony of 'adoubement' ('dubbing', more properly 'equipping'), became a recognition of noble status, French society had fully developed a noble class. This was a development he placed around the year 1200, when downward diffusion of titles and upward diffusion of lifestyle finally came together.[95] Duby seemed unaware in 1966 that he was proposing simultaneously two models of class formation, models which did not sit well together. On the one hand he was giving Sombart's theory its first successful road test; on the other hand he was simultaneously affirming the old orthodoxy that it was privilege that

[94] Duby, 'The diffusion of cultural patterns', 174–5.

[95] G. Duby, 'The transformation of the aristocracy: France at the beginning of the thirteenth century', in, *The Chivalrous Society*, 178–85, first published as 'Situation de la noblesse en France au début du xiiie siècle', *Tijdschrift voor Geschiedenis*, 82 (1969), 509–15. Mrs Postan's translation of the title of the article is rather misleading.

defined class, and saying that 'adoubement' was from 1200 the point where privilege began. He did not appear to notice that Sombart's theory proposed a rather mobile society with class boundaries that continued to shift, while the old theories of noblesse were devised to explain a static society, where the privileged class eventually ossified to the point that it sparked resentment and social revolution. Duby seemed happy to allow that social divisions were fluid up to 1200, but then wanted them to have solidified around the knight.

Class Mobility

The use of knighthood in marking the boundaries of noble class is studied in greater detail in the next chapter. What we need to end with is some discussion about a particular issue that it raises. How open were class boundaries in the middle ages? As we have seen in Chapter 1, British historiography tends to assume – indeed, to take pride in – social mobility. We are told that it was the openness of the English medieval elite that gave its particular strength. Maitland believed that it was a side effect of the establishment of primogeniture: disinherited thirteenth-century noble younger sons either had to starve or go into the trade or law.[96] Class boundaries are therefore still assumed to have been porous at least at the top end of society in medieval England, and most recent commentators seem ready to believe that the same applied elsewhere in Europe. Research indicates that boundaries were at their most porous where there is the most evidence of medieval social discomfort: that is, between the urban wealthy and the knights (see below p. 241).[97] Urban financiers often found favour with princes, and, for a very few, favour and money might take them to the very heights of society. If Artaud de Nogent is a prime example of this in twelfth-century France, his English counterpart would be Robert fitz Harding (died 1171). Robert's family had been on the fringes of the court

[96] F. Pollock and F.W. Maitland, *The History of English Law* (2 vols., 2nd edn., Cambridge, 1898) ii, 274. His idea is still being argued by anthropologists, as in D. Birdwell-Pheasant, 'Family Systems and the Foundations of Class in Ireland and England', *The History of the Family*, 3 (1998), 17–34. For a summary of arguments relating to extinction and recruitment in the English aristocracy, M. Bush, *The English Aristocracy: A Synthesis* (Manchester, 1984), 43–7, who sees much in common in its mobility with that of Continental aristocracies.

[97] See general comments on the European context, in M. Aurell, *La noblesse en Occident (v^{e}-xve siècle* (Paris, 1996), 72–5.

of Edward the Confessor (his grandfather was Ælnoth the Staller[98]), but he began his career as a local landowner in and around Bristol in the reign of Stephen. Using his property base in Bristol, and, we must assume, a high level of financial acumen, Robert accumulated a mass of country estates in the 1150s and 1160s. By the favour of Henry II as duke and king, Robert came to control a castle at Berkeley in Gloucestershire, to found an abbey in his native town and to begin a long-lived baronial lineage.[99]

There is no small amount of English evidence that the urban elites were capable of moving on up past the frontier of nobility after the 1180s. In part this was because town and country societies were not closed to each other, as we have already seen with Robert fitz Harding. An even better example is that of the descendants of the Cornish thegn, Theodulf. His son Æthelsige lived and prospered in the reign of Henry I of England, and he was both a leading citizen of the town of Launceston and the owner of a rural estate in the nearby village of South Petherwin. Æthelsige moved effortlessly within the borough community and the county court of Cornwall alike, and had close connections with the household of the earl of Cornwall, a distant but acknowledged relation by marriage. He was important within the growing town of Launceston, but cannot be narrowly classified as an urban patrician. But there is no doubt that it was on the foundation of his influence within the town that his family fortunes grew, allowing his sons Jordan and Peter to become, respectively, a county knight and a royal chaplain.[100] Social mobility in the twelfth and thirteenth centuries grew out of the interpenetration of town and country elites, allowing those families which could increase their wealth by trade and finance to convert it easily into even greater quantities of land, until a gen-

[98] This identification is not, however, uncontested, see C.P. Lewis, 'The Formation of the Honor of Chester, 1066–1100', in, *The Earldom of Chester and its Charters*, 47–8.

[99] R.B. Patterson, 'Robert fitz Harding of Bristol: Profile of an Early Angevin Burgess-Baron Politician and his Family's Urban Involvement', *Haskins Society Journal*, 1 (1989), 101–22. A similar contemporary example would be Gervase of Cornhill (*civis meus Londoniensis*), granted an estate in Hertfordshire by King Stephen held at knight service, *Regesta Regum Anglorum*, iii, *1135–54*, ed. R.H.C. Davis and H.A. Cronne (Oxford, 1969) no. 244. Gervase, who may have lived as late as 1183, who was a second or third generation London patrician, had begun his land acquisitions before 1130 and also seems to have risen through a combination of royal service, money lending and land dealing, J.H. Round, 'Gervase de Cornhill', in, *Geoffrey de Mandeville* (London, 1892), 304–12; S. Reynolds, 'The Rulers of London in the Twelfth Century', *History*, 57 (1972), 346–7.

[100] Peter of Cornwall, 'The Visions of Ailsi and his Sons', ed. R. Easting and R. Sharpe, in, *Mediaevistik,* i (1988), 206–62.

eration came which no longer needed the transfusion of urban resources to keep them solvent.

Several members of London patrician dynasties were created knights in the first quarter of the thirteenth century: notably members of the families of Cornhill, Blunt, Buccointe and Tolosan.[101] Before they produced knights, these families were typically already well-established in property, both in London and in the counties around the capital. Once knighted, the tendency was for these patricians to further invest their money in the purchase of land and adopt the style that went with the title of knight, if they had not done so already. One example amongst several is that of Sir Andrew Blunt, son and grandson of established city merchants and financiers, with court connections going back at least to the 1160s, when his grandfather Bartholomew was a provisioner to Henry II. The Blunts' trade was principally that of furriers or skinners, and their large stone hall and domestic precinct with a chapel and gatehouse was opposite the site of the present Mansion House on the north side of the street called Poultry in the City. Andrew was the son of Robert Blunt (died *c.*1219), alderman and sheriff; he was nephew of Henry Blunt, or Henry of London, who rose to become archdeacon of Stafford, elect of Exeter and archbishop of Dublin (1213–1228), and this, as much as any court connection, might have been enough to get Andrew knighted by the 1220s. He acquired a large estate at Penkridge in Staffordshire from his uncle the archbishop, and bought or inherited others in Essex (where his father had already been an active estate-builder) and at Beversbrook in Wiltshire. Yet he remained active in London (where he had property in eight city parishes) and in the fur trade (he is described as a *parmentarius* (skinner) on one occasion), and married a member of another family of London knightly patricians, the Buccointes. On his death in 1259 Andrew divided his urban and country estates between his two sons, Hugh and Henry. Both sons were knighted in their turn and the two lines of descendants they originated lived as county gentry for many generations thereafter, the only connection of the Wiltshire branch with the City being the rents that their urban properties continued to provide until the end of the fourteenth century.[102]

[101] See generally for Europe, H. van Werveke, 'The Urban Patriciate', in, *Cambridge Economic History of Europe* iii, *Economic Organization and Policies in the Middle Ages*, ed. M.M. Postan, E.E. Rich and E. Miller (Cambridge, 1963), 32; and for London, G.A. Williams, *Medieval London: From Commune to Capital* (London, 1963), 50ff.

[102] For the Blunts, W. Page, *London: Its Origins and Early Development* (London, 1929), 258–64; *Victoria County History of Staffordshire* v, 108–9; *Victoria County*

Urban families in London produced half a dozen knights before 1250, but even very small English towns could generate knightly lineages. In the late twelfth century one Uthred of Weaversthorpe was a principal landowner within the remote port of Scarborough in Yorkshire. His children and grandchildren were bailiffs of the borough and made gentry marriages and purchases of land in the county. Two of his great-grandchildren took knighthood before 1300 and lived among the Yorkshire gentry as Sir Robert Uthred of Kilnwick and Sir John Uthred of Gowthorpe. Sir Robert worked hard to raise his profile within the county, and gained a military reputation by taking the field with Edward I's armies in Scotland. His son was the famous warrior, Sir Thomas Uthred KG (died 1365), an associate of kings and princes and a hero of Crécy, who continued to augment his income with rents from Scarborough left him by his urban forbears and to support the family chantry founded in the Dominican church there.[103]

Men who made a success of careers as urban landowners, money lenders or merchants were naturally drawn, for reasons both of pragmatism and social ambition, to invest their money in land. It is a mechanism that was evident in England already in the Domesday Survey. Wulfstan of York noticed the upward mobility of merchants as early as the first decade of the eleventh century. It has been observed by historians in studies of regional towns and cities in the twelfth and thirteenth centuries.[104]

History of Wiltshire ix, 96. For Archbishop Henry, E. St John Brooks, 'Archbishop Henry of London, and his Irish Connections', *Journal of the Society of Antiquaries of Ireland*, lx (1930), 1–22. For Andrew Blunt's will, Corporation of London Record Office, Husting Roll 2 (58). Further references and property reconstruction in, Centre for Metropolitan History, Social and Economic Study of Medieval London, under tenement history, 132/12 (Parish of St Mildred Poultry) with thanks to Professor Derek Keene and Olwen Myhill.

103 For the Uthred family origins, D. Crouch, 'Urban Government and Oligarchy', in, *Medieval Scarborough: Studies in Trade and Civic Life*, ed. D. Crouch and T. Pearson (Yorkshire Archaeological Society, Occasional paper 1, 2001), 43–5; For Thomas's remarkable career, and his father's integration into the Yorkshire gentry, A. Ayton, 'Sir Thomas Ughtred and the Edwardian Military Revolution', in, *The Age of Edward III*, ed. J.S. Bothwell (Woodbridge, 2001), 107–32.

104 For the Domesday evidence relating to Lincoln and Ipswich, R. Fleming, 'Rural Elites and Urban Communities in Late Saxon England', *Past and Present*, no. 141 (1993), 35–6. For Wulfstan's comment that successful traders might naturally seek the status of the (presumably, landed) thegn, see his tract *Geþyncðo* in *English Historical Documents* i, c.*500–1042*, ed. D. Whitelock (London, 1955), 432. For regional examples, E. Miller, 'Rulers of Thirteenth Century Towns: the Cases of York and Newcastle upon Tyne', in, *Thirteenth-Century England*, i, ed. P.R. Coss

Possession of landed estates led to intermarriage with local elites and the taking up of knighthood by some. It is not possible to say precisely how large a proportion of the knights of England were drawn from wealthy, urban-based families. But such evidence as there is does point to it being a noticeable minority within the group. France is a more difficult case, but such studies as there have been reveal some of the same developments as England experienced.

The populous and wealthy cities of Artois and French Flanders have naturally drawn the attention of scholars, partly because their growth and influence was so phenomenal and partly because the great economic historian, Henri Pirenne (1862–1935), published so much pioneering work on the region and its cities. It was in fact Pirenne who popularised the idea of talking (in Classical terms) of the 'patricians' and 'patriciat' of the greater medieval cities although he himself said that the terms were not a happy borrowing from Antiquity. Pirenne portrayed medieval cities deeply divided by material wealth, with the wealthy few forming a plutocracy which dominated the poorer citizens. By the end of the twelfth century the Flemish patricians built stone residences marked out by battlements and towers, clear allusions to the noble lifestyle they coveted.[105] But did they go further and look to pass the barrier of nobility in the thirteenth century by seeking knighthood?

In Galbert of Bruges's account of the tumult in Bruges in 1127, we get incidental glimpses of the already existing interpenetration of urban and rural elites in Flanders. He notes an unnamed citizen of Bruges who had married a sister of his to a local knight.[106] At St-Omer at the end of the eleventh century we get an interesting glimpse of how this social interpenetration of elites might occur. The confraternity of the patron saint of the

and S.D. Lloyd (Woodbridge, 1986), 135–41, noting the spectacular rise of Richard of Embleton, from obscurity to knighthood. Coss, *Lordship, Knighthood and Locality*, 35–7, 217–18, noting the rise of the Coventry family to knighthood around 1220 from urban service to the earls of Chester at Coventry in the twelfth century.

105 See the summary in H. Pirenne, *Les villes et les institutions urbaines* (2 vols., 2nd edn., Paris, 1939) i, 215ff. It is worth noting that the urban elite of twelfth-century Bayeux in Normandy also built stone residences with towers, *Vita sancti Gaufridi secundi abbatis Saviniacensis* in, *Analecta Bollandiana*, i (1882), 391. For the prevalence of such 'urban castles' in southern cities, M. Aurell, 'La chevalerie urbaine en Occitanie, fin xe siècle – debut xiiie siècle', in, *Les sociétés urbaines en France méridionale et en péninsule Iberique au moyen âge* (Collection de la maison des pays Ibériques, 43, Paris, 1991), 75–7.

106 Galbert of Bruges, *The Murder of Charles the Good*, trans. J.B. Ross (repr. Toronto, 1982), 215.

town was the basis of its civil organisation, and the annual social gathering offered by the confraternity included not just the citizens and the local clergy, it also included local *milites*.[107] Although it does seem that the urban elites of Flanders produced knightly lineages in the thirteenth century, in the same way as London, the comparison between them needs to be approached with caution.[108] The striking difference between the urban centres of Artois and Flanders and those of England was their size, which may hinder any real Anglo-French comparison. St-Omer's population was some 40,000 in 1300, and it was not the largest city among half a dozen in a region less than the size of Wales. In England, only London could compare with such a concentration in population, and it had a much larger rural hinterland to emphasise its exceptionality. The fact that these populous cities were packed together must have led to differences in the development of their elites. At Ghent in around 1300 there were some 300 families which could be classified as patrician.[109] One gets the impression from current scholarship that the great north-eastern cities of France formed a much more introspective elite society than those of England. In the later thirteenth century they held their own great aristocratic feasts in their squares and streets, such as the urban jousting of the Epinette organised annually in Lille from 1283 and found also at Mons, Douai and St-Omer.[110] They were held exactly on the same lines as those organised by knights but served a self-contained elite urban society with no interest in rural or curial elites.

Elsewhere in deeper France, the situation may have been closer to that in England. Barthélemy finds some early evidence of mobility, or 'renouvellement des élites', in the acquisition of fees near Vendôme by urban families in the twelfth and thirteenth century. He notes the significance of the reference in the annals of abbey of Holy Trinity that in 1161 the urban rich left the city during a famine and took refuge on their country

[107] A. Derville, 'Les élites urbaines en Flandre et en Artois' in, *Les élites urbaines au moyen âge*, ed. C. Gauvard (Paris, 1997), 121.

[108] Derville, 'Les élites urbaines', 129, citing a 'super-élite urbaine' of knighted patricians, possessing landed estates and yet continuing to serve in urban administration and to operate as merchants and financiers.

[109] Derville, 'Les élites urbaines', 128–9.

[110] E. van den Neste, *Tournois, joutes, pas d'armes dans la villes de Flandre à la fin du moyen âge, 1300–1486* (Paris, 1996), 63–127. There is some comparison here with England as the youth of the urban patriciate of London was willing to engage in courtly hastiludes like the quintain in the 1250s, Matthew Paris, *Chronica Majora*, ed. H.R. Luard (7 vols, Rolls Series, 1872–84) v, 367.

estates.[111] A revealing study of the relationship between town and hinterland at Condom in Gascony reveals a situation not far removed from England. Condom was the centre of an abbatial honour, and the town grew up in the eleventh century at the gates of the monastery. It was the market centre for a region populated with the knightly families who were the abbey's tenants. But here there was little apparent relationship between the urban elite and the local knights other than financial. The situation at Condom seems very similar to the situation between the comparable English city of Coventry and its hinterland, as described by Peter Coss.[112] In the rural heart of France as much as England the wealthiest urban families invested in land outside the walls, no doubt, but very few indeed aspired towards nobility: such an impulse was more common amongst the super-rich of the metropolises.

Upward social mobility was most likely where there was money. It happened occasionally outside the worlds of trade and urban rent-rolls too. Military skill could raise a man from very humble rural origins to the side of kings, and sometimes we see it happening. Richard son of Siward began his career as (possibly) a young Yorkshire homicide on the run in 1215, he found a refuge as a soldier for Count William de Forz of Aumale, achieved knighthood in the household of the young Earl William Marshal (1219–1231) and by the earl's favour secured marriage to a widowed countess. In 1236, as one of the most famous warriors of his generation, he carried the sceptre at the coronation of Queen Eleanor of England. All of this because he had a marketable military skill. And as he rose, his relatives rose with him, a nephew called Thomas Siward secured an estate in Ireland by the favour of the Earl Marshal and an illegitimate son was accommodated with a manor in Glamorgan. Although he fell on hard times before his death in 1248, Richard remained a man whose skills and fame made him friends, and when England failed him, he was able to exploit friendships in Scotland.[113]

Administrative skill and ruthlessness could lead to a similarly spectacular rise. Matthew Paris discussed the example of the impoverished

[111] D. Barthélemy, *La société dans le comté de Vendôme de l'an mil au xive siècle* (Paris, 1993), 765–6.

[112] R. Mussot-Goulard, 'Les chevaliers et la ville: Condom du xie siècle au xiiie siècle', in, *Les sociétés urbaines en France méridionale et en péninsule Iberique au moyen âge* (Collection de la maison des pays Ibériques, 43, Paris, 1991), 175–81; Coss, *Lordship, Knighthood and Locality*, 61–92.

[113] D. Crouch, 'The Last Adventure of Richard Siward', *Morgannwg*, xxxv (1991), 7–30, esp. p. 10.

knight, Paulinus Peyvre (died 1251), who used his literacy, court office and ill-gotten gains to expand the estate of two carrucates he inherited into a great honor of 500 carrucates, equal to the estates of an earl. Paulinus, like Robert fitz Harding before him, erected a sumptuous and palatial residence to advertise his wealth, building a great house, chapel and gardens at Tuddington in Bedfordshire, which was so magnificent that it drew sightseers. His case is paralleled in Louis IX's France by the poet and bailiff, Philip de Remy, who by similar means expanded the small family estate inherited from his father. To celebrate his success he built a handsome new house near Compiègne which he proudly called 'Beaumanoir', and from which his family subsequently took its surname.[114] This particular avenue to landed prosperity through bureaucracy became almost an early thirteenth century social topos, and has been thoroughly analysed by John W. Baldwin in the case of Philip Augustus's minor protégé, Pierre du Thillay, a lesser landowner of the Parisis who was enriched by his post as an administrator in conquered Normandy.[115]

A similar sideways avenue into the landed elite was by means of a family relationship with a man who achieved high office in the church. Since late twelfth-century sources are hostile towards peasants who achieve high ecclesiastical office (and drag their relatives into society with them) then this had been observed and was resented. Walter Map famously berated the nobility of the 1180s for failing to provide sons for the Church and so allowing sons of peasants to intrude themselves in the ecclesiastical hierarchy and corrupt its integrity.[116] An anonymous poet, writing around 1190 for the court of Richard the Lionheart, said much the same:

Don't make a bishop of your shepherd's son. Take instead the son of a king, a duke or a count, or even the son of a poor vavassor . . . do not make a lord out of your serf, leave the peasant to do his proper work. A peasant has nothing to do with honour. At the end of the day he will return to his own nature.[117]

114 For Paulinus, *Chronica Majora* v, 242–3; For Philip, see documents collected in H-L. Bordier, *Philippe de Remi, sire de Beaumanoir* (Paris, 1869), 95–104; B.N. Sargent-Baur, 'Dating the Romances of Philippe de Remi: Between an Improbable Source and a Dubious Adaptation', *Romance Philology*, 50 (1996/7), 257–75.

115 J.W. Baldwin, 'Pierre du Thillay, Knight and Lord: The Landed Resources of the Lower Aristocracy in the Early Thirteenth Century', *Francia*, 30 (2003), 9–41.

116 Walter Map, *De Nugis Curialium*, ed. and trans. M.R. James, rev'd C.N.L. Brooke and R.A.B. Mynors (Oxford, 1983), 12.

117 *La Chanson d'Aspremont*, ed. L. Brandin (2 vols, Classiques français de moyen age, 1923–4) ii, ll. 19214–26.

Nothing better indicates the coalescence of a social hierarchy with class boundaries than the outrage of people who saw them being breached. But the fact that it was possible to breach them, and that people strove to do so, is itself further testimony to medieval concepts of class. Social ambition needs social ladders with well-defined rungs. The rhetoric of class mobility and the mechanisms of cultural diffusion all indicate that society had found its rungs in the generation between 1170 and 1200.

CHAPTER 8

Medieval People and Social Division

Medieval people were well aware that they lived in a society in which wealth and status was distributed unequally. It was part of their world and accepted, that some ruled, and others were ruled. It was also part of the Christian theology that people were taught and which they memorised, for the Magnificat told every believer that in this world the mighty ruled, but that the humble were raised in the next. But whatever the long term prospects of the poor, there was no arguing with the view that there was social inequality amongst men and women under God. Some went further and said that social ambition was consequently a bad thing and liable to lead to anarchy; as did Hildegard of Bingen in the 1140s:

God also keeps a watchful eye on every person, so that a lower order will not gain ascendancy over a higher one, as Satan and the first man did, who wanted to fly higher than they had been placed.[1]

The early Marx called this quietism not an awareness of social class, but a low-level awareness of 'estates' within society: it was the way things were, and medieval people lived with it.

Outside this perception of dominant and dominated groups within society, medieval people were also acutely aware of their own individual status, and measured it in all sorts of ways we are still able to reconstruct. The problem for us is that although medieval people knew their individual worth, it does not follow that this medieval sensitivity included a sensi-

[1] *Scivias*, trans. C. Hart and J. Bishop (New York, 1990), vis. IV. She was replying to criticisms as to why aristocratic women alone were accepted in her abbey of Rupertsburg.

tivity to what we call levels of social class within an overall social structure. For a medieval person to draw his status from a group to which he belonged was perfectly possible. As we will see later, knights were a recognised social group in the eleventh and twelfth century, and belonging to it gave a man status. But were knights a class? Did they have a hierarchical relationship with other groups in society? Were they organised nationally? Did all knights possess a comparable level of income? Until they approached these sharper definitions, it could be said that knights were not a social class; it will be suggested later that they did not approach this level of social coherence until well into the thirteenth century.[2]

Before 1200 it could hardly be said that there was any tool of social debate that would sharpen the basic medieval awareness of social standing into something which could cut and trim their vision of society into a hierarchical structure of groups defined in relation to each other. Although medieval discussion about the social structure in which people lived increased in volume and quantity after 1170 it never became a social debate, in which basic positions were debated and shared. In the middle ages there were simply not schools and seminars which could discuss social thinking, and so there were no means for thinking men to reach any sort of common understanding and vocabulary to explore their society. This may seem an obvious point, but it is as well to start by saying it. Other than what we can draw out from surveys and accidental observations, our understanding of medieval society depends on idiosyncratic observations made by a range of people in different circumstances and places, and with different agendas.[3]

Religious Models of Society

It is possible to take what medieval writers say and reconstruct a medieval awareness of class, but as Marx said, it will be, for much of the middle ages, class *für sich*, (unconscious of itself). Most medieval writers did not see themselves as living in a class-bound society riven with social antagonisms. They had high authority for this. The gospel image is of

[2] For some pertinent comments on the difficulty of applying concepts of social class to the middle ages, G. Constable, 'The Orders of Society', in, *Three Studies in Medieval Religious and Social Thought* (Cambridge, 1995), 251–4. I try to use the concept sparingly, but I think it is possible to use it in dealing with a comprehensive schema of a self-conscious society which subdivided itself hierarchically.

[3] See comments in H. Martin, *Mentalités Médiévales* ii, *Représentations collectives du xie au xve siècle* (Paris, 2001), 129.

Christendom as the branches of one vine, which is Christ (John 15: 1). St Paul offered the powerful image of Christian society as one body of many parts, with Christ as the head (1 Corinthians 12: 12–31). In the light of these images, medieval intellectuals, like John of Salisbury, saw their society as, in theory, ideologically united and knit together by its common Christianity (which made it all the worse for heretics and Jews). Writers saw society as made up of multiple groups working together, but did not necessarily see those social groups arranged in a commonly-understood hierarchy. Indeed, by one gospel-based scheme of society it was the last who were first, Christ's poor who were in some respects the top layer: the poor were closer to salvation because they shared the social circumstances of the Lord and his disciples. There were members of royal families and great magnates who believed in all sincerity that they ranked lower in God's eyes than the commonest beggar because in the world to come this world's social order would not be repeated.[4] Social reversal after death was a commonplace in moral reflection during the middle ages. There was also the further reflection, drawn from biblical wisdom literature, and particularly from Ecclesiastes and certain of the psalms, that riches and social position were nothing more than empty vanity. There were bishops who were quite willing to tell kings and magnates to their faces that 'the higher you climb and the higher you get, the further is the fall, and the worse is the death', and to caution them against scheming to extend their land, for 'there'll be a day when you'll need just six feet of it'. They knew that the great of the earth would agree with them in their heart of hearts.[5]

Christ's poor were not to be despised, but to be honoured. There are many examples of medieval aristocrats acting on this belief. So, in 1151, Bishop Bartholomew of Beauvais described a great public assembly at Boran in his diocese when he inaugurated a fellowship *(fraternitas)* for all those wishing to associate with a house for poor women established in the town. Many present, including the count and countess of Beaumont-sur-Oise, offered gifts and promptly joined the fellowship so as to be more

[4] In the *Couronnement de Louis*, ed. E. Langlois (Classiques français du moyen âge, 1984), ll. 1007–12, William of Orange meditated on the day of judgement when he foresaw the social order ending, when acolytes and minor clerks will come before priests and bishops, and a stable boy will come before a count. It has to be noted, however, that Peter of Cornwall's grandfather, Ailsi (a man of the early twelfth century), visualised heaven as a place where orders (*ordines*) and hierarchy (*gradus*) were maintained, and each had its separate choir, 'The Visions of Ailsi and his Sons', ed. R. Easting and R. Sharpe, in, *Mediaevistik* i, (1988), 233.

[5] *Le Livre des Manières*, ed. R.A. Lodge (Geneva, 1979), ll. 35–6, 123–4.

assured of God's mercy.[6] A passing reference in an act of the great Anglo-French magnate, Count Robert II of Meulan (1166–1204), tells us that it was his habit to offer alms of food and drink for the poor outside his hall whenever he himself dined.[7] He had clearly meditated hard on the parable of Dives and Lazarus, and was trying to assure himself of a place with Lazarus in the bosom of Abraham. Kings and queens particularly shared this need to associate with Christ's poor. Assiduous association with the poor and sick was a religious exercise particularly associated with Queen Margaret of Scotland (*c.*1070–93) and her daughter, Queen Mathilda II of England (1100–18). Between them these two great ladies, the elder honoured as a saint, inaugurated a model of religious and charitable royalty in Britain.[8] Louis IX of France (1226–1270) was just as assiduous, not just for himself but for his aristocracy. He urged on Jean de Joinville the need to honour the poor when he found that Joinville was disgusted at the idea of washing their feet in the Maundy Thursday liturgy. Joinville certainly absorbed the lesson, for he mentioned with approval Jean l'Ermin, the master of King Louis's artillery, who refused to have a clamorous crowd of the poor driven from the tent where he was dining, as they were offering a great gift, the chance to give alms and receive salvation.[9]

It was because Count Theobald IV of Blois, Chartres and Champagne (died 1152), the elder brother of King Stephen of England, honoured the poor that he had such a high posthumous reputation: at the end of the century he was taken by Gerald of Wales as the very model of a Christian prince. When Bernard of Clairvaux wished to manipulate Theobald, he knew that he would always react to charges that he was being ungenerous. Arnold, the Cistercian abbot of Bonneval, who knew him well, said that 'he put aside the indulgence of the court and the pride of rank in favour of humility and plain living'. He lavished praise on Theobald for feeding the poor and sick from his own table, for visiting hospitals, for handing out clothes and shoes to the poor in the cold of winter and free grain to the

[6] *Chartes et documents du prieuré de Saint-Martin de Boran*, ed. J. Depoin and J. Vergnet, in, *Mémoires de la société academique du département de l'Oise*, xxiv (1924), 202.

[7] *Chartes de l'abbaye de Jumièges*, ed. J-J. Vernier (2 vols., Rouen, 1916) ii, 207–9, the original is Rouen, Archives départementales de la Seine-Inférieure, 9 H 29.

[8] L.L. Huneycutt, *Matilda of Scotland: A Study in Medieval Queenship* (Woodbridge, 2003), 103–7.

[9] Jean de Joinville, *Vie de Saint Louis*, ed. J. Monfrin (Paris, 1995), 14, 220. This view as to the utility of the poor was being preached as early as the ninth century, in a sermon attributed to Theodulf of Orleans, *PL* 105, c. 281–2.

starving in time of famine.[10] Theobald, according to one source, went so far as to carry about with him ointment and shoes to give to any wandering beggars he passed. He fraternised with the poor and lepers 'so as to give an example of consideration, religious devotion and humility, and so the poor might pray for him all the more sincerely and flock to the funeral of so great and yet so humble a man as he was' and he was indeed commemorated on his death as 'a prince of great holiness and generosity to the poor'.[11] Theobald's great wealth, royal lineage and political achievements were overlooked by contemporaries in favour of the fruits of his faith, hope and charity. It was for that reason as much as any that the Champenois of a century later called him 'Count Theobald the Great'.

One very persistent religious frame of social reference was that of the 'Three Orders'. With a history stretching from the ninth century through to the Reformation and beyond (in its later guise of the 'Three Estates') this model suggested that society was a unity broken down into three 'orders' *(ordines)* each with its own complementary function. The choice of the word 'orders' implies that these groups were 'ordained' by God.[12] Indeed, it implies that the members of each order – as was understood about the orders of priest or deacon – were called to a distinct and inescapable vocation. The three vocations were those who fought *(bellatores)*, those who prayed *(oratores)* and those who worked *(laboratores)*. The first mention of it as a coherent social scheme for humanity under God occurs in the ninth century, although as Giles Constable has pointed out, there had long been in western society a fertile theological seedbed in which such tripartite schemes could grow, and if you want to go as far as Georges Dumézil, 'ternarity' was hard-wired into the mind of Indo-European societies. The scheme occurs fully-formed in England in the mid 890s, in King Alfred's translation of Boethius's *Consolation of Philosophy*, when the king talks of the resources necessary for a functional kingdom being: praying men *(gebedmen)*, fighting men *(fyrdmen)* and working men *(weorcmen)*. Alfred's direct source for the idea is unknown, but it is usually suggested that he did have a source, and that he was drawing on ideas in circulation in the Frankish realms a generation or so earlier, ideas that inspired a

[10] *Sancti Bernardi Vita Prima, auctore Ernaldo*, in *PL*, 185.1, cols. 299–300.

[11] *The Letters of St Bernard of Clairvaux*, trans. B.S. James (Stroud, 1998), nos. 39–44; Robert de Torigny, *Chronica*, in, *Chronicles of the Reigns of Stephen, Henry II and Richard*, ed. R. Howlett (4 vols., Rolls Series, 1884–89) iv, p. 164. Theobald's predilection for the poor and lepers is also recorded by Cardinal James de Vitry, *The Exempla of Jacques de Vitry*, ed. and trans. T.F. Crane (New York, 1890), 43–4.

[12] Constable, 'The Orders of Society', 254.

similar, but unrelated, scheme presented by Heiric of Auxerre at around the same time as Alfred wrote. The scheme occurs a respectable number of times in the tenth century, in the works of writers from Eynsham, St-Omer, Liège, Cluny and Fleury, and although they use the scheme differently, nonetheless it seems they were all trading in a common intellectual currency.[13]

The 'Three Orders' was a medieval intellectual's scheme for understanding God's purpose in society, but it certainly appealed to lay people too. In the 890s Alfred the Great had found the scheme an excellent way of expressing the importance of a king and his people being united in pursuing the business of the realm, a realm threatened by the invasion of powerful pagan armies. Around 1002, in a very different England, Aelfric of Eynsham used the idea to attack clergy who got so confused in their idea of their proper place that they led troops in the field. The problem for us with the 'Three Orders' is that it bore only a limited resemblance to medieval society as medieval people experienced it, which is why writers could use it in so many different ways, according to their own perceptions and agenda. The 'Three Orders' was an ideological scheme that did not match the material facts of society as it was lived; it was a way for writers to criticise society, not necessarily to describe it.

The importance of the 'Three Orders' for the arguments being pursued here, then, is mostly historiographical. It was a concept which fascinated Georges Duby for many years, and in his great work, *Les trois ordres ou l'imaginaire du féodalisme* (1978) he looked at the way medieval writers used the 'Three Orders', and then took it as the keystone of a complex and original reconstruction of medieval society. For our purposes, it is most significant that he found in it yet more support for his idea of a 'feudal transformation' around the year 1000. Duby's argument went as follows. Two noble bishops of the province of Reims, Gerard of Cambrai (1012–51) and Adalbero of Laon (977–1031), cousins and contemporaries, both made social statements using the model of the 'Three Orders'. Gerard's was included in an address made before a consistory in 1024;

[13] *King Alfred's Old English Version of Boethius* De Consolatione Philosophiae, ed. W.J. Sedgefield (Oxford, 1899), 40. For Alfred's scheme, its chronology and its possible sources, T.E. Powell, 'The "Three Orders" of Society in Anglo-Saxon England', in, *Anglo-Saxon England*, 23, ed. M. Lapidge and others (Cambridge, 1994), 103–32. For summaries of the 'Three Orders' debate, its importance in the tenth century and its potential sources, J-P. Poly and E. Bournazel, *The Feudal Transformation, 900–1200*, trans. C. Higgitt (New York, 1991), 143–9; H. Martin, *Mentalités Médiévales* ii, 126–9.

Adalbero's was included in a poem addressed to King Robert II of France perhaps in 1023, or perhaps as late as 1027 (Duby believed Adalbero's rhetoric was inspired by Gerard's). Both bishops, Duby said, were facing the consequences of the grasping of unprecedented power by local castellans. They embraced the imagery of the 'Three Orders' because they were watching their society fracture, and becoming further distant from the harmony of the heavenly Jerusalem that was the Carolingian ideal. The world where kings and princes worked with bishops and effectively kept the peace had gone: Gerard wanted it back; Adalbero, a depressed octogenarian, believed it was gone for good.[14]

We have already seen how the 'descent of the ban' and the evolutionary view of family (the two main pillars on which the 'feudal transformation of the year 1000' rest) have weak foundations. Duby's attempt to deploy the 'Three Orders' as an additional prop to the structure does not work either. He may well be right about the concerns and intentions of Gerard and Adalbero in the 1020s, but commentators have pointed out that he does not take enough account of other earlier and contemporary uses of the scheme. Its general use by writers in the tenth century indicates that intellectuals before the year 1000 saw things badly wrong with society in their times too. As E.A.R. Brown puts it, 'the trifunctional vision flourished when what Duby refers to as "féodalisme" and "féodalité" did not'.[15] The fact that the 'Three Orders' model was used by servants of the powerful West Saxon monarchy in England shows quite clearly that it could be used in circumstances when royal power was effective as much as when royal power was ineffective. That is an alternative explanation for its use in northern France by Gerard and Adalbero. What they were doing in the 1020s was not lamenting feudal anarchy, perhaps, but the harsh efficiency of the princely order in the province of Reims.

Materialistic Divisions

Though it is so far removed from modern sociological schemes of class organisation, medieval theories that stress the unity and interdependence of society, and put the poor and homeless ahead of princes in status are a

[14] G. Duby, *The Three Orders: Feudal Society Imagined*, trans. A. Goldhammer (Chicago, 1980), 16–55. Summaries, with commentary, can be found in E.A.R. Brown, 'Georges Duby and the Three Orders', *Viator* 27, (1986), 54–61; Poly and Bournazel, *The Feudal Transformation*, 148–51; Powell, 'The "Three Orders" of Society in Anglo-Saxon England', 129–32

[15] Brown, 'Georges Duby and the Three Orders', 57.

healthy reminder to us of Max Weber's teaching that in any scheme of society, social worth and status are not necessarily tied to control over the means of production: they respond to other social priorities. That said, there is no doubt that medieval people knew that some people were more important than others; and usually for them, wealth and social influence were the criteria in judging why this was. Vernacular sources will talk without further qualification of the 'greignor' (greater) or 'menor' (lesser) people in any group or assembly. Latin sources will do the same, as when King Stephen of England (1135–54) forbade any person, important or not, *(nullus persona parva uel magna)* to trouble Reading Abbey in the possession of its lands.[16] We assume that they mean greater or lesser in terms of wealth and possessions, and the economic distinction would probably be accurate in most cases.

To justify stating this as a general rule, we can observe that in making lists, medieval people generally placed the wealthiest and most obviously potent people first. It was a reflex, unconscious probably for the most part. Take for instance the eye-witness account of the election as king of Philip of France in the cathedral of Reims in May 1059.

'Then, with King Henry's consent, the archbishop elected Philip, his son, to be king; after him followed the legates of pope (although it was fully explained and stated at that point that the pope's consent was not required for the election; the legates simply assisted in the ceremony for the sake of doing honour to the king and expressing their friendship). After them the election was made by the archbishops, bishops, abbots and clergy; then followed Guy, duke of Aquitaine; Hugh, son and representative of the duke of Burgundy; the representatives of the marquis Baldwin (of Flanders) and Geoffrey, count of Anjou. There were also present and consenting these counts: Ralph of Valois, Herbert of Vermandois, Guy of Ponthieu, William of Soissons, Reginald, Roger, Manasses, Hilduin, William of Auvergne, Hildebert of La Marche, Fulk of Angoulême, and the viscount of Limoges. After them followed the knights and the people, those of consequence and those not, consenting in one great shout. They agreed to the election, crying out three times: 'We agree! We wish it so! Let it be done!'.[17]

[16] *Regesta Regum Anglo-Normannorum*, ed. H.W.C. Davis and others (4 vols., Oxford, 1913–69) iii, no. 675.

[17] Translated from, *Ordines Coronationis Franciae*, ed. R.A. Jackson (Philadelphia, 1995), 230–2.

The list, and indeed the entire ceremonial, was carried out to a plan of strict precedence after the consent of the boy's royal father. This precedence was not just applied to the Church – all following in order the primate of Gaul, the archbishop of Reims – but also to the laity. A duke assented and was followed by a duke's son, he by a marquis (a superior count), then the sovereign counts and the dependent counts, and the magnate election concluded with a superior viscount. The knights and common people were also allowed their voice, but though separated in the list, were not allowed to assent as individuals. It is fine testimony to the hierarchical frame of an eleventh-century mind.

We find much the same in the later 1080s in the lists of contents that the compilers of Domesday Book created at the beginning of each county section. The compilers had a variety of loose returns in front of them, and, being human, they felt an impulse to put them in some order before making a fair copy. So what were the bases of their choice? To take Gloucestershire as an example, there (as in every shire) the king precedes all, and after him comes the clerical orders of archbishops, bishops, followed by the lands of monasteries and, at the end, comes a humble priest. The laity that then follow are headed by three counts (although a stray Norman bishop intrudes at this point) and then forty-seven lay estates are listed, of which the last ten are just one or two manors, and the penultimate estate is the manor of a Frenchwoman, the widow of Geri de Loges. The final entries are an undifferentiated group of sixteen landholders called 'the king's thegns', none of whom are French, but are Englishmen and women, an English nun and last of all a Welshman: all people whom we may assume were of relatively low status.[18] It is fair to say that the list betrays other agendas in status than wealth – women and ethnic groups are marginalised, and hereditary titles count for something – but an overarching consideration is the amount of land each holds.

Domesday Book is unique in the size of the survey it records and it is insular in its concerns, but there are contemporary French documents that allow us access to the same thought-world. Not long after 1094 a list of tenants of the diocese of Bayeux was made which gave the amount of knight service at which they had been assessed. It listed thirty-eight individuals and its author chose to put them broadly in the order of amount of service owed. Robert fitz Hamo, the first name mentioned, owed ten knights; the last person listed held a half-fee. The list is not in precise

[18] *Domesday Book seu Liber Censualis Willelmi primi regis Angliae*, ed. A. Farley and others (4 vols., London, 1783–1816) i, fos 162a–170d.

numerical order, but all those owing five fees and over occur amongst the first thirteen places, and all those owing one fee or less occur in the last fourteen places. The mind of the draughtsman of the list was clearly running on the relative importance of the assessment of the land, and the wealth it represented. In this case a hereditary title meant nothing: he mentioned the earl of Chester, but the earl is tenth on the list and follows two viscounts, who themselves follow untitled tenants.[19]

In the case of twelfth- and thirteenth-century England we are in the happy position of having a number of large surveys which give similar examples of hierarchical thinking. The best and one of the biggest examples is the survey that King Henry II ordered in 1166 to be carried out into the tenants of the great honors of England. Each lord was required to return a written list of holders of their knight's fees under their seals, and some years later these loose documents were organised (like Domesday Book) into a fair copy by an Exchequer clerk. He copied out 166 surviving returns which offer more than three entries; they are drawn from most of the counties of England. Of these over half (87) are constructed on the same basis as the Bayeux inquest of the 1090s. It should also be noted that in each county, when the exchequer clerk registered the returns, he copied the biggest first and the smallest last. From this evidence we can say that it was a natural and widespread medieval impulse to award status on the basis of the extent of landed wealth and possessions. It was by no means the only measure, but it was an important one. There are some informative exceptions in the 1166 returns. When Westminster abbey listed its tenants, the first named had only one fee, but since this tenant was no less a man than the king himself, the reason for his being placed there is obvious. Robert, lord of Okehampton, also placed a man with a single fee at the head of his list, but that man was his elder half-brother, Earl Reginald of Cornwall, so personal prestige, royal charisma and family links could swamp numbers of possessions as a measure of status at times. There is at least one medieval statement – in the *History of William Marshal* in the mid 1220s – that men bearing hereditary titles should properly begin lists of names of knights.[20]

[19] The most accessible edition occurs in *The Red Book of the Exchequer*, ed. H. Hall (3 vols., Rolls Series, 1896) ii, 645–6; for a more extensive edition, H. Navel, 'L'enquête de 1133 sur les fiefs de l'Evêché de Bayeux', *Bullétin de la société des antiquaires de la Normandie*, xlii (1935), 5–80.

[20] *Red Book of the Exchequer* i, 186–445. For the exceptions cited, pp.188, 251. An incidental observation worth making is that lay magnates were more likely to put lists in numerical order than ecclesiastical ones: perhaps because they drew their lists from

Early Social Categories

1. The Magnates

So it is that we have an abundance of evidence from eleventh and twelfth-century sources that early medieval people understood that there were élites within their society which controlled the bulk of its wealth. They had a large variety of Latin and French nouns to describe this group, but they are all synonyms for the controlling few in whose hands was concentrated landed wealth, money and the power to attract followers. They might be called in Latin *principes, primores, proceres, maiores, magnates, nobiliores, illustres, primates* and *optimates:* words which resonate with leadership, priority and distinction. The French language appropriated several of these words, notably *princes* and *magnats*. Chroniclers throughout our period had no doubt of the importance of these men and the way that, despite their fewness, their voice in the affairs of realms was amplified by the golden megaphone of their wealth. So we find around 1000 Richer of Reims describing the gathering of a great Frankish army by King Eudes to meet the Viking threat, with the king collecting the Frankish and Aquitainian *principes* amongst the host to discuss the campaign and to seek their support for battle, urging them on by praising their courage and that of their forbears.[21] If we leap three hundred years we find the English chronicler, William Rishanger, describing a remarkably similar scene at Salisbury in 1297 where King Edward I had gathered the *majores* of England to seek support for a campaign in Gascony. They turned him down flat, perhaps because he was not as good at flattering them as had been King Eudes of France in his day amongst his magnates.[22]

The existence of magnates (I will opt for that particular synonym) is an undeniable fact of medieval social structure. Whatever the ideology of descent and honour used to justify their social hegemony, the essentials of

the oral evidence of open inquisitions in their honor courts, and their jurors had an acute sense of lay consequence. For the priority owed to titled counts in lists, see *History of William Marshal*, ed. T. Holden, S. Gregory and D. Crouch (3 vols., Anglo-Norman Text Society, 2002–6) i, ll. 4538–40, where the author finds the name of the count of Soissons at the end of a list he was reproducing, viz: 'the only reason I put him last is that he was last named in my written source; his name would have been better written at the top of my list'.

[21] *Richeri Historiarum Libri Quatuor*, ed. G. Waitz (Hanover, 1877), 6–7. The incident described happened over a century before Richer wrote, but the social attitudes it reveals are what is important about it.

[22] *Willelmi Rishanger Chronica et Annales*, ed. H.T. Riley (Rolls Series, 1865), 169.

it were materialistic. Walter of Arras put it in his dour and proverbial way around the year 1170:

Everything that the rich achieve – king, count and magnate (li haut home) *is paid for by the poor* (li caitif): *the rich of this world squabble, but the poor foot the bill for the damage.*[23]

There may have been poor knights and squires, but a poor magnate was a contradiction in terms. Wealth was not the only way to get the king's ear, but the possession of outstanding wealth and resources was the only way that a layman could force himself on the king's consciousness. Some kings and princes deliberately attempted to focus this economically and socially dominant group on their own court. The best explored medieval example of this is the court of Henry I of England (1100–35). Henry was said by a later generation to have kept lists of his magnates, which detailed the allowances made to them when they attended court, and the personnel of his court was itemised and immortalised in a surviving tract called the *Constitutio Domus Regis*. The 'counsellors' of King Henry I of England were a small group of men (not forgetting also his admired and respected queen, Mathilda). It included eminent clerics but the rest of his *consultores* or *consiliarii* were English or Norman barons of great possessions whom he consulted widely on a variety of issues, whether or not he took their advice (which sometimes conflicted in any case). Henry's meticulous concern for his magnates' opinion on any and every subject tells us that he perceived and intended to exploit an influential social group at the head of the society of his realm.[24] Henry made of his magnates a self-conscious club, gave them a meeting place and appointed himself their general secretary and treasurer. In this sense he gave them a class identity.

The same mechanism is found elsewhere and earlier. Henry I of England was simply doing as his father had done in Normandy in his day, although more remorselessly and systematically. The identification of magnates with the princely court is implicit in French political culture, not least in the transference out of the Charlemagne cycle into real political life in the reign of Louis VII (1137–80) of the idea of there being 'peers of France' – a group of great lay and ecclesiastical magnates with a right to

[23] *Ille et Galeron*, ed. Y. Lefèvre (Classiques français du moyen age, 1988), ll. 1353–58.

[24] See in particular on Henry I and his confidants, J.G. Hudson, 'Henry I and Counsel', in, *The Medieval State: Essays presented to James Campbell*, ed. J.R. Maddicott and D.M. Palliser (London, 2000), 109–26; for the smallness of the group, and the principles of recruitment at that same royal court, C.W. Hollister, 'Magnates and "Curiales" in Early Norman England', *Viator*, 4 (1973), 115–22.

speak first in council. The appearance of the word 'peers' (*pares, per*) was a way of describing the phenomenon. It was so obviously a good idea that it was being asserted by the 1220s that there were corresponding 'peers of England' with a similar automatic claim to the king's ear. Even a small principality like Philip the Noble's marquisate of Namur was boasting its elite group of 'peers' at the beginning of the thirteenth century.[25] In the 1230s, writers knew that the entourages of emperors, kings and princes were populated with counts and dukes, court nobility (*demainne*) and peers (*per*).[26] The word 'peer' is a symptom of class division. Peers shared aspirations and access to power which were denied to other landowners.

The wealth of the magnate gained him automatic notice from his sovereign. The magnate's inferiors were certainly well aware that there was an upper level of society between them and the king. Alexander Neckam around 1200 talked of the magnates in the same terms as others talked of kings, and talked in particular of the favour (*gratia*) that the magnates could dispense. Their favour had to be courted by hopeful men, and courtiers sought from them a tiny fraction of their wealth. Neckam had a lot to say about how parsimonious, grudging and demanding a magnate could be to those who hung around his household hoping for these benefits.[27] What the magnates demanded was a level of deference from those who acknowledged their social eminence. Certain of them could make their displeasure clear if they did not receive their due. Around 1110 Guy of Merton, a scholarly but socially inept Augustinian canon, attracted unfavourable comment as prior of Taunton 'because he did not know how to entertain guests, men of influence *(potentes)* by whom the Church's work was furthered, and he did not honour them as was proper'. The

[25] For the peers of France, J-P. Poly and E. Bournazel, *The Feudal Transformation, 900–1200*, trans. C. Higgitt (New York, 1991), 200–2; for the 'peers of England', D. Crouch, *The Image of Aristocracy in Britain, 1000–1300* (London, 1992), 104–5 citing the case of William de Beauchamp of Bedford, who in 1250 appealed to the rights of 'the other earls and barons, his peers, in England', National Archives (formerly PRO), KB26/141, m.25d. There was also an effort in the mid 1220s and 1230s, led by successive Marshal earls of Pembroke in opposition to the king, to assert that only their 'peers' (meaning their fellow barons) might judge them, *Patent Rolls, 1225–32*, 82; Matthew Paris, *Chronica Majora*, ed. H.R. Luard (7 vols., Rolls Series, 1872–83). For Nicholas de Condé, in 1204 'par castri Namucensis', *Actes de Philippe Ier dit le Noble, comte et marquis de Namur (1196–1212)*, ed. M. Walraet (Academie Royale de Belgique, 1949), 133–4.

[26] *Gaydon*, ed. F. Guessard and S. Luce (Paris, 1862), ll. 31–2.

[27] *De magnatibus*, in, Alexander Neckam, *De Naturis Rerum Libri Duo*, ed. T. Wright (Rolls Series, London, 1863), 314.

bishop of Winchester was petitioned to find a more urbane head for the community.[28] In the 1170s the courtier-bishop, Stephen de Fougères, who knew similar people all too well, reflected satirically on the common end to which magnates would come: the days of ease and deference would pass, and deferential knees would no longer bend to them as they walked the streets and market places.[29] But respect for lay hierarchy was naturally strong in the overtly hierarchical liturgy of the Church. Daniel of Beccles in the late twelfth century said that the pax (a silver tablet engraved with the face of Christ) should be given first to kiss to the 'most noble' person in the congregation, and that clergy should take special care to defer to such people.[30]

The social consequence of the existence of magnates had subtle but widespread effects on the society in which they lived. It is only necessary to return to the reign of Henry I of England to find telling social comments relating to them. In the mid-1120s William of Malmesbury wrote these perceptive words:

> *The excellence of great men has one laudable feature which perhaps more than any other recommends it; it inspires the affection even of those who are far off, so that men of lower degree adopt as their own the virtues of those above them, reverencing the footsteps of qualities (exempla) they cannot hope to follow.*[31]

Those most admired in society, according to the monk-historian of Malmesbury, offered a pattern of conduct for lesser men to follow. He was thinking in terms of civic virtue, no doubt, but that same mechanism of emulation applied in other areas of conduct and lifestyle. Any socially ambitious and rising man could copy what the magnates did, and, providing that he was not laughed at (as Neckam laughed at the inept social

28 M.L. Colker, 'The Life of Guy of Merton by Rainald of Merton', *Medieval Studies*, 31 (1969), 258.

29 *Le Livre de Manières*, ll. 1231–4.

30 *Urbanus Magnus Danielis Becclesiensis*, ed. J.G. Smyly (Dublin, 1939), 9. Curiously, Ulrich von Liechtenstein describes exactly this happening in an aristocratic congregation at mass in a church in Istria in 1226, *Service of Ladies*, trans. J.W. Thomas (Chapel Hill, 1969), 110–11.

31 *Gesta regum Anglorum*, ed. R.A.B. Mynors, R.M. Thompson and M. Winterbottom (2 vols, Oxford, 1998–9) i, 10. Stephen de Fougères says something similar in the 1170s, viz. 'a duke or a king is a pattern (*rele*) and an example (*esxanple*) to knights and to burgesses, both to the villein and the courtly man', *Le Livre de Manières*, ll. 149–51.

climbers of Angevin England), he could be acknowledged as a man of rank, an aristocrat.

2. The Middle Ground, 1000–1180

It may be that medieval people contemplated with satisfaction the ideological unity of Christendom, but this did not prevent the eleventh-century mind holding the belief that society could be broken down into more component groups than that of the magnates. The basis of the analysis was materialism: different degrees of wealth led to different degrees of status. The fact that it recognised other social groups than the magnates helps us to find the boundaries of the medieval conception of aristocracy, although it is not until the last quarter of the twelfth century that clear boundaries finally emerge. Leaving aside then the magnate and the other important case of the peasant, we find a social middle ground between them occupied by a number of named groups, membership of which gave people a certain amount of status. Knights are the most obvious in clerical sources because one of their defining characteristics was their objectionable violence, and so St Bernard – who had ambitions to reform knighthood – defined the laity as the 'princes, knights and people'.[32] But knights were by no means the only group visible to contemporaries in the intermediate ground between magnates and peasants. From France there come several documents that speak of a perception of diverse status levels, however ill-defined. At some time between 1001 and 1020 the dominant landholders of the Burgundian dioceses of Vienne and Bugey swore an oath to keep the peace. Comprehended within the twenty-six articles of the oath is a perception of the lay part of their society as made up of male and female peasants, prévôts (village administrators), merchants, knights of two levels of status (free and unfree), noblemen and noblewomen, as well as specialist freemen like the bargemen of the Rhône and the huntsmen employed in the forests.[33]

The twelfth century can produce similar statements. There is a particularly revealing list given by the Norman writer Wace of Bayeux around 1160. He also showed an awareness that there was a varied social middle ground. In describing the wasting of the land around Paris by the Vikings centuries earlier he said that the magnates – the dukes, counts and great

[32] As noted by J. Flori, *L'Essor de Chevalerie* (Geneva, 1986), 212.

[33] For date, commentary and translation, D. Barthélemy, *L'an mil et la paix de Dieu: La France chrétienne et féodale, 980-1060* (Paris, 1999), 421–6.

men *(homme puisant)* – were unable to protect the countryside. As a result the burden of local defence fell on the country knights *(li chevalier des villes)*, the free peasants *(li bons païsant)*, the tenant landowners *(vavasor)*, the village stewards *(major)*, unfree peasants *(villain)* and servants *(serjant)*.[34] To Wace, there was a magnate group at the top of society, identified by its national responsibilities. Below were other groups of local status in a hazy relationship with each other. Wace divided his social groups by a sort of rationale of responsibility: the uppermost class was associated with the prince and shared his interests and national social leadership. He believed that there were other people of influence who could draw swords, but their interests were focussed on their own neighbourhood and region, and they depended on their superiors for direction. Below them were groups who normally would not fight, whose duty was only to follow.

In post-Conquest England around 1100 we find the same loose socio-economic perceptions of status as we found in France in 1060. We find a charter of Hugh I earl of Chester (died 1101) which talks of the social make-up of Cheshire in typically vague French terms: his chief barons, lesser barons, knights, townsmen, other sorts of free men and peasants. Although the wergeld system was still current in the reign of Henry I, and had even been modified to take account of the presence of Frenchmen in England, Earl Hugh's clerk made no resort to its antiquated terminology and status levels. One Anglo-Norman clerk chose to translate the old English names for social ranks into Latin to make them more applicable, and so the 'ceorl' experienced demotion to 'villein', and a 'thegn' became generalised as a 'man fully noble', but by then this was not much more than antiquarianism.[35] Any Anglo-Norman writer seeking to comprehend some or all of society in the general address of a document had liberty to sit for a while chewing the end of his quill before putting together his own idiosyncratic list. Eighty years later the same was still true. A writer near the end of the twelfth century put together just such a list when he imagined the king of Leinster seeking to recruit adventurers to join his army to

[34] *Le Roman de Rou*, ed. A.J. Holden (3 vols, Société des anciens textes français, 1970–73) i, pt 2, ll. 758–64.

[35] *The Charters of the Anglo-Norman Earls of Chester, c.1071–1237*, ed. G. Barraclough (Record Society of Lancashire and Cheshire, 126, 1988), 4 (from the pancarte of St Werburgh of Chester). For a wergeld list of *c.*1116, which derived from the sort of texts Wulfstan used, although modified for post-Conquest conditions, *Leges Henrici Primi*, ed. L.J. Downer (Oxford, 1972), 236–42. For the process of translating the system, Maitland, *History of English Law* ii, 459–60

regain his kingdom: he called on earls and barons, knights, squires *(vallez),* serjeants *(serjanz),* mercenaries *(soudeiers),* whether mounted or not.[36]

What this indicates is that eleventh and early twelfth century writers had no perception of class then as being hierarchical. As a result they cannot have had much if any understanding of class *an sich,* as Marx economically put it (meaning 'a class aware of itself as a social level'). Writers observed some social groups; they could recognise that they had characteristics and their own status; and they believed that their readers would recognise them too. But what they did not do was to rank these groups by order of status within society, other than decide that below the king there was no one higher than the magnate, and that no one in society was lower than the unfree peasant. In any group, medieval people would have had little problem with rating individuals by their own importance, bringing into play a range of factors, economic and social. When it came to selecting husbands for the women of their family, they had no trouble recognising when the status of the intended husband did not match that of the bride-to-be. To contemplate such an unequal match would be to 'desparagier' the wife.[37] But they did not extend this to social groups, hence the problem of the status of the urban elites and the squires: both were recognised social groups of the middle ground, but individual merchants and squires drew no particular status from being identified as members of their group. This was even more pointedly true of the knightly group, which included great nobles and humble mercenaries. But by 1200 this amiable confusion was clearing.

Inventing Social Boundaries

1. Social Hierarchy

Twelfth-century writers grew increasingly keen to split humanity up into categories, and what was new was the way they did so increasingly with ideological concerns. There is a distinct type of tract 'On the differing orders of men' which comes to our notice with the work of Bernard of Cluny in the second quarter of the century. This was not the sort of essay in social nostalgia and imaginary hierarchy that Wulfstan and Adalbero of Laon had written a century earlier. What Bernard wrote was a grim and

[36] *The Deeds of the Normans in Ireland*, ed. and trans. E. Mullally (Dublin, 2002), ll. 427–9.

[37] *Garin le Loherenc*, ed. A. Iker-Gittleman (3 vols, Classiques français du moyen âge, 1996–7) i, ll. 2617–21 (reference datable to 1160 × 80), and see pp. 310–11.

heavy tract 'on the contempt of the things of this world'. The early part fits into the school of social rhetoric inspired by Ecclesiastes, but in his second book Bernard shifted his emphasis. He talked now of men, and divided them into several types, which he calls *gradus* (ranks) or *ordines* (conditions). He did so simply to demonstrate the vanity of the endeavours of each, and the corruption of the present day. He listed bishops, kings, priests, other clergy, 'savage' knights, noblemen, justices, merchants and peasants. What Bernard did not do is to say whether he perceived them in any hierarchical relationship. His comments show that he was in two minds about the social importance of knights, but when he dealt with them at length he was willing to consider that knights might be nobles, and therefore men of consequence above others. Bernard considered merchants to be of consequence because of their wealth, and the importance of peasants rested on their agricultural productivity.[38] It seems clear that Bernard was responding at length to traditional pastoral sermons, which addressed a perceived group in society as to what were its proper duties so that it could morally improve itself.[39]

An anonymous French author of a briefer but very similar mid-twelfth-century 'Satire on Greed', written a little later than Bernard's work, took a slightly different tack, closer to Wulfstan a century earlier. For him there are proper ranks *(gradus)* in which people should be content, but the problem was that they were not staying in them; wealth and greed was causing social dissolution, or so he said. His conditions of men *(ordines)* included bishops, merchants or financiers, 'wicked' knights, peasants and monks. The author was very heated about financiers, whom he saw climbing to high rank with the aid of the kings and princes who needed their money, 'as if they were their sort'. Knights, being desirous of luxury and lavish dress, lived above their means, and financed it all by theft. Even peasants bickered and feuded as they tried to increase their lands and their wealth.[40] A much more pointed and extensive essay on the same lines was offered by Bishop Stephen de Fougères in his 'Book of Conduct'. This is

[38] Bernard of Cluny, *De contemptu mundi*, ed. and trans. R.E. Pepin (East Lansing, MI, 1991), 90–6.

[39] Constable, 'The Orders of Society', 274, notes examples back to the eighth century, although Bernard of Cluny's composition was of course on an entirely different scale and written to a distinct scheme. A good example of such precursors is a ninth-century sermon attributed to Theodulf of Orleans (794–821), *De omnibus ordinibus huius saeculi*, in *PL*, 105, cols. 280–2, which urges the rich and powerful, the poor and slaves to be content each in their role.

[40] *Poésies inédites du moyen age*, ed. M. Édélestand du Méril (Paris, 1854), 313–17.

organised as a series of miniature sermons to a number of groups in turn: kings, clergy, bishops, archbishops, popes, cardinals, knights, peasants, merchants and noblewomen. Stephen was clear that the knights had a definite social place amongst the laity. They were employed by greater men and had inferiors: their tenants and peasants. Their arms and training gave knights the ability to intervene in disputes and protect the Church, and they constituted a 'haute ordre' – or at least they had done, for he believed that they were in decline. Stephen talked at length about merchants and tradesmen as another social group, answering, like knights, directly to dukes and counts. The merchant too had inferiors, the poor in towns and those who wanted to borrow his money, but unlike the knight, the merchant had no duties other than that of behaving decently and decorously within his urban community.

The key indicator of the emergence of a hierarchy of social class in the twelfth-century mind is the work of Andrew the Chaplain, a clergyman on the fringes of the courts of King Philip II of France (1179–1223) and his sister, Countess Mary of Champagne (died 1198). He was a close contemporary of the two last authors, and in a very different sort of satire written about the socially corrupting influence of love, or lust, he also offered a social categorisation. But he went one step beyond his predecessors and made it deliberately hierarchical. Written in the mid-1180s, Andrew's *Tractatus de amore* ('On Love') is not an easy work to analyse.[41] Its first book was written as a series of dialogues between men and women of differing social levels; and it is on the face of it a treatise on sexual seduction. But it was written in an age when adultery was punished with great savagery in lay society and bitterly condemned by the Church. So rather than interpret it as an ironical and amoral literary exercise by a wildly eccentric northern French clergyman, I take it here to have been intended as a social satire. Andrew initially proposed three social levels, although he implied a fourth. In Latin he called his three types (in ascending social order) *plebeius, nobilis* and *nobilior*. The range of synonyms and allusions Andrew used makes it perfectly clear that we are meant to take the *plebeius* to be an urban merchant, the *nobilis* to be a knight and the *nobilior* to be a count. There is a fourth and lower social group implied, however. In an appendix to the first book, Andrew opened (a little distastefully) the possibility of an agricultural labourer experiencing love in a way that he admitted that the leisured urban merchant did. Andrew concluded that

[41] For a commentary on interpreting Andrew, C.B. Bouchard, *Strong of Body, Brave and Noble*, 139–41.

whatever urges the peasant experienced, he had best sublimate them in the hard, manual work of tilling his fields.[42]

The mind of Andrew the Chaplain in the 1180s comprehended a society which was divided into a hierarchy of social conditions (which he also called *ordines*). All of them are familiar from earlier writers we have already discussed, the difference is that Andrew saw them as ranked in ascending levels *(gradus)* and as being exclusive, for they had boundaries *(metae, fines)* which should not be crossed. What made them exclusive? Like other writers, Andrew believed that social groups had common mental and physical characteristics: for instance women of the lower orders were not particularly bright and would believe any flattery, whereas urban males were graceless and tended to be physically awkward and ill-proportioned. According to him, peasants were unkempt, hairy and devoid of the higher feelings.[43] But the main boundary was marked by a man's occupation, and bore most heavily on the urban rich. Merchants were rich and could afford all the trappings and luxuries that materially defined the higher aristocrat, and the fact that they could do so troubled the boundary of noble class. It is not just Andrew who tells us that merchants had social aspirations. The leading citizens of London were traditionally called 'barons'. In the early twelfth century this meant little, as all sorts of groups of men in England (such as suitors in the county courts and the attendants at the exchequer table) were called 'barons'. The Latin word originally meant no more than *preusdommes* did in the vernacular: mature men of affairs (the same sense as the vernacular cognate word, *ber*). But by the 1170s its sense had shifted to mean a socially elite group of men around a prince or magnate. Then the fact that Londoners were called 'barons' seemed to imply great status, and the Londoner, William fitz Stephen, writing around 1173, proudly (and inaccurately) proclaimed that though other towns had *civites* (citizens), London in its greatness had *barones*.[44]

The social anomaly of wealthy commoners made them a group which some people clearly believed had to be undermined at every opportunity.

[42] Andrew the Chaplain, *On Love*, ed. and trans. P.G. Walsh (London, 1982), 222.

[43] On physical ugliness and lack of nobility, Crouch, *Image of Aristocracy in Britain*, 18.

[44] William fitz Stephen, 'A Description of the Most Noble City of London', trans. H.E. Butler, in F.M. Stenton, *Norman London: An Essay* (London, 1934), 27; Crouch, *Image of Aristocracy*, 25, 111–14. Compare William of Malmesbury's earlier comment about Londoners 'who are in effect magnates (*quasi proceres*) because of the greatness of their city in England ...' (*c*.1143), *Historia Novella*, ed. E. King (Oxford, 1998), 94.

Andrew the Chaplain worked hard to do this in the 1180s, and he was not alone. James de Vitry and Jean de Joinville both repeat a story which originated in Andrew's generation. In Champagne in the 1170s there was a particularly wealthy merchant called Artaud of Nogent, a close associate of Count Henry the Liberal (1152–1181), the husband of Andrew's patron. Artaud built a grand castle and was an important member of the count's council, and acted and dressed in every way like a magnate. But, according to the story, he was brutally cut down to size when the count was petitioned by a poor knight for help to pay the dowries of two daughters. Artaud spoke up too loudly against the petition, and the count retaliated against his presumption by granting Artaud and his goods to the poor knight, on the grounds that Artaud was his 'villein' to dispose of as he wished.[45] The story's later popularity tells us how useful it was in reinforcing the limits of nobility, but also how insecure those limits actually were when confronted by wealth that could buy the material attributes of aristocracy. As for London and its barons, Matthew Paris put into Henry III's mouth a nasty put-down of their pretensions: 'those London peasants *(rustici)* who call themselves barons sicken me with their wealth'. He also recorded that when young men of the city élite presumed to beat the younger members of the royal court at Westminster in a quintain match, the courtiers provoked a riot by calling the London boys 'scabby peasants and soapmakers'.[46]

For Andrew the Chaplain the closed aristocracy above the urban rich could be marked off by one further feature. Nobility *(nobilitas)* was the conscious property of the two highest of the orders he described, and it was greedily envied by the urban classes. It constrained the knight and the count to be polite, but always to be aware of the social gulf between themselves and the rest. Nobility was rooted both in birth and upbringing, and although Andrew reluctantly conceded that nobility of manners could be possessed or acquired by those outside the aristocracy, to the knight and count they were innate and natural. However, this was an age of criticism of nobility of birth, as we have already seen (see p. 148ff.), and Andrew had to tread carefully about using 'nobility' as a boundary. So he admitted that there was a counterbalancing quality of moral distinction *(probitas)* to that of nobility. Andrew also admitted that the prince, who was above all

[45] *Die exempla aus den Sermones feriales et communes des Jakob von Vitry*, ed. J. Greven (Heidelberg, 1914), 17; Jean de Joinville, *Vie de Saint Louis*, ed. J. Monfrin (Paris, 1995), 46.

[46] Matthew Paris, *Chronica Majora*, ed. H.R. Luard (7 vols., Rolls Series, 1872–84) v, 22, 367.

the orders of society, could confer nobility on a man of great probity (or as the vernacular had it, a *preudomme*), whatever his class. When Andrew said this, he took the critical step of saying that ennoblement was linked with the act of knighting. It is the insecurity of social structures, which he wished to be firm and established, that seems to energise Andrew's prose as much as it had energised that of Wulfstan of York nearly two centuries earlier.

There are one or two thirteenth-century versions of the sort of social tracts we have already looked at, although the genre seems to have lost popularity after 1200. This in itself may be a symptom that hierarchical social organisation had become accepted and understood by all, even if was not always respected. But one major example is an English tract *de diversis ordinibus hominum* ('on the differing conditions of men'), which dates from the period between 1220 and 1240. The big difference from its predecessors is that it directly ranks all its conditions in a hierarchy, from top down. The sequence runs: pope, cardinals, kings, bishops, abbots, monks, friars, counts, knights, priests, clerks, urban merchants, free landholders and servile peasants. As with Stephen de Fougères, the author's intention is to sermonise on the inadequacy of each of these social types. Unlike Stephen, he saw them arranged in an order of precedence, and if the ecclesiastical element is removed, his perception of the secular order is clear. There was no longer any vagueness for this author as to where knights stood in relation to merchants. As with Andrew the Chaplain, knights were associated with counts as noblemen in the service of the king and public order. Merchants were, for him, men devoted to making money and spending it, with no saving grace and less status. With this work it is clear that thirteenth-century people were taking it as matter of course that they were living in a society of distinct social groups hierarchically organised by levels of status.[47]

2. Knighthood

If it had been established by 1200 that society was organised into a hierarchy of classes of descending status, most commentators would say that the process had a lot to do with the knight. As we have already seen, Andrew the Chaplain in the 1180s indicated that for a commoner to be ennobled, it was sufficient for the prince to knight him. The conferring of

[47] *De diversis ordinibus hominum*, in, *The Latin Poems commonly attributed to Walter Mapes*, ed. T. Wright (Camden Society, old ser., 1841), 229–36.

knighthood was therefore the boundary of noble class for this late twelfth-century writer. He was not alone in his generation in believing it. Around the year 1190 a writer associated with the court of King Richard the Lionheart of England came out with the following revolutionary suggestion:

Let no man henceforth consider that he may make knights in his own land. They should come to the royal court when it is assembled. The king will give to each a sword and a shield, arms and horses, weapons and money in return for their chief allegiance.[48]

The fact that the suggestion was made at all indicates that by 1190 people had realised that in their society the conferring of knighthood by itself admitted men to the noble class. That is why the writer suggested that the king should control it. He believed that knighting was now too socially sensitive a matter to let anyone other than the prince decide who should be so dignified. Knighthood by then conferred noble status, and exalted the person of the knight. In the army of Louis IX at Acre in 1252, a sergeant-at-arms who laid a hand on a knight risked having it severed at the wrist as a penalty, even if he was a member of the royal household.[49]

How had this come to happen? It has been argued above that eleventh-century writers perceived no social hierarchy of classes – although they were alert enough to individual status and were aware of social groups – so for them knighthood could not admit a man to a superior social class. To be a knight in the eleventh century was to possess a degree of status, but it did not make a man an aristocrat. To see this we only have to look at the knights who feature in the 'Conventum' of Hugh the Chiliarch of *c.*1030. Hugh's knights formed the garrisons of his castles, and commanded a degree of status. When captured, they might be ransomed for large sums of money. But, as we have seen, rival magnates did not necessarily treat them with consideration as their equals, and some of Hugh's knights were gruesomely mutilated by their captors. The Church's rhetoric against knights as the agents of local violence in the eleventh century certainly did a lot to depress their social standing, equating them with brigands and outlaws. To be poor and a knight was by no means unusual in the eleventh century, and

[48] *La Chanson d'Aspremont*, ed. L. Brandin (2 vols, Classiques français du moyen age, 1923–4) i, ll. 108–9. In 1245 the English royal council decided that all men holding land directly from the king should receive knighthood from him, while men holding land from others might get themselves knighted by anyone they wished, M. Powicke, *Military Obligation in Medieval England* (Oxford, 1962), 80.

[49] *Vie de Saint Louis*, 252.

Domesday Book records hundreds of men called *milites* with very little land indeed to their names.[50] William de Poitiers, once himself a knight, talked in the late 1070s of knights of varied status in the Conqueror's army, knights of 'middling nobility' and 'common knights'.[51]

The uneven social ground on which knights stood before 1190 has long been apparent to historians. There are a number of early observations which leave us confused as to whether early knights were socially important or not, or simply perceived as a socially neutral occupational category. One of the earliest and most famous is the observation by Richer of Reims as to why Charles of Lorraine failed to achieve the support of the magnates for his claim to the crown of the Western Franks in 987. It was because he had married 'a woman who was not of his degree *(ordo)*, a woman from people of the condition of knight *(de militari ordine)*'.[52] The criticism is of course ambiguous. Marrying the daughter of a family of professional warriors was clearly held to be beneath a king, but it had still been good enough for a duke of Carolingian descent. A surviving original charter of Count Geoffrey II of Perche-Mortagne, dated to 1082, does not seem ashamed at all of describing the count as 'girded with the belt of knighthood, and count of Mortagne'.[53] Another charter, of much the same date, is even more revealing of attitudes to knighthood. The Breton lord of Monmouth, Wihenoc, was described by a clerk of the abbey of Saumur as a 'miles' but the clerk also referred to the 'milites' who held land from him.[54] The word 'miles' could be used proudly by and of magnates, but also of their dependents, without any sense of disparagement. More than anything else this reveals that knighthood was *not* perceived as a social level before 1100, but as an occupation with skills and status which the highest in the land, as well as their inferiors, delighted to share in.

A further complication in assessing what the word 'knight' signified in social terms is its place in the coming-of-age ceremony of free males. The

[50] S. Harvey, 'The Knight and Knight's Fee in England', *Past and Present*, xlix (1970), 15, 21, and see further discussion of this evidence in D.F. Fleming, 'Landholding by Milites in Domesday Book' in, *Anglo-Norman Studies*, xiii, ed. M. Chibnall (Woodbridge, 1990), 83–98,

[51] William of Poitiers, *Gesta Guillelmi*, ed. and trans. R.H.C. Davis and M. Chibnall (Oxford, 1998), 158.

[52] *Richeri Historiarum Libri Quatuor*, ed. G. Waitz (2 vols, Paris, 1845) ii, 156, considered in, J.M. van Winter, 'Uxorem de militari ordine sibi imponens' in, *Miscellanea in memoriam J.F. Niermeyer* (Gröningen, 1961), 119–20.

[53] '... ego Gaufridus militari balteo accinctus atque castri Mauritanie comes', K. Thompson, 'Les premiers temps de Saint-Denis de Nogent-le-Rotrou et leurs réécritures', *Bibliothèque de l'École des chartes*, 160 (2002), 658.

[54] Archives départementales de Maine-et-Loire H 3710, no. 1.

ceremony of 'adoubement' (meaning 'equipping') was used at several junctures in medieval masculine life, but its most well-known purpose was when a senior male declared that a boy was a man, by girding him with a sword and conferring horse and other military equipment on him. There are a number of instances of eleventh-century princes and magnates going through this ceremony when they came of age. Fulk le Réchin was girded with a sword at Angers at Pentecost 1060 by his uncle, Geoffrey of Anjou. Before 1065 the young Norman aristocrat, Robert of Rhuddlan, was girded with a sword in England by the French-educated King Edward the Confessor, in whose court he was living. Count Henry, the son of William the Conqueror, received from Archbishop Lanfranc hauberk, helmet and swordbelt on his coming of age in 1086, when the Anglo-Saxon chronicle observed that he had been 'dubbed as a rider'. By 1130 being made or belted as a knight was a synonym for coming of age in England amongst landed families of greater and lesser degree.[55] Princes and magnates were rejoicing in this ceremony as an important family occasion well before the 1060s, so much is clear. This in itself tells against knighthood as being useful as a marker for the boundary of aristocracy in the eleventh century. What would be more revealing about the social value of the knighting ceremony is some idea of how it might have been restricted at the poorer end of society. Unfortunately no such sources exist to tell us that, other than what little we can extrapolate from the diverse levels of wealth and poverty of 'milites' before 1100.

Knighthood and noble status came together at some time before 1190, when there are strong indicators that the two had been linked, not least in Andrew the chaplain's implication that knightly *adoubement* was the lower boundary of nobility. If there was one thing that was the catalyst in narrowing knighthood to a noble elite it may have been the possession of a landed estate. An indicator of how the possession of land and an independent income was affecting the status of the knight comes from the court of King Richard I of England. In 1194 he issued regulations for the conduct of tournaments in England. These included the amount that a member of each rank of society needed to pay to get a licence to join a particular tournament. The tariff ran at twenty marks for an earl, ten marks for a baron, four marks for a knight with land and two marks for a land-

[55] *Chroniques des comtes d'Anjou et des seigneurs d'Amboise*, ed. L. Halphen and R. Poupardin (Paris, 1913), 236; Orderic Vitalis, *The Ecclesiastical History*, ed. M. Chibnall (6 vols., Oxford, 1969–80) iv, 120, 136; *The Peterborough Chronicle*, ed. C. Clark (2nd edn., Oxford, 1970) *s.a.* 1086. For coming of age and knighthood in England, Crouch, *Image of Aristocracy*, 143.

less knight. Any knight seems to have had the right to turn up, but the landed knight was treated differently. Although the regulations do not say anything about how much land was acceptable as a qualification, we can assume that a landed knight had to have an estate that allowed him – with whatever other resources he had – sufficient income not to miss several payments of four marks in a year. Landless knights were automatically assumed to be men of less consequence than those with land: so a fissure had opened up in the previously undifferentiated knightly continuum in society.[56] We see other symptoms of this. Knights who had substantial landed estates were men in whom the royal administration was interested. In England from the 1160s onwards, they were the men who made up juries of inquisition in the counties. By 1220 we find a case in Herefordshire where a man who had been knighted was removed from a jury because 'he is in a household and has no land'.[57]

The possession of land was not the only fissure opening up levels of social status within the knightly group and breaking it up to correspond to the evolution of hierarchical class in society. If a landed estate and knighthood was hardening as the lowest boundary for nobility by 1190, there was another boundary closing at the top end of the group who called themselves knights. As the tournament regulations of 1194 make clear, there was a group called 'barons' who were on a higher status level than the landed knights: they were Andrew the Chaplain's *nobiliores*. Like Wihenoc of Monmouth in 1081, such barons might be proud to be called knights, but by 1194, when the title of 'knight' was being taken to be the *lowest* grade of nobility, such men would not be satisfied to find themselves on an equal footing with owners of one manor, when they were lords of baronies of dozens and even hundreds of manors. Yet 'baron' was not a formal title at this time, and would not become so for over a century. Men of baronial status had to find a way of distancing themselves from knights who were their inferiors, and they found it in the possession of their banners. Banners were ensigns of magnate power. Only a man followed by a retinue of knights would need to have one. Therefore a superior grade of knighthood had evolved by the 1180s, when a distinction was drawn between a knight, and a knight 'carrying a banner'.

The idea of a special level of magnate knighthood grew up simultaneously in France and England. The first inkling of it appears in the

[56] T. Rymer, *Foedera, Conventiones, Litterae et Acta Publica*, ed. A. Clarke and F. Holbrooke (7 vols., London, 1816–69) i, pt 1, 65.

[57] *Curia Regis Rolls* ix, 157.

fragments of a roll made to record a tournament held at Lagny in Champagne in 1179, where knights carrying banners *(portant banière)* were distinguished from others, and were paid attendance money not just for themselves but for the knights they brought with them.[58] In 1193 an equivalent Latin phrase was used of Abbot Samson of Bury St Edmunds when he led his knights to the siege of Windsor castle, and it was used again in 1207 in the surveys of the tenants of his new realm carried out for King Philip II of France. In the mid-thirteenth-century such a magnate-knight might be called in Latin a *vexillifer,* as Matthew Paris did, or in French a *banière,* as Joinville did. In the second half of the century the title 'banneret' *(banneretus)* became more and more usual, and increasingly employed in English governmental records.[59] The appearance of bannerets in the late twelfth century, at the same time that Andrew the Chaplain was portraying a society divided into hierarchical classes, and at the same time that retained and landless knights were being treated as inferior to landed knights, is deeply significant. Between 1170 and 1200 knighthood was established as the lower boundary for the noble class. Knights who were dependents and had no stake in local society began to be edged out of consideration. Those men who were not earls or counts, but still led contingents of knights, were credited with a superior form of knighthood to distinguish them from the common knights they led in the field. The two separate acts of creating knights and bannerets had become a means of drawing class distinctions even within the body of men acknowledged to be noble.

3. Extending Hierarchy, 1240–1300

By 1220 it was already possible to talk of an Anglo-French lay society which saw itself ranked below the king hierarchically downwards: there were the noble dukes, counts and other magnates, enjoying their superior knighthood of banneret; below them were the noble knights admitted into their status by equipping with arms and golden spurs; the ignoble and unarmed wealthy, the merchant and vavassor, occupied a middle ground; below them were the free but inconsiderable common people, and at bottom was the contemptible peasant. By 1300 this hierarchy had firmed up further, to produce a social group on the fringes of nobility below the

[58] *History of William Marshal* i, ll.4750–76.

[59] See references collected in Crouch, *Image of Aristocracy*, 115–17, and for Joinville, *Vie de Saint Louis*, 56.

knight, the level of the squire, or *damoiseau*. By 1300 society had been codified in the same way as had been conduct. It had been analysed and categorised, and most people knew where they stood in regard to this analysis. Class *an sich* had thus appeared in France and England, and was understood in the same way in both realms. The way it had happened is explained best by Duby's model of cultural diffusion, although there is certainly every reason to continue to credit the arrival of the noble knight with a central place in the whole business.

The process did not end in 1220. We can see it working its way out in the general impact of the establishment of knighthood as the frontier of nobility. This hit particularly hard the aspiring social group of the wealthy merchant, but also the members of families which had produced knights in past generations, but which were unable or unwilling to afford the expense that it now involved. As we have seen, across England, the wealthiest and most influential of the urban elites simply took on knighthood in the thirteenth century, and it seems that nothing was done to stop them. As several historians have pointed out, the costs and responsibilities of knighthood in England in the thirteenth century were burdensome enough to persuade many men who could have become knights because of their birth and means, not to bother. The king and his advisors from 1224 onwards felt forced to take the measure of setting up local enquiries as to which men they felt were avoiding knighthood and imposing penalties if they continued to resist the honour (which were often avoided by the payment of fines). The orders compelling knighthood in 1241 and 1242 demonstrate that in its desperation to recruit knights, the royal council was willing to define a man who should be a knight, not by birth, but by the possession of land worth twenty pounds in annual rent. In 1253 this was adjusted upwards to thirty pounds.[60] In these circumstances the king was not going to resist the wealthy and well-connected merchant's desire to take on the distinction.

The situation of the man from a noble family who was not a knight was more fraught and liminal. If a knight was noble by virtue of his descent and his knighting, what about his sons, particularly his younger sons? The eldest son might feel it obligatory to take on knighthood, but his younger brothers would not necessarily feel the need and they were in point of descent, if not in point of means, no less noble than their elder. It was at

[60] M. Powicke, 'Distraint of Knighthood and Military Obligation under Henry III', *Speculum*, 25 (1950), 457–70; idem, *Military Obligation in Medieval England*, 71–81.

this point that squirehood began to mutate into a social group within the class hierarchy. In the twelfth century the words *escuier, damoisel* or *vaslet* indicate that people recognised a group of attendants and trainees associated with the knight. But these men were no means formed a defined group with boundaries. Some, probably the majority, were no more than riding servants; some were boys in expectation of knighthood; some were men of respectable property who joined noble retinues and took up household offices, but who did not aspire to be knights. But definition crept up on the squire nonetheless. William Marshal's biographer recalls that the squires of the 1170s did not expect too much from their masters, whereas by the 1220s squires insisted on not just a mount from their master, but a pack horse too.[61] By 1200, squires had acquired a recognisable costume: short livery coats provided by their masters and a distinctive cropped haircut, to distinguish them from the robed and long haired knights they served. When they fought or attended the tournament, squires were armed with quilted leather coats *(doublentines),* short swords *(coutels),* clubs and broad-brimmed iron caps *(capeliers).*[62]

The poet Henry de Laon, writing between 1220 and 1250, has a lot to say about the aspirations of the squire in his generation. A particularly telling point he observed was that squires on the tournament circuit were behaving more and more like knights. In the twelfth century, magnates who took to the tourney field had come accompanied by a household guard of a score of knights who would look out for them on the field and fend off men trying to capture them. By 1250, knights in France were riding on to the field in the same way, guarded by half-a-dozen squires, who, Henry says, demanded the same arms and standard of mount that a knight would and who, just like knights, demanded the right to ransom the horses of men they threw down.[63] The squire had in this way established himself within the military nobility, and thrown off his former subordination.

Investigation of thirteenth-century landholders called squires reveals the same thing as the tournament evidence. The squire, for instance, was increasingly a title used by holders of fees in the Vendômois after 1240, and by the end of the century most holders of fees in that region called themselves squires, not knights.[64] By 1250 squires were insisting that they

[61] *HWM* i, ll. 767–8.

[62] *Gui de Warewic* i, ll. 6192–8; *Lancelot do Lac*, i, 542; *Jehan et Blonde*, ll. 4023-6.

[63] A. Långfors, '*Le dit des hérauts* par Henri de Laon', *Romania*, xliii (1914), 224.

[64] D. Barthélemy, *La société dans la comté de Vendôme de l'an mil au xive siècle* (Paris, 1993), 943–4.

and their wives be described in documents as *domicellus* and *domicella,* in the same way as a knight and his lady were *dominus* and *domina,* and some were beginning to commission armorial seals.[65] Squires were also holding their own aristocratic festivities. The mid-thirteenth-century French romance *Sone de Nansay* is known for its detailed and accurate depictions of contemporary noble festivals. Its author describes a 'Round Table' or jousting festival, held in the Gâtinais. It was held at magnificent expense exclusively for squires. It was organised for them and their ladies just as it was for the knights, which indicates that the competitors were not youthful apprentices but adult squires who did not care to seek knighting. The competing squires got to keep the horses of those they defeated in their jousts, just as knights did. Significantly for us, the hero's mentor said that this was the way that the Round Table was organised in many countries.[66]

However, despite that urbane assertion, there is less evidence from England in the thirteenth century that squires were taking on noble attributes in the way that they were in France. The words *domicellus* and *armiger/scutifer* were not used in England in the manner of honorable titles, as in France. In an extensive review of the fourteenth-century evidence of the use of the word *armiger* and the spread of heraldry below the knights, Peter Coss argues that the rank of squire failed to establish itself firmly in England as a social category until the middle third of the fourteenth century.[67] But a nominalist approach such as this has its limitations. If we look at noble behaviour and style, it is clear that it had spread to families below those who took up the title of knight well before 1300. We find noble festivals arranged for squires by the end of the thirteenth century. In June 1288 at Boston Fair a 'bohort' (or mock tournament) was held for squires. It should have been a harmless and good-natured enough masque, with one side dressing up in monk's habits and the other in the robes of regular canons. But a certain squire called Robert Chamberlain used it as a cover to attempt to plunder valuables being displayed in the great fair. He was caught and hung by the town authorities, refusing to the end to name his accomplices.[68] As it is described, it was clearly an event organised

65 Crouch, *Image of Aristocracy*, 169 and n; P. Adam-Even, 'Les sceaux d'écuyers au xiiie siècle', *Archives héraldiques suisses*, lxvi (1951), 19–23.

66 *Sone von Nausay*, ed. M. Goldschmidt (Bibliothek des literarischen Vereins in Stuttgart, ccxvi, Tübingen, 1899), ll. 619–25, 1163–98.

67 P.R. Coss, *The Origins of the English Gentry* (Cambridge, 2003), 216–37.

68 *The Chronicle of Walter of Guisborough*, ed. H. Rothwell (Camden Society, 3rd ser., lxxxix, 1957), 224–5.

for men of leisure and status, even though one of them turned out in the end to be a criminal.

There were therefore men in the 1280s in England called squires who behaved as nobles, and were treated as nobles, even though other people called squires did not perhaps have such pretensions. A reductionist position can be sustained which argues that a noble group below the knight was forming in England in the second half of the thirteenth century. People had that perception as early as the 1240s. The rules for household management compiled by Bishop Robert Grosseteste describes a household containing knights, but also other *gentis hommes* (men of good family) who had sufficient status to receive livery robes alongside the knights.[69] Social hierarchy was clearly on the way when Bishop Robert wrote in such terms. It had not yet arrived in England by 1300, for squirehood there was less consolidated than in France. But, as Peter Coss has demonstrated, the process of establishing a social hierarchy was inexorably proceeding, as the members of each social group sought to establish a place in the sun. Aristocratic society in 1300 was not what it had been in 1100. Social class had arrived.

[69] *Walter of Henley and other Treatises on Estate Management and Accounting*, ed. D.M. Oschinsky (Oxford, 1971), 402.

CHAPTER 9

The Precocity of England

Any English historian might well be brimming with objections to the model of social change in the last chapter. The question that will no doubt occur is the one as to whether pre-Conquest England had well-defined and hierarchical social ranks. And it would seem at first sight that we find for once in England not just a different situation, but a radically different situation. Not only were there recognised social groups, but at least one early eleventh-century commentator arranged them in a deliberate hierarchy of status: this was Archbishop Wulfstan of York (1002–1023). Wulfstan compiled and composed a series of texts relating to status during (or possibly after) the social upheavals which accompanied the Scandinavian assaults on England during the reign of Æthelred II (*c.*979–1014). Wulfstan collected a series of old texts, apparently going back in part to the ninth century, relating to wergeld, payments made to the families of murder victims and men maimed in violence, which were fixed according to the status of the deceased.

Wergeld is the English variant of an early judicial practice common to most western European peoples. It appears amongst the early Franks, and the Welsh had their version of it, called galanas. It was a pragmatic way of punishing men for the consequences of their violence. It was also a way of defusing the problem of feud (which we looked at in Chapter 4). It was an honourable way out of the cycle of violence that a murder could begin. For us later historians it is also an interesting lens through which to observe a past society. But it could serve the same purpose for contemporaries too, and Archbishop Wulfstan's treatise on social ranks used the lens of wergeld for the purpose of constructing a social polemic on his own times. Constructing schemes of wergeld fines according to the status of the victim naturally forced those who did it into a hierarchical frame of mind: what is more, it forced them to think not in terms of individuals, but for convenience sake, in terms of status groups. They were inherently artificial.

In pursuit of his purpose Wulfstan made abstracts of antique texts concerning the wergelds he found in the laws of Mercia and the north of England, and produced a hierarchy of lay ranks running down from king, to atheling (that is a royal heir), to ealdorman, royal reeve, thegn, ceorl with five hides of land, and lesser ceorl. The artificiality can be seen here in the fact that the 'ealdorman' was a title which was already being superseded in Wulfstan's day. To make his analysis all the more complete, Wulfstan produced a parallel ecclesiastical hierarchy from the northern laws, and also inserted into the lay hierarchy the wergeld of a free British landholder (again, an antiquated concept when he wrote).[1] His wergeld list was founded on the antique view of society which interlinked material wealth in land with other measures of status, such as blood, office and closeness to the king. Atheling, reeve and thegn are all assumed to have attained a high and undefined level of wealth, and the distinctions between them were solely those of relative status.

But Wulfstan's purpose was more than antiquarian. The key to this can be seen in his treatment of the lesser title of ceorl. It was portrayed as a complex status level. The ceorl's basic status related to his position as a free warrior possessing arms and armour, which apparently assumed that he might make a living without possessing land. But many if not most ceorls were also landowners, and not just landowners but rising ones. They seem to have been regarded as particularly likely to accumulate land, and with it higher status. So a ceorl could have the same wergeld as a thegn if he had enough land to warrant it, just as a Briton's wergeld varied according to the amount of land he possessed. The status of a simple ceorl did not reflect on his children, for if they prospered then the wergeld envisaged the promotion of his offspring into the ranks of the thegns. The fact that land and prosperity might increase meant that the wergeld system assumed the people within its social groups could be socially mobile. Wergeld, as Wulfstan explained it, did not assume that society was static or that status was fixed by heredity.

What was Wulfstan's purpose in writing his tract? He wrote in troubled times, and, like his French contemporaries, Gerard of Cambrai and Adalbero of Laon, he seems not to have liked the social mobility that those troubled times allowed; significantly, he was another soul who comforted

[1] For a translated text, *English Historical Documents*, c.*500–1042*, ed. and trans. D. Whitelock (London, 1955), 431–5, and see now the commentary on Wulfstan's text in, P. Wormald, *The Making of English Law: King Alfred to the Twelfth Century* i, *Legislation and its Limits* (Oxford, 1999), 391–4.

himself by meditating on the idealised society of the three orders.[2] He collected wergeld texts as relics of what he apparently believed were more stable earlier English societies, as part of a conservative political agenda. He did not fully realise, perhaps, that his antiquarian endeavours indicated that earlier societies were in fact socially mobile. To make his point, Wulfstan wrote an introduction to his collection, the famous tract called *Geþyncðo*, which reflects sadly that: 'Once it used to be that people and rights went by dignities and councillors of the people were then entitled to honour, each according to his rank, whether noble or ceorl, retainer or lord'. *Geþyncðo* (which means 'concerning rank') attempted to create a vision of an ideal society with everyone in his established place *(Geþyncðum)*. If people moved up a place, as ceorls were wont to do, then they did so through a recognised process of accretion of land and status. If a ceorl got five hides of land, acquired a fortified hall with a chapel and gatehouse and achieved office at court then clearly he had to be treated as a thegn. That was all right and proper. Wulfstan was by no means a snob who intended placing obstacles in the way of social mobility. He was even happy that a merchant who regularly engaged in distant trade across the seas (he suggested the definition of three voyages) and who made a fortune, might be treated as a thegn too. What Wulfstan apparently loathed, by the implication of his rhetoric, was a situation that seems to have happened in the England conquered and ruled by Sweyn (1013–14) and Cnut (1014–1035), where low-born and uneducated warriors rose to royal favour and earldoms at the king's whim and in defiance of public opinion.

The question for us is whether the idealised social hierarchy that Wulfstan sketched out in *Geþyncðo* was a commonly-held view of society in England in the tenth-century. This is not an easy question to answer. As has already been said, there is no doubt that in eleventh-century France and England alike there was a pragmatic materialistic understanding of people's status, which made clerks naturally put people in order of wealth and status in their lists. *Geþyncðo* certainly demonstrates that outlook as much as does the archbishop of Reims's list of the dignitaries at the coronation of Philip I in 1059. But does what Wulfstan said amount to an eleventh-century view of society as an ordered hierarchy of social groups, with the innate characteristics and stages of social class? Clearly not. Wergeld lists, the similar 'galanas' lists of medieval Wales, Hrabanus Maurus's list of dignitaries at the Carolingian court and Wulfstan's tract

[2] Wormald, *The Making of English Law*, 459–61.

Geþyncðo, all belong to a family of attempts to bring some definition to societies in which people's economic status was normally and acceptably mobile. They focus on the easily-defined criteria of land and office, not the deeper criteria of ideology, education and behaviour that was ultimately to define medieval magnates, knights, squires, burgesses, gentlemen and peasants into a less liberal and less mobile social hierarchy of class in thirteenth-century England and France.

Eleventh-century England was not therefore exceptional or precocious. It did not possess, any more than contemporary France, a hierarchical society of ranked social groups. The evidence of wergeld lists is not enough to say that it possessed social class, only that it had a pragmatic understanding of levels of wealth and wanted status to follow on from it. The Domesday Survey of 1086 confirms this view. The intrusion of foreign nobles with foreign ranks of count and baron obviously made for confusion within post-Conquest society. The Domesday clerks were themselves part of that foreign world. It can only be significant that there is one clear attempt in the text to translate the English social world into a French one. The wives of dead English pre-Conquest earls were described as *comitissae*, in other words it was demoting the former English earls to be equivalent to the counts of northern France, rather than the imperial dukes with which the pre-Conquest English equated them.[3] As far as the other pre-Conquest English ranks are concerned, Domesday still treats them as relevant, but in such a way that they cannot be considered steps in a social hierarchy. Thegns, in particular, appear in most counties in the survey, often listed as a group, as with the numerous 'king's thegns' in Dorset. This interesting group of Dorsetshire English manorial lords held a varying number of manors, from one to several. It included, however, a priest, a reeve and three royal huntsmen, which indicates that it could hardly have been considered a social group with common characteristics, but rather a group organised on the basis of income and its relationship with the king.[4] This is reinforced by the references in Yorkshire, Derbyshire and Nottinghamshire Domesday to the fact that thegns who held more than six manors continued to stand, as before 1066, in a different relationship to the king when they succeeded to their estates, paying a relief of eight pounds in cash, rather than the three marks owed by lesser thegns. Again, it indicates a group defined fiscally and tenurially, and not socially.[5] We

[3] D. Crouch, *The Image of Aristocracy in Britain, 1000–1300* (London, 1992), 56–9, 76–7.
[4] *Domesday Book* i, fo. 84r–v.
[5] Ibid. i, fos. 280v, 298v.

have to dismiss the idea of a hierarchy of social class existing precociously in England before 1100. There were enough other reasons to think England precocious in different areas.

PART FOUR

NOBLE LORDSHIP

CHAPTER 10

The Feudal Debate

Enlightenment and Romantic Feudalisms

Feudalism is a construct, an intellectual model which may or may not reflect the past reality it tries to describe. As modern constructs go it is quite an antique. As a historical model of medieval society it grew out of the work of antiquarian lawyers early in the sixteenth and seventeenth centuries. It makes other constructs like 'bureaucracy' and 'capitalism' seem youthful bycomparison. Feudalism has had now well over two centuries to thrive and mutate in historical discourse and in the process it has become a remarkably ferocious intellectual hydra. Sometimes it is more interesting *in itself* than the mechanics of the society it has purported to describe in different ways at different times. Ironically, the way the term 'feudalism' has been used sometimes tells us a lot more about the perceptions of people in the periods that used it than it tells us about medieval society.

As is now well known, the first guise of 'feudalism' as a social – rather than as a legal – construct was in the use of the phrase 'le gouvernement féodal' by Charles Louis de Secondat, the Baron Montesquieu (1689–1755), in 1748, in his *L'Esprit des Lois*. But the idea that the European middle ages had been 'feudal' was of course already long established. The English legal scholar and antiquarian, Sir Henry Spelman (*c*.1564–1641) had concluded that tenure and feudal law was basic to Western medieval societies, and was indeed their defining characteristic. Fiefs and feudal law were believed to be specific to the middle ages.[1] However, even before Spelman, sixteenth-century French jurists had produced theories of the origins of fiefs in the collapse of the Roman empire,

[1] See the pioneering historiographical essay in, R. Boutruche, *Seigneurie et Féodalité* (2 vols., Paris, 1959–70) i, 12ff.

and attributed their invention to their own Frankish ancestors. They believed that fiefs and feudal law had become nothing more than antiquarian survivals long before their own day.[2] Spelman's French contemporaries were also coming independently to the conclusion he had reached, that the middle ages was inescapably and characteristically 'feudal'. The count of Boulainvilliers was building on the tradition of both nations when he wrote that 'féodalité' arose out of the wreck of Imperial Rome. It is not surprising in view of all this that the encyclopedic minds of the Enlightenment would eventually decide that the medieval world was characteristically feudal, and inevitably attempt to define it according to the label that had been pasted on it.

Montesquieu was the first writer to use the adjective *féodal* in the context of a social state. He used it to describe a condition where monarchy had so far degenerated as to be forced to share power with a military aristocracy whose power base was their knights, established on hereditary fiefs. He coined the term to describe eighth-century Carolingian Francia, which he saw as different from what came before, because landholding there had, he thought, become militarised and men had turned to lords for protection, and not the king.[3] Montesquieu deplored 'feudal' society, being a man who put his faith in strong monarchy as the safeguard of national peace. The English Whigs who read him were rather more sympathetic to the 'feudal' aristocracy (such as that which routed King John at Runnymede) which was seen on such occasions as a bulwark against overbearing monarchy. Both sides were agreed at this point what feudal government was, but within only a few years of Montesquieu's death, the state of society described by 'feudalism' had lost the sense he had given it.

The next dimension added to the construct 'feudalism' came in less than a generation, with Adam Smith in 1776. He gave it an economic dimension. Like Montesquieu, Smith believed that a feudal aristocracy was antipathetic to the king and to ordered government. He defined the sort of regime feudal society offered as 'too weak in the head and too strong in the inferior members'. He made much of the change in his native country caused by the 1745 rebellion. To him the defeat of feudal Scotland in the

[2] S. Reynolds, *Fiefs and Vassals: the Medieval Evidence Reinterpreted* (Oxford, 1994), 4–5.

[3] *De L'Esprit des Lois*, ed. R. Derathé (2 vols., Paris, 1973) ii, 403 (Book 31 ch. 32). The foundation of Montesquieu's development of 'feudal society', as pointed out by S. Reynolds, *Fiefs and Vassals* (Oxford, 1994), 4–7, was the assumption by sixteenth-century French legal antiquaries, working from the twelfth-century Lombard *Libri Feudorum*, that early medieval noble society was one dominated by the law of fiefs.

wreck of the Jacobite cause led to a new nation enjoying commercial and agricultural prosperity. Smith saw Scotland's primitive society as characterised by 'feudal institutions' and a 'feudal subordination' which sanctioned private violence. It offered no public peace in which merchants and farmers could thrive, so feudalism was bad for business. But feudal Scotland was succeeded by a commercial society which by its nature demanded regular justice and civil peace. The feudal lords were themselves subverted by capitalism, because they found that the pursuit of luxuries generated by trade and commerce was more attractive than wasting resources on hungry retainers. A feudal society became thus a stage of human development preceding, or at least being an alternative to, a capitalist one.[4]

The third dimension of feudalism has less to do with society and economics than zeitgeist. As has been pointed out, it was first articulated in England by the Georgian orientalist, jurist and radical politician, Sir William Jones (1746–94). Jones quite agreed with Adam Smith, but added touches characteristic of his time; his feudal society had a Gothick, anti-papist background. He talked of the 'dark auxiliaries' of feudalism: 'ignorance and false philosophy' and contrasted them with the 'good principle' of increasing commerce with her liberal allies, true learning and sound reason. To Jones, feudalism was more than a political or economic state, it was an 'evil principle', a corrosive force liable to subject the human spirit, a synonym for oppression and antiquated restraint.[5] This viewpoint – you might call it 'anti-medievalism' – was paralleled in France by Auguste Comte's early nineteenth-century portrayal of the middle ages as a time when the human spirit was enslaved by superstition. This nineteenth-century positivism was to receive its most vivid expression in Mark Twain's *Connecticut Yankee at King Arthur's Court* (1879), where the battle between wilful medieval ignorance and can-do modern technology was made flesh.

As even one of the defenders of the reality of feudalism has admitted when talking of the historiography of George IV's England: 'the concept of feudalism was rather confused'; and it got more so.[6] The medievalism of early-nineteenth-century England, the medievalism that influenced Sir Walter Scott, Pugin and the Tractarians, was just waiting for terms like

[4] Adam Smith, *The Wealth of Nations* (Edinburgh, 1776), 508–14.

[5] S.N. Mukherjee, 'The Idea of Feudalism: From the Philosophes to Karl Marx', in, *Feudalism: Comparative Studies*, ed. E. Leach, S.N. Mukherjee and J.O. Ward (Sydney Studies in Society and Culture, no 2, 1984), 34–5.

[6] Ibid., 35.

'feudalism' or 'feudal system' to give political and social shape to their various versions of medieval history.[7] The word itself first appears in English, so far as study has revealed, in 1817. When it did, the medievalists who used 'feudalism' were describing a different sort of zeitgeist to that of Sir William Jones. Influenced ultimately perhaps by his friend and patron Scott, Robert Southey, for instance, depicted feudal society as a romantic and Arcadian state of manly virtue; rough and vigorous, perhaps, but thoroughly and hopefully Christian.

And so, within eighty years of Montesquieu's statement, 'feudalism' was a state of society, a socio-economic order, a term of partisan abuse, and two contrasting expressions of zeitgeist. In a way we have already seen with the history of chivalry, feudalism was a changing and mutating concept in the nineteenth-century intellectual world because polemicists battered away with it in their contemporary arguments. Before Marx reached London, feudalism was already a concept with a registered office in the city of Babel. Marx in fact did not much add to the confusion. His 'feudalism' was at root that of Adam Smith, a primitive, socio-economic order stifling commercial development. Marx simply articulated his model with more definition and complexity, and made it transitional and evolutionary. He also made it universal. Following on from Voltaire, Marx saw feudalism in every society where the powerful victimised the weak and imposed tribute on them.[8]

The important thing to emphasise at this point was that all these varying suppositions and constructs of feudal society were plastic and their meanings shifted, because they suited the mood of the moment. Montesquieu invented feudal government as an unpleasant concept, because he wished to bolster the Bourbon monarchy in France, and he knew something about the way that the Merovingian monarchy had fallen into decay. Sir William Jones, as an admirer of the French Revolution, had deplored the Bourbon monarchy and had swallowed the Revolution's own propaganda that it had been provoked by feudal privilege run wild. Robert Southey rather liked the feudal world because it was such a contrast to the grim, industrial desert he saw England becoming in the 1840s. Adam Smith and Karl Marx embraced the idea of a feudal society because they were serious economists who knew something about the changes that

[7] On Victorian medievalism in the arts, see generally, J. Badham, '"Past and Present": images of the Middle Ages in the early nineteenth century', in, *William Morris and the Middle Ages*, ed. J. Badham and J. Harris (Manchester, 1984), 17–31;

[8] Boutruche, *Seigneurie et Féodalité* i, 14.

economic life and society had undergone over the centuries. But not one of these men had methodically studied through its survivals the society they thought they understood. Therefore it is hardly surprising that dissatisfaction with the construct 'feudalism' appears in the later nineteenth century when social history became a new intellectual fashion, partly as a result of the polemic of the utopian positivist and anti-medievalist, Auguste Comte (1798–1857).[9]

Britain and the Feudal System after 1900

Spelman had been the first British scholar to speculate on the significance of feudal law in the middle ages. Whatever ideas other British thinkers had about feudalism, Spelman, as one of the founding fathers of legal history, had put his own bookplate on the idea. The academic study of feudalism in England therefore remained the province of legal historians, and feudal law was studied as a peculiar branch of the law of property. The first great compendium of English law, compiled for teaching purposes by the Vinerian professor of Law at Oxford, Sir William Blackstone (1723–80), reinforced this tendency. Blackstone's *Commentaries on the Laws of England* (1765–69) was the essential text for legal education for many generations of English lawyer, and in his second volume he offered a major study 'Of the feodal [*sic*] system'. By this he meant that post-Roman Europe was dominated by a 'feodal constitution' or 'doctrine of tenure' which bound together barbarian princes and their followers in mutual defence, dependence and security. Blackstone did not believe that the 'full vigour and maturity' of this system was established until the eighth century in France. So it bypassed Anglo-Saxon Britain, which did not experience the rigour of feudalism until the Normans arrived with it in their baggage. To Blackstone, the feudal system was a 'fiction of tenure' imposed on the English by their conquerors. It was a bad thing. It usurped ancient English liberties in disposing of property and brought with it the oppressions of aids, tallages and forest law; worse, its fiction that all tenure depended on the king's will fostered royal tyranny.[10]

[9] Writing in 1824, Comte, like his exact contemporary Michelet (see below), thought that feudalism was all very well and good in its day, but he believed that it was an obstacle to the progress of Man, which was what he thought history was all about, *Lettres d'Auguste Comte à M. Valat, Professeur de Mathématiques, Ancien Recteur de l'Académie de Rhodez, 1815–1844* (Paris, 1870), *s.a.* 1824.

[10] *The Sovereignty of the Law: Selections from Blackstone's Commentaries on the Laws of England*, ed. G. Jones (London, 1973), 131–8, 216–25.

At the very end of the nineteenth century, some legal scholars found this rhetorical, windy and unhistorical analysis of feudal society less than convincing. Frederic Maitland had some telling and ironic things to say about this sort of 'feudalism', ignored because their irony made them seem quirky. He sent up the contemporary debate on the introduction of feudalism by remarking that it was Spelman who brought the feudal system to England. It was Spelman, with his concentration on the law of fiefs and the artificial hierarchy it projected, who persuaded his eighteenth-century successors that there was such a thing as a 'feudal system'. When Maitland dismissed what was in fact Spelman's feudal system as 'an early essay in comparative jurisprudence', he did so to dismiss the artificiality of seventeenth- and eighteenth-century writing on feudal law. In 1888 Maitland remarked that:

the feudal system has ... become for us so large and vague that it is quite possible to maintain that of all countries, England was the most, or for the matter of that, the least 'feudal'; that William the Conqueror introduced, or for the matter of that, suppressed the feudal system.[11]

It was not just Maitland among his contemporaries who paused to reflect on the emptiness of the theory of the feudal construct. Edward Augustus Freeman had already aired some disquiet with the model drawn from Blackstone. In his *Norman Conquest*, he drew a distinction between what parts of the construct he could admit. He rejected as 'imaginary' the 'feudal system' as a model of society, and only admitted to consideration the more concrete 'system of feudal land tenures' which he believed had been invented by Ranulf Flambard to finance William Rufus's oppressive government.[12] To Maitland and Freeman, the idea of 'feudal' society as a construct was worrying, because they knew a good deal about medieval society, and knew that the word as used in the senses of their predecessors was incoherent. The circle of scholars around William Stubbs sought to understand medieval society; their predecessors had not done so. Maitland and Freeman were discriminating intellects irritated by the multitude of meanings that 'feudalism' had acquired.

The word might have been less important in Britain had not John Horace Round managed to inject enough interest into the construct to

[11] F.W. Maitland, *Collected Papers*, ed. H.A.L. Fisher (2 vols, Cambridge, 1911) i, 489. As quoted in E.A.R. Brown, 'the Tyranny of a Construct: Feudalism and Historians of Medieval Europe', *American Historical Review*, 79 (1974), 1065–6.

[12] E.A. Freeman, *The History of the Norman Conquest of England* (6 vols, Oxford, 1870-79) v, 377.

keep it alive and mutating. He was not a historian of societies and peoples; his genius lay in genealogy. It is not to belittle Round to say that his talent was for minutiae, because he tackled minutiae on the grand scale. But such a talent is not capable of broad interpretation, and wide concerns of development in society and monarchy were beyond Round's interest, and perhaps also his grasp. The only exception to Round's narrowness of interest is a large one. It is not so much that Round had a brainstorm, but that his minute study of feudal surveys led him to tackle the question already nearly a century old, the question of when knight service was introduced to England. Irritated by the broad and general use of the feudal concept of society, he sallied out into the unexpected terrain of social structures, and straight into a skirmish with some senior historical figures in Britain.

It was true of Round's senior contemporaries, Stubbs, Green, Bright and Freeman, that they subscribed to the same view of feudal society as Montesquieu had, as a social structure dominated by a military aristocracy. So John Richard Green, a very influential writer in terms of readership, pictured feudalism as entering England in the tenth century, corrupting the power of the resurgent West Saxon monarchy. Stubbs, Green's mentor, was more equivocal, but Freeman was in advance of Green, seeing English knight service as bearing a direct relationship to the Anglo-Saxon military service which preceded it. Round disagreed with this 'anti-cataclysmic' view of the Norman Conquest and wanted to narrow the feudal concept to the area he knew best: simple feudal surveys. The Norman Conquest brought feudalism to England, for Round, because feudalism was defined by him as the parcel of customary obligations which went with the grant of the fee. Norman England was, for him, feudal, because it had knight service and a new aristocracy bound by feudal incidents and customs. Round was of course sticking to a strict interpretation of Blackstone's 'doctrine of tenure' and ignoring the more general ideas of feudal nature of early society put about by Spelman and Montesquieu.

Round expressed the narrow view of post-Conquest English society which has subsequently formed the majority opinion in Anglo-American historiography.[13] A more idiosyncratic view promoted by Round (although not invented by him) was that English, or rather Anglo-Norman,

[13] An indirect tribute to Round's intellectual influence on this point is that even attacks on 'feudal' understanding of English history were conducted within the limits of the military understanding of it that he had propagated. For an early example see H.G. Richardson and G.O. Sayles, 'The Shadow of Feudalism' in, *The Governance of Medieval England from the Conquest to Magna Carta* (Edinburgh, 1963), 62–91.

feudalism stood apart from that of France.[14] Round's view was in fact maintained much earlier by William Stubbs (1825–1901) and Jules Michelet (1798–1874). Both of these great men, founders of long-standing English and French schools of history, accepted that post-Conquest England was feudal. But both thought that it was not the anarchic feudalism of the Continent because its social dangers were kept in check by the personal prestige of the first three Norman kings. English feudalism was tamed by the centralising kingship which France lacked at the time. It happened that the views of Michelet, Round and Stubbs on feudal England came together in the work of a Frenchman, Charles Petit-Dutaillis, who provided the synthesis of which Round was incapable. Petit-Dutaillis agreed that England had had no feudalism before 1066. When it was established there by the Normans it had a native eccentricity. The fusion of feudal tenure and strong royal authority counteracted the disintegration evident in Anglo-Saxon England. It prevented the feudal privilege which led to the disintegration of public authority which France had suffered and which characterised later French society.

The Belgian legal historian François-Louis Ganshof (1895–1980) in 1944 repeated and confirmed Petit-Dutaillis's views on the divergent English medieval society without much comment. He noted the lack of allodial, or non-feudal, lordship in England, and the disconnection which 1066 represented. Ganshof pleased an English constituency (and irritated a French one) by recognising and accepting the narrow 'feudalism' argued by Round, and by playing down the wider concept of 'feudal society', which he promoted to a theoretical realm beyond the necessity of consideration.[15] English appreciation of Ganshof was predictably strong. In his 1952 foreword to the translation of the second edition of Ganshof's

[14] The point that Normandy had to have been exceptionally feudalised, if its structure was the template for English military feudalism, was registered by nineteenth-century French historians, see J. Flach, *Les origines de l'ancienne France* (4 vols., Paris, 1886–1917) iii, 88, and confirmed as far as Stenton was concerned, by C.H. Haskins, *Norman Institutions* (New York, 1918), 5ff. For the overturning of this notion, D.R. Bates, 'England and the Feudal Revolution', in, *Il feudalesimo nell'alto medioevo* (2 vols, Settimane di Studio de centro Italiano di studi sull'alto medioevo, xlvii, 2000) ii, 626–7.

[15] F.L. Ganshof, *Qu'est-ce que la féodalité* (Brussels, 1947), of which the latest French reprint was in 1982. Stenton's comments were in the English edition, *Feudalism*, trans. P. Grierson (3rd edn., London, 1964), esp. pp. xv–xvi. For an attack by a French theoretician on Ganshof's legalism and jejune analysis, A. Guerreau, *Le Féodalisme: un horizon théorique* (Paris, 1980), 78–80.

Qu'est-ce que la féodalité, Sir Frank Stenton said with approval that Ganshof's work would deliver English historians

> *from the insidious temptation to regard the peculiarities of the English system as deviations from a continental model. They will realise that English feudalism is the product of English history.*

This of itself tends to prove that Stenton had read and did not approve of some contemporary French 'feudal' scholarship.

The name of Stenton brings us to that critical point in the history of the construct 'feudalism', the point where the construct met the first empirical scholar able fully to conceptualise a medieval society. Stenton's was beyond all argument a unique talent. He possessed all of Round's virtues, and was a historian too. Round's mind was myopic, but Stenton's (to pursue the analogy) was equipped with reading glasses. It was possible at this point, had the spirit so moved Stenton, that he might have overthrown the place of the feudal construct in the minds of British medieval historians, or at least unbalanced it by an intellectual shove. But in 1932 Stenton entitled his study of post-Conquest society *The First Century of English Feudalism*, and the moment was lost. Stenton was bound by ties of early patronage to Round, who had rescued him from an unhappy interlude in schoolteaching and placed him in the *Victoria County Histories*. Stenton was brought to academic notice by Round and to challenge his views on medieval society might have seemed ungrateful. But it may just as well be that the urge to overthrow established views was not in Stenton, and it never occurred to him that the orthodoxy did not quite match his conclusions on late eleventh- and twelfth-century society. So we find in his classic book some lapidary statements: there was a 'new order' established by the Norman Conquest; English feudalism was a creation of the Conquest, and differed markedly from that of Normandy in being constrained by a centralising, bullying dynasty. Again, according to Stenton, Henry II put English society back on course towards a centralised feudal state, after the blip of Stephen's reign. None of these statements came out of Stenton's own head.

Yet Stenton's originality was there beneath the surface. To begin with, he constructed for the first time a picture of medieval society centred on the lord, rather on the king. Instead of barons being seen solely as an antagonistic force in society opposing good and exploiting bad kings, Stenton reconstructed their world and rationally explained their actions. Even more important, his unique ability to deal with the charter sources created quite an unorthodox view of society when taken overall. Earlier historians had made little or nothing of the phenomenon Stenton settled on calling the 'honor'. Stenton's feudal society was not the vertical society of links implied by concentration on the artificial hierarchy of fees and submission. It was a much more centripetal society of aristocratic communities divorced from hierarchy, a society of local power created by a mixture of means of patronage (see Chapters 7 and 11).

The problem for the student is that Stenton's highly original view of society was still expressed in terms of Round's feudal construct. This contradiction is the chief reason why some find the *First Century* so very difficult to read. Stenton's second-hand feudalism sits uneasily on top of what the accumulated evidence of cartularies, charters and chronicles says. His model of society did not fit any of the previous definitions of 'feudal' society, except the broad concept of *Gefolgeschaften* which embraced Frankish war bands as much as twelfth-century Anglo-French retinues. There were further implications about the society he described that Stenton frankly dodged. He was quite content to accept it as unchallenged that Norman feudalism was different from English feudalism, as the dominant historiography of his day assumed. Charles Homer Haskins' survey of Norman institutions pushed Stenton towards that view, without further investigation of his own. He never subjected Norman sources to the same degree of scrutiny with which he favoured English sources; he might have been led to modify his presupposition had he done so.

Stenton provides an example of how the acceptance of a construct of society can defeat the best scholarship. By his methodology, which was impeccable, Stenton had a hitherto unique opportunity to penetrate at least twelfth-century society. His failure was twofold. It was not just that he failed fully to articulate what he saw; what was less forgivable was that what he let what he saw be clothed by ill-fitting ideological cast-offs. The peculiar problem with Stenton and feudalism was his eminence as a scholar and the intellectual watershed on which he lived. His *First Century* guaranteed that the construct would haunt British medieval scholarship into the twenty-first century. Stenton is a villain rather in the mould of Dr Frankenstein. With the best of intentions and in pursuit of true science, he stitched together bits and pieces of dead intellectual flesh and gave it a life it did not deserve.

Stenton's redefinition of feudal society was naturally influential within the English-speaking world. The important *Studies in the History of the English Feudal Barony* (1943) of the American scholar, Sidney Painter, was written entirely and self-consciously within Stenton's model of English aristocracy, projected by Painter on into the early thirteenth century. This is the way that British professional historiography has lived with its feudal construct to the present day, as a grafting of continental tenurial and social bonds on to powerful native kingship to produce something unique; the foundation of the English state.[16] It is reluctant to abandon its feudalism, and this can only be because the idea is used by so many of its past heroes. So feudalism in Britain continues to draws its life from one narrow artery of meaning: the obligations created by the possession of a 'fee'. This narrow tenurial understanding of feudalism is very different from that of the French. It is not unusual in British historiography for feudalism still to be talked of in Blackstone's terms as an 'institution' or 'system', by which is meant a legal framework to express social relations. To do this is to lose sight of the old historical idea of feudalism as a form of society; it also implies that medieval people knew that they were living feudally, within a system of relations dictated by the fee. Judging by the mass of litigation concerning knights' fees in the thirteenth century, medieval people were very sensible of the importance of the fee and its obligations. But I doubt that they thought that this network of obligations was what principally defined their society. There were concerns which were even more pressing on them, such as their relations with neighbours, family and, most importantly of all, their God.

When most British medievalists used the term 'feudal society' they generally meant England between 1066 and 1272 (or Scotland between 1124 and 1745). They meant to evoke a society where customs of castle guard, scutage, wardship, counsel and the feudal summons had real meaning and social consequence. In the last year of the twentieth century David Carpenter published a study arguing for the continuing validity of that sort of understanding of feudalism when dealing with English society even in the late thirteenth century. He argued that 'it continued to make a hugely important contribution to the social and political fabric of England'.[17] Within the limits of English historiography Carpenter is perfectly correct.

16 As remarked on in J.M.W. Bean, *The Decline of English Feudalism* (Manchester, 1968), 1–2. Very revealing in this respect is the overview by H. Cam, 'The Quality of English Feudalism' in, *Law-Finders and Law-Makers in Medieval England: Collected Studies in Legal and Constitutional History* (London, 1962), 44–58, esp. 46–7.

17 D.A. Carpenter, 'The Second Century of English Feudalism', *Past and Present*, no. 168 (2000), 30–71, quotation from p. 32. Carpenter's search for precision in what he is talking about led him to the new phrase 'fiscal feudalism' to denote honorial obligations in the thirteenth century (p. 44). He followed the path of J.M.W. Bean who in 1968 was arguing that from the beginning English feudalism was 'as much a fiscal as a military institution', *Decline of English Feudalism*, 5.

But as we have seen in earlier chapters, what he means by feudalism is the structure built on that community of aristocratic interest called the 'honor' which Stenton identified. Carpenter defines his terms closely, fortunately. Others have been less clear, which is why the concept sows confusion.

It may seem that the feudal concept is harmless if kept as Carpenter keeps it, on a tight conceptual leash. But is it? Firstly it separates British historiography from the European mainstream. It covertly reinforces the idea of the separateness and special nature of medieval England by implying that it had its own national feudalism. Secondly, because of the way it has been used by nineteenth-century historians, feudalism has become inescapably identified with an unsustainable evolutionary idea of medieval society. In English terms this social evolution begins with a non-feudal pre-Conquest society. In 1066 this was succeeded by the eccentric centralising feudalism of the Norman monarchy. This gradually gave way to a third phase of society with more plural social structures based on cash and patronage: but when precisely this happened depends on your chronology. This has been characterised since 1885 as 'bastard' (or debased) feudal. The 'bastard feudal' order supposedly held sway until crushed by Tudor absolutism in the sixteenth century.[18] I have argued elsewhere that medieval society was not so simple, even in the twelfth century, that it could be characterised by a single paradigm. Its social structures were complex, and within it there were many sources of power. My view, first expressed in 1991, is still that unless we jettison the idea that medieval society was 'feudal' we are not going to get close to what it was, and the true originality of Stenton's work will never be recognised.[19]

There is one group of British historians which uses feudalism in a less insular way. Unsurprisingly, this is to be found amongst the intellectual heirs of Eileen Power. She and the economic historians who succeeded her were far more open to social theory, to Marx and Weber.[20] Feudalism for them was most assuredly a social state, and indeed they were very keen to

[18] For alert and critical views of this historiographical scheme, J.M.W. Bean, *From Lord to Patron: Lordship in Late Medieval England* (Manchester, 1989), 1–9; P.R. Coss, 'From Feudalism to Bastard Feudalism' in, *Die Gegenwart des Feudalismus*, ed. N. Fryde, P. Monnet and O.G. Oexle (Veröffentlichungen des Max-Planck-Instituts für Geschichte, 173, 2002), 80–5.

[19] D. Crouch, 'Debate: Bastard Feudalism Revised', *Past and Present*, no. 131 (1991), 166.

[20] See particularly the paper of her husband, M.M. Postan, 'Feudalism and its Decline: a semantic exercise' in, *Social Relations and Ideas: Essays in Honour of R.H. Hilton* (Cambridge, 1983), 73–87.

observe class tensions within feudal society. Economic oppression and feudal resistance to capitalism are themes in some twentieth-century British historiography. When Rodney Hilton and Peter Coss use the term feudalism and the adjective feudal, they use it in the Marxist sense. But other contemporary socio-economic historians can talk of a 'feudal economy' without embracing Marxist social evolutionism. So the non-Marxist Christopher Dyer can evoke a feudal period in the medieval English economy and simply mean that the aristocracy was able to use its social dominance to amass surplus revenue for the purpose of display.[21] A call to jettison the idea of feudalism in these quarters is likely to be met with the curt reply that everybody must be well aware of how it is being used by them, and if everybody used it their way, there would be no confusion. Unfortunately the long history of the feudal construct proves otherwise.

French Feudalism

Feudalism had an existence in France just as abiding but less narrowly defined than in Britain. The mythology of the French Revolution – based on Voltaire's characterisation of the *ancien régime* – was that it had overthrown the oppressive feudal aristocracy of the Bourbon monarchy. The overthrow of feudalism therefore was a concept on which nineteenth-century French republicanism and statehood rested. This guaranteed feudalism academic attention and importance, but (unlike Britain) less sympathy amongst contemporary political commentators. Since the idea of French feudalism was based on the diffuse 'feudal government' theorised by Montesquieu, it was a concept that was used by scholars freely and without much precision. This is the way that Michelet used the feudal concept in the second volume of his epic *Histoire de France* in 1833. Feudalism was for him a social change forced on late Carolingian society by the Viking invasions. Although it created a violent military aristocracy it was better than the alternative: 'Rien de plus populaire que la féodalité à sa naissance'.[22] Michelet's view was a widespread one, and because he was from 1838 a professor of the Collège de France it was very influential. Under his scheme, feudalism became part of the process by which France was created and unified. So, for example, in 1858 Etienne de Certain, a

[21] C. Dyer, *Standards of Living in the Later Middle Ages: Social Change in England, c.1200–1520* (Cambridge, 1989), 6–7.

[22] J. Michelet, *Histoire de France* (rev'd edn, 19 vols, Paris, 1879) ii, 53–4.

scholar working in what was then the École Impériale de Chartes, viewed the evolution of Frankish into French society as a matter of the feudal impulse. Viking invasions in the ninth century worsened the social anarchy that the decadence of the Carolingian dynasty was already producing. The 'régime féodal', part military and part legal system, bad though it was, reestablished 'social order' and offered the bulk of the population some protection in a world descending into chaos.[23]

Michelet's influence did not lessen over time. Marc Bloch's feudalism, although without the ideological tinge of Michelet's, was in the same tradition. But the French understanding of feudalism was no less complex than anywhere else. Other theories developed. A year or two after Michelet's death, a very different intellect, that of Numa Denis Fustel de Coulanges, envisioned a very different feudalism. Fustel was a historian of institutions and laws, and so his feudalism naturally gravitated towards one which was fixed on institutions like vassalage and in particular on the oath of faith sworn by a dependent to his new lord. For Fustel this exclusive oath was in the end what destroyed Frankish society. Under Charlemagne the power this oath gave to lords was combined with the older idea of kingship. It made Charlemagne hugely powerful – a 'super lord' – but it also made his successors vulnerable, as their dependents used the same feudal mechanism to take power for themselves.[24]

This form of institutional feudalism became influential in one part of the French intellectual world. Jacques Flach (1846–1919), professor of jurisprudence at the Collège de France, reproduced Fustel's feudal model in his multi-volume study of early France. Like Fustel he looked to the ancient contract between lord and dependent as the basis of feudalism, and saw it as integral to most early societies.[25] When Ganshof wrote on feudalism in the 1940s and 1950s it was this French legalistic model of feudalism on which he based his work. Because it was devised by legal historians and like-minded anthropologists, it was not surprising that it should be the only form of French feudal model which appealed to British historians trained in the ideas of Maitland. However, it was something of an illusory appeal. This school of French feudal history was based on a much broader conception of feudalism than that of the British, and like

[23] *Les miracles de Saint Benoît*, ed. E. de Certain (Paris, Société de l'histoire de la France, 1858), pp. vi–vii.

[24] N.D. Fustel de Coulanges, *Histoire des institutions politiques de l'ancienne France* (rev'd edn, 5 vols., 1891–2) v, 571–2, 614–18, 666–7; see also, idem, *Les origines du système féodal*, ed. C. Jullian (Paris, 1890).

[25] Flach, *Origines de l'ancienne France* ii, 491–514.

that of Michelet and Guizot, it was devised to explain the corruption and fall of an older society. It also led to an emphasis on the economic subjection of peasantry to lords by the growth of seigneurial controls and rights. This is an area which in Britain tended to be the preserve of economic historians.

The Fustel-Flach model of feudal society persists in France, although subsumed into the broad studies of regions and counties which become important from the 1960s onwards. It is the form of feudalism favoured by Jean-François Lemarignier, a medieval historian at the opposite pole of scholarship to his contemporary, Georges Duby. In his standard textbook, *La France médiévale: institutions et société* (of which the latest edition was issued in 2000) *féodalité* has two principal characteristics. The first is the familiar collapse of royal power and the rise of principalities in post-Carolingian times. The second is what made this *morcellement* possible: the 'feudo-vassalic link'. Lemarignier here, like Fustel and Flach, concentrates on the single social act of entering into dependence as the key to what made society feudal. The principal difference between Lemarignier and his intellectual predecessors is that he adopts the chronology which places the social consequences of the 'feudo-vassalic' oath in the later tenth century. A difference with his contemporaries is that since he sees feudalism as deriving from law and contract, then – like the British – he does not, like other French historians, see the 'ban' as important to the feudal concept. It must be something else.

Lemarignier's feudalism is an example of how modern French ideas on the subject are not monolithic, but almost as diverse as the British. But there is a mainstream idea of feudalism which has tended to marginalise Lemarignier's ideas. They have taken a back seat because they were faced by Marc Bloch's classic reformulation of the feudal model of the eighteenth century. Bloch drew his understanding of feudalism ultimately from Montesquieu, so he saw it in broad terms as a form of civilisation, as a civilisation in a state of dissolution. But as an analytical social historian of the twentieth century Bloch felt responsible for explaining what the eighteenth century had only observed. So he proposed dividing feudalism into two 'ages'. The first was the troubled age of the late Carolingians, beset by anarchy and invasion, the time of the decay of old ideas of the state. It was succeeded around 1050 by a second age. Here feudalism paved the way to the reformation of a new sort of monarchical, national state. It was a time of expanding economy and population, an age in which the new military aristocracy challenged monarchy but was ultimately defeated by the aggressive and centralising Capetian dynasty. Bloch – who liked to see himself as a universal historian rather than as a medievalist – believed feudalism to be an 'ideal type' of society, a coherent phase of civilisation with its own generic character. The principal character of feudalism was that it was an unstable social state. It was a response to an older society in a state of collapse. In turn it caused a social and economic transformation of its own. The feudal ages were a watershed in western civilisation: a painful fusion of Latin and Germanic cultures. But although painful, feudalism was an essential stage leading to the birth of western capitalism and modernity.[26]

The feudalisms of Marc Bloch and of Sir Frank Stenton can be seen from this to be utterly incompatible. There was no attempt at a meeting of minds on Stenton's part. So far as can be ascertained Stenton had not read any of Bloch's comparative and economic studies when he wrote his *First Century of English Feudalism* other than an essay in the Cambridge Economic History. Bloch on the other hand had read Maitland and Stenton with care, but did not see their work as of any relevance to France. He integrated English ideas of feudalism into his great comparative scheme accordingly. He went along with the old French view that English medieval society was different from French. But he put his own stamp on this idea. He suggested that the Norman monarchy established itself in 1066 on the cusp of the shift in feudalism from its phase of dissolution to its phase of reformation: so for him Norman England was the first fruit of the second age of feudalism. Its dynasty was able to create a unique, centralising legal feudalism, very favourable to the formation of a national state. We see the influence of Blackstone as well as Fustel in Bloch's statement that every English tenement was ultimately dependent on the king, who concentrated all feudal links on to himself. We see the influence of Stenton in Bloch's view that the pre-Conquest English state had preserved traditions of common taxation and public order which allowed the Norman kings to form a precocious national monarchy. But to be truly feudal, England must exhibit some signs of aristocratic defiance of the king, and he found this where Stubbs told him it was to be found, in the civil war of Stephen's reign.[27]

Comparative history became particularly prominent in the United States in the 1940s and 1950s and to use feudalism it had to reject both Bloch and Marx. The irony of this is that Bloch was himself the principal

[26] See particularly, *Feudal Society*, trans. L.A. Manyon (2 vols., 2nd edn., London, 1962) ii, 441–6.

[27] Ibid., ii, 429–31,

theorist behind comparative history. Bloch had to be rejected because his feudalism was eurocentric; Marx because he was Marx. So a comparative study of world feudalisms published in the post-McCarthy United States in 1956 did not mention Marx and firmly rejected both of Bloch's stances (that feudalism was a transformational type of society and that it had an economic dimension). It found its way through its dilemma in a reductionist version of Fustel. Feudalism was defined simply and indeed simplistically as a form of government '... in which the essential relation is not that between ruler and subject, nor state and citizen, but between lord and vassal'.[28] Following that sort of evasive and ideologically compromised statement, it is not surprising that the next generation of American historian produced the most celebrated (and frankly, enjoyable) attack ever published on the use of the feudal construct.[29]

The idea of feudalism in France has not developed much beyond where Bloch took it. The feudalism of Georges Duby also signified a society in flux. In full empirical flood in 1953 he emphasised the transforming nature of feudalism, and it can be no surprise that eventually this led him in the 1960s to the idea of the 'feudal transformation' of the year 1000 (see Chapter 7). He was radical enough in 1953 to agree with Bloch and say that 'féodalité' was a poor word for the phenomenon, saying that it was castles and not fees which were the active, transforming agents in society.[30] A feudal society was for Duby, as for Bloch, a society in the process of dissolving and reforming. At one end of the process was the Carolingian empire with its regional governors sent from Aachen and Laon, and at the other the administrative monarchy of Louis IX with its all-powerful baillis (bailliffs) sent from Paris. At one end was a sprawling multiracial empire on the late Roman model, and at the other the French nation state. By 1958, Duby was shifting his ground, and in an essay published that year he described feudalism as more of a noble 'mentalité'.[31] By the 1970s

[28] R. Coulbourn, 'The Idea of Feudalism' in, *Feudalism in History* (Princeton, 1956), 3–11, quotation from pp. 4–5. The essay by J.R. Strayer, 'Feudalism in Western Europe', ibid., 15–25, follows precisely the same line, taking feudalism entirely as a governmental system which simply had economic and social consequences. As such Strayer accepted Michelet's line that feudalism helped create a unified France, but found no theoretical difference between English and French feudalism.

[29] I refer to Brown, 'Tyranny of a Construct', 1063–88; for her unhappiness with Strayer, ibid. 1072–3.

[30] *La société aux xie et xiie siècles dans la région mâconnaise* (repr. Paris, 1982), 285–6. For Bloch's unhappiness with the term, *Feudal Society* i, p. xviii.

[31] G. Duby, 'La féodalité? Une mentalité médiévale', *Annales ESC*, 13 (1958), 765–71, as noted in Brown, 'Tyranny of a Construct', 1074.

feudal society was for Duby politically anarchic, but artistically dynamic and economically and culturally expansive. Everything about society between the eleventh and thirteenth century was feudal, because it shared in the character of the age, its 'bouleversement'. So its art, its economy and even its theology were all tied into its *féodalité*.[32]

Under the influence of Duby, the key feature of feudalism in medieval society became the 'transformation' it worked on society, and the key phase of that transformation was for him around the year 1000. We have looked in earlier chapters at why the features of this interpretation are unsustainable and are gradually being abandoned. There was no transformation in family structures around the year 1000, as we have seen in Chapter 4. In Chapter 7 we likewise laid out the objections to the 'descent of the ban', Duby's particular contribution to feudal theory. It is not surprising then to find that the Fustel-Flach model of feudal rights or 'seigneurie', incubated by Lemarignier, is now beginning to reemerge as an alternative feudalism in France, a development noticed with approval in Britain. It had never of course entirely disappeared. As well as Lemarignier, the massive two-volume work of Robert Boutruche on *Seigneurie et Féodalité* (2 vols., 1959–70) emphasised the old themes of social and economic subjection of the agrarian work force to lords as the key to understanding feudalism: the 'seigneurie foncière' (landlordship) rather than the 'seigneurie banale' (coercive lordship). Of necessity, this idea assumes a continuity of subjection in social and economic structures from the early middle ages onwards, and no break around 1000.[33] At this point the feudal debate breaks up. The only serious argument in favour of talking about feudalism is that it describes a characteristic medieval social order, whose core is its transitional nature. If medieval historians once begin to talk of *continuity* in medieval social structures, then the feudal cause is utterly lost.

[32] See particularly the comments in, G. Duby, *Le temps des cathédrales. L'art et la société, 980–1420* (repr. Paris, 1976), 45.

[33] See for a recent view on this, M. Bur, 'Le féodalisme dans le royaume franc jusqu'à l'an mil: la seigneurie', in, *Il feudalesimo nell'alto medioevo* (2 vols, Settimane di Studio de centro Italiano di studi sull'alto medioevo, xlvii, 2000) i, 53–5, 77–8.

CHAPTER 11

Power and Structures

I would imagine that if it were possible to talk to a reasonably well-educated twelfth-century person about his society, and to assure him that he lived in a feudal age, he might well have been confused. Not that he would have any difficulty with the concept itself. He knew that he lived in troubled and transitional times. He also knew that land could be translated into power. If he were of a legal turn of mind, he would know that customs relating to the knight's fee were an important part of property law, even if they were less important in the raising of armies. His confusion would arise from the fact that – if he were talking to a traditional British historian – he would find that the fee was being used as the central organising principle for his society. As we have seen, late-twelfth-century people knew well that there were such things as human societies and social classes. But they also knew that their society and class structure was rather more complex than the feudal construct allowed in any of its manifestations. There was no one single organising principle in their world, outside its theology.

This chapter will analyse where power lay in medieval society. We will find that if we look past the feudal construct and instead at the way lords ruled men, then medieval England and France do not look very different, the one from the other. Certainly they were not identical as societies, and there was variety within each, but within each we find the same range and complexity of structures. This should not be a surprise. Historians have been assiduous in analysing medieval power structures and some of the mechanisms they have found have already been explored in detail. British historians, reacting against the feudal construct, or led by their own empirically-based studies, have taken the lead here. The outlines of what follows are therefore already well established.[1]

[1] The basis of much of what follows in this chapter has appeared in D. Crouch, 'From Stenton to McFarlane: Models of Societies in the Twelfth and Thirteenth Century', *Transactions of the Royal Historical Society*, 6th ser., 5 (1995), 179–200.

The Honor

The idea of the honor as a centre of power and as an aristocratic community was established for England by Stenton, as we have already seen. The word 'honor' has passed into the technical vocabulary of the British historian, although there are synonyms like 'barony', 'feudal barony' or 'fee' which Sidney Painter and Stenton himself used. In English terms an 'honor' was the community of tenants dependent on the overlord of a number of manors. They were bound to him by a formal act of submission (homage) and an oath of loyalty. They owed him services relating to their tenements, usually but not always military service. Together with his own proprietary estates and woodland, and his rights to levy occasional taxes and raise tolls, the honor was a way to raise revenue and dominate men. It may not have been a 'feudal kingdom in miniature' but it was certainly one way that English earls and barons exerted power from the 1070s, and in some cases on well beyond 1200. The 'honor' is not a technical word generally used by French historians. If it is used, it is applied to the offices (*honores*) held by Carolingian counts and dukes. But 'honor' was a Latin word used the same way in northern French sources as it was used in England. French historians are likely to use the phrases 'seigneurie banale' or 'seigneurie foncière' for the same phenomenon.[2] But there was no material difference between the twelfth-century English 'honor' and the French 'seigneurie', even if they were in different political worlds.

The purpose of the honor was to accumulate revenue and exert power over lesser men. Lords of honors bolstered their power by attracting dependents and by cultivating in them hereditary loyalties which lasted in some cases for four or five generations. Sir Frank Stenton diagnosed some of the symptoms of 'feudal community' as he called it. One of his principal arguments was that the aristocratic tenants of an honor had a community spirit. Just like the clergy of a great collegiate church would be 'fellow canons' (*concanonici*), so the tenants of a lord could be described as 'colleagues' (*compares*). Institution into stalls of the choir of a great church would link one set of men in a common bond, whereas in the honor the

[2] M. Aurell, *La noblesse en Occident, v^{e}-xve siècle* (Paris, 1996), 60–1. For the use of the word 'honor' for the seigneuries of the Vendômois from the late eleventh century onwards, D. Barthélemy, *La société dans le comté de Vendôme de l'an mil au xive siècle* (Paris, 1993), 559–64, who concludes (in empirical style) that the word signified the estates held by a baron. He makes the point that the French use of the word is complicated because of its application by earlier medievalists to Carolingian public offices.

bonds would be attendance at the same man's court and the common oath of loyalty they had taken to him. So John Basset of Oakley in the honor of Wallingford and Walter de Bolbec of the honor of Ramsey abbey could address their charters early in the twelfth century to their *compares* within the honor, when transacting business over property. When they did this they were talking to men in the same condition as themselves in relation to their lord; to men they knew and could associate with as equals. English legal tracts from the first half of the twelfth century assume as a matter of course that each honor contained a body of *pares* who made up the lord's court and ideally should assist him in his judgements.[3] We can occasionally glimpse some of the humanity of that community. A tenant of the earldom of Warwick, Robert de Montfort, retired into the abbey of Thorney in Cambridgeshire in the early years of King Stephen's reign. At some time around 1140, Earl Roger heard that Robert was ill, so he travelled across England to visit his sick friend and dependent. While at Thorney, he good-naturedly eased the arrangements for Robert's reception into the abbey.[4] Similarly we can also glimpse the potential for violence in the honor. In England at some time between 1085 and 1094, Roger the Poitevin, lord of Lancaster, was angered at the abbot of Burton, and sent sixty knights of his household and honor led by his honorial steward to lay waste the abbey's lands at Blackpool and elsewhere. His intention was to draw out the abbot's knights, who were all his kinsmen, to capture, kill or humiliate them. As it happened, according to the abbey's sources, it was Roger's knights who were shamed when the abbot's military household drove them off, despite being heavily outnumbered.[5]

Honorial communities, as much as any other communities, were not necessarily happy or peacable bodies of men. But the fact that occasionally we hear of the men of the honor taking common action both for and against their lord is a good indication that they could be close-knit and even wilful communities. There is some English evidence of this. In December 1135, as soon as they had heard that King Henry I had died, the men of the honor of Pontefract rose up against the intruder that the king had forced on them, killed him and reinstated as lord a member of the Lacy family which had previously held the honor.[6] The

[3] F.M. Stenton, *The First Century of English Feudalism, 1066–1166* (2nd edn, Oxford, 1961), 60–1.

[4] Cartulary of Thorney, Cambridge University Library, Additional ms 3021, fo. 233r,

[5] Geoffrey of Burton, *The Life and Miracles of St Modwenna*, ed. R. Bartlett (Oxford, 2002), pp. xxix, 192–4.

[6] Richard of Hexham, *De Gestis Regis Stephani et de Bello Standardi* in, *Chronicles of the Reigns of Stephen etc.*, ed. R. Howlett, iii (Rolls Series, 1886), 140; W.E.

same thing might happen in Normandy. The great southern honor of Breteuil went through internal wars in 1103, 1119–20 and 1137–8 as two successive generations of its greater tenants fought outsiders to keep or reinstate the descendants of William fitz Osbern as their lords.[7] When lords were driven to rebellion against their prince, this feeling of solidarity was what they hoped to exploit so as to raise a rebel force. Sometimes they were successful. For instance, in the English rebellion of 1173–4 against Henry II, Gervase Paganel lord of Dudley successfully recruited a high proportion of his tenants to ride against the king.[8] In 1215 the large majority of the seventy or so honorial tenants of William de Mowbray, lord of Axholme, followed him into rebellion against King John.[9] Sometimes lords might be badly disappointed in their followers. When Count Waleran II of Meulan led a rising in Normandy against Henry I in 1123, his greatest Norman follower, the lord of Harcourt, refused his summons to join him.[10] The community spirit of the honor did not necessarily determine the behaviour of its members, and it could work against an unpopular lord. We have still the complaints of Count John of Eu written to Archbishop Rotrou of Rouen between 1164 and 1170 that his men in Normandy had taken against him and were out of control. They had made inroads on his personal estates and were victimising the religious houses under his patronage. The county of Eu was one of the most ancient and coherent of the great Norman honors, and its family was one of the most distinguished and noble houses in France. Yet in certain circumstances, its lord could clearly not control his men or expect their automatic loyalty.[11]

Noble honors existed as much in France as in England in the twelfth century. They behaved as communities in much the same ways in either kingdom. The principal difference between English and French honors was

Wightman, *The Lacy Family in England and Normandy, 1066–1194* (Oxford, 1966), 68–73; the men of Pontefract got away with the assassination, for King Stephen forgave them the offence apparently on the grounds that it occurred before his coronation, D. Crouch, *The Reign of King Stephen, 1135–54* (London, 2000), 40 and n.

[7] Reconstructed in, D. Crouch, *The Beaumont Twins: The Roots and Branches of Power in the Twelfth Century* (Cambridge, 1986), 107–13.

[8] J. Hunt, *Lordship and the Landscape: A Documentary and Archaeological Study of the Honor of Dudley, c.1066–1322* (British Archaeological Reports, British Series, 264, 1997), 66. A high proportion of the tenants of Earl David II of Huntingdon also turned out for their lord in that rebellion, although the turnout was higher among the tenants with modest tenures and no links to other lords, see K.J. Stringer, *Earl David of Huntingdon: A Study in Anglo-Scottish History* (Edinburgh, 1985), 25–6, 132.

[9] J.C. Holt, *The Northerners* (Oxford, 1961), 43–4.

[10] Crouch, *Beaumont Twins*, 20, 125–6.

[11] Cartulary of the Counts of Eu, Bibliothèque nationale, ms latin 13904, fo. 45r–v.

their different origin. The history of most English honors began abruptly in the period between 1066 and 1070. It is true that there was sometimes a predecessor to a few Anglo-Norman honors. Some honors were created out of block grants of the estates of an English predecessor, but the new honor had little other sort of continuity with it. The new French lord inherited no capital of lineage or loyalty from his predecessor. There would come a time in the late twelfth century when Anglo-Norman lords of English honors liked to fancy that the history of their honors could be traced back to a distant Anglo-Saxon past. The best instance of this is the way that the earl of Warwick around 1200 commissioned a dynastic romance projecting back the honor of Warwick to the times of King Athelstan, and implying a continuity between the imaginary Anglo-Saxon Earl Roalt and himself through the English lineage of the lords of Wallingford. But this sort of fancy belonged to the competition for distinction and dignity in a later age.

Even in Normandy a French honor was in origin an older and less artificial entity than an English one. The duchy was only created by the Scandinavian dynasty of Hrolfr of Rouen in the first half of the tenth century, but the principal honors of Upper and Central Normandy were already in being by around 1020, as is clear in that the network of castles on which they were centred was then in existence. The creation of the Norman honors occurred within the span of one long human life. They may well have existed decades earlier than 1020 for all we know, as there was no absolute necessity for an honor to have a central castle in order to exist. How Norman honors began is not a question ever likely to be answered, but in other better-documented areas of France there are some clues. In Georges Duby's research into the county of the Mâconnais he found it was subdivided by the twelfth century into the sort of complexes of castles, seigneurial estates and forests, and tenements which a British historian would call an honor. There were then six large secular honors, and three major ecclesiastical ones. The difference from Normandy was that Duby was able to say something about their origins. He found that – beginning in 980 and continuing to 1030 – men who were already minor powers in the region, from their personal wealth and estates and from the holding of offices like viscounties, began to attract lesser men into their allegiance. The employment of knights and the building of a castle or castles marked the point where their local predominance had got to the point where the honorial lords could assert their independence from the count of Mâcon.[12]

[12] G. Duby, *La société aux xi*[e] *et xii*[e] *siècles dans la région mâconnaise* (repr. Paris, 1982), 140ff, and for a map showing the seigneurial geography of the county, ibid.,

In Normandy we see only the end of the process, for we know nothing of the founders of the Norman honors. In Normandy also the honorial lords were not in general tempted to ignore the power of the duke, other than in its southern Marches.

The significant and defining difference between an English and a French honor was the manner of its creation and the effect that had on its structure. Since a French honor was created by a powerful local man on his own account and to serve his own ambition, it generally had a core area where every local landowner acknowledged his sway. The documentation is such in France that we sometimes are given a picture of it in the process of happening. So a memorandum of 1037 in the acts of the abbey of St-Aubin of Angers tells us that, thirty years before that date, Count Fulk Nerra of Anjou had built a castle and bourg on the river Mayenne at a place then called Hondainville. It was renamed Château-Gontier. Within a few years the count had decided to bestow Château-Gontier on one of his knights, Rainald son of Ivo. Rainald immediately got to work to try and maximise his revenue from the town, pleading his poverty. The abbey came under pressure to give up some of the revenues it had long had in the nearby estate of Bazouges to help Rainald support his dignity as lord. With the count's support Rainald got what he wanted. Here we glimpse part of what must have been a wider onslaught by the new lord of Château-Gontier on his neighbours, to being them into a relationship that recognised his local dominance.[13]

Where it is possible to plot twelfth-century honors on the map, as has been done for Upper Normandy, for Duby's Mâconnais, Fossier's Picardy and Barthélemy's Vendômois, we see exclusive blocks of estates lying next to each other like a feudal mosaic. A man could literally go to the top of his castle tower and be master of all he surveyed. In England this was not the usual case. Honors were created by an act of the king's patronage, not by the enterprise of an individual. Three principal types of honor emerged, with different structures. The estates of an English honor might be concentrated and exclusive, as in the honors of Dudley, Lancaster, the Sussex rapes, Chester and the Welsh marches. A second type might also have a solid core but then be diffuse and interspersed with lands of other lords,

518–19. Barthélemy, *La société dans le comté de Vendôme*, 564ff examines the same process in an another well-documented county. He finds the appearance of what he calls 'honors' at much the same time, although their lords did not aim for 'independence' from the count they followed, whether he was count of Vendôme or of Anjou.

[13] *Cartulaire de l'abbaye de St-Aubin d'Angers*, ed. le comte Bertrand de Brousillon (4 vols, Paris, 1903) i, 1–3.

such as the honors of Leicester, Warwick, Stafford or Clare. A third type had no core but was scattered randomly across several counties, such as the estates of the Arsic, Marshal or Musard families. The process for England is now well understood. We know that the Conqueror was keen to create compact and militarily effective castellanies in regions he considered to be threatened. There he deliberately replicated the familiar French pattern by sending in a baron with his licence to appropriate all the estates in a defined area. Elsewhere he simply appropriated the estates of one or more dispossessed English landowners and awarded them to a follower. Sometimes this produced a core area and sometimes it did not. The result was that over most of England there was no obvious and coherent pattern of honorial geography. Great lords had to live cheek-by-jowl with other powerful lords.

I would suggest that the difference in honorial geography in England and France had long-term social consequences. British historians have generally believed that honors became less important in the social structure of England as generation succeeded generation. Quite early on, the empirical point was made that tenants of the intermeshed English honors were free to become tenants of other honors, if it served their own local purposes. The wealthier the tenant, the more he was likely to be courted by other lords. So each honor was not a simple and self-contained structure. Some of a lord's tenants would have taken an oath of loyalty to other lords. Honorial studies in England have found this to be a widespread phenomenon and in some cases, tenants can be proved to have switched attention when it suited them from one of their lords to another. This introduced an element of volatility into the honor's structure at an early date. The Laws of Henry I mention it as a factor in social relations in the second decade of the twelfth century. A second influence was the rival influence of the king. Royal power in England was present in every shire, and there was no area, outside Cheshire and the Marches, where the king could not travel and exert himself. His justices sat in every communal court which he did not specifically exempt, and all offences against public order were offences against him. Many of the king's great officers were recruited from the tenants of his tenants, happy to seek out sources of high patronage. So again, the honor was compromised by an alternative power structure. A more long-term but corrosive influence, however, was the slow wearing away of feelings of community as generation followed generation.

When a charter was written in late eleventh- and twelfth-century England, it was provided with a list of people present at the time it was commissioned. Analysis of the attestations to the written acts of consecutive holders of English earldoms throughout the twelfth century has revealed a slow leaching away of families who were prominent in its early history. In my study of the earldom of Warwick from its creation in 1088 to the extinction of its first dynasty in 1242 this was the clear and hardly unexpected pattern. The earldom under its first earl, Henry I (1088–1119), was dominated by four major tenants, three of them lords of castles in the county of Warwick, at Hatton, Beaudesert and Studley. Under his son, Roger (1119–53), a further major tenant family emerged in the family of Clinton, initially enemies to the earl, then by a politic marriage, his kin. Until the tenure of the earldom by Roger's son William (1153–84), its charters reveal that the relationships begun in his grandfather's day were still active ones. William's retinue included men who answered for three quarters of the knight service assessed on his honor in 1166. But the charters of his brother Earl Waleran (1184–1204) include men answering for only a third of that service, while Waleran's son, Earl Henry II (1204–1229) was attended by men answering for a fifth. What these figures reveal is a crude measure of the relationship between the earl as lord of the men of his honor. By the fourth generation the personal link had largely ceased to function in the way that it had done. There were a number of reasons why that should be. Of the five greatest families of the honor, Clinton had become extinct, and the lords of Hatton and Studley had fallen into financial ruin and political insignificance. The lords of Beaudesert had become politically independent, and one family, that of the Ardens, alone remained actively attached to their lord's retinue. The decline of the honor as community was in that sense inevitable and perfectly natural.[14] It hardly needs to be explained by the personal animosity and internal tensions we see at Breteuil and Eu in contemporary Normandy. The later earls seem to have seen it happen, and quietly developed strategies to exert local power by different and no less effective means, as we will see later.

Some qualifying observations need to be made here. Within an overall pattern of decline, some dynastic loyalties might be persistent. Thomas of Arden, lord of Ratley, was as important in the affairs of the earldom of Warwick in the year 1200 as we assume his great-grandfather, Thurkil of Arden, had been over a century earlier. A more striking example occurs in the honor of Striguil[15],

[14] D. Crouch, 'The Local Influence of the Earls of Warwick, 1088–1242: A Study in Decline and Resourcefulness', *Midland History*, xxi (1996), 1–23.

[15] 'Striguil' is an Anglicisation of the Welsh 'Ystrad Gwy', or 'valley of the Wye', it was the Marcher honor based on Chepstow.

which was created for William of Eu before 1086, and comprised many manors scattered across Somerset, Gloucestershire, Wiltshire and a number of other counties. Its greatest tenant in 1086 was Ralph Bloet (I) with forty-three hides of land in Hampshire, Wiltshire, Gloucestershire and Somerset. He and his descendants maintained their place in the followings of three successive dynasties holding Striguil. His great-grandsons, Sir Ralph Bloet (IV) of Silchester (died 1243) and Sir William Bloet of Salisbury (viv. 1261), were in their days prominent followers of the Marshal lords of Striguil. But the personal connection between the Bloets and their overlords ended in a way that is significant for the argument here. Ralph (IV) died leaving a son, William, under age. He came into the wardship of Earl Walter Marshal of Pembroke, but the earl promptly sold his wardship and the keeping of the boy and his lands to Earl Simon de Montfort of Leicester.[16] There is no subsequent personal connection noted between a Bloet and a lord of Striguil. Indeed, in 1287 William was summoned to attend a royal council as a peer in his own right.

A dynamic loyalty had clearly existed between the Bloets and their lords over four generations, even though the lordship of Striguil changed hands in *c.*1095 and 1189. Still in 1217 a Bloet was the banner bearer of the younger William Marshal at the battle of Lincoln.[17] What abruptly ended the link seems to have been a decision by the lord of Striguil in *c.*1243 to exercise his prerogative as lord to turn William Bloet's wardship to profit, rather than use it to consolidate family ties of affection and dependence. This is a good example of the sort of emotional entropy which eventually eroded the honor as a community. Earl Walter chose to look on the boy William Bloet as a means to make money rather than as a personal responsibility. He might instead have taken the boy into his own household and married him off into another tenant family, if he had been more keen to affirm the Bloet allegiance to the honor of Striguil. But he did not. Judging by the large numbers of thirteenth-century lawsuits sparked by alleged misconduct of guardians, and the way that Magna Carta sought to curb guardians' exploitation of their wards, many lords saw wardship simply as a means of making money.

Emotional entropy is not an easy social process to assess. But it must have been a major cause of the decline of many English honors. It has long

[16] For some details about the Bloets of Silchester, Raglan and Salisbury (in Gwent), D. Crouch, *William Marshal: Knighthood, War and Chivalry, 1147–1219* (2nd edn, London, 2002), 149–50, 220–1. For the wardship of William Bloet, National Archives (formerly Public Record Office), KB26/131, m. 8d.

[17] *History of William Marshal*, ed. A. Holden and D. Crouch, trans, S. Gregory (3 vols, Anglo-Norman Text Society, Occasional Publications Series, 4–6, 2002–6) ii, lines 16913–21.

been the assumption of historians that the honor was in decline at the end of the twelfth century. The two principal reasons for this have been summed up by Peter Coss.[18] Legal historians have assumed, with some reason, that the seigneurial court at the heart of the honor must have gone into decline as the attractiveness of the courts of royal justices grew in the second half of the twelfth century. The writ *precipe*, developed out of earlier writs in Henry II's reign, could be secured by a plaintiff to have his case taken before the king's justices. By the time of Magna Carta, certainly, an action arising from *precipe* was regarded as a direct threat to the legal jurisdiction of an honorial lord. Coss sees the growth of royal power under Henry II as a particular challenge to the great honorial magnates.[19] Another obvious weakness was that there was nothing to stop the tenants of one lord accepting lands from another lord. The problems of jurisdiction caused by this are mentioned as early as the Laws of Henry I. We know from a number of empirical studies of eleventh- and twelfth-century English honors that a proportion of the tenants of a lord, however great and formidable a man he was, would be also the tenants of other lords. The intertwined honorial geography of England made this all the more likely to happen, in that a local man out to build up a coherent estate in his neighbourhood would find that its lands and manors could belong to a number of honors.[20]

None of this is to go so far as to say that the honor in the twelfth century was an unimportant social and political community, indeed we have seen plenty of evidence to the contrary. Coss is careful to say that he sees it as a powerful focus of noble power well into the thirteenth century, and still visible in the fourteenth. Some of the smallest honors were unlikely to have been of much importance, even locally. But even the lord of a modest-sized honor could be as formidable to his neighbours, as was Manasses Arsic, the mid-twelfth-century lord of the Oxfordshire honor of Cogges. His threats to recover his family's grants to the abbey terrified a

[18] See summary in, P.R. Coss, *Lordship, Knighthood and Locality: A Study in English Society, c.1180–c.1280* (Cambridge, 1991), 5–8.

[19] See specifically, P.R. Coss, 'Bastard Feudalism Revised', *Past and Present*, no. 125 (1989), 63. For the relationship between royal and seigneurial justice in England, J. Hudson, *Land, Law and Lordship in Anglo-Norman England* (Oxford, 1994), 253–81; idem, *The Formation of the English Common Law* (London, 1996), 118–56, 186–219.

[20] The classic study of this has become, R. Mortimer, 'Land and Service: The Tenants of the Honor of Clare' in, *Anglo-Norman Studies* viii, ed. R.A. Brown (Woodbridge, 1986), 177–97.

monk of Fécamp sent to Oxfordshire to take care of his abbey's interests in the 1160s.[21] Other than military support of their lord, there were a number of powerful evocations of honorial spirit which were still potent in the years on either side of 1200. One of the most evocative is the fact that the first knightly heraldry, which appeared just after 1200, was often assumed in imitation of the older magnate heraldry of the honor to which the knights belonged.[22]

David Carpenter has recently examined the phenomenon of the honor in the thirteenth century. He was moved to do so by a feeling that its continuing importance has been underestimated by recent historical work. He does not in fact talk much of honors and honorial communities in his study. He describes what he is talking about – in the nineteenth-century British way – as 'feudal society' and 'feudalism'. His study sets out to examine the extent to which the honor still functioned in the thirteenth century; its money payments, seigneurial rights and private courts. The range of Carpenter's evidence and the strength of his argument would certainly deter any historian from being unwise enough to write off the honor as a functioning method of generating baronial income before 1300. However, the key to his argument is that this supposedly hollow and intimidatory 'fiscal feudalism' was more than just a money-making machine. It was a continuing means by which magnates could form relationships with dependents, and was evidence of community, even if a dysfunctional one at times. In fact, in several instances Carpenter finds good evidence of life in some large thirteenth-century honors, like those of Stafford and Tutbury, and smaller ones like Eaton in Bedfordshire and Dudley in the Central Midlands. He believes that this counters the arguments of those who would argue for 'feudal' decline in the thirteenth century, although he accepts that those who do argue for it have never said that honors stopped functioning abruptly in 1200. As he points out, Magna Carta assumes that honorial life was a reality for the English upper classes in 1215.

I still remain convinced that there was a decline in the ability of lords to use the honor as a weapon of social control and local power during the

[21] '*Epistolae Fiscannenses*: lettres d'amitié, de gouvernement et d'affaires', ed. J. Laporte, in, *Revue Mabillon*, 43 (1953), 30.

[22] D. Crouch, *The Image of Aristocracy in Britain, 1000–1300* (London, 1992), 232–4; P.R. Coss, *The Knight in Medieval England, 1000–1400* (Stroud, 1993), 79–81; D.A. Carpenter, 'The Second Century of English Feudalism', *Past and Present*, no. 168 (2000), 53–4.

thirteenth century, and that the decline had begun well before 1215.[23] Here's the thirteenth-century dilemma: if a lord exercised his prerogatives over his tenants, did he lose in loyalty what he gained in cash? We have already seen how the exercise of honorial rights could sabotage rather than affirm generations of the allegiance of lesser to greater men in the example of William Bloet and his lord Earl Walter Marshal in 1243. Another example, which can be followed in greater detail, is that of the Mallory family of Kirkby in Leicestershire. The Mallory example poses a related question: if a child was given to a guardian outside the honor, what would be the emotional effect? Richard Mallory of Kirkby died in the service of Earl Saher de Quincy at the siege of Mountsorrel castle in 1217.[24] The Mallories had been followers of the lords of the honor of Leicester for generations. Richard's great-uncle, Anschetil Mallory of Tachbrook, had been steward of the honor and in 1174 had defended Leicester castle against the king's men when Earl Robert III of Leicester had rebelled. Since Earl Saher had married one of the co-heirs to the earldom of Leicester, the death of Richard Mallory in his service was in the finest family tradition. But Richard had married Cecilia, who can be proved to have been the sister of the rising courtier and Leicestershire man, Stephen of Seagrave (chief justiciar, 1232–34) and when Richard died, his children came somehow into the wardship of their uncle, Stephen. Richard's heir, Thomas Mallory, spent at least six years in Seagrave custody and entered into an affective relationship with his guardians. He appears as a frequent witness to Seagrave acts, and Seagrave influence secured presentation to the royal living of Dilwyn in Herefordshire for his younger brother Robert Mallory, a clerk, in 1230 (Robert would have then been in his early or mid-twenties).[25] Thomas and Robert Mallory demonstrate quite how corrosive an external wardship could be to an honorial allegiance. In the case of the Mallories, it was because they were placed in the household of a powerful maternal kinsman where they were clearly loved and valued.[26]

In my study of the decline of the honor of Warwick, I used the disappearance of tenants from the witness lists of the earl's charters as evidence

[23] The reason why I do not talk here in Carpenter's terms of a decline in 'feudalism' and 'feudal society' will already be obvious from the last chapter, and will be all the more obvious by the time you get to the end of this one. Carpenter wants to talk of a 'second century of English feudalism' I had rather not talk of a 'first century'.

[24] For Richard's death, National Archives, JUST1/949, m.2.

[25] For these relationships, *Patent Rolls, 1225–32*, 418; *A Catalogue of the Muniments at Berkeley Castle*, ed. I. Jeayes (Bristol, 1899), 65, 69, 90.

[26] Carpenter, 'Second Century', 52–3.

that the honorial community was in decline. Since the fates of all five of the major tenant families of the honor can be reconstructed, we know from other sources what had happened to them and why they had disappeared. Extinction and a steep decline in fortunes accounted for the disappearance of three out of the five. Only one was left in attendance on the earl in 1200. The evidence was used to highlight the fragility of the honorial bond as generation succeeded generation. Carpenter, in considering this evidence, raises the question as to whether the evidence of witness lists as to baronial followings can be entirely trusted, the implication being that such analyses are based on partial evidence. Following an unsupported suggestion of Sir James Holt, he suggests that the magnate charter was changing in the early thirteenth century, recording smaller transactions, with by implication fewer, and more domestic, witnesses. The big men attached to a magnate would not turn out for such small affairs. Since the witness lists of charters have long been used to try to reconstruct the circles of dependents around magnates, this is a criticism with some major implications and one which cannot be easily let pass. If Carpenter is right, then a whole avenue of investigation of noble society might be considered to be closed. However, there is reason to believe that charter evidence does give quite a full picture of baronial followings, even in the thirteenth century. On occasion, charter evidence of baronial followings can be cross-checked against other sources. In the case of William Marshal we have the evidence of his charters from 1189 to 1219, but we also have the complementary evidence of his biography. Checking the one against the other we find that the lists of Marshal dependents generated by each source is, if not identical, then closely similar. If this is the case for the Marshal household, one would expect it to be equally true for other magnates. At the end of the thirteenth century, numerous charters allow us to reconstruct in the traditional way the household of Edmund earl of Lancaster (d.1296). In his case there are complementary sources in the royal records to construct a parallel list, which is again very similar.

The evidence still persuades me that magnate honors were in decline after 1180, and it is possible to reconstruct the reasons for the decline. Carpenter is assuredly right in his belief that it is unwise to write off honorial communities too soon as a powerful factor in thirteenth-century society. The fiscal element to honors can be easily demonstrated to have been important. But decline happened, even though it proceeded at a different pace in different honors. Marcher honors could arguably last comfortably as functioning aristocratic communities well into the fourteenth century. But the natural process was always decline: emotional entropy, division of inheritance, the extinction and decline of families, all made it inevitable. So it was that Earl Henry II of Warwick (1204–29), Earl Simon de Montfort of Leicester (1231–65) and Earl Roger de Quincy of Winchester (1235–64) possessed followings which drew a minority of their personnel from families which were honorial tenants and reflected instead their power and ambition in a particular locality; in Montfort's case, around his chief seat of Kenilworth.[27] They had found other ways of constructing political networks, and that way was through recruiting the locality, not the honor.

Locality: Community and Affinity

One of David Carpenter's strongest arguments for the continuing vitality of thirteenth-century honors can be used to suggest something quite different. Carpenter draws attention to some mid-thirteenth-century honors which showed very positive signs of political life: notably the large honor of Tutbury, possessed by the Ferrers earls of Derby and the smaller honor of Eaton Socon, possessed by the Beauchamp family of Bedford. He also noted that although Henry II, earl of Warwick, was not followed in the early thirteenth century by his chief tenants, three of his stewards were knights with a tenurial connection to the honor of Warwick. He draws particular attention to the report of a meeting of the honor court of Warwick held around 1220, which we hear of because it ordered the dispossession of a tenant who had refused to give up her son to the earl's wardship. When that decision was challenged in front of the king's justices, the members of the court were listed. So we find that indeed all but one of them were tenants of some sort of fee held of the honor; the exception was the earl's steward, Sir Henry of Tubney, a tenant of Abingdon abbey and professional administrator.[28] This would fit with Carpenter's

[27] For the following of Roger de Quincy (which favoured Northamptonshire and Cambridgeshire), G.G. Grant, 'The *Familia* of Roger de Quincy, earl of Winchester and constable of Scotland' in, *Essays on the Nobility of Medieval Scotland*, ed. K.J. Stringer (Edinburgh, 1985), 102–28, especially 121–2. For that of Simon de Montfort (which favoured north Warwickshire and Leicestershire), D. Williams, 'Simon de Montfort and his Adherents' in, *England in the Thirteenth Century*, ed. W.M. Ormrod (Grantham, 1985), 174–6; D.A. Carpenter, 'Simon de Montfort: the First Leader of a Political Movement in English History', *History* 76 (1991), 11–13; J.R. Maddicott, *Simon de Montfort* (Cambridge, 1994), 61–71.

[28] *Rolls of the Justices in Eyre being the rolls of pleas and assizes for Gloucestershire, Warwickshire and Staffordshire (recte Shropshire) 1221, 1222*, ed. D.M. Stenton (Selden Society, lix, 1940), 175–6.

conclusion that even in the honor of Warwick the feudal spirit was alive and still capable of exerting a draw on its tenants in 1220.

However, there is another possible conclusion. The membership of the court that day included more than several knights holding fractional fees and serjeantries from the earl. Earl Henry had with him that day Sir Ralph Butler of Oversley (died 1226). The Butlers had not been tenants of the honor of Warwick in 1166, but Sir Ralph appears to have picked up from Earl Henry's father two fees from the honor at Billesley and Upton, Warwickshire.[29] He was a first-generation member of the honor, and perhaps had been deliberately enticed into it by the later earls. If so, the reason would be that the Butlers were one of the most considerable of landowning families in western Warwickshire; but they held their great estates there, focussed on the castle of Oversley, not from the honor of Warwick, but from that of Leicester, of which they were the most considerable tenant. Was the presence of Sir Ralph that day in the earl's court because he was a knight of the honor, or because he was a wealthy regional banneret who had allied with the earl and taken lands from him as an inducement? The same applies to the lesser knights present. Were they present as tenants, or as knights drawn towards the retinue of the major local magnate in the vicinity of their homes?

The 'feudal' spirit was only one influence that might lead a man to serve a lord. There was also the indomitable ambition of some lords to dominate a locality or a community, which could intimidate and attract local men into joining their following. The honors of Tutbury and Eaton Socon, when plotted on the map, are the sort of honor which had a geographically concentrated core. In other words, there were areas of the country where their lords had been powerful for generations, and where their castles, ecclesiastical foundations and manor houses were concentrated. When the local tenants of Tutbury and Eaton attended their lords, was the imperative the homage they had done for their estates, or was it also because their lord was still the most potent magnate in the area they lived in? When such lords looked for local knights to recruit into their following, it would be hardly surprising to find that the knights they recruited were also their tenants since the honor and local ambition in their cases coincided.

[29] The Butler fees in the honor of Warwick are mentioned first when Earl Waleran (1184–1203) assigned Ralph's service as part of the dower of his second wife, Alice de Harcourt, *Curia Regis Rolls* iv, 216. Ralph otherwise held eight fees of the honor of Leicester for a very considerable estate, rated at 46 hides in five counties in 1130, of which twenty were in Warwickshire, *Pipe Roll of 31 Henry I*, 23, 80, 86, 89, 108, 135; *Red Book of the Exchequer*, ed. H. Hall (3 vols., Rolls Series, 1896) ii, 552,

Medieval literature and history is full of the ambitions of magnates to be lords of the area around their chief seats and castles. They would devote energy and patience sometimes over generations to secure control over estates they coveted. A particularly early English case in point is the ambitions of Robert II, earl of Leicester (1118–68), to gain control over Charnwood, the lower Soar valley and the town of Leicester. The honor of Leicester was one of those which had an obvious core, in the town itself and the wapentake of Guthlaxton to south and west, but in places it was interpenetrated by lands of other lords. His ambition meant confrontation with two local magnates whose estates intruded into the core of his own honor, the earl of Chester and the bishop of Lincoln. In the 1120s he began to move against both of his rivals. By a process of confrontation, exchange and negotiation, he had by 1149 managed to break the power of the earl of Chester in the Soar valley and had taken from him his castle of Mountsorrel. He had also by then abstracted the manor of Knighton and the episcopal estates in the eastern suburb of Leicester from the bishop of Lincoln. All this so that he could be exclusive lord of Leicester and unquestionably dominant in its neighbourhood. His grandson, Earl Robert IV (1190–1204), had to weather counter-attacks from later bishops, by law-suits in the royal courts, and his great-grandaughter and her husband, Saher de Quincy, fought the last battle to recover Mountsorrel in 1217.[30]

A similar and famous example, involving appeals to the royal courts, and the manipulation of faction and justice, occurred between 1189 and 1192. William de Roumare, lord of Bolingbroke in Lincolnshire and earl of Lincoln, had ambitions to extend his control over the fens between Spalding and Crowland. In 1189, when the kingdom was troubled by (premature) rumours of Henry II's death, it seems that Roumare persuaded the prior of Spalding, through the agency of Gerard de Camville, to organise a mass invasion of the fens by thousands of his men, who went on to occupy the area and besiege and plunder Crowland Abbey, which till then had owned the land. The confrontation became tied into court faction disputes, because the new abbot of Crowland in 1190 was the brother of the chief justiciar, William de Longchamp. The dispute simmered down during the period of the Longchamp ascendancy, but in 1192, Roumare used the rising influence of his friend Count John, the king's brother, to temporarily get a judgement in Spalding's favour. It took Crowland abbey

[30] E.J. King, 'Mountsorrel and its Region in King Stephen's Reign', *Huntington Library Quarterly*, xliv (1980), 1–10; D. Crouch, 'Earls and Bishops in Twelfth-century Leicestershire', *Nottingham Medieval Studies*, xxxvii (1993), 9–20.

a decade and a lot of money to get its possession of the fens recognised. Whatever the tensions between local people and the abbey, the reason for the violence and persecution was the clever opportunism and powerful connections of a local magnate.[31]

Ambitions like this, and the determination to pursue them, gave political shape to the locality, because ambitious lords had defined an area by seeking to control it. It was a social mechanism independent of the honor; although, as in the case of Leicester, an ambition to extend local power beyond the possibilities the honor presented might be at the root of it. If the honor did not completely define aristocratic politics, neither did it necessarily confine relations between lord and man. If a lord wanted to define an area for his ambition which was bigger than the estates he actually held, then he had to come to terms with lesser men who were not his tenants. This is most obviously the case where a man came to wealth and influence at the royal court, but had no obvious centre of landed power. Such a man was William Marshal (died 1219) who acquired the scattered honor of Striguil by marriage in 1189 and his small paternal honor of Hamstead with estates in several south-western counties in 1194. He finally secured the earldom of Pembroke in the March of Wales in around 1200, with claims on the great honor of Leinster in Ireland. The result was that the Marshal had honors and castles concentrated in South Wales, but a random scattering of estates in Gloucestershire, Somerset, Berkshire and Wiltshire. His solution was to recruit what men he had as tenants into his following, but to recruit other knights and lesser barons particularly from leading families in the region of Gloucestershire and Wiltshire, some of whom were principally tenants of other lords, such as Stephen d'Evreux of Lyonshall, leading tenant of the honor of Weobley. So he erected a network of influence and contacts. He did it consciously, with a particular emphasis on powerful families of banneret status such as d'Evreux, Berkeley and Musard. Influence at court allowed him to secure for a while key components of regional domination, such as the shrievalty (sheriffdom) and castle of Gloucester and the forest of Dean and the castle St Briavels, and the keeping of the royal castles of Marlborough and Bristol. While he had royal favour William Marshal was secure and unassailable in

[31] For the dispute, D.M. Stenton, *English Justice between the Norman Conquest and the Great Charter, 1066–1215* (London, 1965), 148–211, for comments on the part of William of Roumare in instigating the business. W. Liu, 'Competing for Justice beyond law between Croyland and Spalding, 1189–1202', *Anglo-American Law Review*, 29 (2000), 67–96.

what was a largely non-honorial lordship in the Severn valley and Cotswolds.[32]

These political interest groups gathered around magnates are called 'affinities' by later medievalists. Such a political construction was transitory and could be constructed for a variety of purposes in a variety of ways. Huw Ridgeway's reconstruction of the affinity of William de Valence, lord of Pembroke (died 1296), found that his followers were drawn not from a distinct locality but almost entirely from the knights of the royal court and the tournament circuit, where Valence wanted to be dominant and secure.[33] There was no reason why any sort of affinity should last beyond its creator's life. But that did not mean that it was not a powerful fact of political life in its day. It could not have existed at all if knights of the time did not already recognise that their behaviour and allegiance was not confined by the membership of an honor. Richard Mortimer's study of the behaviour of the twelfth-century tenants of the honor of Clare in Suffolk demonstrated that they too had local ambitions, and would seek to consolidate their own position where they could by taking lands outside the honor. In the case of William Marshal's affinity after 1189 we see the end result: a politically dynamic and continually shifting world of allegiances, not a society static and confined by tenure.

As well as locality, community was another way in which magnates could exert themselves. England had a number of communal identities which could be exploited, of which the most extensive and powerful was the shire. The shire had a court to express the communal will of its free landowners, and a sheriff to wield executive and police powers. There is plenty of evidence that twelfth- and thirteenth-century people identified with their shires, and where such a feeling existed we might ask whether there were also magnates who wanted to take advantage of it. A few certainly did. William Rufus and Henry I seem to have been willing in rare cases to appoint sheriffs who were dependents of great magnates powerful in their shires. So Earl Henry I of Warwick (1088–1119) had as sheriff of his county for a time his leading baron, William fitz Corbezun. But it was much more likely that the sheriff was a man tied to the royal court in those reigns. In Stephen's reign the king deliberately allowed earls in 1139 to nominate and control their own sheriffs in a large number of counties, and the office remained subordinate to that of earl in some cases up till 1155.

[32] Crouch, *William Marshal*, 166–76.
[33] H. Ridgeway, 'William de Valence and his Familiares, 1247–72', *Historical Research*, 65 (1992), 246–50.

This experiment was soon reversed and thereafter it was very rare for magnates to be permitted to control the office.

If magnates were rarely able to control the office of sheriff – other than in the special cases of the counties of Chester and Cornwall – did this mean that they had no ambitions to seek to dominate the county? Some may have tried. The recruitment principle for the affinity of Earl Henry II of Warwick (1204–29) was to retain knights who can be identified as prominent jurors in the county court of Warwickshire. If the earl was seeking to win over some of the county's leading administrators, he was trying at least to monitor county business through them. For the most part, however, historians conclude that medieval local communities focussed on town, neighbourhood and local courts were generally inward-looking and caught up with their own local concerns.

Comparing France and England

The question of how local French social structures compared with English is not an easy one to answer. We have one intriguing contemporary witness, a Norman monk of Fécamp ordered abroad to the Oxfordshire of the 1160s to attempt to recoup the abbey's interests in the manor of Cogges. He was daunted and homesick, and aghast at the difficulties in recovering his abbey's rights. He was also fearful at the unconcealed threats of the local magnate, Manasses Arsic, who swore that he would recover the grants made to Fécamp by his ancestors. These were not the sort of complaints that were confined just to England. However, the monk was quite clear that things were simpler back home in Normandy. He confessed his bewilderment at the maze of rights and dues imposed on Englishmen by a hierarchy of officers, lay and ecclesiastical: '. . . the land has as many lords as neighbours, and what is more burdensome than anything, you can get nothing by which to pay the host of dues'.[34] If local political structures were simpler in France, it may have been because of the geographically concentrated nature of the secular honors which grew up in the tenth century (see above). This increased the local power of magnates, and made it difficult for external princely officers to impose their own layer of dues, courts and obligations. The determination of King Henry I to extend the intrusive and universal nature of princely power he found in England into Normandy was one of the reasons why the Norman magnates rebelled against him in 1123. Amaury, count of Evreux, was

[34] '*Epistolae Fiscannenses*', 29–30.

affronted because: '. . . he had to watch bailiffs and provosts running wild in his province. They imposed unaccustomed taxes, perverted justice as the fancy took them, did many wrongs to both high and low'.[35]

Cross-Channel studies of comparative Anglo-French local societies are rare in English, and unknown in French. Those that exist inevitably concern Normandy, the French province most closely linked with England. Their aristocracies were interlinked by history and descent. As we have already seen, studies so far have emphasised the obvious differences in honorial geography between England and Normandy. Norman honors were concentrated and territorially exclusive; Norman knight service was held on very liberal terms compared to English; a Norman knight's fee in general was drawn from an extent of land several times larger than that which supported an English fee.[36] This would lead us to expect that Norman magnates were less oppressed by the ducal regime in terms of financial demands, even if the rights of wardship probably bore down just as hard on them. Comparison of military service with other areas of France are difficult to accomplish, but it is a reasonable proposition that they resembled more Normandy than England.

We may assume that honorial or seigneurial courts were very much alive as centres of lordship in twelfth-century France outside Normandy. The British historian, Kathleen Thompson, has carried out a study of the county of Perche-Mortagne, south of Normandy, based on the sort of criteria used within English historiography. The records of the county of Perche during the reign of Count Rotrou III (1144–91) certainly indicate that his court was the centre of justice and administration in his small realm. The picture of a community of interest around a lord is not dissimilar from the sort of communities we find around English magnates. The Perche evidence is of particular interest because the counts were honorial lords in England too. They seem, like many other cross-Channel magnates, to have had less difficulty comprehending conditions in two realms than the harassed monk of Fécamp.[37]

Another good comparison is the lordship of Coucy in the Laonnais just to the north of the Capetian royal domain, as comprehensively analysed by Dominique Barthélemy: one of the few French honorial studies resembling

[35] Orderic Vitalis, *The Ecclesiastical History*, ed. M. Chibnall (6 vols, Oxford, 1969–80) vi, 330.

[36] T.K. Keefe, *Feudal Assessments and the Political Community under Henry II and his Sons* (Berkeley CA, 1983), 94.

[37] K. Thompson, *Power and Border Lordship in Medieval France: The County of Perche, 1000–1226* (Woodbridge, 2002), 100–1.

those carried out in Britain (in terms of territory Coucy, and its outlying castle of Marle, equalled the extent of the earldom of Pembroke). Coucy's origins were in a castle built as one of several by the archbishop of Reims in 922 to protect his secular lordship. By the mid-eleventh century, one Aubrey, a son of the count of Beaumont-sur-Oise, had used it to construct the core of a new honor, and from Aubrey it passed into the famous lineage that held it in the male line till 1311. There is evidence that Enguerrand I was busy extending his lordship over the surrounding villages west of Laon in the 1070s. By 1120 a group of knightly castellans are found dependent on Coucy, making up what a British historian would call a honorial baronage, men of local influence dependent on the lord's court, forming a community of service around him. Just as with Stenton's contemporary English honorial barons, the greater tenants of Coucy were in 1138 called *pares* ('peers'), when they were not called *barones*. Just as in England, they appear in contexts where they are supporting their lord in his seigneurial court.[38]

But of course there were differences between France and England, and at Coucy the community of the honor did not weaken in the thirteenth century, but carried on; its knightly lineages serving successive Enguerrands, where they did not ruin themselves financially and fall into squirehood. Barthélemy has reason to refer to his honor of Coucy as 'un petit royaume' with its lord exercising absolute power within its bounds.[39] In England, only the Marcher honors matched that sort of status at that time. But even in France there were influences countering that sort of independence. Capetian power had spread to the borders of Coucy by the reign of Philip Augustus, and some of the Coucy vassals had also become vassals of the king. Royal baillis were intervening around the frontiers of the honor of Coucy by the 1230s. In 1259, in a portentous dispute over Enguerrand IV's judicial rights with the Laonnais abbey of St-Nicolas-aux-Bois, King Louis IX intervened within Coucy itself to settle the dispute. Coucy was a 'kingdom' no more.

French and English magnates were alike in several ways in the twelfth and thirteenth centuries. One of these was that their ambitions quite often exceeded the confines of their honors, and that drew them into extra-

[38] D. Barthélemy, *Les deux ages de la seigneurie banale: Coucy xie–xiiie siècle* (2nd edn., Paris, 2000), esp. pp. 153–7. Barthélemy makes the point that this is by far the earliest mention of *pares* within a French seigneurie, but it is contemporary with the English examples listed by Stenton.

[39] Ibid, 486, paralleling Stenton's idea of the English honor as a 'feudal kingdom in miniature (an image he dropped on mature consideration).

honorial forms of relationship. The evidence to analyse this is not as plentiful as in England, but it exists. One such source can be found on the inquests carried out by Philip Augustus's officers around 1205 into the northern French Capetian conquests. The king had taken over lordship of the French Vexin, and in the inquest concerning his new province we find references to a number of 'liege fees' formerly held from the count of Meulan by surrounding lesser magnates: the lords of Blaru, Maule, La Roche-Guyon, Poissy and Rosny. The nature of these liege fees appears to have been payments in cash to secure the primary allegiance of these lords, and so effectively extend the count's power up and down the valley of the Seine, far beyond his territorial lordship. From the analysis of the acts of the counts, it seems that these relationships had all been set up in the first half of the twelfth century.[40] It would be tempting to call these liege fees 'feudal' links, but in fact the essence of them was to 'feudalise' extra-honorial relationships. The holders of the liege fees of Meulan were lesser honorial magnates who acted in their own interest independently of any prince.

This sort of contract of dependency may have been widespread in the French lands in the twelfth and early thirteenth centuries, but examples only survive in exceptional circumstances. However, the collected acts of Matthew II, duke of Lorraine (1220–1251) include ten Latin and French 'agreements' (*conventiones*) by which counts and lesser magnates around Metz recognised and defined their dependency on his power. In one case, that of Amadeus of Neufchâtel, the contract was being renewed which Amadeus had made with the duke's father, Theobald (1213–1220).[41] It was clearly not therefore a hereditary relationship, but one entered into by individual negotiation, and it did not apparently involve land. In other cases, a relationship was being defined with Metz by a magnate who had links with other surrounding princes. The count of Châlon in Burgundy, for instance, reserved his allegiance with the king, the duke and count of Burgundy and the count of Nevers in declaring that he was the 'liege man' of Duke Matthew. In return for this somewhat equivocal allegiance, the count had two villages in Lorraine confirmed to him.[42] A curious word used in many of these agreements was that the dependents were 'taking

[40] *Recueil des historiens des Gaules et de la France*, ed. M. Bouquet and others (24 vols., Paris, 1869–1904) xxiii, 712; D. Crouch, *The Beaumont Twins: the Roots and Branches of Power in the Twelfth Century* (Cambridge, 1986), 58–60.

[41] *Actes de Mathieu II duc de Lorraine (1220–1251)*, ed. M. le Mercier de Morière (Recueil des documents sur l'histoire de Lorraine, 17, 1893), 256–7.

[42] Ibid., 260–1.

back' (*reaccipere*, or *repriser*) lands from the duke, which implies that the relationship was being renegotiated after either his or their succession, and might therefore have been terminated at convenience.

The *conventio* (the negotiated contract of lordship between equals or near-equals) so prominent in the power relationships of mid twelfth-century and late thirteenth-century England, did therefore exist in France, although you have to look hard to find it. There is however one remarkable and informative survival, which derives from the circle of Count Waleran II of Meulan (1104–1166). In late 1141 and 1142 the count was picking up the pieces of his career in Normandy and France after the collapse of his ambitions in England. To bolster his affinity in Normandy, he chose to target his cousin, Robert, lord of Le Neubourg. Robert was a minor magnate of central Normandy but, more importantly for Waleran, was very influential at the court of Geoffrey of Anjou. For both these reasons Count Waleran chose to negotiate a *conventio* with Robert, by which he became his man. It involved the annual payment to Robert of 378*li.* in rents, several small properties and exemption from tolls in his lands. In return Robert dropped whatever claims he had against the count and offered his support and that of his castle of Le Neubourg against all the count's enemies, reserving only his allegiance to the 'lord of Normandy'.[43]

The Meulan-Le Neubourg *conventio* of the 1140s is a document which in form and purpose closely resembles the indenture, looked upon as the key to social and political relationships amongst the aristocracy of later medieval England. Both belong to different stages of the same documentary family. But this resemblance of form is all a long way from assuming that there was such a phenomenon as 'bastard feudalism' in France. Indeed, the classes of evidence used to reconstruct bastard feudalism in England does not survive in France, even if such a structure ever existed there. But there is some reason to think that the 'affinity' – or lordship constructed within localities and power structures – did exist in France. It would have been disguised for the most part, in that locality and honor were more or less coterminous in the parts of France that have so far been examined by historians. But in the cases of the count of Meulan and the duke of Lorraine-Metz, we see a lord reaching out beyond his territorial lordship to form relationships which may have been intended to be personal between the two parties.

[43] D. Crouch, 'A Norman "conventio" and bonds of lordship in the middle ages', in, *Law and Government in the Middle Ages: Essays in Honour of Sir James Holt*, ed. G. Garnett and J.G. Hudson (Cambridge, 1994), 299–324, text, pp. 321–4.

Aristocratic society in France can be compared with that in England, although the two were clearly not identical. Honorial geography was far more complex and dispersed in England, and so there was a key difference in the experience of lordship. English magnates had to be more inventive and hardworking in the relationships of dependence that they formed. They also had to contend with a king who was ever present in their particular localities in the twelfth century; although the more influential and inventive English magnates turned that into an advantage, colonising local government offices and local courts with their men. French honorial units seem to have been more long-lasting and important than those of England. Yet despite those two quite hefty differences, the two societies' power structures still resembled each other. This was because the imperative to seek to command distinct localities was the same in each, and led to the same strategies. The aim of a magnate in both was actively to recruit local knights and lesser magnates into his following by a variety of means: exploiting local loyalty; giving money or land; or intimidating with the menace of greater power, it was all the same. Through the magnate's eyes, the Perche and Wiltshire looked much the same as spheres for their ambition; and from the perspective of the knights of either region, magnates loomed up above them in just the same way.

CHAPTER 12

Noble Women : The View from the Stands

In the last two chapters we have been looking at power and ideas of how it was exerted in medieval society. The basic problem with the old feudal construct was that it was too simplistic a model by which to understand medieval society. The eighteenth and nineteenth-century scholars who used it to try to understand the middle ages were all too convinced of the primitive simplicity of the medieval aristocrat. Michelet and Burckhardt, for instance, were both doubtful as to whether a medieval person was even able to understand that he was an individual set apart from other individuals. The rational and humanistic post-Enlightenment mind was also bound to be somewhat dismissive of a medieval mentality which was so uncritically religious and, as they looked at it, superstitious. Mark Twain's imagining of a priest-ridden Arthurian society confronted with the technology of the industrial revolution is humorous, no doubt, but it was shamelessly constructed to assert the superiority of modern America over a dark, Catholic and brutal European past. Nineteenth-century writers admired medieval art and architecture, but the only thing they admired about medieval aristocrats was their fearlessness and childlike, chivalrous generosity. Conan Doyle's portrayal of the noble Sir Nigel Loring, for instance, pictured a simple, direct soul chaperoned and manipulated by his rather brighter plebeian servants.

The twentieth century was by no means so patronising. Indeed, the last century has been admirable in the way that it has deployed detailed research and a variety of approaches to rediscover the complex individuals who were its medieval ancestors. Perhaps this emerging realisation of the complexity and richness of medieval culture and society was the reason why the narrow feudalism of Adam Smith and William Blackstone had begun to irritate medievalists even before 1900. French ideas of what was medieval feudal society were not so confining and simplistic, which may be why the construct remains still largely unchallenged in France. In Britain it was not till the inspired work of K.B. McFarlane in the middle of the century that a model of medieval society emerged which respected its plural and complex structures. But it was not till the 1980s that the old feudal construct was finally hunted down and cornered by dissatisfied historians. Even so, it is still pleading for its life.

What perhaps was needed to give the whole question of power in medieval society some intellectual depth has only recently appeared in medieval historiography, and that is the study of women and power. The old feudal construct had absolutely no time for women. Sir Frank Stenton's great empirical study of medieval English society devoted no space to them, for in terms of a feudal society reconstructed from law and conveyances, females were largely an irrelevance. They did not carry the sword, hold public office or inherit land, except by default. Women were marginal characters, and were usually only written about by marginalised female historians. Such women as appeared in medieval historiography were those few who defied expectations, like the militant Joan of Arc, or who confirmed stereotypes, like the beautiful and wayward Eleanor of Aquitaine. Yet, as any systematic medieval historian soon realises, the sources for the history of medieval women are by no means thin. In my own research indexes, the subject of 'women' is one of the largest of my files. This in itself is some indication that women were not as marginal in medieval society as might appear from the legalistic historiography which dominated in the late nineteenth and early twentieth centuries. The second half of the twentieth century has realised this. One result of this has been to give some deeper thought to the nature of power and influence in medieval society, so as to be able to give some background to the fact that women were clearly a lot more influential than the old feudal models allow.

Women in Historiography

The study of the noblewoman is, as I said, a relatively recent movement in history. The serious study of medieval women began in the 1970s. There was historical work on women published before that time, and a number of deeply-rooted presuppositions about medieval women were formed in the distant past.[1] But the study of medieval noblewomen has chiefly been

[1] There were earlier English and French essays on the history of women, stretching back to the encyclopedists of the Enlightenment, see P. Stafford, 'Women and the

the contribution of this present generation of historians. The history of the noblewoman is by no means detached from the history of the rest of the nobility. Let us take the example of the oldest of the presuppositions to which I have just referred. We have already seen, while dealing with the historiography of kinship, how the theory of family formation in the 1860s was based on a model of emerging patriarchy (see Chapter 4). If the theory of kinship had a master narrative which taught that male control over the family increased as civilisation grew and matriarchy receded into the pastoral past of the hunter gatherers, then it had to be true that women's position worsened as regards control of property. And when in the middle ages inheritance was supposedly concentrated more and more in the hands of the eldest son, then his sisters became ever more disadvantaged and oppressed.

The first historians of medieval noblewomen were among the first generation of women academics. They were working on the margins of university life, and it is not surprising that some of them were drawn to study the marginal social life of their medieval predecessors. The first academic study in English specifically to address the subject of women in the middle ages is reckoned to have been Georgiana Hill's *Women in English Life from Medieval to Modern Times* (1896). Hill's long perspective was well-adapted to demonstrating the worsening position of women through history, culminating in the dire position of her mother's generation. By comparison, her medieval women seemed less constrained in their lives than those of the nineteenth century. But this was only by comparison. The greatest woman historian of the twentieth century, Eileen Power, took much the same line. She approached women's history through her work on female religious, literature and the economy. She wrote several studies specifically addressed to the subject of women in the middle ages, written and redrafted through the 1920s and 1930s but not published until they appeared posthumously as *Medieval Women* (1975). Between these and her 1926 essay 'The Position of Women' her views can be reconstructed with a degree of coherence.[2]

Writing at a time after women had achieved suffrage and independent control of their property, the middle ages was for Power, more obviously than for Hill, a time of female subjection to overlord, parents and

Norman Conquest', *Transactions of the Royal Historical Society*, 6th ser., 4 (1994), 221–3, for an informative sketch.

[2] E. Power, 'The Position of Women' in, *The Legacy of the Middle Ages*, ed. C.G. Crump and E.F. Jacob (Oxford, 1926), 401–33; eadem, *Medieval Women*, ed M.M. Postan (Cambridge, 1975).

husband. There were slight compensations. The independent noblewoman, widow, regent or heir – the *femme sole* – did have the advantage of the protection of the principle of feudal tenure. If legal tenure defined social class, as Maitland believed, then it was equally potent when it devolved on a woman, as it possibly could. But otherwise the only choice for a young woman was marriage or the convent, and Power did not find women of the middle ages blessed by that sort of choice. In today's way of looking at women's past, Eileen Power's studies of women would be regarded as heavily 'gendered'. Her studies were based more on established expectations of women than on detached investigation. The same was true of other writing on women of the 1950s and 1960s. Lady Stenton's *The English Woman in History* (1957) is a series of illustrative studies which shares Power's approach to the declining position of medieval women, and does not get beyond the literature of expectations where she deals with the middle ages.

The polemical approach to women's history did not survive the 1970s. Women's history lost its marginal academic status as women academics entered mainstream academic history in increasing numbers. The focus of study changed. Barbara Hanawalt has identified a key point in the sudden rise in the number of academic dissertations devoted to women submitted in the United States after 1975.[3] In due course these naturally became the basis for monographs and undergraduate courses. They fed new academic debate and raised new questions. It follows from all this that the historiography of noble women has as yet shallow roots compared to the other debates we have been following. But this at least gives it some advantages. The study of medieval women began seriously in the intellectual ferment of the 1980s. Its scholarship lacks the deep-rooted presuppositions we find in early chapters, presuppositions so deep-rooted that many of the participants in the debate are often unaware of their antiquity and origins. This has given the discussion of this relatively new aspect of medieval nobility a more theoretical and often a more vital and original outlook than others.

The development of scholarship on women in France follows a similar chronology to that of Britain and the United States, although for different reasons. Late nineteenth-century French historians have been characterised as either romantically obsessive about significant female characters like Eleanor of Aquitaine, Blanche of Castile or (naturally) Joan of Arc. If

[3] B.A. Hanawalt, 'Golden Ages for the History of Medieval English Woman', in, *Women in Medieval History and Historiography*, ed. S. Mosher Stuard (Philadelphia, 1987), 14.

they were not that, then they were Rankean administrative historians who ignored women, like Petit-Dutaillis, because they were absent from the record.[4] Both traditions tended to subvert the idea of women in history. For a romantic historian of France, women's importance resided in their relationship with a male: so Bertrade de Montfort was important only in relation to her lover, King Philip I. For the empirical student of Capetian government, as for the English constitutional historian, women were not relevant to the narrative, and so were wholly ignored.

The Annales movement of the 1920s and 1930s produced no major study of women in history. Considering the movement's ambitions to produce total history, and to look in on history and society from the margins, this omission is very strange indeed. It could be accounted for by the fact, common to both Britain and France, that medieval women had traditionally been approached through biographies. Annales historians deprecated the use of biography and the significance of the individual, and this might be the source of the omission. Whatever the case, the first significant French move towards discovering a history of women occurred not among the socio-cultural historians of the Annales sort, but amongst legal historians. The Société Jean Bodin chose to hold its annual meetings in 1956 at Leyden and at Dijon in 1957 on the 'Status of Women'. The proceedings were published subsequently in multiple volumes. They provided what was the first concerted intellectual effort by academics anywhere to examine the changing status of women in customary, canon and Roman law down the centuries.[5] But the legal historians' lead was not followed by general historians for more than a decade.

As with the United States, the investigation of medieval women in France changed gear in the early 1970s. In the USA this can be put down to social and professional change both inside and outside the historical profession. In France, where historical schools tend to dictate investigation, the change can be traced to one individual. In this case it was the decision by Georges Duby in 1973 to devote his seminar at the Collège de France to the history of kinship and reproduction. This move rapidly led the great man towards male and female relations – barely explored except by canonists – and to the place of women in society. Duby was a Cistercian of the mind: he had an unerring instinct for a historiographical wilderness

4 S. Mosher Stuard, 'Fashion's Captives: Medieval Women in French Historiography' in, *Women in Medieval History and Historiography*, ed. S. Mosher Stuard (Philadelphia, 1987), 62–8.

5 *La Femme* (3 vols, Recueils de la Société Jean Bodin, xi–xiii, Brussels, 1959–62).

that could be made to bloom. So in 1976–77 Duby devoted his seminar at the Collège de France to the subject of marriage and inaugurated what would become a major and fruitful theme in his scholarship, leading to a number of major studies in the next two decades.[6] But his change in historiographical direction was noted elsewhere, and a wide-ranging conference on 'Women in the civilisations of the tenth to the thirteenth century' in 1976 at the CNRS centre for the study of medieval history and culture at Poitiers followed self-consciously where Duby was leading.[7] The difference between French and Anglo-American histories of women is therefore that the move into the study was male-led in France. Other than that, the histories of women that developed in the last quarter of the twentieth century were not dissimilar in the Francophone and Anglophone worlds. The period was one where at least the Anglophone historians read the French as a matter of course. There has not been for once an opportunity for national historiographies to diverge.

The Minimalist View

A characteristic of the current historiography of women is the study of the ability of medieval women to act within their world. The ability to be an independent actor is what most distinguishes a medieval from a modern woman. It is not perhaps surprising therefore that it is this aspect of female life that has monopolised historical study; it points up the historical distinction between the two periods. But to what degree was the medieval woman repressed by society? As we have already seen, and will see again, the structures of power in medieval society were rather more complex than the old feudal models would have us believe. The potential for women to be actors may therefore have been greater than was once thought possible. The feudal construct of society put landholding and its military and social bonds at the centre of eleventh and twelfth-century society. Judged by that yardstick, women could never have been of much consequence in society, as they only came to control land in default of men and could never have ridden to war. So, as Susan Johns says, there remains embedded in the historiography a 'minimalist' view, which tends to regard medieval noblewomen as generally ineffectual: too disabled by family and social

[6] See Duby's own account in *The Knight, the Lady and the Priest*, trans. B. Bray (London, 1983), pp. xvii–xix, and also the historiographical review in, E. Santenelli, *Des femmes éplorées? Les veuves dans la société aristocratique du haut moyen âge* (Lille, 2003), 13–14.

[7] Proceedings published in *Cahiers de Civilisation Médiévale*, 20 (1977).

constraints to act.[8] In traditional French historiography, dominated by nineteenth-century ideas of family change and lineage formation, this minimalist view of women's position was taken for granted. It is the basic assumption of most of Georges Duby's work on women, and has been widely influential also in America until recently.[9] In traditional British historiography, dominated by the idea of tenure as the key to understanding society, the minimalist position also dominates, because by its view only a small number of women ever achieved free control of land.[10]

We find this minimalist scheme addressed with sober empirical logic in Sir James Holt's presidential address to the Royal Historical Society in 1984. It is a particularly significant essay on women in medieval society because it draws also on French work.[11] The presuppositions of both British and French historiography are all present. Women's significance depended only on the property and rights they brought with them, because property and rights were central to medieval society. They were important because they produced heirs who would in turn transmit the property on to the next generation. Here we find the French influence: Holt assumed with Duby that society had been restructured 'within a few generations at most' into male-dominated lineages. Women, younger sons and bastards paid the price for this social mutation. But, although derivative, Holt's arguments are powerful ones. No unattached Anglo-Norman woman, other than a widow, ever does appear as an independent landowner in the eleventh or twelfth century. A substantial amount of female inheritance took place in default of male heirs, but the fact that these women were married meant that their inheritances were never theirs exclusively to enjoy. Holt makes the point that a party within the male-dominated

[8] S.M. Johns, *Noblewomen, Aristocracy and Power in the Twelfth-Century Anglo-Norman Realm* (Manchester, 2003), 5–6.

[9] J-A. McNamara and S. Wemple, 'The Power of Women through the Family in Medieval Europe, 500–1100' in, *Women and Power in the Middle Ages*, ed. M. Erler and M. Kowaleski (Athens GA, 1988), 137–8. As usual David Herlihy was in advance of almost everybody else in diagnosing this historiographical trend, 'Did Women have a Renaissance? A Reconsideration', *Medievalia et Humanistica*, 13 (1985), 1–22.

[10] J.A. Green, 'Aristocratic Women in Early-Twelfth Century England' in, *Anglo-Norman Political Culture and the Twelfth-Century Renaissance*, ed. C.W. Hollister (Woodbridge, 1997), 59–82 gives a balanced and empirical study of female succession, but (pp. 60–1) within a framework which emphasises lack of female control.

[11] J.C. Holt, 'Feudal Society and the Family in Early Medieval England: IV. The Heiress and the Alien', *Transactions of the Royal Historical Society*, 5th ser., 35 (1985), 1–28.

society in England obliged the king to modify such female successions as there were to its advantage. The king – perhaps Stephen around 1136 – decreed that inheritance was to be shared out between several daughters on the death of their father without sons, rather than going exclusively to the eldest of them. This satisfied a male ambition to make female inheritance within a family to go as far as possible amongst the husbands and sons of the heirs. Holt naturally puts it all down to being an effect of the 'mutation familiale', because he assumed that it gave opportunities to provide for the newly disinherited group of younger sons, disadvantaged by emerging primogeniture.

Anybody sympathetic to the idea of the minimalist position of women in twelfth-century society need only read Holt's masterly retelling of the well-attested story of Grace of Saleby to feel thoroughly justified. This Lincolnshire girl was supposedly born to an aged Lincolnshire landowner and his young wife, Agnes, early in the 1190s. I say 'supposedly' because an enquiry uncovered the fact that Agnes was in fact barren, and had feigned pregnancy with the aid of padding, faked a childbirth and smuggled a baby into her chamber. She had the baby baptised as Grace 'with appalling candour' and employed the real mother as nurse. All this so that Agnes could avoid coming into the custody of her hated brother-in-law when her husband died, as he did soon after the supposed birth. When he died, Agnes and Grace came by royal grant into the wardship of the minor courtier, Adam de Neville, and Adam passed on Grace through marriage to another courtier so as to profit from the wardship of her lands, apparently when she was still less than four years old. In 1194, William of Hartshill, Grace's supposed uncle and the object of her mother's hatred, launched a lawsuit to gain what he considered his rights. He failed, and in 1205 after Adam's subsequent death, the girl became the wife of a third courtier, Brian de Lisle, 'apparently undeterred by the accumulation of fatalities which were coming to be associated with the wretched Grace'. She had become a widow before she was ten and had earned her guardian a total of 500 marks in payments for her two marriages. The impression from this sort of source is that a woman's importance lay only in that she was a means of access to land and rights.[12]

There were limits to society's willingness to treat women as an animated title deed, as Holt points out. There was a very real and highly vocal concern in the twelfth century amongst noble families that their daughters should not come into the hands of men beneath their rank because of the

[12] Ibid., 22–3.

customary right of lords to marry off fatherless heirs. The word used was 'disparagement': their spouses were not of their *parage*, in this case meaning 'not socially equal'. As early as 1100 King Henry I had made a politic acknowledgement that he ought to consult with the families of his tenants-in-chief about the marriage of their daughters. In 1215 King John was forced to repeat this promise to consult and also to declare that he would commit no *disparagacio* when he arranged marriages. He was also obliged to say that he would never force a widow into a remarriage, and only retain a right to give his consent if she did indicate that she wished to marry.[13] This was not only an English concern. Twelfth-century romances written in the north of France not infrequently feature wicked kings who marry noble widows and heirs to low-born courtiers, and clearly have a contemporary relevance to French magnates.[14] This resistance movement indicates, as Holt says, that not every ward had the same experiences as Grace of Saleby. Many wardships of heiresses were kept within families and some were bought by their widowed mothers.[15]

A particularly English aspect of the minimalist stance on the social status of women also emerges from traditional historiography. The growth of centralising royal power has been taken to be the characteristic of the English 'feudal' monarchy since the beginning of the nineteenth century, and such a power naturally concerned itself with women as with every other potential source of income. The bureaucracy that grew up to enforce royal rights and collect royal revenues was going to be very interested in controlling the revenue and patronage offered by widows and heirs. This is epitomised by the despatch of royal justices into the shires in 1185 to make a national enquiry as to the women and children who ought to have been in royal wardship. It produced what is called the *Rotuli de Dominabus*, a county-by-county listing of such women and wards and

13 J.C. Holt, *Magna Carta* (Cambridge, 1965), 212–13, 319–20. Holt argues that 'disparagement' first occurs as a technical term around 1194, a condition imposed by the Exchequer to exclude parvenus from taking advantage of the king's concession of freedom for a family to marry off an heir. By *c.*1218 it plainly had passed into the vernacular in the sense we use it, for the Arthurian romance of Fergus has King Arthur being petitioned to find a husband for the heroine 'et que ne fust *desparagie*', *The Romance of Fergus*, ed. W. Frecoln (Philadelphia, 1983), l. 6362.

14 As in, *Raoul de Cambrai*, ed. S. Kay (Paris, 1996), ll. 214–16, where Countess Alice is married to Giboin of Le Mans, 'coupling a mongrel with a greyhound'; *Garin le Loherenc*, ed. A. Iker-Gittelman (3 vols., Classiques français du moyen âge, 1996-7) i, ll. 2617–21, where a count of Flanders married off his sister rapidly, having heard that the king planned to marry her to one of his kitchen servants.

15 Holt, 'Feudal Society and the Family in Early Medieval England: IV', 23.

their assets, of which the returns for twelve counties survive. This survey, and the intrusive inquest that produced it, could be interpreted as another example of twelfth-century English royal government being ambitious to penetrate to the heart of society and to intervene even at the level of the noble family.[16]

Duby's work ran along parallel lines, although it was expressed in his distinctive idiom and drew on his particular literary methods. Using early medieval theological writers, he constructed in 1981 a bleak picture of a misogynistic middle ages. Woman was weak and treacherous, so said her critics. Marriage was a way of controlling her behaviour and limiting her indiscriminate lust. There was always a fear of the dishonour into which they would drag their families. She might get pregnant by another man and present her husband with a child of other blood, who would steal the inheritance away from his lineage. She was always suspected of seeking to escape marriage and take her own inheritance elsewhere. It was the duty of a man to curb and control her.[17] Duby was happy to transfer this theological model to twelfth-century literary texts and circumstances. As with Holt, we see the same fixation on lineage and property in Duby's work, but also he concentrated, as a French historian tended to, on power and privilege. It has to be said, however, that his particular take on minimalism in female status led him astray. This is nowhere more evident than in his 1984 interpretation of what happened in Leinster in 1208. William Marshal had gone with his pregnant wife to Ireland. He had been called back to England by King John, and had to go. He feared that his Irish vassals intended rebellion against him, so he left his wife in charge, the heir of the great Strongbow, the conqueror of Leinster. But first he gathered the vassals together and harangued them about the demands on their loyalty which the countess's lineage imposed. Then he left, leaving her to the protection and counsel of his loyal household. Duby warped this incident to fit the misogynistic model he had created.

> *... we sense his anxiety at having to let her out of his sight for even a moment. Will she escape him, will he find himself empty-handed once again? Let her be closely guarded, let care be taken that no one will carry her off. Let her not proceed, still so young, to God knows what secret shamelessness, fornicating so openly that he would be constrained to separate from her.*[18]

[16] As for instance, S.L. Waugh, *The Lordship of England: Royal Wardships and Marriages in English Society and Politics, 1217–1327* (Princeton, 1988), 113–15.

[17] Duby, *The Knight, the Lady and the Priest*, 45–7.

[18] G. Duby, *William Marshal: the Flower of Chivalry*, trans. R. Howard (London, 1985), 129.

The unfortunate consequences of Duby's methodology can be seen in this piece of historical nonsense, as much as the weakness of the model he was trying to urge on us.

The greatness of Duby as a historian in part lies in his ready recognition of when he was adrift. He was already modifying his extreme position in 1985, the year after the publication of his *Guillaume le Maréchal*. A conference in Madrid that year had opened his eyes to the complexity of sources for the history of women, and the alternative models that it could support, as well as the crudeness of the categories he had been using. In particular, he was beginning to appreciate that he had not thought through his ideas of female powerlessness, because he had followed the path of traditional historiography which related power to land. Women had power of another sort: the power of the chamber, the power of the nursery.[19] In the early 1990s, in the years before he died, he returned again and again to the subject of women and power. In the end he never got very far from his original model of female subjection. But at least in looking closer at the sources, he did find that noblewomen were not quite as powerless as he had first suggested. Admittedly it was uncommon, he said, and it was resented, but women did on occasion wield *potestas*, the power to command and punish. Sometimes it was even acknowledged that they acquitted themselves well. The other source of female power, he said, was the control of the private chambers. It was not *potestas*, it was a power-base over domestic servants, the power of sexual seduction, and through control over the lord's sons, a potential source of subversion against her husband's authority.[20]

Maximising the View

To use nineteenth-century models of feudal society is to limit severely the scope of enquiry into the nobility of women. If you do it like Holt in a typically British way, and focus on feudal tenure, or like Duby in a typically French way, and focus on power, then the resulting picture is bound to be a bleak one. The only escape from such deterministic models is to go back to the evidence. An alternative approach is to construct case studies on female lives, and let the accumulated evidence speak freely to suggest new

[19] G. Duby, 'Pour une histoire des femmes en France et en Espagne' in, *Mâle moyen âge: de l'amour et autres essais* (Paris, 1990), 118–26.

[20] G. Duby, 'Women and Power' in, *Cultures of Power: Lordship, Status and Process in Twelfth-Century Europe*, ed. T.N. Bisson (Philadelphia, 1995), 69–85.

questions. At the back of all this was a new genre of studies of queenship, which emerged strongly with the expansion of women's history in the 1970s. Queens were of course exceptional women, and at the far end of the spectrum of female power. They were exceptional in terms of personal wealth; in opportunities to exercise patronage in offices in the Church and royal household; and in the exercise of real power as regents and queen dowagers. The twelfth century even saw ruling queens in Castile, Jerusalem, and – very nearly – in England. Queens were exceptional also in the amount of the sources which could be deployed to reconstruct their lives and their acts. As well as considering queenship and its various aspects, it was possible for book-length biographies to be constructed on the lives of several queens, and several distinguished examples have been published.[21]

Queens were not noblewomen, any more than kings were magnates. A barrier of ideology and ritual separated the queen as effectively from the rest of society as it did the king. But queens operated on noblewomen in the same way as kings did on noblemen: they provided avatars of desirable dignity, and were a useful source of trappings to which the noble might aspire. But most importantly, queens demonstrate the plenitude of power to which a medieval woman might aspire, and the degree of power was indeed impressive, even in a queen consort sitting mutely beside her husband on a throne (as Duby portrayed her). Duby himself was challenged to his face on the matter of female rulership, in K-F. Werner's analysis of real female authority.[22] As a result, questions which can be legitimately asked of the power of queens, have tended to be applied also to other, lesser women. So it has become natural to ask what place women really played in the command of armies, the management of estates, the patronage of lesser aristocrats and of artists.[23]

As a result there has recently grown up a complementary literature of studies of duchesses and countesses. There have been studies of notable and well-documented noblewomen, such as Countess Adela of Blois (died 1137) and the countesses of Flanders, Clemence (died 1133) and Sybil (died 1165). The liberally documented countesses of Barcelona have had

[21] See for a brief survey, J.C. Parsons, 'Family, Sex and Power: the Rhythms of Medieval Queenship' in, *Medieval Queenship*, ed. J.C. Parsons (Stroud, 1994), 1–11.

[22] Duby, 'Women and Power', 69; K-F. Werner, 'Les femmes, le pouvoir et la transmission du pouvoir' in, *La femme au moyen âge* (Maubeuge, 1990), 365–79.

[23] L.L. Huneycutt, 'Female Succession and the Language of Power in the Writings of Twelfth-Century Churchmen', in, *Medieval Queenship*, ed. J.C. Parsons (Stroud, 1994), 189–201, esp. p. 190.

several important studies devoted to them. In addition, the very idea of the title and status of the countess has been analysed by a number of writers.[24] These studies tend to emphasise the same traits in female power as do queenship studies. The delegation of executive power to women in the absence of their husbands is a major theme, because it is the opposite pole to the minimalist interpretation of female power. Countess Clemence ruled Flanders in the absence of her husband, Count Robert II, on crusade between 1096 and 1100. In his absence the young countess exercised full power; dealing with popes and kings; issuing acts under her own seal, minting coins in her own name, presiding over the comital court and its officers, and governing the Flemish church and people with some style.[25] While Clemence was ruling Flanders, Adela was ruling Blois-Chartres to universal acclaim: indeed, she was so effective that the return of her husband made little apparent difference to her power (especially as he did not have that good a crusade) and the period of her effective power over Blois-Chartres lasted beyond his death in 1103 and into the majority of her sons. She devised a succession policy that ultimately extended the power of Blois over England and Normandy, and she lived to see a brief 'Blessensian empire' dominating northern France and the Atlantic coasts.[26]

These episodes of female rulership were not just confined to the turmoil of the First Crusade in Northern France. While Count Thierry of Flanders was absent on the second Crusade, 1146-48, Countess Sibyl was left in charge of his realm, as on other occasions too. She acquitted herself well in affairs of church and state. She did not allow her pregnancy to get in the

[24] D. Crouch, *The Image of Aristocracy in Britain, 1000–1300* (London, 1992), 75–80; R. DeAragon, 'Dowager Countesses, 1069–1230', *Anglo-Norman Studies*, xvii, ed. J. Gillingham (Woodbridge,1995), 87–100; Johns, *Noblewomen, Aristocracy and Power*, ch. 4.

[25] T. de Hemptinne, 'Les épouses des croisés et pèlerins flamands aux xie et xiie siècles: l'exemple des comtesses de Flandre Clémence et Sibylle' in, *Autour de la Première Croisade: Actes du Colloque de la 'Society for the Study of the Crusades and the Latin East'*, ed. M. Balard (Paris, 1996), 89–92. For the long tradition of female rulership in Flanders, K.S. Nicholas, 'Countesses as Rulers in Flanders' in, *Aristocratic Women in Medieval France*, ed. T. Evergates (Philadelphia, 1999), 111–37.

[26] See the studies by K. LoPrete, 'The Anglo-Norman Card of Adela of Blois', *Albion*, 22 (1990), 569–89; eadem, 'Adela of Blois and Ivo of Chartres: Piety, Politics and the Peace in the Diocese of Chartres', *Anglo-Norman Studies*, xiv (1992), 131–52; eadem, 'Adela of Blois as Mother and Countess' in, *Medieval Mothering*, ed. J.C. Parsons and B. Wheeler (New York, 1996), 313–33; eadem, 'Adela of Blois: Familial Alliances and Female Lordship' in, *Aristocratic Women in Medieval France*, ed. T. Evergates (Philadelphia, 1999), 7–43, which stem from her unpublished 1992 doctoral thesis.

way of a successful war she carried on in defence of Flanders, invaded by a hostile coalition led by Baldwin IV of Hainault.[27] Sibyl, who died in the Holy Land in the monastery of St Lazarus in Bethany, attracted universal praise, perhaps because she was willing enough to resign power when her husband returned home from his perpetual travelling as much because of her sanctity. But the fact that her predecessor Countess Clemence attracted criticism because of her continuing engagement in the affairs of Flanders after her regency and second marriage to the duke of Brabant, is further evidence of the pervasiveness of female power. Clemence manipulated relations between Hainault and Flanders in order to challenge the new count Charles, who had succeeded her last surviving son, Baldwin VII, in 1119. Because her dower lands included twelve Flemish castles, because of her prestige and Capetian blood, and because her brother was pope, there seemed little limit to her ambitions.

Aside from examples of women as active rulers, the example of queenship leads us to look at the cultural power exerted by women. The place of queens in fostering liturgy, music, history and piety has been the subject of several evocative studies. Margaret, queen of Scotland (died 1093), and her daughter, Mathilda II, queen of England (died 1118), comprise consecutive generations of women who made powerful changes in their own worlds. Her biographer makes Margaret responsible for giving the Scottish court a complete cultural makeover in dress, attitudes to religious patronage and manners. Mathilda II of England, with far greater resources, furthered the career of clerics, scholars, historians and poets (or at least some of them had hopes that she would). In her short reign she altered the entire religious orientation of the English court towards almsgiving and confession. Both she and her mother were also active regents for their husbands.[28] The same power, on a lesser scale, was exercised by noblewomen. Geoffrey Gaimar, for instance, wrote his *Estoire des Engleis* for Constance fitz Gilbert, a Lincolnshire noblewoman who wanted to read English history in the French vernacular. It was vernacular culture where noblewomen had the greatest impact, as is perhaps natural when the world of Latin scholarship was closed down for them by exclusively male schools and universities.[29]

[27] T. de Hemptinne, 'Women as Mediators between the Powers of *Comitatus* and *Sacerdotium*' in, *The Propagation of Power in the Medieval West*, ed. M. Gosman, A. Vanderjagt and J. Veenstra (Mediaevalia Groningana, xxiii, 1997), 265–80

[28] See now L.L. Huneycutt, *Matilda of Scotland: A Study in Medieval Queenship* (Woodbridge, 2003), chs. 1, 5, 6.

[29] For an extensive survey of female literary patronage, Johns, *Noblewomen, Aristocracy and Power*, 31–43.

Some contributed to vernacular literature themselves, like the well-published but mysterious Anglo-French noblewoman who called herself 'Marie de France'. Andrew the Chaplain is the most powerful witness to female cultural power. Whatever the intention of his 'Tract on Love' there is no doubt that it was a work written to attract the notice of noble female patrons, and to excite their self-importance. He imagined a world where powerful women like Countess Mary of Champagne, Countess Elizabeth of Flanders and Countess Ermengarde of Narbonne, exercised jurisdiction over the entire late twelfth-century Francophone world on matters of morality, love and courtly behaviour. Andrew's literary vision was not necessarily a misleading counterfeit of reality, just an exaggeration.

The apotheosis of this vision of female cultural power is to be found in the Burgundian version of the Lancelot romance, called the *Lancelot do Lac*, written around 1220. Its brilliant and anonymous author made the central character Vivien, the Lady of the Lake. She abducts the child-prince Galaaz, who will come to be Lancelot, and brings him up in an alternative world beneath the Lake, a world of castles, forests and noble knights, but ruled by the Lady and her female counsellors. The Lady broods on the world above. Her female ambassadors dance through its Arthurian complexities, engineering wars and undermining those she dislikes. She has no love for Arthur, but detests even more the oafish and sinister Claudas, who is Arthur's mortal enemy. She prepares Galaaz herself for knighthood, although she is a little uneasy in the role. But he must be knighted, as he is to be her unwitting weapon in the world above the Lake, first to destroy Claudas, and then, in time, Arthur. Vivien is a hypnotic character, learned, cultured and wise, and fully sensible of what is good, great and beautiful. But she is obsessed with power, with manipulation and with the exercise of her own mystical sorcery, so all that is great in her must inevitably turn ultimately to destruction. It is hardly necessary to push the argument that Vivien is an avatar and critique of medieval feminine power: power which reaches out from the inner chambers of palaces and which can entrap and manipulate men and shape them and their world towards its own concealed ends.[30]

There was therefore female power of a sort in medieval society, and it has to have been a continuous factor from the eleventh to the fourteenth century, especially because the manifestations we have looked at had little to do with property and dower. We could take many examples of such women and the image of power they projected. A representative one for

[30] *Lancelot do Lac*, ed. E. Kennedy (2 vols., Oxford, 1980).

our purposes here would be Agnes, countess of Meulan (died 1181). Agnes was the daughter of Count Amaury I de Montfort of Evreux (died 1137). In *c.*1142 a marriage was arranged for her by King Louis VII, who bestowed her on Count Waleran II of Meulan, as a means of tying him closer to the Capetian cause.[31] Waleran was then aged around thirty-eight, already a widower, and Agnes was probably in her late teens. She brought to the marriage the Garlande family honor of Gournay-sur-Marne in the Ile-de-France, and a few estates in Normandy. She did all that was expected of her, producing five sons who lived to adulthood. Her material image and legal identity survives on her seal, a more or less standard contemporary image of a gowned lady, a bird of prey perched on her left wrist and a lily in her right hand.[32] Unlike most of her contemporaries, however, we do have a pen-portrait of her by Stephen of Rouen *c.*1167. It is not exactly conventional and reveals some telling details:

His [Waleran's] widow is a great beauty, his equal in nobility, in deportment, intellect, birth, character and faith. The countess is accounted equal to the count. She resembles very much the father to whom she was born. She is like him in mind and fortune, in good will and eagerness, in feelings, speech, generosity, understanding and enterprise.[33]

Descriptions of Agnes are, as one would expect, keen to stress her nobility and noble virtues: the nobility she conveyed from her own Montfort and Garlande lineage to the house of Meulan, for she was the replica of her father. Her distinctly feminine virtues of chastity and nobility are expressed by the lily and hawk in her seal image.[34] But Stephen's word-play is that 'the countess is accounted equal to the count', and equal in all areas, whether nobility, dignity, character, intellect and religious feeling.

31 For the marriage and its circumstances, D. Crouch, *The Beaumont Twins: the Roots and Branches of Power in the Twelfth Century* (Cambridge, 1986), 52, 64–5.

32 Archives Nationales, L 877, no. 20.

33 *Carmen elegiacum de Waleranno comite Mellenti* in, *Chronicles of the Reigns of Stephen, Henry II and Richard I*, ed. R. Howlett (4 vols., Rolls Series, 1886–89) ii, 767.

34 On reading such images, B. Bedos Rezak, 'Women, Seals and Power in Medieval France, 1150–1350' in, *Women and Power in the Middle Ages*, ed. M. Erler and M. Kowaleski (Athens GA, 1988), 61–82; Johns, *Noblewomen, Aristocracy and Power*, ch. 7. The hawk on the wrist is an element in the conventional depiction by Thomas of Kent of Queens Olympias and Cleopatra, where it can only denote nobility, *Le Roman de Toute Chevalerie*, ed. B. Foster (2 vols., Anglo-Norman Text Society, 1976–7) i, ll. 105–24, 715–23.

Strange words to use if noblewomen in medieval society, as in the Duby world view, were customarily controlled, subjugated and marginalised.

Women at Large

The title of this chapter is 'The View from the Stands'. The point it makes is that the role of medieval women was often to be spectators. They watched as their husbands and brothers went off to war. While the men were absent, as often as not the women were left to hold things together, and wait for their return. But the title is not a metaphor. Medieval women often really did sit in the stands to spectate. The great medieval sporting obsession was the tournament. But the tournament was by no means an entirely male affair. It is coming to be recognised that women played almost as important a part. Noble women attended the greater tournaments in no small numbers. From at least the 1170s it was the custom for tournament patrons to arrange for carpenters to erect stands for the spectators: they placed them at the gates of the towns which were hosting the events. In front of the line of stands were erected the palisades and banks of the lists, beyond which the action of the tournament was played out. From their elevated stands and draped benches, the ladies present could look over the lists and observe the opening jousts of the day. Then in late morning or at midday they could marvel at the main event, the grand charge of the tournament, when two teams of hundreds of knights thundered towards each other across the open ground and then fought in a great mêlée.[35]

The role of the spectator is not necessarily a passive one. Women on the day of the tournament were expected to be quite as vocal an audience as in any modern sporting event. They would sit for hours in their sheltered seats and reminisce about past encounters.[36] They would comment loudly and sometimes sarcastically on the performance of the day. They would shriek when a knight went down in a welter of blood in a dangerous fall: 'God, what misfortune! He's dead!'. They would consult together with the heralds and decide who was to be honoured, and they would offer prizes. The heralds loved to draw them into the action. Leaping on to the banks of the lists at Chauvency in the duchy of Lorraine in 1280, a king of

[35] For stands at tournaments, and their history, see D. Crouch, *The Tournament: Sport, Celebrity and Society* (London, 2005), ch. 5.

[36] An interesting example of women as transmitters of social memory, a role considered broadly in, E.M.C. van Houts, 'Introduction' in, *Medieval Memories: Men, Women and the Past, 700–1300*, ed. E.M.C. van Houts (London, 2001), 1–16.

heralds (or senior herald) extemporised a speech to the ladies above, who had just watched two knights and their horses knocked on to their backs by a fierce joust. They had imperilled their lands and their bodies for you, he said, their wounds were suffered to earn your love. He lyricised for several minutes over the groaning bodies behind him, that they were there entirely for the sake of love, for from love derived all the great chivalric virtues. The ladies had tears in their eyes as he begged them then to be tender to those poor men behind him, and their like.[37]

What was going on at Chauvency and many hundreds more such places in the twelfth and thirteenth century? The tournament betrays a world of considerable social interaction between men and women. In the evening receptions and dinners, women mingled and chatted with the men, they sang and danced. This was not a society where women were cloistered away from men. They rode with them, sang with them and danced with them. It is clear that the tournament would have been a pretty barren event without the society, the criticism, the memory and the praise of women, much more so than in the rather more masculine world of nineteenth-century sport. There were power relationships going on, but they were muted and the participants were equal. Some relics of that equality of standing survive. Around 1188, Huon d'Oisy, a noble poet of the Cambrésis and former husband of a countess of Boulogne, devised an evening entertainment for a Champenois tournament. It was song about a fantastical tournament where the wives of the knights decided they would themselves experience the blows that men undertook for their sake. So they armed and mounted and took the field. The *Tournoi des Dames* is utterly straightfaced, apart from a few knowing asides, and the partygoers must have found it hilarious, for the women described were all characters they knew. They were present when Huon sang it, as we learn from these verses: 'Isabel – whom we all know – gallops on to the field, and attacks like a mad thing, crying over and over again her war cry, 'Let's get 'em, Châtillon!'.'[38]

Here was a world of fun and remarkably free association between the sexes. It was probably not a relaxed world, because there was danger in free association between men and women. Cardinal James de Vitry spelled it out:

There is plenty of the seventh deadly sin, called Lust, since the tournament goers are out to entice shameless women, if they achieve

[37] Jacques Bretel, *Tournoi de Chauvency*, ed. G. Hecq (Mons, 1898), 31–4.

[38] Huon d'Oisy, *Li Tournoi des Dames*, in, A. Jeanroy, 'Notes sur le tournoiement des dames', *Romania*, 28 (1899), 240–4.

prowess in arms; they are also accustomed to carry certain female tokens, as it they were their banners.[39]

The entire plot of the romance of the later thirteenth-century romance of the Castellan de Couci, a historical novel set in the tourneying society of Richard the Lionheart's time, is about the adulterous passion between Reginald the castellan, and the wife of a local lord. It was only possible because the two could meet frequently under cover of the 'lonc sejour', the tournament season in the north east of France.[40] It was just the same sort of world where Andrew the Chaplain's courtly and sexually-charged dialogues between men and women might occur in reality. It was the world where Count Alfonso of Poitiers, the brother of Louis IX, might organise gambling sessions in his palace at Acre in 1250, and invite *gentilz homes* and *gentils femmes* to crowd in and join the fun.[41] However, it is equally likely that unattached noblemen rarely went beyond flirting, even if they went that far. The social and physical penalties for proven adultery were not pleasant. William de Lorris gives sound advice for men and women in such social situations in his Roman de la Rose:

Serve and honour all women; take every care to be at their service. If you hear some slanderer (mesdisant) *who is putting down a particular woman, rebuke him and tell him to keep quiet. So far as you can, behave in a manner which is pleasing to ladies and girls, so that they hear and speak nothing but good about you. That is the way your reputation will increase.*[42]

The medieval woman was not by any means unable to act within her world. It is true that women were dependent on fathers, husbands and sons, but the social constraints we see in the twelfth and thirteenth century were not harsh. It is also true that we know of examples of bad relationships between men and women. There was wife-beating, like the assaults of Count Robert of Mortain on his wife which St Vitalis of Savigny discov-

39 *The Exempla of Jacques de Vitry*, ed. and trans. T.F. Crane (New York, 1890), 63.

40 Jakemes, *Le Roman du Castelain de Couci et de la Dame de Fayel*, ed. M. Delbouille (Société des anciens textes français, 1936). James de Vitry by contrast praises a noblewoman who had the maid beaten and ducked in stream who conveyed advances from a would-be lover, *Exempla of Jacques de Vitry*, 106.

41 Joinville, *Vie de Saint Louis*, ed. J. Monfrin (Paris, 1995), 206.

42 *Le Roman de la Rose*, ed. D. Poirion and J. Dufournet (Manchecourt, 1999), ll. 2115–24. The same advice is to be found in Raoul de Houdenc, *Le Roman des Eles*, ed. and trans. K. Busby (Utrecht Publications in General and Comparative Literature, 17, Amsterdam, 1983), ll. 325–36.

ered and stopped.[43] But there is no reason to think that such behaviour was either sanctioned or permitted by contemporaries. Women, even noblewomen, had little public role, other than at the very tip of the social world among princesses and queens. But there were ways female social influence could be exerted, through social means, through intercession and approval. Male and female lives were not separate in the medieval world, far from it. Noblewomen were not socially enclosed. They travelled extensively with their husbands and on their own. Up until the first decades of the twelfth century, this was a society where it was common for male aristocrats unapologetically to maintain households for sexual partners in addition to their wives. To find such partners, there had to be a degree of free association. When they were widows, they had to ask no one's congé to organise their lives. It is only by identifying female status with control of land and rights that one can sustain a vision of women as powerless; but they were never that.

To that extent, the modern study of the woman's place in medieval aristocratic society is one of the most revealing avenues into the interior of that society. It indicates its complexity and subtlety, for it is only in a complex and subtle society full of shades of meaning and ambiguities that the legally powerless could acquire and exercise such influence as they did. It discredits any model of that society which relies exclusively on landholding. It also provides further reason to abandon ideas of a 'mutation' in French society, whether in 900, 1000 or 1180. There was no adoption of ideas of male-dominated lineage in the eleventh or twelfth centuries. Female lineage remained important throughout this period, and the situation of women neither improved or worsened. If women were capable of making their mark on medieval society by wit and native resource, then men too could exploit the complexities and ambiguities of their habitus. When we recognise that complexity, then we will finally understand medieval society.

[43] *Vita beati Vitalis*, ed. E.P. Sauvage in, *Analecta Bollandiana*, i (1882), 363.

Select Bibliography

This bibliography contains works cited more than once in the text, or works of particular significance to the argument. Manuscript sources are cited in full within the chapter notes.

A History of the Family, trans. S.H. Tenison and others (2 vols, Cambridge, 1996), originally published as, *Histoire de la famille*, ed. A. Burguière and others (Paris, 1986).

A Medieval Prince of Wales: the Life of Gruffudd ap Cynan, ed. and trans. D. Simon Evans (Llanerch, 1990).

Actes de Mathieu II duc de Lorraine (1220–1251), ed. M. le Mercier de Morière (Recueil des documents sur l'histoire de Lorraine, 17, 1893).

Actes de Philippe Ier dit le Noble, comte et marquis de Namur (1196–1212), ed. M. Walraet (Académie Royale de Belgique, 1949).

Adam-Even, P. 'Les sceaux d'écuyers au xiiie siècle', *Archives héraldiques suisses*, lxvi (1951), 19–23.

Adams, J.D. 'Modern Views of Medieval Chivalry, 1884–1984', in, *The Study of Chivalry: Resources and Approaches* (Kalamazoo MI, 1988), 46–9.

Age of Chivalry: Art in Plantagenet England, 1200–1400, ed. J. Alexander and P. Binski (London, 1987).

Agricoltura e mondo rurale in occidente nell'alto medioevo (Settimane di Studio del centro Italiano di studi sull'alto medioevo, xiii, Spoleto, 1966).

Ailes, A. 'Heraldry in Medieval England: Symbols of Politics and Propaganda', in, *Social Display and Status in the Middle Ages*, ed. P.R. Coss and M. Keen (Woodbridge, 2002), 83–104.

Ailes, A. 'The Knight, Heraldry and Armour: the Role of Recognition and the Origins of Heraldry' in, *Medieval Knighthood*, iv, ed. C. Harper-Bill and R. Harvey (Woodbridge, 1992), 1–21.

Ailred of Rievaulx, *Genealogia regum Anglorum*, in, *PL* 195.

Alan of Lille, *Anticlaudianus*, in, *Satirical Poets of the Twelfth Century*, ed. T. Wright (2 vols, Rolls Series, 1872, translated in, *Anticlaudianus*, trans. J.J. Sheridan (Pontifical Institute of Medieval Studies, Toronto, 1973).

Alexander Neckam, *De Naturis Rerum Libri Duo*, ed. T. Wright (Rolls Series, 1863).

Ami et Amile, ed. P.F. Dembowski (Classiques français du moyen âge, 1987).

Andrew the Chaplain, *On Love*, ed. and trans. P.G. Walsh (London, 1982).

Anger's Past: The Social Uses of an Emotion in the Middle Ages, ed. B.H. Rosenwein (Ithaca NY, 1998).

Anglo-Norman Political Culture and the Twelfth-Century Renaissance, ed. C.W. Hollister (Woodbridge, 1997).

Annales de Theokesburia, in, *Annales Monastici*, ed. H.R. Luard (5 vols., Rolls Series, 1864-9) i.

Antiquus cartularius ecclesiae Baiocensis, ed. V. Bourienne (2 vols., Société des historiens de Normandie, 1902–3).

Appadurai, A. 'Commodities and the Politics of Value', in, *The Social Life of Things: Commodities in Cultural Perspective* (Cambridge, 1986), 3–63.

Aurell, M. 'La chevalerie urbaine en Occitanie, fin xe siècle – debut xiiie siècle', in, *Les sociétés urbaines en France méridionale et en péninsule Iberique au moyen âge* (Collection de la maison des pays Ibériques, 43, Paris, 1991), 71–110.

Aurell, M. *La noblesse en Occident, v^e^–xve siècle* (Paris, 1996).

Aurell, M. 'La parenté en l'an mil', *Cahiers de civilisation médiévale: x^e^–xiie siècle*, 43 (2000), 128–39.

Aurell, M. *Les noces du comte: mariage et pouvoir en Catalogne (785–1213)* (Paris, 1994).

Ayton, A. 'Sir Thomas Ughtred and the Edwardian Military Revolution', in, *The Age of Edward III*, ed. J.S. Bothwell (Woodbridge, 2001), 107–32.

Barthélemy, D. 'Debate: the "Feudal Revolution"??, *Past and Present*, no 152 (1996), 199.

Barthélemy, D. 'Kinship', in, *A History of Private Life* ii, *Revelations of the Medieval World,* ed. P. Ariès and G. Duby and trans. A. Goldhammer (London, 1988).

Barthélemy, D. *La mutation de l'an mil a-t-elle eu lieu? Servage et chevalerie dans la France des x*[e] *et xi*[e] *siècles* (Paris, 1997).

Barthélemy, D. *La société dans la comté de Vendôme de l'an mil au xiv*[e] *siècle* (Paris, 1993).

Barthélemy, D. *L'an mil et la paix de Dieu: La France chrétienne et féodale, 980–1060* (Paris, 1999).

Barthélemy, D. *Les deux âges de la seigneurie banale: Coucy xi*[e]*-xiii*[e] *siècle* (2nd edn., Paris, 2000).

Bartlett, R. *England under the Norman and Angevin Kings, 1075–1225* (Oxford, 2000).

Bartlett, R. *The Making of Europe: Conquest, Colonization and Cultural Change, 950–1350* (London, 1994).

Bassett, S. 'In search of the origins of Anglo-Saxon kingdoms', in, *The Origins of Anglo-Saxon Kingdoms* (Leicester, 1989), 3–27.

Bates, D. 'England and the Feudal Revolution', in, *Il feudalesimo nell'alto medioevo* (2 vols, Settimane di Studio de centro Italiano di studi sull'alto medioevo, xlvii, 2000) ii.

Bates, D. *Normandy before 1066* (London, 1982).

Bates, D. 'West Francia: the Northern Principalities', in, *The New Cambridge Medieval History* iii, *c.900–c.1024*, ed. T. Reuter (Cambridge, 1999), 398–419.

Baudrey de Bourgueil, *Historia Hierosolymitina*, in, *PL*, 154.

Bean, J.M.W. *From Lord to Patron: Lordship in Late Medieval England* (Manchester, 1989), 1-9.

Bean, J.M.W. *The Decline of English Feudalism* (Manchester, 1968).

Benedeit, *The Anglo-Norman Voyage of St Brendan*, ed. I. Short and B. Merrilees (Manchester, 1979).

Berg, M. *A Woman in History: Eileen Power, 1889–1940* (Cambridge, 1996).

Bernard of Clairvaux, *De laude novae militiae*, in *PL* 182.

Bernard of Cluny, *De contemptu mundi*, ed. and trans. R.E. Pepin (East Lansing MI, 1991).

Biller, P. 'Confession in the Middle Ages', in, *Handling Sin: Confession in the Middle Ages*, ed. P. Biller and A.J. Minnis (York Studies in Medieval Theology, 2, 1998).

Birdwell-Pheasant, D. 'Family Systems and the Foundations of Class in Ireland and England', *The History of the Family*, 3 (1998), 17–34.

Bisson, T.N. 'Lordship and Tenurial Dependence in Flanders, Provence and Occitania (1050–1200)' in, *Il feudalesimo nell'alto medioevo* (2 vols, Settimane di Studio de centro Italiano di studi sull'alto medioevo, xlvii, 2000) i, 389–439.

Bisson, T.N. 'Nobility and Family in Medieval France', *French Historical Studies*, 16 (1990), 597–613.

Bisson, T.N. 'The "Feudal Revolution" ', *Past and Present*, no. 142 (1994), 6–42.

Blair, J. 'Anglo-Saxon minsters: a topographical review' in, *Pastoral Care before the Parish*, ed. J. Blair and R. Sharpe (Leicester, 1992), 226–66.

Blair, J. *Early Medieval Surrey: Landholding, Church and Settlement before 1300* (Stroud, 1991).

Blair, J. 'Introduction' in, *Minsters and Parish Churches: The Local Church in Transition, 950–1200* (Oxford University Committee for Archaeology, 1988), 1–19.

Bloch, M. *Feudal Society*, trans. L.A. Manyon (2nd edn., London, 1962).

Bloch, M. *Les caractères originaux de l'histoire rurale française* (Oslo, 1931).

Bloch, M. 'Pour une histoire comparée des sociétés européennes', *Revue de synthèse historique*, 46 (1925), translated as, 'A Contribution to the Comparative History of European Societies', in, *Land and Work in Medieval Europe: Selected Papers by Marc Bloch*, trans. J.E. Anderson (London, 1967), 64–7.

Bonnassie, P. *La Catalogne du milieu du xe à la fin du xie siècle* (2 vols., Toulouse, 1975–6).

Bouchard, C.B. 'Family Structure and Family Consciousness among the Aristocracy in the Ninth to Eleventh Centuries', *Francia*, 14 (1986), 639–58.

Bouchard, C.B. *Strong of Body, Brave and Noble: Chivalry and Society in Medieval France* (Ithaca, 1998).

Bouchard, C.B. 'The Origins of the French Nobility: A Reassessment', *American Historical Review*, 86 (1981), 501–32.

Bouchard, C.B. *Those of My Blood: Constructing noble families in Medieval Francia* (Philadelphia, 2001).

Bourdieu, P. *Distinction: A Social Critique of the Judgement of Taste*, trans. R. Nice (London, 1984)

Bourdieu, P. *L'amour de l'art* (Paris, 1966).

Bourdieu, P. *Outline of a Theory of Practice*, trans. R. Nice (Cambridge, 1977).

Boussard, J. 'L'origine des familles seigneuriales dans la région de la Loire moyenne', *Cahiers de civilisation médiévale*, 5 (1962), 303–22.

Boutruche, R. *Seigneurie et Féodalité* (2 vols., Paris, 1959–70).

Brown, E.A.R. 'The Tyranny of a Construct: Feudalism and Historians of Medieval Europe', *American Historical Review*, 79 (1974).

Brown, E.A.R. 'Georges Duby and the Three Orders', *Viator* 27, (1986), 54–61.

Bur, M. *La formation du comté de Champagne, v. 950–v. 1150* (Mémoires des annales de l'Est, no. 54, Nancy, 1977).

Bur, M. 'Le féodalisme dans le royaume franc jusqu'à l'an mil: la seigneurie', in, *Il feudalesimo nell'alto medioevo* (2 vols, Settimane di Studio de centro Italiano di studi sull'alto medioevo, xlvii, 2000) i, 53–78.

Bur, M. 'L'image de la parenté chez les comtes de Champagne', *Annales*, 38 (1983), 1016–39.

Bur, M. 'Vers l'an mil, la motte, une arme pour une révolution', *L'information historique*, 44 (1982), 101–8.

Burgess, G.S. 'The Term "Chevalerie" in Twelfth-century French', in, *Medieval Codicology, Iconography, Literature, and Translation: Studies for Keith Val Sinclair*, ed. P.R. Monks and D.D.R. Owen (Leiden, 1994), 343–58.

Burke, P. *History and Social Theory* (Cambridge, 1992).

Bush, M. *The English Aristocracy: A Synthesis* (Manchester, 1984).

Bush, M.L. *Noble Privilege* (Manchester, 1983).

Cam, H. 'The Quality of English Feudalism' in, *Law-Finders and Law-Makers in Medieval England: Collected Studies in Legal and Constitutional History* (London, 1962), 44–58.

Carmen elegiacum de Waleranno comite Mellenti, in, *Chronicles of the Reigns of Stephen, Henry II and Richard*, ed. R. Howlett (4 vols., Rolls Series, 1886–89).

Carpenter, D.A. 'The Second Century of English Feudalism', *Past and Present*, no. 168 (2000), 30–71.

Carron, R. *Enfant et parenté dans la France médiévale, x[e] – xiiie siècles* (Geneva, 1989).

Cartae Antique Rolls, 11–20, ed. J. Conway Davies (Pipe Roll Society, 1960).

Cartulaire d'Afflighem, ed. E. de Marneffe, in, *Analectes pour servir à l'histoire écclésiastique de la Belgique*, iie section, *Série des cartulaires et des documents étendus* i, pt 1 (Louvain, 1894).

Cartulaire de l'abbaye de Notre-Dame de Ourscamp, ed. M. Peigné-Delacourt (Amiens, 1865).

Cartulaire de l'abbaye de St-Aubin d'Angers, ed. le comte Bertrand de Brousillon (4 vols., Paris, 1903).

Cartulaire du chapitre de Saint-Laud d'Angers, ed. A. Planchenault (Angers, 1903).

Chansons des Trouvères, ed. S.N. Rosenberg, H. Tischler and M-G. Grossel (Paris, 1995).

Chartes de l'abbaye de Jumièges, ed. J-J. Vernier (2 vols., Rouen, 1916).

Chartes et documents du prieuré de Saint-Martin de Boran, ed. J. Depoin and J. Vergnet, in, *Mémoires de la société academique du département de l'Oise*, xxiv (1924).

Cheney, C.R. 'A monastic letter of fraternity to Eleanor of Aquitaine', *English Historical Review*, li (1936).

Cherry, J. 'Heraldry as Decoration in the Thirteenth Century' in, *England in the Thirteenth Century*, ed. W.M. Ormrod (Stamford, 1991), 123–34.

Chibnall, M. *The World of Orderic Vitalis* (Oxford, 1984).

Chivalry: A Series of Studies to Illustrate its Historical Significance and Civilizing Influence, ed. E. Prestage (London, 1928).

Chrétien de Troyes, *Cligés*, ed. A. Micha (Classiques français du moyen âge, 1957).

Chrétien de Troyes, *Le Chevalier au Lion (Yvain)*, ed. M. Roques (Classiques français du moyen âge, 1982).

Chrétien de Troyes, *Le Conte de Graal*, ed. F. Lecoy (2 vols., Classiques français du moyen âge, 1972–5).

Chronicle of Jocelin of Brakelond, ed. H.E. Butler (London, 1949).

Chroniques des comtes d'Anjou et des seigneurs d'Amboise, ed. L. Halphen and R. Poupardin (Paris, 1913).

Chroniques des comtes d'Eu in, *Recueil des historiens des Gaules et de la France*, ed. M. Bouquet and others (24 vols., Paris, 1869–1904) xxiii, 440–3.

Clanchy, M.T. *Abelard: A Medieval Life* (Oxford, 1997).

Clanchy, M.T. *From Memory to Written Record* (2nd edn., Oxford, 1993).

Clarke, P.A. *The English Nobility under Edward the Confessor* (Oxford, 1994).

Coad, J.G. 'Recent Work at Castle Acre Castle' in, *Château Gaillard: Études de Castellologie médiévale* xi (Caen, 1983).

Cohen, G. *Histoire de la chevalerie en France au moyen âge* (Paris, 1949).

Colker, M.L. 'The Life of Guy of Merton by Rainald of Merton', *Medieval Studies*, 31 (1969).

Colker, M.L. 'Latin Texts concerning Gilbert, founder of Merton Priory', *Studia Monastica*, 12 (1970), 241–72.

Colker, M.L. 'The "Margam Chronicle" in a Dublin Manuscript', *Haskins Society Journal*, 4 (1992), 123–48.

Constable, G. 'The Orders of Society', in, *Three Studies in Medieval Religious and Social Thought* (Cambridge, 1995).

Coss, P.R. 'Debate: Bastard Feudalism Revised', *Past and Present*, no. 131 (1991).

Coss, P.R. 'From Feudalism to Bastard Feudalism', in, *Die Gegenwart des Feudalismus*, ed. N. Fryde, P. Monnet and O.G. Oexle (Veröffentlichungen des Max-Planck-Instituts für Geschichte, 173, 2002), 91–9.

Coss, P.R. 'Knighthood, Heraldry and Social Exclusion', in, *Heraldry, Pageantry and Social Display in Medieval England*, ed. M. Keen and P.R. Coss (Woodbridge, 2002), 39–68.

Coss, P.R. *Lordship, Knighthood and Locality: A Study in English Society, c.1180-c.1280* (Cambridge, 1991).

Coss, P.R. 'The Formation of the English Gentry', *Past and Present*, no. 147 (1995).

Coss, P.R. *The Knight in Medieval England, 1000–1400* (Stroud, 1993).

Coss, P.R. *The Lady in Medieval England, 1000–1500* (Stroud, 1998).

Coss, P.R. *The Origins of the English Gentry* (Cambridge, 2003).

Coulbourn, R. 'The Idea of Feudalism' in, *Feudalism in History* (Princeton, 1956), 3–11.

Coulson, C. *Castles in Medieval Society: Fortresses in England, France and Ireland in the Central Middle Ages* (Oxford, 2003).

Coulson, C. 'Peaceable Power in English Castles' in, *Anglo-Norman Studies*, xxiii, ed. J. Gillingham (Woodbridge, 2000), 69–95.

Coutumiers de Normandie, ed. E-J. Tardif, i (Rouen, 1881).

Crouch D. and de Trafford, C. 'The Forgotten Family in Twelfth-Century England', *Haskins Society Journal*, 13 (2004), 41–52.

Crouch, D. 'Debate: Bastard Feudalism Revised', *Past and Present*, no. 131 (1991).

Crouch, D. 'A Norman "conventio" and bonds of lordship in the middle ages', in, *Law and Government in the Middle Ages: Essays in Honour of Sir James Holt*, ed. G. Garnett and J.G. Hudson (Cambridge, 1994), 299–324.

Crouch, D. 'Earls and Bishops in Twelfth-century Leicestershire', *Nottingham Medieval Studies*, xxxvii (1993), 9–20.

Crouch, D. 'Loyalty, Career and Self-Justification at the Plantagenet Court: the Thought World of William Marshal and his Colleagues' in, *Culture Politique des Plantagenet (1154–1224): Actes du Colloque tenu à Poitiers du 2 au 5 mai 2002*, ed. M. Aurell (Poitiers, 2003), 229–40.

Crouch, D. *The Beaumont Twins: the Roots and Branches of Power in the Twelfth Century* (Cambridge, 1986).

Crouch, D. 'The Historian, Lineage and Heraldry', in, *Heraldry, Pageantry and Social Display in Medieval England*, ed. M. Keen and P.R. Coss (Woodbridge, 2002), 17–37.

Crouch, D. *The Image of Aristocracy in Britain, 1000–1300* (London, 1992).

Crouch, D. 'The Local Influence of the Earls of Warwick, 1088–1241: A Study of Decline and Resourcefulness', *Midland History* xxi (1996), 179–200.

Crouch, D. *The Reign of King Stephen, 1135–1154* (London, 2000).

Crouch, D. *The Tournament* (London, 2005).

Crouch, D. 'The Troubled Deathbeds of Henry I's Servants: Death, Confession and Secular Conduct in the Twelfth Century', *Albion*, 34 (2002), 24–36.

Crouch, D. *William Marshal: Knighthood, War and Chivalry, 1147–1219* (2nd edn., London, 2002).

Crouch, D. 'From Stenton to McFarlane: Models of Societies of the Twelfth and Thirteenth Centuries', *Transactions of the Royal Historical Society*, 6th ser., 5 (1995).

Cultures of Power: Lordship, Status and Process in Twelfth-Century Europe, ed. T.N. Bisson (Philadelphia, 1995).

Curia Regis Rolls.

Dalton, P. *Conquest, Anarchy and Lordship: Yorkshire 1066–1154* (Cambridge, 1994).

Davies, D.J. *Death, Ritual and Belief* (London, 1997).

Davies, R.R. *The Age of Conquest: Wales, 1063–1415* (Oxford, 1991).

Davies, W. *Wales in the Early Middle Ages* (Leicester, 1982).

Davis, R.H.C. 'What happened in Stephen's Reign, 1135–54', *History*, xlix(1964), 1–12.

De diversis ordinibus hominum, in, *The Latin Poems commonly attributed to Walter Mapes*, ed. T. Wright (Camden Society, old ser., 1841).

De duodecim abusionibus saeculi, in, *PL* 4.

De fundatione monasterii sancte Fidis Sletstatensis, ed. O. Holder-Egger, in *MGH, Scriptores*, xv, pt 2 (Hanover, 1888).

De similitudine temporalis et spiritualis militis, in, *Memorials of St Anselm*, ed. R.W. Southern and F.S. Schmitt (London, 1969).

Debord, A. *Aristocratie et pouvoir: le rôle du château dans la France médiévale* (Paris, 2000).

Derville, A. 'Les élites urbaines en Flandre et en Artois' in, *Les élites urbaines au moyen âge*, ed. C. Gauvard (Paris, 1997), 121.

Devailly, J. *Le Berry du x*[e] *siècle au milieu du xiii*[e] *siècle: étude politique, religieuse, sociale et économique* (Paris, 1973).

Die exempla aus den Sermones feriales et communes des Jakob von Vitry, ed. J. Greven (Heidelberg, 1914).

Die Gegenwart des Feudalismus, ed. N. Fryde, P. Monnet and O.G. Oexle (Veröffentlichungen des Max-Planck-Instituts für Geschichte, 173, 2002).

Dits et contes de Baudouin de Condé et de son fils Jean de Condé, ed. A. Scheler (3 vols., Brussels, 1866–7).

Domesday Book seu Liber Censualis Willelmi primi regis Angliae, ed. A. Farley and others (4 vols., London, 1783–1816).

Duby, G. 'La féodalité? Une mentalité médiévale', *Annales ESC*, 13 (1958), 765–71.

Duby, G. 'Au xiie siècle: les "jeunes" dans la société aristocratique dans la France du nord-ouest', in, *La société chevaleresque* (repr. Paris, 1988), 129–42, repr. in English, *The Chivalrous Society*, trans. C. Postan (London, 1977), 112–22.

Duby, G. 'La notion de chevalerie dans les chansons de geste de xiie siècle: étude historique de vocabulaire', *Le Moyen Âge*, 81 (1975), 211–44, 407–44.

Duby, G. *La société au xi*[e] *et xii*[e] *siècles dans la région mâconnaise* (repr. Paris, 1982).

Duby, G. 'La vulgarisation des modèles culturels dans la société féodale' in, *La société chevaleresque* (repr. Paris, 1988), 194–205, translated by R. Hilton as, 'The Diffusion of Cultural Patterns in Feudal Society', *Past and Present*, no. 39 (1968).

Duby, G. *Le Chevalier, la Femme et le Prêtre* (Paris, 1981), published in English as, *The Knight, the Lady and the Priest: the Making of Modern Marriage in Medieval France*, trans. B. Bray (London, 1983).

Duby, G. 'Le Roman de la Rose', repr. in, *Mâle moyen âge: de l'amour et autres essais* (Paris, 1990), 83–117.

Duby, G. *Le temps des cathédrales: l'art et la société, 980–1420* (repr. Paris, 1976).

Duby, G. *Les trois ordres ou l'imaginaire du féodalisme* (Paris, 1978), repr. in English as *The Three Orders: Feudal Society Imagined*, trans. A. Goldhammer (Chicago, 1980).

Duby, G. 'Lignage, noblesse et chevalerie au xiie siècle dans la région mâconnaise: une révision', repr. in *La société chevaleresque* (Paris, 1988), 83–116, repr. in English, *The Chivalrous Society*, trans. C. Postan (London, 1977), 59–87.

Duby, G. *Mâle moyen âge: de l'amour et autres essais* (Paris, 1990).

Duby, G. 'Pour une histoire des femmes en France et en Espagne' in, *Mâle moyen âge: de l'amour et autres essais* (Paris, 1990), 118–26.

Duby, G. 'Recherches sur l'évolution des institutions judiciaires pendant le xe et le xie siècle dans la sud de la Bourgogne', *Le Moyen Age*, 52 (1946), 149–94; 53 (1947), 15–38.

Duby, G. 'Remarques sur la littérature généalogique en France aux xie et xiie siècle', repr. in *La société chevaleresque* (Paris, 1988), 167–80, published in English as, 'French genealogical literature: the eleventh and twelfth centuries', in *The Chivalrous Society*, trans. C. Postan (London, 1977), 149–57, esp. 150, 153–4.

Duby, G. *The Chivalrous Society*, trans. C. Postan (London, 1977).

Duby, G. 'The transformation of the aristocracy: France at the beginning of the thirteenth century', in, *The Chivalrous Society*, 178–85, first published as 'Situation de la noblesse en France au début du xiiie siècle', *Tijdschrift voor Geschiedenis*, 82 (1969), 509–15.

Duby, G. 'Une enquête à poursuivre: la noblesse dans la France médiévale', *Revue historique*, 226 (1961), 1.

Duby, G. 'Women and Power' in, *Cultures of Power: Lordship, Status and Process in Twelfth-Century Europe*, ed. T.N. Bisson (Philadelphia, 1995), 69–85.

Duby, G. *Guillaume le Maréchal ou le meilleur chevalier du monde* (Paris, 1984).

Durkheim, E. 'La famille conjugale', *Revue Philosophique*, 91 (1901), 1–14.

Dyer, C. *Standards of Living in the Later Middle Ages: Social Change in England, c.1200–1520* (Cambridge, 1989).

Elias, N. *Über den Prozess der Zivilisation* (2 vols., Basel, 1939), published in English as *The Civilizing Process*, trans. E. Jephcott (Oxford, 1994).

Ellis, W.S. *The Antiquities of Heraldry* (London, 1869).

Engels, F. *The Origin of the Family, Private Property and the State* (London, 1884).

English Historical Documents i, *c.500–1042*, ed. D. Whitelock (London, 1955).

'*Epistolae Fiscannenses*: lettres d'amitié, de gouvernement et d'affaires', ed. J. Laporte, in, *Revue Mabillon*, 43 (1953), 29–31.

Ernald of Bonneval, *Sancti Bernardi Vita Prima auctore Ernaldo*, in *PL*, 185.1.

Eudes de St-Maur, *Vie de Bouchard le Vénérable*, ed. C. Bourel de la Roncière (Paris, 1892).

Feaver, G. *From Status to Contract: A Biography of Sir Henry Maine, 1822–1888* (Longman, 1969).

Feudalism in History, ed. R. Coulbourn (Princeton, 1956).

Fink, C. *Marc Bloch: A Life in History* (Cambridge, 1989).

Flach, J. *Les origines de l'ancienne France* (4 vols., Paris, 1886–1917).

Fleming, D.F. 'Landholding by Milites in Domesday Book' in, *Anglo-Norman Studies*, xiii, ed. M. Chibnall (Woodbridge, 1990), 83–98.

Fleming, R. 'Rural Elites and Urban Communities in Late Saxon England', *Past and Present*, no. 141 (1993).

Fleming, R. 'The new wealth, the new rich, and the new political style in late Anglo-Saxon England', *Anglo-Norman Studies*, xxiii, ed. J. Gillingham (Woodbridge, 2000), 1–22.

Flori, J. *La Chevalerie* (Paris, 1998).

Flori, J. *La Chevalerie en France au Moyen Âge* (Paris, 1995).

Flori, J. *L'Essor de la Chevalerie, xi*[e]*-xii*[e] *siècles* (Geneva, 1986).

Flori, J. *L'idéologie du glaive: préhistoire de la chevalerie* (Geneva, 1983).

Flori, J. *Richard Coeur de Lion: Le roi-chevalier* (Paris, 1999).

Fossier, R. *Histoire sociale de l'occident médiéval* (Paris, 1970).

Fossier, R. *La terre et les hommes en Picardie jusqu'à la fin du xiii*[e] *siècle* (2 vols., Paris, 1968.

Fossier, R. 'Land, Castle, Money and Family in the Formation of the Seigneuries', in, *Medieval Settlement: Continuity and Change*, ed. P.H. Sawyer (London, 1976), 159–68.

Fossier, R. 'The Feudal Era (Eleventh-Thirteenth Century)', in, *A History of the Family*, trans. S.H. Tenison and others (2 vols., Cambridge, 1996), 407, originally published as, *Histoire de la famille*, ed. A. Burguière and others (Paris, 1986).

Freed, J.B. 'Reflections on the Medieval German Nobility', *American Historical Review*, xci (1986), 553–75.

Freed, J.B. *The Counts of Falkenstein: Noble Self-Consciousness in Twelfth-Century Germany* (Transactions of the American Philosophical Society, 74, pt 6, 1984).

Freeman, E.A. *The History of the Norman Conquest of England* (6 vols., Oxford, 1870–79).

Fustel de Coulanges, N.D. *Les origines du système féodal*, ed. C. Jullian (Paris, 1890).

Fustel de Coulanges, N.D. *Histoire des institutions politiques de l'ancienne France* (rev'd edn, 5 vols., 1891–2).

Galbert of Bruges, *The Murder of Charles the Good*, trans. J.B. Ross (repr. Toronto, 1982).

Ganshof, F.L. *Qu'est-ce que la féodalité* (Brussels, 1947), published in English as, *Feudalism*, trans. P. Grierson (3rd edn., London, 1964).

Garin le Loherenc, ed. A. Iker-Gittleman (3 vols, Classiques français du moyen âge, 117–19, 1996–7).

Gautier, L. *La chevalerie* (Paris, 1884), published in English as *Chivalry*, trans. D.C. Dunning (London, 1965).

Gaydon, ed. M.F. Guessard and S. Luce (Anciens Poètes de la France, Paris, 1862).

Genealogiae comitum Flandriae, ed. L.C. Bethmann, in *Monumenta Historicae Germanniae: Scriptores* ix.

Geoffrey Gaimar, *L'Estoire des Engleis*, ed. A. Bell (Anglo-Norman Text Society, 1960).

Geoffrey of Burton, *The Life and Miracles of St Modwenna*, ed. R. Bartlett (Oxford, 2002).

Geoffrey of Monmouth, *Historia Regum Britanniae* i, *Bern Burgerbibliothek, MS 568*, ed. N. Wright (Cambridge, 1984).

Gerald of Wales, *Expugnatio Hibernica*, ed. A.B. Scott and F.X. Martin (Dublin, 1978).

Gervase of Tilbury, *Otia imperialia: Recreation for an Emperor*, ed. and trans. S.E. Banks and J.W. Binns (Oxford, 2002).

Gesta Stephani, ed. and trans. K.R. Potter and R.H.C. Davis (Oxford, 1976).

Gillingham, J. '1066 and the Introduction of Chivalry into England', in, *Law and Government in Medieval England and Normandy: Essays in Honour of James Holt*, ed. G. Garnett and J.G. Hudson (Cambridge, 1994).

Gillingham, J. 'Conquering the Barbarians: War and Chivalry in Twelfth-century Britain', *Haskins Society Journal*, 4 (1992), 67–84.

Gillingham, J. 'Kingship, Chivalry and Love. Political and Cultural Values in the Earliest History written in French: Geoffrey Gaimar's Estoire des Engleis', in, *Anglo-Norman Political Culture and the Twelfth-Century Renaissance*, ed. C.W. Hollister (Woodbridge, 1997), 33–58.

Gillingham, J. 'Thegns and Knights in Eleventh-Century England', *Transactions of the Royal Historical Society*, 6th ser., 5 (1995), 129–53.

Girouard, M. *The Return to Camelot: Chivalry and the English Gentleman* (New Haven, 1981).

Goody, J. *The Development of the Family and Marriage in Europe* (Cambridge, 1983).

Grant, G.G. 'The *Familia* of Roger de Quincy, earl of Winchester and constable of Scotland' in, *Essays on the Nobility of Medieval Scotland*, ed. K.J. Stringer (Edinburgh, 1985), 102–28.

Green, J.A. *The Aristocracy of Norman England* (Cambridge, 1997).

Green, J.A. 'Aristocratic Women in Early-Twelfth Century England' in, *Anglo-Norman Political Culture and the Twelfth-Century Renaissance*, ed. C.W. Hollister (Woodbridge, 1997), 59–82.

Guerreau, A. *Le Féodalisme: un horizon théorique* (Paris, 1980).

Gui de Warewic: roman du xiiie siècle, ed. A. Ewert (2 vols., Classiques français du moyen âge, 1932).

Guibert de Nogent, *De vita sua*, ed. E.R. Labande (Paris, 1981), translated as, *Self and Society in Medieval France*, trans. J.F. Benton (Toronto, 1985).

Guilhiermoz, P. *Essai sur les origines de la noblesse* (Paris, 1902).

Guiliato, G. 'Le château reflet de l'art défensif en Lorraine de xème au début du xiiième siècle', *Annales de l'Est*, 6th ser., 1 (2003).

Guizot, F. *The History of Civilization in Europe*, trans. W. Hazlitt (repr. Harmondsworth, 1997).

Hanawalt, B.A. 'Golden Ages for the History of Medieval English Woman', in, *Women in Medieval History and Historiography*, ed. S. Mosher Stuard (Philadelphia, 1987).

Handling Sin: Confession in the Middle Ages, ed. P. Biller and A.J. Minnis (York Studies in Medieval Theology, 2, 1998).

Hareven, T.K. 'The History of the Family and the Complexity of Social Change', *American Historical Review*, 96 (1991), 95–124, repr. and revised as 'Recent Research on the History of Family', in, *Time, Family and Community: Perspectives on Family and Community History*, ed. M. Drake (Oxford, 1994), 13–43.

Harvey, S. 'The Knight and Knight's Fee in England', *Past and Present*, xlix (1970).

Haskins, C.H. *Norman Institutions* (New York, 1918).

Haskins, C.H. *The Normans in European History* (New York, 1915).

Hearnshaw, F.J.C. 'Chivalry: its Place in History', in, *Chivalry: A Series of Studies to Illustrate its Historical Significance and Civilizing Influence*, ed. E. Prestage (London, 1928), 29–33.

Hemptinne, T. de 'Les épouses des croisés et pèlerins flamands aux xie et xiie siècles: l'exemple des comtesses de Flandre Clémence et Sibylle' in, *Autour de la Première Croisade: Actes du Colloque de la 'Society for the Study of the Crusades and the Latin East'*, ed. M. Balard (Paris, 1996), 83–95.

Hemptinne, T. de 'Women as Mediators between the Powers of *Comitatus* and *Sacerdotium*' in, *The Propagation of Power in the*

Medieval West, ed. M. Gosman, A. Vanderjagt and J. Veenstra (Mediaevalia Groningana, xxiii, 1997), 265–80.

Henderson, G. 'Romance and Politics on Some Medieval English Seals', *Art History*, i (1980).

Henry of Huntingdon, *Historia Anglorum*, ed. and trans. D. Greenway (Oxford, 1996).

Herbert of Bosham, *Vita S. Thomae,* in, *Materials for the History of Thomas Becket, archbishop of Canterbury*, ed. J.C. Robertson and J.B. Sheppard (7 vols., Rolls Series, 1875–85).

Herlihy, D. 'Did Women have a Renaissance? A Reconsideration', *Medievalia et Humanistica*, 13 (1985), 1–22.

Herlihy, D. 'Family Solidarity in Medieval Italian History', in, *The Social History of Italy and Western Europe* (London, 1978).

Herlihy, D. *Medieval Households* (London, 1985).

Herlihy, D. *The History of Feudalism* (London, 1971).

Hermann of Laon, *De miraculis sanctae Mariae Laudunensis*, in, *PL*, 156.

Heslop, T.A. 'The Seals of the Twelfth-Century Earls of Chester' in, *The Earldom of Chester and its Charters*, ed. A.T. Thacker (Journal of the Chester Archeological Society, 71, 1991), 179–97.

Hilton, R. *A Medieval Society: The West Midlands at the End of the Thirteenth Century* (Cambridge, 1966).

Hincmar, *De regis persona et ministerio*, in, *PL* 125.

Hintze, O. 'Wesen and Verbreitung des Feudalismus', *Sitzungsberichte der Preussischen Akademie der Wissenschaften, phil.-hist Klasse*, 20 (Berlin, 1929), 321–30, translated as 'The Nature of Feudalism', in, *Lordship and Community in Medieval Europe: Selected Readings*, ed. F.L. Cheyette (Huntington, NY 1975), 22–31.

Histoire des ducs de Normandie et des rois d'Angleterre, ed. F. Michel (Société de l'histoire de France, 1840).

Histoires d'outre-Manche: tendances récentes de l'historiographie britannique, ed. F. Lachaud, I. Lescent-Giles and F-J. Ruggiu (Paris, 2001).

History of William Marshal, ed. T. Holden, S. Gregory and D. Crouch (3 vols., Anglo-Norman Text Society, Occasional Publication Series, 4–6, 2002–6).

Hollister, C.W. 'Magnates and "Curiales" in Early Norman England', *Viator*, 4 (1973), 115–22.

Holt, J.C. 'Feudal Society and the Family in Early Medieval England: I. The Revolution of 1066', *Transactions of the Royal Historical Society*, 5th ser., 32 (1982).

Holt, J.C. 'Feudal Society and the Family in Early Medieval England: IV. The Heiress and the Alien', *Transactions of the Royal Historical Society*, 5th ser., 35 (1985), 1–28.

Holt, J.C. 'Politics and Property in Early Medieval England', *Past and Present*, no. 57 (1972) 3–52.

Holt, J.C. *The Northerners* (Oxford, 1961).

Holt, J.C. 'The Prehistory of Parliament', in, *The English Parliament in the Middle Ages*, ed. R.G. Davies and J.H. Denton (Manchester, 1981), 1–28.

Holt, J.C. *Magna Carta* (Cambridge, 1965).

Household and Family in Past Time, ed. P. Laslett and R. Wall (Cambridge, 1972).

Hudson, J.G. *Land, Law and Lordship in Anglo-Norman England* (Oxford, 1994).

Hudson, J.G. 'Henry I and Counsel', in, *The Medieval State: Essays presented to James Campbell*, ed. J.R. Maddicott and D.M. Palliser (London, 2000).

Hudson, J.G. *The Formation of the English Common Law* (London, 1996).

Huizinga, J. *The Waning of the Middle Ages*, trans. F. Hopman (repr. Harmondsworth, 1990).

Huneycutt, L.L. 'Female Succession and the Language of Power in the Writings of Twelfth-Century Churchmen', in, *Medieval Queenship*, ed. J. Carmi Parsons (Stroud, 1994), 189–201.

Huneycutt, L.L. *Matilda of Scotland: A Study in Medieval Queenship* (Woodbridge, 2003).

Hunt, J. *Lordship and the Landscape: A Documentary and Archaeological Study of the Honor of Dudley, c.1066–1322* (British Archaeological Reports, British Series, 264, 1997).

Hurd, R. *Letters on Chivalry and Romance* (London, 1762).

Hyams, P. 'What did Henry III of England think in bed and in French about Kingship and Anger', in, *Anger's Past: The Social Uses of an Emotion in the Middle Ages*, ed. B.H. Rosenwein (Ithaca NY, 1998), 92–124.

Il feudalesimo nell'alto medioevo (2 vols, Settimane di Studio de centro Italiano di studi sull'alto medioevo, xlvii, 2000).

Ille et Galeron, ed. Y. Lefèvre (Classiques français du moyen âge, 1988).

Ioannis Saresberiensis Policraticus, ed. C.C.I. Webb (2 vols, Oxford, 1909).

Jaeger, C.S. 'Courtliness and Social Change', in, *Cultures of Power: Lordship, Status and Process in Twelfth-Century Europe*, ed. T.N. Bisson (Philadelphia, 1995).

Jaeger, C.S. *The Origins of Courtliness: Civilizing Trends and the Formation of Courtly Ideals, 939–1210* (Philadelphia, 1985).

Jakemes, *Le Roman du Castelain de Couci et de la Dame de Fayel*, ed. M. Delbouille (Société des anciens textes français, 1936).

Jean de Joinville, *Vie de Saint Louis*, ed. J. Monfrin (Paris, 1995).

Johns, S.M. *Noblewomen, Aristocracy and Power in the Twelfth-Century Anglo-Norman Realm* (Manchester, 2003).

Jones, G.R.J. 'Settlement patterns in Anglo-Saxon England', *Antiquity*, 35 (1961), 221–32.

Jones, G.R.J. 'The multiple estate as a model favourable for tracing early stages in the evolution of rural settlement', in, *L'Habitat et les paysages ruraux d'Europe*, ed. F. Dussart (Liège, 1971), 251–67.

Jordan Fantosme's Chronicle, ed. R.C. Johnston (Oxford, 1981).

Kaeuper, R.W. *Chivalry and Violence in Medieval Europe* (Oxford, 1999).

Keefe, T.K. *Feudal Assessments and the Political Community under Henry II and his Sons* (Berkeley CA, 1983).

Keen, M. *Chivalry* (New Haven, 1984).

Kennedy, E. 'The Quest for Identity and the Importance of Lineage in Thirteenth-Century French Prose Romance', in, *The Ideals and Practice of Medieval Knighthood*, ii, ed. C. Harper-Bill and R. Harvey (Woodbridge, 1988), 70–86.

King Alfred's Old English Version of Boethius De Consolatione Philosophiae, ed. W.J. Sedgefield (Oxford, 1899).

King, E.J. 'Mountsorrel and its Region in King Stephen's Reign', *Huntington Library Quarterly*, xliv (1980), 1–10.

Kuper, A. *The Invention of Primitive Society: Transformations and Illusions* (London, 1988).

La Chanson d'Aspremont, ed. L. Brandin (2 vols., Classiques français du moyen âge, 1923-4).

La Chanson de Roland, ed. F. Whitehead (2nd edn., Oxford, 1946).

La Chevalerie Vivien, ed. A-L. Terracher (Paris, 1909).

La Chronique de Gislebert de Mons, ed. L. Vanderkindere (Brussels, 1904).

La Femme (3 vols, Recueils de la Société Jean Bodin, xi–xiii, Brussels, 1959–62).

La Vie de Saint Alexis, ed. M. Perugi (Geneva, 2000).

L'abbaye Toussaint d'Angers des origines à 1330. Étude historique et cartulaire, ed. F. Comte (Société des Études Angevines, 1985).

Lachaud, F. 'La "Formation de la *Gentry*", xie-xive siècle: un nouveau concept historiographique?', in, *Histoires d'outre-Manche: tendances récentes de l'historiographie britannique*, ed. F. Lachaud, I. Lescent-Giles and F-J. Ruggiu (Paris, 2001), 13–36.

Lair, J. *Étude sur la vie et la mort de Guillaume Longue-épée duc de Normandie* (Paris, 1893).

Lambert of Ardres, *The History of the Counts of Guines and Lords of Ardres*, trans. L. Shopkow (Philadelphia, 2001).

Lancelot do Lac, E. Kennedy (2 vols., Oxford, 1980).

Lancelot: roman en prose du xiiie siècle, ed. A. Micha (9 vols., Geneva, 1978–83).

Långfors, A. '*Le dit des hérauts* par Henri de Laon', *Romania*, xliii (1914).

Laslett, P. 'The History of the Family', in, *Household and Family in Past Time*, ed. P. Laslett and R. Wall (Cambridge, 1972), 16–21.

Le Conventum (vers 1030): un précurseur aquitain des premières épopées, ed. G. Beech, Y. Chauvin and G. Pon (Geneva, 1995).

Le Couronnement de Louis, ed. E. Langlois (Classiques français du moyen âge, 1984).

Le Goff, J. *La civilisation de l'Occident médiévale* (Paris, 1964), translated by J. Barrow as, *Medieval Civilisation, 400–1500* (Oxford, 1988).

Le Jan, R. 'Continuity and Change in the Tenth-Century Nobility', trans. J. Nelson, in, *Nobles and Nobility in Medieval Europe: Concepts, Origins, Transformations*, ed. A.J. Duggan (Woodbridge, 2000), 53–68.

Le Jan, R. *Famille et pouvoir dans le monde franc (viie–xe siècle): Essai d'anthropologie sociale* (Paris, 1995).

Le Play, F. *La réforme sociale en France deduite de l'observation comparée des peuples européens* (2 vols., Paris, 1864).

Le Roman de la Rose, ed. D. Poirion and J. Dufournet (Manchecourt, 1999).

Le Roman de Thèbes, ed. and trans. F. Mora-Lebrun (Paris, 1995).

Le Roy Ladurie, E. *Les paysans de Languedoc* (2 vols., Paris, 1966).

Leges Henrici Primi, ed. L.J. Downer (Oxford, 1972).

Lemarignier, J-F. 'Quelques remarques sur l'organisation écclésiastique de la Gaule du viie à la fin du ixe siècle principalement au nord de la Loire', in, *Agricoltura e mondo rurale in occidente nell'alto medioevo* (Settimane di Studio del centro Italiano di studi sull'alto medioevo, xiii, Spoleto, 1966).

Les élites urbaines au moyen âge, ed. C. Gauvard (Paris, 1997).

Les miracles de Saint Benoît, ed. E. de Certain (Paris, Société de l'histoire de la France, 1858).

Les sociétés urbaines en France méridionale et en péninsule Ibérique au moyen âge (Collection de la maison des pays Ibériques, 43, Paris, 1991).

Lewis, C.P. 'The Early Earls of Norman England', in, *Anglo-Norman Studies*, xiii ed. M. Chibnall (1990), 208–13.

Leyser, K. 'The German Aristocracy from the Ninth to the Early Twelfth Century: A Historical and Cultural Sketch', *Past and Present*, no. 41 (1968).

Li Torneiemenz Antecrit, ed. G. Wimmer and trans. S. Orgeur (2nd edn., Paris, 1995).

Liber Eliensis, ed. E.O. Blake (Camden Society, 3rd ser., xcii, 1962).

Liber Epistularum Guidonis de Basochis, ed. H. Adolfsson (Acta Universitatis Stockholmensis, Studia Latina Stockholmensia, 18, 1969).

Llewellyn, N. *The Art of Death* (London, 1991).

LoPrete, K. 'Adela of Blois and Ivo of Chartres: Piety, Politics and the Peace in the Diocese of Chartres', *Anglo-Norman Studies*, xiv (1992), 131–52.

LoPrete, K. 'Adela of Blois as Mother and Countess' in, *Medieval Mothering*, ed. J.C. Parsons and B. Wheeler (New York, 1996), 313–33.

LoPrete, K. 'Adela of Blois: Familial Alliances and Female Lordship' in, *Aristocratic Women in Medieval France*, ed. T. Evergates (Philadelphia, 1999), 7–43.

LoPrete, K. 'The Anglo-Norman Card of Adela of Blois', *Albion*, 22 (1990), 569–89.

Lordship and Community in Medieval Europe: Selected Readings, ed. F.L. Cheyette (Huntington NY, 1975).

Mabillon, J. *Annales ordinis sancti Benedicti occidentalium monachorum patriarchae*, v (Paris, 1738).

Maddicott, J.R. 'Magna Carta and the Local Community, 1215–1259', *Past and Present*, no. 102 (1984), 25–65.

Maine, H.J.S. *Ancient Law* (London, 1861).

Maine, H.J.S. *Village Communities in East and West* (3rd edn., London, 1876).

Maitland, F.W. *Collected Papers*, ed. H.A.L. Fisher (2 vols., Cambridge, 1911).

Maitland, F.W. *Domesday Book and Beyond,* (repr. London 1960).

Martin, H. *Mentalités Médiévales* ii, *Représentations collectives du xi*[e] *au xv*[e] *siecle* (Paris, 2001).

Matthew Paris, *Chronica Majora*, ed. H.R. Luard (7 vols., Rolls Series, 1872–84).

McFarlane, K.B. 'Bastard Feudalism', reprinted in, *England in the Fifteenth Century: Collected Essays*, ed. G.L. Harriss (London, 1981), 23–44.

McFarlane, K.B. *The Nobility of Later Medieval England* (Oxford, 1973).

McLaughlin, M. *Consorting with Saints: prayer for the dead in medieval France* (Ithaca NY, 1994).

McNamara. J-A. and Wemple, S. 'The Power of Women through the Family in Medieval Europe, 500–1100' in, *Women and Power in the Middle Ages*, ed. M. Erler and M. Kowaleski (Athens GA, 1988).

Michelet, J. *Histoire de France* (rev'd edn, 19 vols., Paris, 1879).

Miller, E. 'Rulers of Thirteenth Century Towns: the Cases of York and Newcastle upon Tyne', in, *Thirteenth-Century England*, i, ed. P.R. Coss and S.D. Lloyd (Woodbridge, 1986).

Mills, C. *The History of Chivalry or Knighthood and its Times* (London, 1825).

Montesquieu, *De L'Esprit des Lois*, ed. R. Derathé (2 vols., Paris, 1973).

Moore, R.I. 'The Peace of God and the Social Revolution', in, *The Peace of God: Social Violence and Religious Response in France around the year 1000*, ed. T. Head and R. Landes (Ithaca NY, 1992).

Mortimer, R. 'Land and Service: The Tenants of the Honor of Clare' in, *Anglo-Norman Studies* viii, ed. R.A. Brown (Woodbridge, 1986), 177–97.

Mukherjee, S.N. 'The Idea of Feudalism: From the Philosophes to Karl Marx', in, *Feudalism: Comparative Studies*, ed. E. Leach, S.N. Mukherjee and J.O. Ward (Sydney Studies in Society and Culture, no 2, 1984).

Murray, A. 'Confession before 1215', *Transactions of the Royal Historical Society*, 6th ser., 3 (1993), 51–82.

Murray, A. *Reason and Society in the Middle Ages* (Oxford, 1978).

Murray, A.C. 'Theories of Germanic Kinship Structure in Antiquity and the Early Middle Ages', in *Germanic Kinship Structure: Studies in Law and Society in Antiquity and the Early Middle Ages* (Toronto, 1983), 11–32.

Musset, L. 'L'aristocratie normande au xie siècle', in, *La noblesse au moyen age xie–xve siècle: essais à la mémoire de Robert Boutruche* (Paris, 1976), 71–96.

Mussot-Goulard, R. 'Les chevaliers et la ville: Condom du xie siècle au xiiie siècle', in, *Les sociétés urbaines en France méridionale et en péninsule Iberique au moyen âge* (Collection de la maison des pays Ibériques, 43, Paris, 1991), 175–81.

Navel, H. 'L'enquête de 1133 sur les fiefs de l'Eveché de Bayeux', *Bullétin de la société des antiquaires de la Normandie*, xlii (1935), 5–80.

Nicholas, K.S. 'Countesses as Rulers in Flanders' in, *Aristocratic Women in Medieval France*, ed. T. Evergates (Philadelphia, 1999), 111–37.

Noble, P. 'Anti-clericalism in the Feudal Epic', in, *The Medieval Alexander Legend and Romance Epic: Essays in Honour of David J.A. Ross*, ed. P. Noble, L. Polak and C. Isoz (Nendeln, 1982), 149–58.

Nobles and Nobility in Medieval Europe: Concepts, Origins, Transformations, ed. A.J. Duggan (Woodbridge, 2000).

Oeuvres complètes de Rutebeuf, ed. E. Faral and J. Bastin (2 vols., Paris, 1959–60).

Ogburn, W.F. *Social Change with respect to Culture and Original Nature* (London, 1923), 56–7.

Orderic Vitalis, *The Ecclesiastical History*, ed. M. Chibnall (6 vols., Oxford, 1969–80).

Ordines Coronationis Franciae, ed. R.A. Jackson (Philadelphia, 1995).

Page, W. *London: Its Origins and Early Development* (London, 1929).

Painter, S. *French Chivalry: Chivalric Ideas and Practices in Mediaeval France* (Baltimore, 1940).

Parsons, J. Carmi 'Family, Sex and Power: the Rhythms of Medieval Queenship' in, *Medieval Queenship*, ed. J. Carmi Parsons (Stroud, 1994), 1–11.

Patrologiae cursus completus: series Latina, ed. J-P. Migne (221 vols., Paris, 1847–67).

Patterson, R.B. 'Robert fitz Harding of Bristol: Profile of an Early Angevin Burgess-Baron Politician and his Family's Urban Involvement', *Haskins Society Journal*, 1 (1989), 101–22.

Peter of Cornwall, 'The Visions of Ailsi and his Sons', ed. R. Easting and R. Sharpe, in, *Mediaevistik: Internationale Zeitschrift für interdisziplinäre Mittelalterforschung*, i (1988), 206–62.

Petit-Dutaillis, C. *Studies and Notes Supplementary to Stubbs' Constitutional History*, trans. W.E. Rhodes and W.T. Waugh (Manchester, 1915).

Philip de Beaumanoir, *Coutumes de Beauvaisis*, ed. A. Salmon (3 vols, Paris, 1970–4).

Philip de Novara, *Les Quatre Ages de l'Homme*, ed. M. de Freville (Société des anciens textes français, 1888).

Philip de Remy, *Jehan et Blonde*, ed. S. Lécuyer (Classiques français du moyen age, 1984).

Philip de Remy, *La Manekine*, ed. H. Suchier (Société des anciens textes français, 1884).

Philip the prior, *De miraculis sanctae Frideswidae*, in, *Acta Sanctorum*.

Phillpotts, B. *Kindred and Clan in the Middle Ages and After: A Study in the Sociology of the Teutonic Races* (Cambridge, 1913).

Pirenne, H. *Les villes et les institutions urbaines* (2 vols., 2nd edn., Paris, 1939).

Pitt, A. 'Frédéric Le Play and the Family: Paternalism and Freedom in the French Debates of the 1870s', *French History*, 12 (1998).

PL (see *Patrologiae cursus completus: series Latina*).

Poésies complètes de Bertran de Born, ed. A. Thomas (Toulouse, 1888).

Poésies inédites du moyen âge, ed. M. Édélestand du Méril (Paris, 1854).

Pollock, F. and Maitland, F.W. *The History of English Law* (2 vols., 2nd edn., Cambridge, 1898).

Poly, J-P. *Le chemin des amours barbares: génèse médiévale de la sexualité européenne* (Paris, 2003), 350–1.

Poly, J-P. and Bournazel, E. *La mutation féodale, x^e–xiie siècles* (Paris, 1980), trans. C. Higgitt as, *The Feudal Transformation, 900–1200* (London, 1991).

Postan, M.M. 'Feudalism and its Decline: a semantic exercise' in, *Social Relations and Ideas: Essays in Honour of R.H. Hilton* (Cambridge, 1983), 73–87.

Postan, M.M. *The Medieval Economy and Society* (repr. Harmondsworth, 1975).

Pouchelle, M-C. 'Le sang et ses pouvoirs en moyen âge', in, *Affaires du sang*, ed. A. Farge (Paris, 1988), 17–41.

Powell, T.E. 'The "Three Orders" of Society in Anglo-Saxon England', in, *Anglo-Saxon England*, 23, ed. M. Lapidge and others (Cambridge, 1994), 103–32.

Power, E. *Medieval Women*, ed. M.M. Postan (Cambridge, 1975).

Power, E. 'On Medieval History as a Social Study', in, *The Study of Economic History*, ed. N.B. Harte (London, 1971), 111–22.

Power, E. 'The Position of Women' in, *The Legacy of the Middle Ages*, ed. C.G. Crump and E.F. Jacob (Oxford, 1926), 401–33.

Powicke, M. 'Distraint of Knighthood and Military Obligation under Henry III', *Speculum*, 25 (1950), 457–70.

Powicke, M. *Military Obligation in Medieval England* (Oxford, 1962).

Prentout, H. *Essai sur les origines et la fondation du duché de Normandie* (Paris, 1911).

Price, R. 'Boulainvillier and the Myth of the Frankish Conquest of Gaul', *Studies on Voltaire*, 199 (1981), 155–85.

Proverbes français antérieurs au xve siècle, ed. J. Morawski (Classiques français du moyen âge, 1925).

Radulfi de Diceto decani Lundoniensis Opera Historica, ed. W. Stubbs (2 vols, Rolls Series, 1876).

Ralph Glaber, *Historiarum Libri Quinque*, ed. and trans. J. France (Oxford, 1989).

Ramon Llull, *Libre que es de l'ordre de cavalleria, Obres essencials*, i, ed. P. Bohigas (Barcelona, 1957).

Raoul de Cambrai, ed. S. Kay and trans. W. Kibler (Paris, 1996).

Raoul de Houdenc, *Le Roman des Eles*, ed. and trans. K. Busby (Utrecht Publications in General and Comparative Literature, 17, Amsterdam, 1983).

Reading Abbey Cartularies, ed. B. Kemp (2 vols, Camden Society, 4th ser., 31, 33, 1986–7).

Recueil des historiens des Gaules et de la France, ed. M. Bouquet and others (24 vols, Paris, 1869–1904).

Red Book of the Exchequer, ed. H. Hall (3 vols., Rolls Series, 1896).

Regesta Regum Anglo-Normannorum, ed. H.W.C. Davis and others (4 vols., Oxford, 1913–69).

Renoux, A. 'Les fondements architecturaux du pouvoir princier en France (fin ixe siècle-debut xiiie siècle)' in, *Les princes et le pouvoir au moyen âge* (Paris, 1993), 167–94.

Reuter, T. 'Debate: the "Feudal Revolution"', *Past and Present*, no. 155 (1997).

Reuter, T. 'The Medieval Nobility', in, *Companion to Historiography*, ed. M. Bentley (London, 1997), 177–202.

Reynolds, S. *Fiefs and Vassals: The Medieval Evidence Reinterpreted* (Oxford, 1994).

Reynolds, S. 'The Rulers of London in the Twelfth Century', *History*, 57 (1972).

Rezak, B. Bedos 'Women, Seals and Power in Medieval France, 1150–1350' in, *Women and Power in the Middle Ages*, ed. M. Erler and M. Kowaleski (Athens GA, 1988), 61–82.

Richard of Devizes, *Chronicon*, ed. and trans. J.T. Appleby (London, 1963).

Richard of Hexham, *De Gestis Regis Stephani et de Bello Standardi* in, *Chronicles of the Reigns of Stephen etc.*, ed. R. Howlett, iii (Rolls Series, 1886).

Richardson H.G. and Sayles, G.O. *The Governance of Medieval England: from the Conquest to Magna Carta* (Edinburgh, 1963).

Richeri Historiarum Libri Quatuor, ed. G. Waitz (Hanover, 1877).

Ridgeway, H. 'William de Valence and his Familiares, 1247–72', *Historical Research*, 65 (1992), 246–50.

Robert de Torigny, *Chronica*, in, *Chronicles of the Reigns of Stephen, Henry II and Richard I*, ed. R. Howlett (4 vols, Rolls Series, 1885–9).

Roger of Howden, *Chronica*, ed. W. Stubbs (4 vols, Rolls Series, 1868–71).

Rolls of the Justices in Eyre being the rolls of pleas and assizes for Gloucestershire, Warwickshire and Staffordshire (recte Shropshire) 1221, 1222, ed. D.M. Stenton (Selden Society, lix, 1940).

Roman de la Rose, ed. D. Poirion and J. Dufournet (Manchecourt, 1999).

Rymer, T. *Foedera, Conventiones, Litterae et Acta Publica*, ed. A. Clarke and F. Holbrooke (7 vols., London, 1816–69).

Sainte-Palaye, Jean-Baptiste de la Curne de, *Mémoires sur l'ancienne chevalerie* (2 vols., Paris, 1759–60), translated as *Memoirs of Ancient Chivalry*, trans. Susanna Dobson (London, 1784).

Santenelli, E. *Des femmes éplorées? Les veuves dans la société aristocratique du haut moyen âge* (Lille, 2003).

Sassier, Y. 'De l'ordre seigneuriale à l'époque féodale', in, *Pouvoirs et institutions dans la France médiévale*, ed. O. Guillot, A. Rigaudière and Y. Sassier (2 vols., 3rd edn., Paris, 1999).

Scaglione, A. *Knights at Court: Courtliness, Chivalry and Courtesy from Ottonian Germany to the Italian Renaissance* (Berkeley CA, 1991).

Scammell, J. 'The Formation of the English Social Structure: Freedom, Knights and Gentry, 1066–1300', *Speculum*, 68 (1993), 601–18.

Schmid, K. 'The Structure of the Nobility in the earlier Middle Ages', in, *The Medieval Nobility*, ed. and trans. T. Reuter (Amsterdam, 1978), first published as 'Über die Struktur des Adels im früheren Mittelalter', *Jahrbuch für fränkische Landesforschung*, 19 (1959), 1–23.

Schmid, K. 'Zur Problematik von Familie, Sippe und Geschlecht, Haus und Dynastie beim mittelalterlichen Adel: Vortragen zum Thema "Adel und Herrschaft in Mittelalter" ', *Zeitschrift für die Geschichte des Oberrheins*, 105 (1957), 1–62.

Schmitt, J.C. *Ghosts in the Middle Ages: the Living and the Dead in medieval society*, trans. T.L. Fagan (Chicago, 1998).

Schulze-Busacker, E. *Proverbes et expressions proverbiales dans la littérature narrative du moyen âge français: recueil et analyse* (Paris, 1985).

Searle, E. *Predatory Kinship and the Creation of Norman Power, 840–1066* (Berkeley, 1988).

Smith, A. *The Theory of Moral Sentiments* (London, 1759).

Smith, A. *The Wealth of Nations* (Edinburgh, 1776).

Sombart, W. *Luxury and Capitalism* (Ann Arbor, 1967), originally published as *Luxus und Kapitalismus* (Munich, 1910).

Sone von Nausay, ed. M. Goldschmidt (Bibliothek des literarischen Vereins in Stuttgart, ccxvi, Tübingen, 1899).

Stafford, P. 'La Mutation Familiale: A Suitable Case for Caution', in, *The Community, the Family and the Saint: Patterns of Power in Early Medieval Europe*, ed. J. Hill and M. Swan (Turnhout, 1998), 103–25.

Stafford, P. 'Women and the Norman Conquest', *Transactions of the Royal Historical Society*, 6th ser., 4 (1994), 221–49.

Stenton, D.M. *English Justice between the Norman Conquest and the Great Charter, 1066–1215* (London, 1965).

Stenton, F.M. *Anglo-Saxon England* (3rd edn., Oxford, 1971).

Stenton, F.M. *The First Century of English Feudalism, 1066–1166* (2nd edn., Oxford, 1961).

Stephen de Fougères, *Le Livre de Manières*, ed. R.A. Lodge (Geneva, 1979).

Strayer, J.R. 'Feudalism in Western Europe', *Feudalism in History* (Princeton, 1956), 15–25.

Strickland, M. 'Slaughter, Slavery or Ransom: the Impact of the Conquest on Conduct in Warfare', in, *England in the Eleventh Century*, ed. C. Hicks (Stamford, 1992), 41–60.

Strickland, M. *War and Chivalry : the Conduct and Perception of War in England and Normandy, 1066–1217* (Cambridge, 1996).

Stringer, K.J. *Earl David of Huntingdon: A Study in Anglo-Scottish History* (Edinburgh, 1985).

Stuard, S. Mosher 'Fashion's Captives: Medieval Women in French Historiography' in, *Women in Medieval History and Historiography*, ed. S. Mosher Stuard (Philadelphia, 1987), 62–8.

Stubbs, W. *The Constitutional History of England* (3 vols, Oxford, 1874–78).

Suger, *Vita Ludovici Grossi regis*, ed. H. Waquet (Paris, 1964).

The Anonymous Ordene de Chevalerie, ed. and trans. K. Busby (Utrecht Publications in General and Comparative Literature, 17, Amsterdam, 1983).

The Book of Chivalry of Geoffroi de Charny, ed. and trans. R.W. Kaeuper and E. Kennedy (Philadelphia, 1996).

The Cartulary and Charters of Notre Dame of Homblières, ed. W.M. Newman, revised T. Evergates and G. Constable (Cambridge, Mass., 1990).

The Charters of the Anglo-Norman Earls of Chester, c.1071–1237, ed. G. Barraclough (Record Society of Lancashire and Cheshire, cxxvi, 1988).

The Chronicle of John of Worcester iii, *The Annals from 1067 to 1140*, ed. P. McGurk (Oxford, 1998).

The Chronicle of Richard of Devizes of the Time of King Richard the First, ed. and trans. J.T. Appleby (London, 1963).

The Chronicle of Walter of Guisborough, ed. H. Rothwell (Camden Society, 3rd ser., lxxxix, 1957).

The Deeds of the Normans in Ireland, ed. and trans. E. Mullally (Dublin, 2002).

The Exempla of Jacques de Vitry, ed. and trans. T.F. Crane (New York, 1890).

The Gesta Guillelmi of William of Poitiers, ed. and trans. R.H.C. Davis and M. Chibnall (Oxford, 1998).

The Gesta Normannorum Ducum of William of Jumièges, Orderic Vitalis and Robert of Torigni, ed. and trans. E.M.C. van Houts (2 vols., Oxford, 1992–95).

The Later Letters of Peter of Blois, ed. E. Revell (Auctores Britannici Medii Aevi, xiii, 1993).

The Letters and Poems of Fulbert of Chartres, ed. and trans. F. Behrends (Oxford, 1976).

The Letters of Osbert de Clare, prior of Westminster, ed. E.W. Williamson (Oxford, 1929).

The Letters of Peter of Celle, ed. J. Haseldine (Oxford, 2001).

The Letters of St Bernard of Clairvaux, trans. B.S. James (Stroud, 1998).

The Medieval Alexander Legend and Romance Epic: Essays in Honour of David J.A. Ross, ed. P. Noble, L. Polak and C. Isoz (Nendeln, 1982).

The Medieval Nobility, ed. and trans. T. Reuter (Amsterdam, 1978).

The Peace of God: Social Violence and Religious Response in France around the year 1000, ed. T. Head and R. Landes (Ithaca NY, 1992).

The Peterborough Chronicle, ed. C. Clark (2nd edn., Oxford, 1970).

The Propagation of Power in the Medieval West, ed. M. Gosman, A. Vanderjagt and J. Veenstra (Mediaevalia Groningana, xxiii, 1997).

The Red Book of the Exchequer, ed. H. Hall (3 vols., Rolls Series, 1896).

The Romance of Fergus, ed. W. Frescoln (Philadelphia, 1983).

The Study of Chivalry: Resources and Approaches (Kalamazoo MI, 1988).

The Treatise on the Law and Customs of the Realm of England commonly called Glanvill, ed. G.D.G. Hall (London, 1965).

Theodulf of Orleans, *De omnibus ordinibus huius saeculi*, in *PL*, 105.

Thomas of Kent, *Le Roman de Toute Chevalerie*, ed. B. Foster (2 vols., Anglo-Norman Text Society, 1976–7).

Thompson, K. 'Les premiers temps de Saint-Denis de Nogent-le-Rotrou et leurs réécritures', *Bibliothèque de l'École des Chartes*, 160 (2002), 641–66.

Thompson, K. *Power and Border Lordship in Medieval France: The County of Perche, 1000–1226* (Woodbridge, 2002), 100–1.

Thorne, S.E. 'English Feudalism and Estates in Land', *Cambridge Law Journal* (1959), 193–209.

Trautman, T.R. *Lewis Henry Morgan and the Invention of Kinship* (Berkeley, 1987).

Turner, R.V. *Men Raised from the Dust* (Philadelphia, 1988).

Ulrich von Liechtenstein, *Service of Ladies*, trans. J.W. Thomas (Chapel Hill, 1969).

Urbanus Magnus Danielis Becclesiensis, ed. J.G. Smyly (Dublin, 1939).

van den Neste, E. *Tournois, joutes, pas d'armes dans la villes de Flandre à la fin du moyen âge, 1300–1486* (Paris, 1996).

van Houts, E.M.C. 'Introduction' in, *Medieval Memories: Men, Women and the Past, 700–1300*, ed. E.M.C. van Houts (London, 2001), 1–16.

van Proeyen, M. 'Sang et hérédité: à la croissée des imaginaires médicaux et sociaux', in, *Le sang au moyen âge (Actes du quatrième colloque internationale de Montpellier, Université Paul Valéry (27–29 novembre 1997)*, ed. M. Faure (Montpellier, 1999), 69–85.

van Werveke, H. 'The Urban Patriciate', in, *Cambridge Economic History of Europe* iii, *Economic Organization and Policies in the Middle Ages*, ed. M.M. Postan, E.E. Rich and E. Miller (Cambridge, 1963).

van Winter, J.M. 'Uxorem de militari ordine sibi imponens' in, *Miscellanea in memoriam J.F. Niermeyer* (Groningen, 1961).

Vita beati Herluini, in, *PL*, 150.

Vita beati Simonis comitis Crespeiensis, in, *PL* 156.

Vita sancti Gaufridi secundi abbatis Saviniacensis in, *Analecta Bollandiana*, i (1882).

Wace of Bayeux, *Le Roman de Brut*, ed. I. Arnold (2 vols, Société des anciens textes français, 1938–40).

Wace of Bayeux, *Le Roman de Rou*, ed. A.J. Holden (3 vols, Société des anciens textes français, 1970–3).

Wagner, A.R. *Heralds and Heraldry* (Oxford, 1939).

Walch, J. *Les maîtres de l'histoire, 1815–1850* (Geneva, 1986).

Wallwork, E. *Durkheim: Morality and Milieu* (Cambridge, MA, 1972).

Walter Map, *De Nugis Curialium*, trans. M.R. James, rev'd edn C.N.L. Brooke and R.A.B. Mynors (Oxford, 1983).

Walter of Arras, *Eracle*, ed. G. Raynaud de Lage (Classiques français du moyen âge, 1976).

Walter of Henley and other Treatises on Estate Management and Accounting, ed. D.M. Oschinsky (Oxford, 1971).

Waugh, S.L. *The Lordship of England: Royal Wardships and Marriages in English Society and Politics, 1217–1327* (Princeton, 1988).

Weber, M. *The Theory of Social and Economic Organization*, trans. A.M. Henderson and T. Parsons (New York, 1947).

Welty, G. 'Social Antagonism: the General and Specific Theory', *Revue Internationale de Sociologie*, 20 (1984), 100–18.

Werner, K-F. 'Les femmes, le pouvoir et la transmission du pouvoir' in, *La femme au moyen âge* (Maubeuge, 1990), 365–79.

Werner, K-F. *Naissance de la noblesse: l'essor des élites politiques en Europe* (2nd edn, Paris, 1998).

White, S.D. *Custom, Kinship and Gifts to Saints: the Laudatio Parentum in Western France, 1050–1150* (Chapel Hill, 1988).

White, S.D. 'Feuding and Peace-Making in the Touraine around the Year 1000', *Traditio*, 42 (1986), 195–263.

White, S.D. 'Maitland on Family and Kinship', Proceedings of the British Academy, 89 (1996).

White, S.D. 'The "Feudal Revolution": Reply', *Past and Present*, no 155 (1997), 207–17.

White, S.D. '*Pactum legem vincit et amor judicium*. The Settlement of Disputes by Compromise in Eleventh-Century France', *American Journal of Legal History*, 22 (1978), 281–308.

Willelmi Rishanger Chronica et Annales, ed. H.T. Riley (Rolls Series, 1865).

William de Jumièges, *Gesta Normannorum Ducum*, ed. and trans. E.M.C. van Houts (2 vols, Oxford, 1992–95).

William fitz Stephen, 'A Description of the Most Noble City of London', trans. H.E. Butler, in F.M. Stenton, *Norman London: An Essay* (London, 1934).

William of Malmesbury, *Gesta regum Anglorum*, ed. R.A.B. Mynors, R.M. Thompson and M. Winterbottom (2 vols, Oxford, 1998–9).

William of Malmesbury, *Historia Novella,* trans. K.R. Potter, ed. and rev'd E. King (Oxford, 1998).

William of Poitiers, *Gesta Guillelmi*, ed. and trans. R.H.C. Davis and M. Chibnall (Oxford, 1998).

Williams, A. 'A Bell-house and a Burh-geat: Lordly Residences in England before the Norman Conquest' in, *Medieval Knighthood* iv, ed. C. Harper-Bill and R. Harvey (Woodbridge, 1992), 221–40.

Williams, G.A. *Medieval London: From Commune to Capital* (London, 1963).

Wilson, A. 'A critical portrait of social history', in, *Rethinking Social History*, ed. A. Wilson (Manchester, 1993),

Wormald, P. *The Making of English Law: King Alfred to the Twelfth Century* i, *Legislation and its Limits* (Oxford, 1999).

INDEX

This includes subjects, medieval and modern writers and selected key characters. It is not intended to be a comprehensive index of persons and does not generally include place names.